The Iranian Revolution
and the
Muslim World

The Moshe Dayan Center for
Middle Eastern and African Studies,
The Shiloah Institute
Tel Aviv University

The Moshe Dayan Center, through The Shiloah Institute and its other constituent units, seeks to contribute by research, documentation, and publication to the study and understanding of the modern history and current affairs of the Middle East and Africa. The Center, with the Department of Middle Eastern and African History, is part of the School of History at Tel Aviv University. This study appears in the Center's Collected Papers Series.

The Iranian Revolution and the Muslim World

edited by
David Menashri

Westview Press
BOULDER • SAN FRANCISCO • OXFORD

Westview Special Studies on the Middle East

This Westview softcover edition is printed on acid-free paper and bound in library-quality, coated covers that carry the highest rating of the National Association of State Textbook Administrators, in consultation with the Association of American Publishers and the Book Manufacturers' Institute.

Published in 1990 in the United States of America by Westview Press, Inc., 5500 Central Avenue, Boulder, Colorado 80301, and in the United Kingdom by Westview Press, 36 Lonsdale Road, Summertown, Oxford OX2 7EW

Library of Congress Cataloging-in-Publication Data
The Iranian revolution and the Muslim world/edited by David
  Menashri.
    p. cm.—(Westview special studies on the Middle East)
  Includes index.
  ISBN 0-8133-7751-X
  1. Iran—Relations—Middle East. 2. Shīʾah—Iran. 3. Middle
East—Relations—Iran. I. Menashri, David. II. Series.
DS63.2.I68I73 1990
303.48′255056—dc20   90-40602
                                                                    CIP

Printed and bound in the United States of America

The paper used in this publication meets the requirements
of the American National Standard for Permanence of Paper
for Printed Library Materials Z39.48-1984.

10   9   8   7   6   5   4   3   2   1

Contents

Preface

Iran's Islamic revolution was one of the most important events of recent times—certainly in regional, quite possibly in global, history. The revolutionary *élan* of its activists, its unique method of seizing power, its goals and policies once it had taken over government—all these have not ceased to amaze and fascinate students and observers of contemporary history. They have made Khomeini's Iran (and the Shi'i community as a whole) a special focus of interest for policy-makers as well as for researchers.

Like many other great revolutionaries, Khomeini and his men had set their minds on carrying their creed and practice over into other countries— most particularly, of course, into other Muslim societies. Indeed, this "export drive" became one of the main objects of the regime. By its stunning success, by riding the groundswell of mounting religious sentiment and appealing to the *malaise* of so many Muslims in the modern world, it soon became (and in some cases remained) a source of emulation and a pattern of imitation. Regimes susceptible to similar trends found themselves compelled, unexpectedly, to take counter-measures.

The present volume focuses on Iran's attempts to export its type of revolution and on the response this elicited throughout the Middle East. It opens with an analysis of the revolutionary vision, relating it to both the Shi'i historical context and to Khomeini's actual foreign (and war-time) policies. It goes on to assess the measure of success of these policies, nurtured by the broad resonance the revolution found in many places throughout the Middle East, but simultaneously circumscribed by as many theological and political trends opposed to it.

In preparing and publishing such a volume, one must, naturally, draw on the support and counsel of many individuals and institutions. I am especially indebted to Itamar Rabinovich, the former head of The Moshe Dayan Center and now Rector of Tel Aviv University, and to Asher Susser, the present head of the Center, for their invaluable encouragement throughout the various states of the project. The Moshe Dayan Center provided the necessary support and auspices, first for gathering the contributors and their papers together and later for the publication of this volume. Jacob Goldberg, Joel Kraemer, Martin Kramer, and Itamar Rabinovich offered most useful advice.

I am also grateful to the following: Ami Ayalon, Shahram Chubin, Uriel Dann, Hélène Carrère d'Encausse, Werner Ende, Yair Evron, Thomas Friedman, Gideon Gera, Moshe Gil, Gad Gilbar, Jo-Anne Hart, Johannes J. G. Jansen, Farhad Kazemi, Zalmay Khalilzad, David Kushnir, Uri Lubrani, Ergun Özbudun, Yehudit Ronen, Barry Rubin, Haim Shaked, Shimon Shamir, Aryeh Shmuelevitz, Asher Susser, Binnaz Toprak, Aharon Yariv, David Yerushalmi, and Michael Zand.

The organizational talents and the zeal of Amira Margalit were instrumental in securing the success of this volume. Edna Liftman, with her great experience and efficiency, was extremely valuable in the complex work of turning the papers into a published volume. Thanks should similarly go to Elinore Segal and Ilana Greenberg for their support—always in good spirit. I am especially thankful to Lydia Gareh for the extremely painstaking preparation of the manuscript for telemedia conversion and to Margaret Mahlab, who typed the manuscript. I wish to offer special thanks also to the staff of Westview Press, for the masterly handling of the publication of this volume. Thanks should go mainly to Barbara Ellington, Jane Raese, Mick Gusinde-Duffy, Rebecca Ritke, and Michelle Welsh. And, finally, special thanks are extended to Daniel Dishon for the valuable editing of the manuscript. He has been a sophisticated and keen reader, and his imprint is felt throughout this volume. I am grateful to them all.

It is also my pleasant duty to thank all those who made the project possible: The Israel Academy of Science and Humanities; The Canada-Israel Foundation for Academic Exchanges; The United States Information Service and the French Embassy at Tel Aviv; the Faculty of Humanities at Tel Aviv University, and Tel Aviv University Conference Committee.

Transliteration has proved a thorny problem in a work that includes names and terms drawn from most major Muslim languages. Therefore, given the multiplicity of authors and their individual preferences, complete consistency as regards transliteration could not possibly have been achieved. As a rule, we have kept the system of transliteration simple by omitting all diacriticals and vowel quantities. The medial *ayn* and *hamza* have, however, been retained. In transliterating, the authors have made frequent allowances for pronunciation. Thus, for example, we used *mostaz'afun* or *Hokumat-e Islami* for Persian, but *mustad'afun* or *al-Hukuma al-Islamiyya* for Arabic; *Jihad* (when the word referred to holy war), but *Jehad-e Sanzandegi*. In the case of well-known proper names, or Islamic terms for which a different orthography has become established in English usage, we have consciously departed from the system of transliteration, for example: Abd al-Nasser, Husayn, Islam, Mujtahid, Hojjat al-Islam, or Ayatollah. (All this does not include quotations from, or reference to, sources using other systems; those have been quoted in their original form.)

David Menashri
Tel Aviv

Abbreviations Used in Notes

AFP Agence France Presse (Paris)
DR Daily Report: Middle East and Africa
EIU Economist Intelligence Unit
FT The Financial Times
IHT International Herald Tribune
IJMES International Journal of Middle Eastern Studies
IRNA Islamic Revolution News Agency
JI Jomhuri-ye Islami
JP The Jerusalem Post
JPRS Joint Publication Research Services, Near East and North Africa
KUNA Kuwaiti News Agency
MECS Middle East Contemporary Survey
MENA Middle East News Agency
MES Middle Eastern Studies
MI Al-Mukhtar al-Islami
NYT The New York Times
SANA Syrian Arab News Agency
SPA Saudi Press Agency
SWB British Broadcasting Corporation: Summary of World
   Broadcasting: Middle East and Africa
TASS Telegrafnoe Agentstvo Sovetskovo Soiuza
TI Al-Tali'a al-Islamiyya
UPI United Press International

Introduction

David Menashri

The Islamic Revolution in Iran—one of the most significant events in the modern history of the Middle East—has had reverberations far beyond the boundaries of its home country and the immediate region. It aroused enthusiasm throughout the Muslim world and became a force to be reckoned with by local as well as foreign governments. For its leaders, Islamic Revolution was not just a name; it was a vision soon to be turned into reality. And it was by no means meant for the people of Iran alone, or for Shi'is only, or even just for Muslims. Its ultimate goal was to launch what Ramazani called an "ideological crusade"[1] aimed at bringing the message of Islam to all peoples, everywhere.

Yet, upon their seizure of power, the new leaders did not seem to have a clear-cut, comprehensive scheme for "exporting" their vision. They seemed confident that the very success of their movement would launch a chain reaction in other Muslim societies, but this did not happen. Over time, significant differences emerged in the attitudes and opinions of revolutionary leaders, and the burden of running the state combined with other pressures to cause what were sometimes significant deviations from the initial dogma.[2] In practical terms, the leaders' attempts to export their vision became influenced by the internal situation in Iran, by each "importing" society's particular circumstances and by circumstances caused by regional or international events (such as the war with Iraq or the US military presence in the Gulf). The initial expectations, it turned out, had been too optimistic.

At first, the main idea was to merely present the revolution as an example for other movements and to rely on its impact. The revolution was exported, among other ways, by means of broadcasts in different languages,[3] books and indoctrination material, conferences, and the organization of huge delegations for the *hajj*. More active steps were the creation or encouragement of dissident movements in different Muslim countries (such as in some of the Gulf emirates), the dispatching of the *Pasdaran-e Enqelab-e Islami* (Revolutionary Guards, or, literally, the Guardians of the Islamic Revolution) to Lebanon and even the use of certain aspects of the war (such as the ideology used as legitimization for the continuation of the war, the arguments used for mobilization, or the suicide-type of some of the military operations).[4]

1

These active measures earned revolutionary Iran no more than minimal success. The Islamic states concerned quickly came to perceive Iran as a threat and set out to crush any sign of Islamic fundamentalism in their countries. While in most countries such fundamentalist movements continue to exist, their present size and influence does not seem impressive. The main impact of the Iranian revolution has been found in tightly knit numerically small movements, mostly within Shi'i populations; but even there the measure of Iranian control—or even influence—is far from clear. None of the fundamentalist movements currently seem to pose an immediate challenge to the stability of the Muslim regimes.[5] Even in the case of movements for which Tehran may claim greater success (such as *al-Da'wa* [hereafter Da'wa] and *al-Amal* ["Action"; Amal] in Iraq or the *Hizballah* [hereafter Hizballah] and *Amal* [so called after its Arabic initials: Amwaj al-Muqawama al-Lubnaniyya—Battalions of Lebanese Resistance—and better known in the West by the Arabic meaning of the initials: "Hope"; Amal] in Lebanon), the "exact connections" between these movements and the Iranian revolution are "obscure."[6]

In fact, Sunni radicalism, which draws on older Sunni sources, preceded the Iranian revolution. Sunni radicals were not demonstrably influenced by early Iranian-Shi'i revolutionary thinking, nor do their writings refer to radical Shi'i doctrines. Their position did not change significantly following the victory of the revolution in Iran.[7] Even when Sunni radicals expressed views similar to those of Khomeini, it should not be assumed that they did so only under the influence of Khomeini or Khomeinism. After all, as Johannes Jansen argues in his chapter, some notions "are common to all Muslim revolutionaries." Iran was "only one, and not even the most important," among the many forces that determined the path of these Islamic movements.[8] A decade after the revolution, its impact cannot be ignored, but the fact remains that Iran is still its first and only exemplar.

When discussing Iran as a role model, we have to consider two distinct aspects: the example it has set in toppling a strong regime, both advancing westernization and supported by the West, and its success or failure in solving the problems that led to the revolution in the first place.

Although groups with different ideologies took part in the revolution, unquestionably the main force was Islam and the *ulama* were the masters of the day. Fundamentalists will undoubtedly continue to see the victory of the revolutionary movement as a successful model and a source of inspiration, even if the Iranian revolution eventually comes to grief. One way or another, the revolution has proven the power and capability of a popular movement led by the *ulama* and motivated by Islam to overthrow a hated regime and make a mockery of superpowers (mainly the United States). Other movements and leaders will always be able to find explanations and excuses for the revolution's failure to meet its followers' initial expectations; in fact, much of the sympathy or enthusiasm of radical Sunni movements centered on the advent, rather than the subsequent fate, of the revolution (see chapter by Chubin). Moreover, even losing credibility at home did not mean that the "oppressed elsewhere could not continue to hope for global salvation through Khomeinism," just as Stalinism continued to be viewed by many devoted Communists in Europe as the hope of the masses long after it lost credibility in the Soviet Union (see chapter by Jansen).

To what degree has the revolution set an example by its own achievements? In this regard, its record has been much less impressive. If one accepts that the roots of the revolution were much deeper than what people in the West would describe as "religious," then we must ask whether such broad aims were achieved fully or partially.[9] Clearly there was no greater freedom in Islamic Iran than there was under the Shah, and the social and economic pressures on the *mostaz'afin* (the disinherited) have not been eased since the revolution; on the contrary, the revolution has added many new problems. The regime can offer many explanations for Iran's social and economic dilemmas: the war, the animosity of the superpowers, the drop in oil income, and so on. But are these conditions not, at least in part, the result of the revolution? How long will such explanations convince the people? The fact is that for many Muslims the new Iranian regime has come to be identified with poverty, fanaticism and lack of freedoms; in short, it has become a "disgrace to Islam." Some Muslim critics go as far as declaring the revolution not a genuine Islamic ideology but, rather, a distortion of true Islam. After some initial hesitation, leaders of most "Islamist" movements turned critical of Khomeini, his world view and his regime's modus operandi (see chapter by Ende). For the more traditionalist movements and leaders, there was no such thing as "Khomeini's Islam" but rather a choice between Khomeini or "the true message of Islam" (see chapter by Toprak).

One success—of an entirely different order—is that the revolution has focused attention on Shi'i Islam and Iran. It has not only resulted in an "unprecedented degree in interest in Shi'ism, but has also led scholars to take a new look at some basic questions about the nature of the Ithna Ashari tradition" (see chapter by Savory). Yet, events in Iran aroused not only curiosity abroad but also a "fear of Islam."[10] Western opinion was often "marred by prejudice and distortion."[11] Sunni reports about Shi'ism were, for the most part, no more flattering. Despite some progress in the 1970s, Shi'ism did not become a central topic in Islamic research until the revolution in Iran "forced all and sundry to take a fresh look at it." Ultimately, Kohlberg may well be right when he suggests that the "resurgent interest in Twelver Shi'ism is bound to prove a positive contribution of the revolution, whatever else one may think of it."[12] But while encouraging interest in Shi'ism, the Islamic revolution did not change the (mostly distorted) basic attitudes toward it in the West or among Sunnis. By and large, both groups tend to identify Shi'ism with disorder, executions, lack of freedoms, martyrdom, fanaticism, terrorism, hostage-taking and the like. Its ecumenical vision notwithstanding, the revolution did not contribute to a Sunni-Shi'i *rapprochement* (see mainly chapters by Goldberg, Rekhess, Ende, and Toprak).

A comprehensive examination of the impact of the Islamic Revolution throughout the Muslim world cannot, I believe, be made at this point. This book sets out, therefore, to delineate the revolution's impact mainly on the Muslim Middle East and examine the first decade of the revolution. Even so, the contributors could not help singling out some of the Muslim communities of the region at the expense of some others.

The book begins with an examination of the notion of exporting Ithna Asharism. Roger Savory asks whether Ithna Asharism is innately revolutionary or, on the contrary, quietist. For all its importance of historical depth, the question has no clear-cut answer. Ithna Asharism, like Islam at large, goes through both quietist and activist periods. It is likely to try to expand when an opportunity presents itself, but in the past Ithna Asharism has expanded through "the random exploitation of political opportunities" by individual rulers rather than as the result of "state policy." This being so, Savory concludes that Khomeini has gone "beyond traditional Ithna Ashari messianism."

As my own chapter shows, the shift toward a supra-national vision was not merely a deviation from "traditional" Ithna Ashari politics but also from Khomeini's own dogma prior to his Iraqi exile as well as from his usual practice once he had seized power. The chapter provides some explanation for the change first from an Iranian patriotic vision to an Islamic (or even worldwide) vision then back to a more pragmatic, patriotic "national" policy.

Farhad Kazemi and Jo-Anne Hart examine the interaction between the Islamic Republic's foreign policy (including the notion of exporting the revolution) and domestic affairs. Instead of the old status quo regime, the revolution installed one committed to universalistic religious ideology. But in practice, the new rulers were interested first and foremost in establishing "a viable Islamic government and securing its future." To do so, the Islamic Republic often manipulated foreign relations "to suit its domestic purposes."

Shahram Chubin's chapter examines the impact of the war with Iraq on Iran's foreign relations, specifically with the Gulf states. Chubin explores the ways in which the war "conditioned and constrained" the Islamic Republic during its different phases. The initial "militant enthusiasm" gradually changed to a policy of self-interest as a result of the military stalemate and Iran's need to escape "self-inflicted isolation." Nevertheless, a first phase of "dialogue and fence-mending" (1984–1986) was followed by a new cycle of "crises [and] estrangement" and a second "return to a balance" (1987–1988).

To bring the message of the revolution to the people at home as well as to the outside world the regime used all available channels. The educational system, the mass media, Friday sermons and so on, were pivotal means at home. Broadcasts and publications in different languages (Turkish and Arabic, for example), and Islamic meetings (Friday Imams' Congress, Unity Week, the *hajj*, and so forth) brought the message to a wider Islamic audience.[13] The iconography of Iranian bank notes and stamps illustrates such indoctrination efforts. Peter Chelkowski shows how bank notes utilize the symbols of the new political mythology by appealing both "to the visual sense [and] to religious sensibility." Comparison of *motifs* used by the revolutionary regime with those of the Pahlavis graphically shows the departure from the glorification of pre-Islamic Iran to Khomeini's Islamic revolutionary themes.

The second part of the book deals with the repercussions of the revolution in several Shi'i communities where, as was to be expected, the revolution had a considerable impact. These communities (in Iraq, Lebanon, Kuwait, Saudi Arabia, and Bahrain), sharing common religious-sectarian beliefs with Iran and each suffering social and economic deprivation, seemed the most fertile ground for Khomeini's dogma. Yet there were difficulties in duplicating the Iranian revolution's success in those communities. One problem was the socio-economic differences between pre-revolutionary Iran and the other Shi'i communities. Another was that collaboration by the *ulama* with other sectors of the society in common struggles against the central government was a uniquely Iranian tradition. But more important was that even where conditions did "lend themselves to partial emergence of neo-fundamentalist ideology, clerical elites were not capable, even with Iran's assistance, of overcoming the domestic forces arrayed against them."[14] No wonder then, that the most successful example of "exporting the revolution" occurred in Lebanon, where the central government was too weak to prevent the emergence of a comparatively strong revolutionary Shi'i movement. Despite the important emotional and psychological influence that the Iranian revolution undoubtedly had on Shi'i populations (more so, one can assume, than on other Muslim communities), the effect on them could not yet be translated into political gains for revolutionary Iran.[15]

Undoubtedly, the Lebanese Hizballah comes closest to being a successful export of the revolution. As a movement of Shi'i Muslims who "wish to restore Islam to a place of pre-eminence in the political, social, and economic order of the Muslim world," it gained—as Martin Kramer shows—considerable support from Tehran. Iran's example and support were decisive in the Hizballah's success. But the long history of Shi'i social and economic deprivation and the indoctrination by revolutionary clerics as well the circumstances of the civil war were also powerful factors. As Kramer maintains, the revolutionary notion of "pan-Islam worked for Iran in Lebanon because Lebanon was itself unworkable."

All similarities (such as social deprivation and political discrimination) notwithstanding, the case of the Shi'i community in Iraq was rather different. In Iraq, the power of the government and its determination to block any possible Shi'i uprising decided the issue. Iraq had to deal with Iran's most explicit and undisguised attempts to export the revolution; one of Iran's principal conditions for terminating the war was the establishment of an Iraqi Islamic republic. The Iraqi government, as Amazia Baram shows, was determined to prevent just that. Yet the few surviving activists of the Iranian-inspired Da'wa movement in Iraq persisted (as the Hizballah did) in their allegiance to the "original" vision of the Ayatollah—more so than Khomeini's disciples or even the Ayatollah himself.

Khomeini believed there was no difference between Muslims; his doctrine was meant for all Muslims, whatever their ethnic or sectarian affiliation.

But in the lands of Sunni Islam, people took a different view. Some prominent *ulama* viewed Khomeinism as a heresy; others (such as the Saudis) condemned it for political reasons; others again (like the leaders of Syria and Libya), though not necessarily supporting its ideology sought an alliance with the Islamic regime. Some radical Sunni movements, however, came to view Khomeini's ascent as an example of a successful Islamic revolution and were encouraged and influenced by it.

Jacob Goldberg's chapter examines the Saudi-Iranian "Islamic" struggle. Saudi Arabia and its claims to be a leading Islamic state were more loathsome to Tehran than the self-professed secular Ba'th regime of Syria. How Tehran and Damascus—those strange bedfellows—came to be allies despite the ideological gulf between them and despite their political disagreements (concerning Lebanon and Iran's aims in the war against Iraq, for example) is illustrated in the chapter by Yosef Olmert, who examines the Syrian side.

The case of a radical Palestinian Sunni movement is the subject of Elie Rekhess's chapter, which explores the meeting points and the divergences between the doctrines of Khomeini and those of the (originally Gazan) *al-Jihad al-Islami* (hereafter Islamic Jihad). He speaks of the Islamic Jihad as "a militant Sunni movement, steeped in Sunni action and traditions, yet inspired and embolded by the Shi'i revolution in Iran." Even though the Iranian revolution was not the sole (or even the prime) *motif* shaping Islamic Jihad thinking, it "gave the spread of fundamentalist Islam its final impetus."

Johannes Jansen examines the Iranian revolution in the writings of Egyptian Muslims. He demonstrates that Egyptian writers on religious subjects show some familiarity with the movement and ideology of Khomeini, though certainly no intimate knowledge of it. Even the opposition newspapers that claim abundant "ideological sympathy with Khomeinism" often display no more than "a purely political sympathy for Khomeinism."

Concluding this section of the book, Werner Ende examines Sunni polemical writings on the Shi'a and the Iranian revolution and addresses two important subjects: the main issues of Sunni-Shi'i controversy in modern times and how they have been handled by Sunni polemicists in recent years. He finds that "some *motifs* have passed into desuetude, but no new ones have been added." Khomeini's ecumenical ideology notwithstanding, and despite certain pro-Shi'i tendencies in modern Sunni thought, "Sunni-Shi'i disagreements appear to be as strong as ever."

Finally, the Islamic Revolution also had some impact on neighboring non-Arab states such as Afghanistan, which was locked in a struggle—sometimes assuming Islamic coloration—against the Soviets; Turkey, which has taken the secularization process further than any other Middle Eastern country; and the Soviet Union, where Muslims have been under Communist rule for over sixty years. In other countries such as Pakistan, India, Indonesia, the Philippines (not reviewed in the volume), and even Muslim communities in the West, the influence of Khomeini's movement was clearly felt as well.

In his chapter, Zalmay Khalilzad lists four major considerations influencing Iranian policy toward Afghanistan: strategic reasoning, factional policies in

Iran, sectarianism, and ideologies. Ideology alone cannot explain Iranian policy in Afghanistan: the policy is neither "Islamic internationalism," nor even "Shi'i internationalism" because "being Shi'i alone was not sufficient to gain Iranian support."

The impact of the revolution was also felt in Turkey. Nevertheless, Ergun Özbudun claims that the "secularization (or privatization) of Islam" is still on firm ground. Religious observance and the secular state "are no longer incompatible." Although basically in agreement with him, Binnaz Toprak stresses a "change of outlook towards Islam at the level of the political elite . . . in an overt departure from radical Kemalist secularism." Militant Islam may have been on the rise since 1980, but "the numerical strength of groups with a revolutionary outlook is very limited." Only a small minority within the Islamic movement "supports the Iranian regime or similar revolutionary action."

In Soviet Transcaucasia and Central Asia, as Yaacov Ro'i shows, the beginnings of national discontent go back long before the Iranian revolution. Nevertheless, the revolution in Iran clearly strengthened these feelings. Soviet Muslims were aware of the victory of Islam in Iran, and broadcasts from Tehran carried the message throughout the southern regions of the USSR. Although "Islamic fundamentalism appears to hold little attraction" for the population and Muslims there do not consider events "primarily through an Islamic prism," Khomeini and his ideology have become "a meaningful political symbol for many."

The revolution in Iran has undoubtedly been a pivotal event for the Muslim world as a whole. Despite language barriers and ethnic, sectarian and other differences, Muslims everywhere took notice of it and thought of it—at least initially—as a portent of the potential of Muslim people to return history to its "natural" path and restore Muslims to their "accustomed" predominance. In most cases the trend toward greater radicalism had begun earlier, had drawn on other philosophies, and was motivated by locally distinct circumstances. For the most part, the roots of discontent transcended purely "religious" reasons (in the Western sense of that word), and in different places the response was varied (depending on local socio-economic conditions, the authority of the central government, or the international circumstances). Yet the dramatic victory of the revolution in Iran and the overpowering figure of Ayatollah Khomeini captured the imagination of Muslims everywhere. This victory will remain an asset to Islamic radicalism regardless of the future of the Iranian revolution.

The assessment of Tehran's actual achievement in exporting its vision depends on how one chooses to perceive the situation. Overall, the chapters in this volume concur that, following an initial burst of enthusiasm, there was a sobering up: The influence of the revolution reached its peak in 1979, then gradually decreased in most places.[16] After all, a decade later, the Iranian revolution remains the first and only example of its kind.

But this analysis may be somewhat misleading. For one thing, even in places where the Iranian revolution did not elicit similar movements, it may have influenced the policies of local regimes. It is difficult to measure what local policies, considered feasible when first conceived, were cancelled because in the new atmosphere they might have been considered provocative, or what part overt and covert preventive measures played in holding local Islamic movements at bay. More important, the apparent limited success of the revolution beyond its home borders does not reflect its emotional and sentimental impact on the minds of individual Muslims or Muslim societies— a point made over and over again in most chapters of this volume. The revolution certainly contributed to the pride and self-confidence of Muslims, whether Sunnis or Shi'is, regardless of their nationality or political orientation. From Indonesia to the Muslim communities in the West, the victory of the Iranian revolution was tantamount to the victory of Islam and signaled Islam's potential to lead oppressed people to confront corrupt regimes and foreign exploitation. Moreover, Khomeini became a symbol to which Muslims may yet turn in the future. Pictures of the Imam were displayed in teahouses, mosques, and public buildings in Sunni as well as Shi'i regions. Although "translating this . . . emotional support into a popular movement [is] another matter,"[17] such an impact must not be discounted or ignored.

In this sense, the Islamic revolution should perhaps not be compared to the American, French, or Soviet revolutions but rather to the Japanese victory over Russia early in the twentieth century. Both of these movements held the hope that the peoples of the East could overcome the threatening power of the West. The Iranian revolution did more than that: It indicated to an ideology capable of guiding the struggle (Islam) and a leadership capable of heading it (the *ulama*). Yet there remains a crucial difference: The victory of Japan was not only the result of reforms and progress but it was also followed by further rapid advances. In that regard, the first decade of Islamic rule—although ten years are not sufficient to pass definite judgment—does not seem impressive. The domestic situation in Islamic Iran, its foreign relations, and its conduct of the war against Iraq made it difficult to hold up the Islamic regime as a model for others to imitate.

At this stage it remains moot whether the revolution will ultimately be seen as Islamic, Shi'i, or Iranian. Nor is it clear whether Khomeini's successors will uphold the mission of exporting the revolution. Looking at internal developments in Iran, either in terms of the power struggles or the social and economic situation, one would expect Iran to concentrate on domestic affairs. Yet as long as the Islamic regime is in power, exporting the revolution is likely to remain an important enterprise. Whether it will be actively pursued or only taken up when opportunities present themselves depends very much on the domestic situation and the regional and international environment.

Notes

1. Ruhollah Ramazani, *Revolutionary Iran: Challenge and Response in the Middle East* (Baltimore: 1986), 19–31.

2. For deviations from the revolutionary vision in other major fields, see my article "Khomeini's Iran: Doctrine and Reality," in Efraim Karsh (ed.), *The Impact and Implications of the Iran-Iraq War* (London: 1989), 42–57.

3. For such measures, see for example Marvin Zonis and Daniel Brumberg, "Khomeini, the Islamic Republic of Iran, and the Arab World," *Harvard Middle East Papers*, V (1987), 32.

4. This is not to say that the war against Iraq was initiated and/or intentionally prolonged to help exporting the revolution; but once war had broken out, Iran used it to spread the revolution.

5. Ramazani, 53.

6. James Piscatori, *Islam in a World of Nation States* (Cambridge: 1986), 114.

7. Emanuel Sivan, *Radical Islam* (New Haven: 1985), particularly 187–89 in the postscript to the Hebrew edition (Tel Aviv: 1986).

8. Shireen Hunter, "Iran and the Spread of Revolutionary Islam," *Third World Quarterly*, XII/2 (April 1988), 730–49.

9. I have discussed this subject briefly in *Iran: A Decade of War and Revolution* (New York: 1990), 1–4. For a discussion of the social and economic problems in the first decade of the revolution, see ibid., in various chapters and mainly in the postscript as well as in my article "Khomeini's Iran: Doctrine and Reality," 42-57 (cf. note 2). See also Shaul Bakhash, *The Reign of the Ayatollahs* (New York: 1985).

10. Piscatori, 2.

11. Etan Kohlberg, "Western Studies of Shi'a Islam" in Martin Kramer (ed.), *Shi'ism, Resistance and Revolution* (Boulder: 1987), 31-44.

12. Kohlberg, 41.

13. For example, the Foundation of the Mostaz'afin in New York distributed among Iranologists the books of Morteza Motahheri and Husayn Modarresi, and recently a fancy edition of Khomeini's will and testament was distributed among Western scholars in English, Persian and Arabic. These are, of course, only a few examples.

14. Zonis and Brumberg, 42.

15. The Shi'is of Iraq, it should be stressed, did not welcome the Iranian troops entering Iraq after 1983, just as the Arabs of Khuzestan showed no signs of enthusiasm when Iraq invaded their territory in 1980. Such a response may reflect their apprehension of a possible change of fortunes, but the question remains whether the Arabs of Khuzestan really wished to join their fellow Arabs, or the Shi'is of Iraq their coreligionists, across the border. More likely, both simply wanted to improve their situation in their own country. If the second theory is true, it reflects the supremacy of the notion of the modern nation-state.

16. One clear exception is the case of the Muslims of the USSR. Here, as Ro'i shows, the influence of Islam and the Iranian revolution seems to be on the increase.

17. Zonis and Brumberg, 71.

PART 1

Islamic Universalism and Iranian Impetus

1

The Export of Ithna Ashari Shi'ism: Historical and Ideological Background

Roger M. Savory

Ten years ago, the Islamic Revolution in Iran, led by Ayatollah Ruhollah Khomeini, burst upon a largely unsuspecting world. It soon became clear that it was one of the major revolutions of this century. Indeed, assessed on the basis of its long-term implications not only for the Persian Gulf, the Middle East, and the whole Dar al-Islam, but also for the rest of the world as well, it could claim to be the most significant since the Bolshevik Revolution of 1917.

Until the Islamic Revolution in Iran, the Shi'i tradition had been largely ignored by Western scholarship, with some notable exceptions. Most scholars appeared willing to look at Shi'ism through Sunni eyes, that is, to view it, at best, as a relatively unimportant minority sect of Islam, and, at worst, as a sect so deviant as actually to be outside the pale of Islam. The Khomeini Revolution has not only resulted in an unprecedented degree of interest in Shi'ism, but has also led scholars to take a new look at some basic questions about the nature of the Ithna Ashari tradition. For example, is militancy an essential part of the Ithna Ashari tradition or is it an aberration? S. A. Arjomand and others maintain that the normative Ithna Ashari tradition is quietist, and that militancy, and extremism of the *ghuluww* type, represent the exception to the rule. Those who hold this view consequently regard the ideology of the Islamic Republic of Iran as a deviation from the norm and Khomeini's doctrine of *velayat-e faqih* ("the rule of the jurisconsult"), a doctrine which is the cornerstone of this ideology, as a *bid'a*, that is, as an innovation tantamount to heresy.

Closely linked to this question is whether Ithna Ashari Shi'ism implies the rejection or the subjugation of earthly power. This is not simply an academic question, but a fundamental political question relevant to the permanence of the Khomeini regime. If one argues that Ithna Ashari Shi'ism implies the subjugation of earthly power, then the Islamic Revolution, by overthrowing the shah, who represented the pre-Islamic tradition of secular monarchy, has achieved its objective, and the religious leaders may, therefore, presumably look forward to a lengthy period of power. If, on the other hand, one argues that Ithna Ashari Shi'ism implies the rejection of all earthly power, and that its ideology is purely millenarian and messianic, then Khomeini, by claiming to have instituted a regime which anticipates the just rule of the Twelfth Imam, may run the risk of being judged to have fallen short of the standards of perfect equity expected from the Mahdi. The fact that Khomeini seemed to encourage the attribution to himself of the title 'Imam', with some messianic overtones, increases the likelihood that, at some point, disillusionment with the Islamic regime may occur.

Finally, there is the whole vexed question of Iranian nationalism and of the part played in it by the traditions of Darius and Muhammad respectively. Through the legend that Husayn, the younger son of Ali, married Shahrbanu, the daughter of the last of the Sasanid kings, Yazdgird III, Ithna Ashari Shi'ism was lifted out of its purely Islamic context and merged with the Iranian historical tradition. As Eugène Aubin put it:

> Le Chiisme offrit une expression à cette nationalité qui s'obstinait à survivre; il fit une nation compacte de peuple le plus divers de l'Asie moderne, et, à défaut d'autre ressource, l'idée persane se réincarna sous une forme religieuse.[1]

Under Khomeini, has this alliance, which was at best a *mariage de convenance*, ended in divorce? Is Khomeini in the process of forging something which one might call Ithna Ashari nationalism, consisting of some elements of Iranian nationalism but resolute in its rejection of secularism? All these inter-related questions bear indirectly on this paper, which attempts to discover to what extent there is any historical justification, in the Ithna Ashari tradition, for the Islamic Republic of Iran's policy of seeking to export its brand of revolutionary Islam to other parts of the Islamic world.

Is Ithna Asharism Innately Revolutionary?

Until the Islamic Revolution, it was frequently assumed that Ithna Asharism was too closely identified with the Iranian national identity to be exportable to other parts of the Muslim world. This assumption may, of course, still prove to be well-founded. If it proves to be incorrect, it may be discovered that it is other elements of Khomeini's syncretist ideology, rather than undiluted Ithna Asharism, that have made the mixture palatable to non-Iranian Muslims. What is now generally conceded, I think, even by the most optimistic Arab states in the Persian Gulf area, is that the attempt by the Khomeini regime to export its Islamic revolutionary ideology does constitute a danger to other states in the region. The wish to export one's ideology, to foist it upon unwilling recipients, postulates that the ideology in question is revolutionary in nature. Before attempting to address the question of the export of Ithna Ashari ideology, therefore, perhaps one should first ask whether or not Ithna Asharism is innately revolutionary.

As Bernard Lewis has correctly said, there are present in the Islamic tradition, as a whole, strands of both quietism and activism,[2] and the same is true of Ithna Ashari tradition. There is, however, a crucial difference in the balance struck between quietism and activism in the Sunni and the Shi'i traditions, respectively. Over twenty years ago, Vladimir Minorsky captured the essence of Ithna Ashari ideology when he referred to "Shi'ism, with its overtones and its aroma of opposition, of martyrdom, and revolt." These attributes, Minorsky said, had always been "quite well" matched with the Persian character.[3] Given these basic characteristics of Ithna Ashari Shi'ism, a *prima facie* case could be made for its being a revolutionary creed. The circumstances attending its birth ensured that it would be a party, initially only a political party, opposed to the government of the day. This undeniable fact has left an enduring mark on Ithna Ashari ideology. There has always been a strong strand of negativism in Shi'i thought. It has always been much easier to say what Ithna Asharism is *against*, than to say what it is *for*. In the long-term, the leaders of the Islamic Republic of Iran may need to change this historically negative outlook into a more positive one. In the initial stage, however, they have been quite satisfied with a negative one.

If one accepts that opposition is a basic characteristic of Ithna Asharism, then the chances of this opposition being expressed in the form of a revolt are high. In the mediaeval Islamic world, as in mediaeval Christendom, dissidence was bound to be expressed by revolt, since there were no mechanisms for the peaceful transfer of political power. One may say, then, that Ithna Asharism had, from its inception, at least the *potential* for revolutionary activity. Arjomand, however, in a series of recent publications, considers that the dominant influence in Ithna Ashari thought is "legalistically and theologically rationalized Shi'ism," which is quietist. What he terms "millenarian extremism" he regards as aberrant and unrepresentative of 'true' Shi'ism, however that may be defined.[4] I believe that an even stronger case can be made for the proposition that Shi'is were quietist only during those periods when they had no hope of attaining political power. After 940/1, when Ithna Asharis abandoned the hope of the imminent return of the Twelfth Imam, such quietism could be rationalized in the light of their millenarian expectations. *Sub specie aeternitatis*, it might seem foolish to invite repression on the part of the dominant Sunni rulers of the Islamic world on a scale which might result in the annihilation of Ithna Asharism. It is interesting to note that the other major branch of the Shi'a, the Isma'ilis, achieved political power early, and, by the tenth century, ruled an important part of the heartlands of Islam. It was only *after* the Fatimids had lost political power that they attached greater importance to their millenarian expectations. Ithna Asharis were assisted in this attitude of quietism, when quietism seemed inevitable, by their doctrine of *taqiyya*, or 'prudential dissimulation', which not infrequently saved them from persecution. I would contend, then, that what Arjomand sees as "pious withdrawal from the political sphere"[5] was, in reality, an attitude dictated by political necessity. Having failed to seize political power from the Sunni caliphs by force of arms, the Ithna Asharis bided their time and continued to operate 'underground'.

In the course of their armed opposition to the Sunni caliphs, the Ithna Asharis acquired martyrs. Indeed, Ithana Asharis firmly believed that most of their Imams were done to death on the orders of the caliphs.[6] In this way, Ithna Asharis came to lay increasing emphasis on the third characteristic of their creed noted by Minorsky: martyrdom.

Targets of Ithna Ashari Activism in the Middle Ages

If it is agreed that Ithna Ashari ideology contained within itself at least the potential for revolutionary activity, at whom was this activity to be directed? In the early days of Islam, Ithna Ashari political activism was directed primarily at the Sunni caliphs, who were deemed to be usurpers. Ithna Asharis came close to success during the Abbasid Revolution, but had victory snatched from their grasp when Ali al-Riza, the eighth Imam, whom the Abbasid Caliph Ma'mun had designated as his successor in 817,[7] died the following year. Ithna Ashari historians allege that he was poisoned either by or on the orders of Ma'mun, but Tabari does not allude to the possibility of murder.[8] In 940/1, the last of the four *vakil*s or vicegerents of the Mahdi died without designating a successor, and Ithna Asharism entered the period of the 'greater' occultation (*ghaybat-e kubra*), which is still in progress. Ithna Ashari messianic aspirations were postponed till the millennium. It took the Ithna Ashari community some time to decide who was to lead it, in the absence of an Imam or of a vicegerent of the Mahdi. Ultimately, the community agreed that the Ithna Ashari *mujtahid*s, those scholars most learned in jurisprudence and theology, should act as the representatives on earth of the Mahdi, and should exercise a 'general agency' (*niyabat-e amma*) on his behalf, until his second coming. This decision coincided roughly with the establishment of the Buyid (Buwaihid) dynasty at Baghdad in 945, and the extension of the dominion of the Buyid rulers over Iraq-e Arab and most of Iraq-e Ajam.

The century of Buyid control of the caliphate (945–1055), which was felicitously termed by Minorsky the 'Iranian intermezzo', still poses some questions which await satisfactory answers. *Prima facie*, one would have expected the Buyid rulers, who were by all accounts some kind of 'moderate' Shi'is, to have seized the opportunity to establish an Ithna Ashari caliphate. Why did this not happen? Various arguments have been advanced to explain this. First, it is suggested that the Fatimids pre-empted the Ithna Ashari position by establishing a Shi'i caliphate in Cairo. It would have been difficult, this argument runs, to establish a rival Shi'i caliphate. I find this argument unconvincing. The two major branches of the Shi'a, the Isma'ilis or 'Seveners' and the Ithna Asharis or 'Twelvers', had diverged after the death of the sixth Imam Ja'far al-Sadiq, in 757, and had gone their separate ways. Their ideology had developed along very different lines, and there was no collaboration or community of interest between the two groups. On the theoretical level, it seems to me that the establishment of an Ithna

Ashari caliphate by the Buyids should not have been beyond the bounds of possibility. There would have been no question of weakening a theoretical 'common Shi'i front' against the Sunnis.

A second argument commonly advanced is that, since the majority of the population in Iraq-e Arab was Sunni (and probably also at that date the majority of the population in Iraq-e Ajam) the Buyids decided that it would be politically unwise to provoke political opposition by installing a Shi'i caliph in Baghdad. This argument has greater validity, but does not address one central problem. Supposing the Buyids had decided to install an Ithna Ashari caliph. Where would they have found a candidate? An essential part of the selection of an Ithna Ashari imam was *nass*, or designation by the preceding Imam. This was vital in Ithna Ashari theory because of the belief that the imams were in possession of a body of esoteric truth transmitted from Ali and ultimately from the Prophet. As already mentioned, the fourth *vakil* of the Mahdi died in 940/1 without designating a successor, merely declaring that "the matter was now with God."

The Ithna Ashari ship, temporarily bereft of a helmsman, was eventually placed under the control of the *mujtahids*. The legitimacy of the claim of the *mujtahids* to act as the representatives on earth of the Mahdi was gradually accepted by the Ithna Ashari community. The claim of the *fuqaha* to be, in the absence of the Hidden Imam, the only legitimate rulers of the state, was a claim of an altogether different magnitude. It is *this* claim, as already adumbrated by the tenth century, uttered mainly *sotto voce* but, on occasion, out loud in Safavid times,[9] and brought to its ultimate and logical conclusion by Khomeini, which has prevented the development of a political consensus in Iran to the present day. Once it had been conceded by the Ithna Ashari community that the *mujtahids*/*fuqaha* possessed what Arjomand calls "exclusive hierocratic authority,"[10] it was a logical progression to the position that all other forms of authority were illegitimate, and to the claim that they, and they alone, were the legitimate rulers of an Ithna Ashari state (in the absence, of course of the Mahdi). Perhaps it was not only the practical difficulty of identifying a legitimate candidate to lead the Ithna Ashari community that gave the Buyids pause. Perhaps it is not too far-fetched to suggest that the Buyid rulers were astute enough to realize, however dimly, that the investiture of an Ithna Ashari caliph would strike a serious, if not fatal, blow at their own authority.

The Postponement of Revolutionary Aspirations Until the Millennium

Whatever the reason for Buyid 'moderation', there is no doubt that, by the middle of the tenth century, the thrust of Ithna Ashari political activism had been directed away from the short-term goal of overthrowing the Sunni caliph, and had been transferred to the messianic plane.[11] Ithna Ashari jurists devoted much time and effort to formulating concepts of the 'just ruler', but their lucubrations remained theoretical until the establishment of the Safavid state in 1501. With the advent of the Safavids, the whole question of the legitimacy of any form of sovereignty, other than that of the Hidden Imam, immediately became a vital part of *realpolitik*. Moreover, since the Safavids had come to power as the consequence of some two centuries of the dissemination of the *da'wa* or political and religious propaganda, the existence of a well-organized network of *da'is*, 'missionaries' or 'propagandists', for the first time opened up the possibility of extending Ithna Asharism outside the boundaries of Iran. I know of no attempt by the state to export Ithna Ashari ideology on any significant scale beyond the confines of Iran and the Ithna Ashari enclaves in Mesopotamia, prior to the establishment of the Safavid state.

There does not appear to be any justification for such an idea in the works of Ithna Ashari jurisprudents during the mediaeval period. The principal concerns of the mediaeval jurists related to those issues, among others, which I set aside at the beginning of this paper as bearing only indirectly on the question of the export of Ithna Ashari ideology. The jurists were concerned to establish without doubt the need for an imam to lead and give right guidance to the Ithna Ashari community. They discussed the role of *saltane* ('temporal' rule) and the legitimacy of rulers such as *amir*s and *sultan*s, in the light of the general Islamic obligation of rulers to uphold and promulgate the rule of justice and equity. They asked whether it was proper for a member of the religious classes to accept judicial office under an unjust (*ja'er*) sultan. They discussed the paramount need to preserve the unity of the *umma*, the Islamic community, whether this unity was threatened by infidels outside the boundaries of Dar al-Islam, or by internal dissension. They discussed the right of the *ulama* to exercise the "general agency" (*al-niyaba al-amma*) on behalf of the Hidden Imam. Embedded in these discussions was the germ of the concept enunciated by Khomeini of *velayat-e faqih*. The only portions of the works of the jurists which seem to bear at all directly on the question of the export of Ithna Ashari ideology are the sections on *jihad*, 'holy war'. *Jihad*, even when waged against infidels, must be justified on ethical grounds and not simply on the desirability of extending the territory of Dar al-Islam, and most Ithna Ashari jurists agree that for the purpose of waging an offensive (as distinct from a defensive) *jihad*, the sanction of the Imam is mandatory.[12] There is, however, a significant interpretation of *jihad*, dating from early Islamic times, which permits its use *"even against dissenting groups within the Muslim community,"* if the latter are engaged in spreading discord in the earth.[13] "In an important *hadith*-report Imam Ali explains this meaning of *jihad* and declares that two groups of people with whom *jihad* is obligatory are the unjust group (*al-fi'a al-baghiya*), and the unbelievers (*al-fi'a al-kafira*)."[14] This interpretation of *jihad* was used by Ithna Ashari jurists to justify the *jihad* launched by the Caliph Ali against his opponents.[15]

As is well known, the original theory of *jihad* did not license Muslims to turn their arms against one another. It is equally clear that throughout Islamic history this rule has been violated. Launching a *jihad* against fellow-

Muslims has, more often than not, been justified by the simple device of declaring one's opponents, albeit Muslims, to be infidels (*kafir*). Khomeini has used this device extensively. In the judicial opinion quoted above, *jihad* against a group of dissenting Muslims is licensed if the latter are "engaged in spreading discord in the earth." The phrase "discord in the earth" (*fasad fi al-ard*) is based upon Qur'an V:33:

> The only reward of those who make war upon Allah and His Messenger and strive after corruption in the land will be that they will be killed or crucified
> . . . (Pickthall's translation).

Because this charge is a moral charge, not a legal one in the Western sense, no defense against it is possible; it is the public prosecutors who define what constitutes *fasad fi al-ard* at any given time.

If one is justified in declaring a *jihad* against one's fellow-Muslims, it would follow logically that one would also be justified in imposing on them, once subjugated, one's particular brand of Islam. It would be possible, therefore, to argue that this interpretation of *jihad* could afford a legal basis for the export of Ithna Ashari Islam. Within the context of this paper, it is interesting that the Safavid *mujtahid* Ali b. Abd al-Ali al-Karaki, known as al-Muhaqqiq al-Thani (d. 1530/1 or 1533/4), in his *Jami al-Maqasid*, a commentary on the *Qawa'id al-ahkam fi ma'rifat al-halal wal-haram* of Allama Hasan b. Yusuf b. Ali b. Mutahhar al-Hilli, "provided in the sphere of *jihad* nothing that could be interpreted as favorable to or justificatory of the Safavid struggle with the Ottomans."[16] In other words, one of the most powerful jurists of the Safavid period apparently did not avail himself of this interpretation of *jihad* to justify the attempt to export the Safavid *da'wa* beyond the confines of Iran.

The Nature of the Safavid *Da'wa*

Before we examine the nature of the Safavid *da'wa*, the first question to be asked is, was this political and religious propaganda state-sponsored or not? If by 'state-sponsored' one means formally disseminated by organs or agencies of government whose sole function is to promulgate propaganda, as is the case for example in the Soviet Union or the Islamic Republic of Iran today, then the answer is 'yes' and 'no'. To begin with, one has to determine whether or not the political entity noted during the early Safavid period as *mamalek-e mahruse* constituted a 'state' in the usually accepted sense of the term or not. H. R. Roemer and I have been discussing this issue for some years.[17] The question arises because of the way in which the Safavids came to power. Shah Isma'il was placed on the throne, not initially of the whole of Iran but only of Azerbayjan, by supporters who were members of a militant Sufi Order called the Safaviyye. This Order had been in existence at Ardebil for 200 years, since the installation of Shaykh Safi al-Din as its head in 1301, and had been transformed into a militant organization, openly aspiring to temporal power, under the leadership of Junayd (1447–1460). The early years of Safavid rule in Iran represent a period of transition from the Sufi organization of the Safaviyye to the more traditional institutions of a mediaeval Islamic state.

What then was the nature of the Safavid *da'wa*? Again, one has to differentiate clearly between the pre-revolutionary and the post-revolutionary *da'wa*.

> The most important element in the ideology of the Safavid revolutionary movement was that its leader, as the supreme director (*morshed-e kamel*) of the Safavid Order, was entitled to the unquestioning obedience of his Sufi disciples (*murids*), the majority of whom belonged to the Turcoman tribes and were known by the general name of *qizilbash*.[18]

These Turcoman tribes constituted the élite of the Safavid army, and it was primarily their fighting élan, inspired by the ideology described above, which was responsible for the success of the Safavid revolutionary movement. Many of these tribesmen lived outside the borders of Iran (in some instances the name of the tribe indicates this), in Syria, eastern Anatolia, and the Armenian highlands around Lake Van. Here is an indication of *da'wa* being directed from within Iran to persons outside Iran, but within the context of this paper two points should be made: first, the *da'wa* prior to 1501 was not state-sponsored, because the Safavid state had not yet been established; second, the content of the *da'wa* in the pre-revolutionary period owed more to militant Sufism, and to devotion to a charismatic leader, than it did to Ithna Asharism in any formal sense. This is not to say, of course, that elements of Shi'i ideology were totally absent. Indeed, one of the problems of the post-Mongol period of Persian history is the difficulty of distinguishing between the Sufi and the Shi'i strands in the *da'wa* of many sects. Perhaps this is why Henri Corbin made his controversial statement:

> True Shi'ism is the same as Tasawwuf, and similarly, genuine and real Tasawwuf cannot be anything other than Shi'ism.[19]

Ali is the point of departure for Ithna Ashari ideology, and Ali also figures prominently in the ideology of many Sufi groups from the thirteenth century to the establishment of the Safavid state. Ali also plays an important part in the ideology of extremist groups such as the Ahl-e Haqq and the Hurufis, and the Safavid *da'wa* of the pre-revolutionary period, laying emphasis, as it does, on the divine or quasi-divine nature of the Safavid leader, has much in common with the *da'wa* of such sects. We know of one instance in which a prominent Safavid *da'i* at Harat was accused of being a Hurufi.[20]

The clearest indication of the extreme nature of the Safavid pre-revolutionary *da'wa* is afforded by the poems written by Isma'il himself under the pen-name of Khata'i.[21] A contemporary Sunni source, the *Tarikh-e Alam-ara-ye Amini* of Fazlollah b. Ruzbihan Khunji, openly accuses the Safavid *murids* of referring to the Safavid leader Junayd as God and to his son as "the son of God" (ibn Allah). In his [i.e., Junayd's] praise they said: "he is the Living One, there is no god but he."[22] Junayd was succeeded as head of the Safaviyye by his son Haydar (1460–88), and, according to the same source, the Sufi 'commissars' (*khulafa*) "came from every direction and foolishly announced the glad tidings of his divinity (*uluhiyyat*)."[23] In other words, this *da'wa* had as its objective not the entrenchment of the jurists as the rulers of the state as the representatives on earth of the Hidden Imam, but the glorification of the leader of the Safaviyye and the winning of support for his claim to become ruler of Iran. The Safavid ruler thus played a dual role: supreme spiritual director (*morshed-e kamel*) of the Safavid Order, and potential king (*padeshah*) of Iran.

That the Safavid *da'wa* was to be imposed by *force majeure* is beyond dispute. In 1494 the Safavid leader Sultan Ali, shortly before his own death in battle with Aq Qoyunlu troops, invested his brother Isma'il with the Sufi *taj* (crown), signifying that Isma'il should succeed him as leader of the Safaviyye. "I desire you," said Sultan Ali, "to avenge me and your father and your ancestors upon the children of Hasan Padeshah [i.e., the Aq Qoyunlu]. For the die of heaven's choice has been cast in your name, and before long you will come out of Gilan like a burning sun, and with your sword sweep unbelief from the face of the earth."[24] "The face of the earth" is probably only a rhetorical exaggeration. Another story in the anonymous history of Shah Isma'il relates that the Aq Qoyunlu sultans, Alvand and Murad, who had amicably divided the Aq Qoyunlu empire between them, were visited in 1500 A.D. by a dervish named Baba Khayrollah, who informed them that a voice from the unseen world had told him that there would shortly come forth from Gilan a person who would increase the dignity and honor of the religion of Muhammad, establish the faith of the Twelve Imams, and restore law and order *in the land of Iran*.[25]

To the extent that Safavid *da'is* operated beyond the bounds of Iran, they could be said to be "exporting" the Safavid *da'wa*. The activities of the *da'i* Qasim al-Anwar at Harat hardly qualify as 'outside the bounds of Iran', even though Harat at the time of Qasim al-Anwar was in Timurid hands.[26] In Anatolia, however, which was certainly outside the boundaries of Iran, the Ottomans took the threat of the Safavid *da'wa* very seriously indeed. The struggle between the Ottomans and the Safavids for control of eastern Anatolia was essentially a struggle for the hearts and minds of the heterodox Turcoman tribes which formed the bulk of the population there. By the middle of the fourteenth century, the extreme *ghuluww*-type *da'wa* of the revolutionary Safavids appealed much more to these tribesmen than did the more orthodox and formalized Islam of the Ottoman religious establishment in Istanbul. The struggle for eastern Anatolia continued after the establishment of the Safavid state and, in 1511 and again in 1512, Shah Isma'il sent significant forces into the area. The fact that the Safavid forces were greeted with enthusiasm by Safavid sympathizers in the region was, without doubt, a major reason for Sultan Selim I's decision to invade Iran in 1514.

After the accession of Isma'il as (as yet only) ruler of Azerbayjan in 1501, the nature of the Safavid *da'wa* underwent an abrupt change. The Safavid leaders had used militant Sufism as the dynamic ideology capable of bringing them to power; now they were to use institutionalized Ithna Asharism to consolidate their rule. The fanatical devotion of the *qizilbash murid*s which had served them so well in the pre-revolutionary period, became something of a liability once the Safavid leaders wanted to consolidate their victory and put in place the administrative structure of their new state.[27]

Ithna Asharism Proclaimed State Religion

One of Shah Isma'il's first acts after his accession at Tabriz was to have the *khutba* read in the name of the Twelve Imams, and to proclaim the Ja'fari (Ithna Ashari) rite the true faith and the official religion of the new Safavid state.[28] The words "I bear witness that Ali is the Beloved of God" (*vali allah*) were incorporated in the call to prayer (*adhan*).[29] This proclamation changed the whole course of Iranian history. For the first time a major Islamic state had officially espoused the Ithna Ashari form of Shi'ism. Despite the long period during which the Safavid *da'wa* had been disseminated, many of Shah Isma'il's followers were nervous about the possible reaction of the population of Tabriz. There were good reasons for their anxiety because, as pointed out above, the Safavid *da'wa* prior to 1501 laid emphasis not on Ithna Asharism but rather on the position of the Safavid leader as *morshed-e kamel* endowed with divine or semi-divine status. Before the proclamation was made, a group of *qizilbash* amirs, and the few Shi'i *ulama* who were in Isma'il's retinue, voiced their apprehension:

> Of the 200–300,000 people in Tabriz, two-thirds are Sunnis; from the time of the *hadarat* (i.e., the Ithna Ashari Imams themselves) until now no one has publicly recited this *khutba,* and we fear that the people may say that they do not want a Shi'i sovereign (*padeshah-e shi'a*), and if, which God forbid! the people renounce Shi'ism, to what remedy can recourse be had?

Isma'il left no doubt that, as far as he was concerned, the sword was mightier than the pen: "By God's help," he said, "if the people utter one word of protest, I will draw the sword and leave not one of them alive." Yet, despite his brave words, the Shah was nervous. He received reassurance from Ali in a dream:

> O son, do not let anxiety trouble your mind . . . let all the *qizilbash* be present in the mosque fully armed, and let them surround the people; if, when the *khutba* is read, the people make any movement, the *qizilbash* will be able to deal with the situation, since they surround the people; then give the order for the *khutba* to be read.

When the *khutba* was read uproar broke out; one-third of the city gave thanks to Almighty God, and it was ordained that all the *khatib*s in the provinces should read the *khutba* of the Twelve Imams.[30]

Despite the uproar, two-thirds of the population of Tabriz, who the *qizilbash* chiefs had correctly estimated still to be Sunnis, apparently accepted the new dispensation without open confrontation. Opposition came, as was to be expected, from the Sunni *ulama*. Some migrated to Khorasan, which was still ruled by the Sunni Timurid monarch Sultan Husayn Mirza. When Isma'il reconquered Khorasan in 1510, they moved still further northeast, into Transoxania, ruled by the khans of the Özbeg confederation. Other Sunni *ulama* were put to death when they refused to recant. As Isma'il, in the course of the first decade of his rule, extended his sovereignty over the whole of Iran,[31] the indoctrination of the people with the basic tenets of the Ithna Ashari creed and the imposition of doctrinal unity, became his primary objectives. Because of the shortage of Shi'i *ulama*, theologians were imported from the Shi'i enclave of Jabal Amil in Syria, and the *sadr*, the official who was the head of the religious institution, was given as part of his duties the task of imposing doctrinal unity. Since he was a political appointee, responsible directly to the Shah, the Shah was able from the beginning to make the religious institution subordinate to the political institution. In this connection, the expression *padeshah-e shi'a*, 'king of the Shi'a', used by the *qizilbash* chiefs, is significant. It clearly suggests that, despite the proposal to make Ithna Ashari Shi'ism the official religion of the new Safavid state, there was no thought in their minds of letting the *fuqaha* govern the state. In other words, the by now firmly established Ithna Ashari theory that, in the continuing absence of the Mahdi, the *mujtahid*s, and they alone, exercised the general agency as the representative of the Hidden Imam on earth, and therefore constituted the only legitimate governing body in an Ithna Ashari state, was not practical politics, as far as the *qizilbash* were concerned.

Nevertheless, the fact that the Ithna Ashari creed had become the official religion was bound to pose a challenge to the legitimacy of the shah as ruler. If the *mujtahid*s were the only legitimate rulers of an Ithna Ashari Shi'i state, was not the shah a usurper? In terms of Ithna Ashari theory, he was. So should he be overthrown? No, said the majority of the *ulama*. Why did they say 'no'? Because they realized that, even if they conceded the right to govern to the shah, their power in a Shi'i state *without* sovereign control was still greater than it would be in a Sunni state in which they would be in a minority position with no political power at all. The *ulama* still continued to uphold the theoretical position, if only in private. The perceptive analysis of the Huguenot jeweller Jean Chardin, who was in Iran at the time of the coronation of Shah Sulayman in 1666, puts the situation in a nutshell:

> The clergy, and all the holy men of Iran, consider that rule by laymen was established by force and usurpation, and that civil government belongs by right to the *sadr* [the head of the religious institution] and to the Church

. . . but the more generally held opinion is that royalty, albeit in the hands of laymen, derives its institution and its authority from God; that the king takes the place of God and the prophets in the government of the People; that the *sadr*, and all other practitioners of the religious law, should not interfere with the political institution; that their authority is subject to that of the king, *even in matters of religion.* This latter opinion prevails; the former opinion is held only by the clergy and those whom they supervise; the king and his ministers close the mouths of the clergy as it pleases them, and force the clergy to obey them in everything. In this way, the spiritual is at the moment completely subordinate to the temporal.[32]

Why did Shah Isma'il declare Ithna Ashari Shi'ism to be the official religion of the Safavid state if he knew that this action was bound to provoke, sooner or later, a challenge to the sovereignty and the legitimacy of the Safavid shahs? A. K. S. Lambton has suggested that political considerations were uppermost in Isma'il's mind. Such a policy would give the new state territorial and political identity and would clearly differentiate it from the powerful Sunni states lying to the west and to the east: the Ottoman Empire and the Özbeg confederation. When Isma'il came to the throne, there were three distinct bases to his power: First, his position as *morshed-e kamel* of the Safaviyye Order. (I have suggested above that this ideology, though eminently successful in instilling in the *qizilbash* a fanatical devotion to their apotheosized leader, was somewhat of a liability in the post-revolutionary period). Second, the divine right of Persian kings, which had nothing to do with Islam, but had been given, after the advent of Islam, an Islamic coloration as *zill allah fi al-ard* ("the shadow of God upon earth"). Amin Banani has noted the similarity between the manner in which the Achaemenid and the Safavid monarchies were established, and he comments:

The ideological formulation of *khwarna/zillallah* were instrumental in elevating the monarch to a position of absolute patrimonial power.[33]

Third, the claim of the Safavid shahs to be the representatives of the Mahdi,[34] in this instance usurping the function which the *mujtahid*s had claimed to exercise for centuries. The second and third of these elements of the power of the Safavid shahs were in fundamental contradiction, representing as they did the tradition of Darius and the tradition of Muhammad (and more especially, of Ali), respectively. This basic dichotomy in the Iranian polity and in the Persian psyche has not yet been resolved.

The reigns of the Safavid shahs prior to the accession of Shah Abbas I, in 1588, constitute something of a transition as far as the ideology which drove the machinery of government is concerned. The revolutionary organization of the Safaviyye, headed by an official called the *khalifat al-khulafa*, and comprising *khalifa*s (dubbed by Minorsky 'commissars'), *abdal*s, *dada*s and *khadem*s, continued to exist in a fossilized form, bereft of political power.[35] It was used by the shahs mainly as a touchstone by which to determine the loyalty or otherwise of a particular official. In an emergency, the shahs could still appeal to the old emotive concept of *shah-sevani*, "love of the shah." The concept of *sufigari*, conduct appropriate to a Sufi, was interpreted as 'loyalty to the state'; conversely, *nasufigari*, "conduct unbecoming a Sufi," denoted 'high treason'. Gradually, as Ithna Ashari doctrine became entrenched in a more formalized way, in all parts of the Safavid state, it was only natural that the *ulama*, the exponents of Ithna Ashari law and theology, should acquire greater power in the state. The spiritual was not quite as completely subordinate to the temporal as Chardin had declared. As early as the reign of Shah Tahmasp (1524–76), *mujtahids* on several occasions challenged the authority of the *sadr* who, as mentioned above, was a political appointee responsible for keeping the *ulama* under control.

> On two occasions the *mujtahed al-zaman* was able to secure the dismissal of a *sadr* to whom he was hostile, and on two other occasions the appointment of a *sadr* was due to the influence of the *mujtahed*.[36]

This suggests that, even at this early stage in Safavid history, the *mujtahids*, aware of the opportunity to enhance their own power afforded by the creation of an Ithna Ashari state, were beginning to flex their muscles. Of particular interest, in view of the attempt by the Iranian government in 1978 to discredit Imam Khomeini by publishing a libelous attack on him in the press, is the attempt by the *sadr* Amir Ne'matollah Hilli, circa 1528–30, to discredit the leading *mujtahid* of the day by planting behind his house an anonymous document containing libelous statements about the *mujtahid*. Plus ça change . . . ! These incidents portended the dramatic increase in the power of the *mujtahids* under the later Safavid shahs.

There is no doubt that Shah Isma'il I was a zealous propagator of the Ithna Ashari creed. It is equally clear that in his eyes Sunni Muslims were every bit as much infidels as were the Christian populations of Georgia and other parts of the Caucasus region. In the later recension of the *Safvat al-Safa* made by Abu al-Fath al-Husayni during the reign of Tahmasp, the author writes that, when Isma'il emerged from Gilan in 1499 to make his bid for power,

> he delivered us from the tyranny of the infidels of that time. Within a short time he cleansed Azerbaijan, Shirvan, Diyar Bakr, Iraq-e Arab, Iraq-e Ajam, Fars and Khorasan of the oppression and corruption of seditious and contumacious people . . . after seven or eight hundred years during which the true Imami [Ithna Ashari] faith had lain in concealment, he revealed and manifested it, and gave currency to and made effective the articles [of that faith], and published and made known to the people of the world [the practice of] the cursing and vilifying of the enemies of the Prophet's house.[37]

Wherever Safavid arms went, the Ithna Ashari creed accompanied them and was imposed on the subject population. In 1508, when Isma'il subjugated southwest Iran and Iraq-e Arab, he had manifested the *yad-e bayda*[38] in order to promote and magnify the creed of the Twelve Imams, despite the dominant position of the Sunnis in those regions.[39] Two years later, in 1510, Shah Isma'il incorporated into the Safavid state the province of Khorasan, which was one of the few areas of Iran that had remained in Timurid hands after Timur's death in 1405. Khorasan was over-run by the rising power in Transoxania, a confederation of Özbeg tribes led by Muhammad Shibani Khan, but the religious orientation of the area remained Sunni. After Isma'il's defeat of the Özbegs in 1510, he made great efforts to extend the Ithna Ashari creed throughout the province. The *khatibs* everywhere recited the names of the Twelve Imams in the *khutba*, and were required to institute the practice of the ritual cursing of Abu Bakr, Umar and Uthman. The *shaykh al-islam* of Khorasan, who refused to comply with these orders, was put to death *pour encourager les autres*. By contrast, any members of the religious classes known to be Shi'is were singled out by the shah and accorded a specially privileged status. The Ithna Ashari form of the *shari'a* was substituted for the Sunni form.[40]

None of this, however, constitutes evidence that the Safavids, after the accession of Shah Isma'il, deliberately set out to export Ithna Ashari ideology. The regions mentioned above either formed part of Iran, historically speaking, or, as in the case of Iraq-e Arab, formed part of the two great pre-Islamic Persian empires, the Achaemenid and the Sasanid. Moreover, the conquest of Iraq-e Arab was imperative on both political and religious grounds: first, Baghdad was still held by military officers loyal to the Aq Qoyunlu dynasty which Isma'il had overthrown on his way to seizing power in Iran; second, control of Iraq-e Arab would enable Isma'il better to monitor the activities of the Musha'sha dynasty in the frontier area of Hawiza, Dezful and Shushtar. The Musha'sha Arabs were one of the extremist Shi'ite groups (*ghulat*) which might have constituted a threat on ideological grounds to the spread of the Safavid *da'wa*. They believed in the divinity of Ali, and one of their rulers is said to have claimed to be the incarnation of Ali, or even to have been the divinity in his own person;[41] third, Isma'il, as a zealous Shi'i, would obviously wish to have under Safavid control the important Shi'i shrines in Mesopotamia, namely, Najaf, Karbala, and Kazimayn. It is no coincidence at all that Imam Khomeini has given so many of the Iranian offensives against the Iraqis the code-name 'Karbala'.

Ithna Asharism in India

From early Islamic times, Shi'is had made their way to India. Since they were usually going there to escape persecution by Sunnis, they did not wish to attract attention to themselves, and practised *taqiyya* in order to blend in with the primarily Sunni background among the Muslims in India. The first dynasty in India to show evidence of Shi'i proclivities appears to have been the Bahmanid dynasty of the Deccan, established in 1347. From their capital at Gulbarga, the Bahmanid rulers waged wars on the two principal Hindu principalities of the southern Deccan, Warangal and Vijayanagar.[42] Eventually, three Shi'i dynasties, all founded by former servants of the Bahmanids, were established in the Deccan: the Adelshahis of Bijapur (1490–1686); the Nezamshahis of Ahmadnagar (1491–1633); and the Qotbshahis of Golconda (1512–1687). The Qotbshahi dynasty was founded by a Qara Qoyunlu officer, Sultan Qoli, who had fled from Persia after the rival Aq Qoyunlu chiefs obtained the upper hand there in 1467. Sultan Qoli had first entered the service of the Bahmanid king, and later set up his own kingdom at Golconda on the ruins of the Warangal Hindu kingdom. Though Sultan Qoli proclaimed Ithna Ashari Shi'ism at Golconda in 1512, he was at pains to disclaim any Safavid connection:

> I also swore by the Prophet and his descendant Ally [Ali], that if I ever succeeded in establishing my independence, I would promote the faith of the Twelve Imams, in parts where the banners of the faithful had never been waved; but let it not be supposed that I took up the idea for Shah Ismael of Persia, for be it known that I professed the religion of the twelve (on whom be the peace of God!) from the period of Sultan Yakoob, as being the faith of my ancestors.[43]

The founder of the Nezamshahi dynasty of Ahmadnagar was a convert to Islam from Hinduism. The son of a Brahman, he had been taken prisoner and brought up as a slave at the court of the Bahmani ruler Ahmad III (1461–63). Although exposed to Shi'i influence at court (the Persian *vazir* Mahmud Gavan was probably a crypto-Shi'i), he does not seem actually to have promulgated Ithna Asharism when he asserted his independence of the Bahmanid ruler in 1491. This step was taken by his son and successor Burhan I, who acceded to the throne when only seven years of age. It is hardly surprising that Burhan's *vazir*, another Persian immigrant named Shah Taher Junaydi, was successful in persuading Burhan to adopt Shi'ism.[44]

The case of the Adelshahi dynasty of Bijapur is especially interesting. It is said to have been founded by Yusuf, a son of the Ottoman Sultan Murad II (1421–51). According to the account of the chronicler Fereshte, at the time of the accession of Yusuf's brother Muhammad (Mehmet) II in 1451, Yusuf was about to be put to death (following normal Ottoman practice) when he was saved by his mother, who had him smuggled out of the country by a merchant. Yusuf was taken to Ardebil, the nerve-center of the Safavid revolutionary movement, and was there indoctrinated with Ithna Ashari ideology. After some years in Iran, Yusuf was instructed in a dream by the prophet Khezr to go to India; there, his royal blood would be recognized and he would become king. Yusuf obeyed the prophet's instructions, and in 1490 established the Adelshahi dynasty of Bijapur. In 1502 he fulfilled "a long-time wish" by having the *khutba* recited in the name of the Twelve Imams, "the first time," says Fereshte, "that any ruler in India had dared to perform these ceremonies in public." However, the ritual cursing of the first three caliphs, encouraged by his fellow-Shi'i ruler at Golconda, was forbidden by Yusuf.[45] Ithna Asharism was not deeply rooted in Bijapur. Each succeeding reign saw the restoration of Sunnism or Shi'ism as the case might be, until the kingdom of Bijapur was absorbed into the Mughal empire in 1686; the same fate befell the Shi'i enclaves at Golconda and Ahmadnagar in 1687 and 1633, respectively.[46]

Two Mughal emperors flirted with Ithna Ashari Shi'ism, one voluntarily and the other perforce. Babur, the founder of the Mughal empire, donned the *qizilbash taj*[47] as the price of receiving military support from Shah Isma'il when he attempted to recover his Transoxanian dominions in 1511/2,[48] but doffed it with alacrity after the disastrous failure of that expedition. Babur's son, the emperor Homayun, was forced by his rivals in India to seek refuge in Iran in 1544. While he was a refugee at the court of Shah Tahmasp, great pressure was brought upon him by the Shah to adopt Ithna Asharism as the *quid pro quo* for Safavid military support in Homayun's attempt to regain the Mughal throne. It seems that Homayun signed some documents attesting to his conversion, but it is obvious that he took this action purely for reasons of political expediency.

None of this evidence adds up to anything like a deliberate effort by the Safavid state to export Ithna Asharism to India. The Safavid rulers were always ready to exploit a particular political situation that might occur. There is evidence that Ithna Asharis who had emigrated from Persia to India seem to have done rather well at various courts in India, and some played a part in converting local rulers to Shi'ism. As to the story of Yusuf, if one accepts the account of Fereshte, it seems that the headquarters of the Safavid revolutionary movement at Ardebil was an effective place for the training of converts to the Safavid cause, but this is already known. The actual decision of Yusuf to leave Iran and move to India is credited to the prophet Khezr, not to the Safavid leaders.

Ithna Ashari emigration from Iran to India continued after the fall of the Safavids. Those Ithna Asharis who aspired to service at the Mughal court, even though they came from *ulama* families in Iran, found it necessary, if they were "to succeed socially," to "concentrate on literary or medical pursuits"[49] rather than on the spreading of Ithna Ashari ideology. In 1722, the year of the fall of Isfahan to the Afghans, another Shi'i kingdom was established in India, this time at Oudh. The first ruler of this kingdom, Mir Muhammad Amin Musavi, whose family hailed from Nishapur in Khorasan, was appointed governor of Oudh by the Mughal Emperor Muhammad Shah (1719–48). During the latter part of the eighteenth and early part of the nineteenth centuries, Lucknow, the capital of the kingdom of Oudh, achieved extraordinary wealth and prosperity, but was also the scene of frequent clashes between Shi'is and Sunnis. After the establishment of the British raj in 1858, the fortunes of the Ithna Asharis declined.[50] It is interesting, as an aside, to note that in recent times the Government of India has fared no better in trying to curb communal violence between Sunnis and Shi'is than did its predecessor, the British raj. After the 1965 Commission of Inquiry into Communal riots, the Government of India, in an effort to be even-handed, banned both the ritual cursing by Shi'is of the first three caliphs, and the eulogizing of them by Sunnis.[51] There is no suggestion, however, that the movement of Ithna Asharis to India in the eighteenth century was the result of sponsorship by the Iranian state. Rather, emigrants seem to have been attracted either by the greener economic pastures of the Mughal empire or by the prospect of escaping from the anti-Shi'i policies instituted by Nader Shah during the latter part of his reign, and from the political turmoil that followed his death.

The Later Safavids and Nader Shah

Throughout his reign, Shah Abbas the Great (1588–1629) kept the religious leaders on a tight leash. His aim, in which he was largely successful, was to build up a multi-cultural state in which an atmosphere of religious tolerance would encourage not only European merchants, but also members of the non-Muslim communities in Iran, especially the Jews and Armenians, to participate in the economic development of the country. This policy of religious tolerance was not followed by all his successors, and, during the last half century of Safavid rule, the *mujtahid*s took advantage of the weak rule of Shah Sulayman (1666–1694) and of Shah Sultan Husayn (1694–1722) to increase their political power and influence in co-operation with the *haram*. According to Banani, "some sources suggest a direct religious rule by means of a concourse of *mujtahid*s above the monarch."[52] The supremacy of the *mujtahid*s ushered in a period of religious bigotry, directed by powerful jurists like Muhammad Baqer Majlesi, who held the office of *shaykh al-islam* from 1687 to 1694, and the newly-created office of *mollabashi* from 1694 until his death in 1699. This was the Muhammad Baqer Majlesi who, according to a member of the Iranian *ulama* writing in 1966, "in conformity with the tenets of the religious law of Islam, was opposed to Sufis, idolators, Jews, Christians, and the fellow-countrymen of Edward Browne."[53]

It was during this period that a great deal of work was done in the fields of Ithna Ashari Shi'i theology and jurisprudence. Did this elaboration and codification of Ithna Ashari doctrine lead to any attempt to export it outside Safavid dominions? I know of no evidence to that effect. It would be strange if any attempt *were* made, in view of the political and military weakness of the Safavid state at that period. Further, it seems that Muhammad Baqer Majlesi and his contemporaries were more concerned with the extirpation of heretics within the Safavid state than they were with exporting Ithna Asharism. The non-Muslim minorities bore the brunt of the religious persecution. Shah Sultan Husayn does not appear to have been personally antagonistic toward religious minorities, but allowed himself to be persuaded to sign oppressive decrees as the result of pressure from powerful religious leaders like Muhammad Baqer Majlesi and his grandson and successor in the office of *mollabashi*, Mir Muhammad Husayn Khatunabadi (died 1739). For example, many Jews were forcibly constrained to convert to Islam, as were many Zoroastrians.

The overthrow of the Safavids in 1722 was followed by the Afghan interregnum (1722–29) and then by the seizure of power by Nader Khan Afshar. Nader Khan at first pretended to reign in the name of the Safavid kings, and adopted the tongue-in-cheek soubriquet of Tahmasp Qoli ('slave of Tahmasp') to indicate his supposed subordinate status, but in 1736 he abandoned this pretense and reigned as Nader Shah until his assassination in 1747. There is a number of contradictions in Nader's attitude toward religious matters. On the one hand, he abolished the office of *sadr*, thereby throwing away his last chance to bring back under control the religious leaders who had exercised a sort of condominium with the shah during the period of Safavid decline. On the other hand, he made an attempt to have the Ithna Ashari rite recognized as the fifth orthodox school (*madhhab*) of Islamic law. In 1743 Nader, in the course of a campaign against the Ottomans in Iraq-e Arab, convened a conference of *ulama* from Iran, Afghanistan, Balkh, Bukhara, Karbala, Najaf and Kazimayn. This conference was unique, in that it was attended by both Sunni and Shi'i *ulama*. The communiqué issued at the end of this summit meeting, as we would say these days, deplored the religious policies of the Safavids, but affirmed the right of the Ja'fari sect to be recognized as the fifth orthodox school of law in Islam; in return, Ithna Asharis were to recognize the legitimacy of the first three caliphs, who traditionally had been the target of ritual cursing on the part of Ithna Asharis.[54] It was to be more than two hundred years before Sunnis again addressed themselves to the question whether Shi'is could be regarded as orthodox Muslims, or even as Muslims at all. In 1959 Shaykh Mahmud Shaltut, the Rector of al-Azhar theological school in Cairo, issued a *fatwa* in which he ruled that Shi'is *were* to be recognized as Muslims.

Although the majority of Nader's troops were Sunni Afghans and Turcomans, there seems to be some doubt whether the assumption that he himself was a Sunni is correct. Lockhart points out that Nader's three sons all had "characteristically Shi'a names": Reza Qoli; Morteza Qoli (later changed to Nasrollah after Nader's victory at Karnal); and Imam Qoli, and suggests that Nader himself may have been born into a Shi'i family.[55] In 1732, Nader, still the power behind the throne, made references to the Twelve Imams and to the Shi'a generally in his denunciation of the Turco-Persian Treaty signed by Tahmasp II, but Lockhart comments:

> It is difficult to believe, at this stage, that his words were inspired by any genuine enthusiasm for, and belief in, the Shi'a faith; it seems more probable that he merely wished to excite and utilise Shi'a fanaticism for his own political ends; so long as the Shi'a ladder was of use to him in his upward progress, he would not kick it away.[56]

Lockhart's skepticism seems to be justified by Nader's subsequent actions. In 1736, Nader went through an elaborate charade which purported to give the leaders of the state a genuine choice as ruler: himself or Tahmasp II. The *mollabashi*, Mirza Abd al-Hasan, unwisely remarked "in the privacy of his tent," 'Everyone is for the Safavid dynasty'. Next day Nader had him strangled. Nader then announced that he was willing to become shah. One of his conditions was:

The Sunni faith should be adopted in place of the Shi'a, whose obnoxious and heretical practices must cease . . . if the people of Persia desire that we [Nader] should reign, they must abandon this doctrine which is opposed to the faith of the noble predecessors and the great family of the Prophet, and [they must] follow the religion of the Sunnis.[57]

Again, Lockhart expresses the opinion that Nader took this step for political reasons, and was not "actuated by any genuine religious conviction," and may not have ever had any "religious beliefs at all." Possible motives for Nader's actions, says Lockhart, were: a desire to weaken the Shi'i *ulama*, who were ideologically committed to the Safavid regime and might conspire to overthrow him; a desire to please his troops, the majority of whom, as already mentioned, were Sunnis; and not improbable an ambition to march on Istanbul, overthrow the Ottoman sultan and to install himself as ruler of the entire Muslim world.[58]

Even before his coronation on 8 March 1736,[59] Nader had sent a diplomatic mission to Istanbul to communicate his peace terms to the Ottoman government. One of the conditions was:

The Persians, having given up their former beliefs and chosen the religion of the Sunnis, were to be recognized as a fifth sect, to be known as the Ja'fari.[60]

A preliminary agreement was reached with the Ottoman commander, Ahmad Pasha, but Nader was eventually forced to drop this demand. In any case, the condition makes no sense as it stands. Obviously Nader had succeeded in putting one over on the worthy pasha! The same confusion exists in one of the articles of the Supplement to the Treaty of Kurdan, signed on 4 September 1746, which states that:

The Persian peoples, having abandoned 'those unseemly opinions which were created in the time of the Safavids, and having in their fundamental beliefs followed the path of the Sunnat', were thenceforward to treat the Orthodox Caliphs [i.e., Abu Bakr, Umar and Uthman] with respect.[61]

Despite the fascinating twists and turns of Nader's attitude toward religion, there is a fair body of evidence to support Lockhart's contention that he was, basically, an irreligious man. His liberal attitude toward Christians[62] makes it certain that he did not hold fanatical Ithna Ashari beliefs. His willingness to perform a *volte-face* on the question of Ithna Asharism, and to try and reimpose Sunnism after more than two and a quarter centuries of Safavid rule, supports Lockhart's theory that "Nadir was international rather than national in his outlook, and his dreams of dominion extended far beyond the confines of the Safavi empire."[63] It is significant that Nader Shah thought that ecumenicity within Dar al-Islam could be achieved only on the basis of Sunnism. Perhaps this holds a lesson for the present regime in Iran. What *is* clear is that, although Nader tried to gain recognition of Ithna Asharism as the fifth orthodox school in Islam, this was a bargaining ploy only, as he made no attempt to export Ithna Ashari ideology beyond the borders of Iran.

The Zands and the Qajars

The death of Nader Shah in 1747 was followed by half a century of civil war as two rival factions, the Zands and the Qajars, fought for supremacy in Iran. Karim Khan Zand (1750–1779) seized possession of most of the country, but failed to wrest Khorasan from the descendants of Nader Shah. The Qajars, who had been rivals of Nader before his accession to the throne, and subsequently entered his service, soon supplanted the Afsharids in Khorasan after Nader's death, and by 1756 had extended their sway over the north of Iran and Azerbayjan. Karim Khan Zand, though head of what Perry has felicitously called a "neo-Safavid" state, only "upheld the Shi'a in a conventional way."[64] Coins were minted in the name of the Hidden Imam, but the Safavid office of *mollabashi* was abolished, and the head of the religious institution was termed *shaykh al-islam*.[65] Preoccupied as he was with his struggle against the rising power of the Qajars, and by nature disinclined to promote religious fanaticism, Karim Khan did nothing to export Ithna Asharism; however, during the brief Zand occupation of Basra (1776–79), coins were minted which included a dedication to the Lord of the Age (*saheb-e zaman*), one of the titles of the Mahdi.[66]

The rule of the Qajar dynasty in Iran, even before being formally established by Aqa Muhammad Khan Qajar in 1796, opened with two campaigns against the 'infidels' of Georgia. The *casus belli* was the repudiation of Persian suzerainty in 1783 by King Erekle (Heraclius) of Georgia, who had placed himself under the protection of Russia. Incidentally, it is interesting to note that Catherine the Great offered "to protect all Iranian subjects, including Muslims, from the tyrannical rule of the usurper Aqa Muhammad Khan."[67] Ironically, a few years later, in 1786, the Russian consul at Enzeli gave Aqa Muhammad Khan arms to enable him to conquer Gilan.[68] Subsequently, the Russians transferred their support to his brother, Morteza Qoli Khan, because Aqa Muhammad Khan refused to accept vassal status.[69] Aqa Muhammad Khan's invasion of Georgia in 1795, and a second Persian invasion in 1797, were instances of *jihad* ('holy war') in the classic sense against the Christian populations of the southern Caucasus, and were characterized by the usual burning, looting and the seizure of prisoners. They were reminiscent of similar expeditions into the southern Caucasus launched by Safavid leaders in the fifteenth, and by Shah Tahmasp in the sixteenth century. Their purpose was the acquisition of booty, and the imposition of vassal status on the Christian rulers of the area. They do not seem to have constituted an attempt to export Ithna Ashari ideology across the Aras river.

The establishment of the Qajar dynasty saw a dramatic recrudescence of the power of the religious classes. The Afghan inter-regnum, and the vagaries of Nader's religious policies, had caused many of the *ulama* to leave Iran and settle at one of the Ithna Ashari shrines in Iraq (known as the *atabat*).[70]

The various measures taken by Nader Shah to weaken the power of the *ulama* are well known: "the confiscation of *waqf* property, the abolition of the post of *sadr*, the restriction of all jurisdiction to *urf* courts, and the strangling of the *shaykh ul-Islam* of Isfahan."[71] It was precisely during this period, between the fall of the Safavids and the rise of the Qajars, that the fortunes of the *ulama* were at a low ebb. It is no coincidence that it was also during this period that the Akhbari school of Ithna Ashari jurisprudence, which denied the interpretative function of the *mujtahid* and restricted the political role of the *ulama*, flourished. By the end of the eighteenth century, however, a time which coincided with the rise to power of the Qajars, the activist Usuli school of Ithna Ashari jurisprudence, led by Aqa Muhammad Baqer Behbahani (1705–1803), had triumphed over the Akhbaris to the extent that "hardly a trace of their former dominance remained."[72] Not only was there a recrudescence of the power of the *ulama* during Qajar times, but their power was also revived in its most militant form. Why was this?

The Qajar shahs no longer possessed the means of controlling the *ulama* which the Safavids had had until the accession of Shah Sulayman. Of the three bases of the power of the Safavid shahs mentioned above: the shah as *morshed-e kamel*; as the representative on earth of the Mahdi; and as the Shadow of God upon earth—only the last remained in Qajar hands. Although the Qajars, like the Safavids, considered themselves to be directly appointed by God, and believed strongly in the divine right of kings, unlike the Safavids they did not consider themselves as ruling on behalf of the Mahdi. Under the Qajars, the *mujtahids* therefore reverted to the role which they had played since the tenth century, of exercising the general agency on behalf of the Mahdi; but the office of *sadr*, a political appointee responsible for 'keeping the religious classes in their place', no longer existed. Too late, Naser al-Din Shah (1848–96) attempted to bring the *ulama* once more under the control of the Crown, by the appointment of an official called the *imam jum'a*. With the greater separation between the functions of the religious institution and the political institution, the power of the *ulama* was enhanced. The *ulama* were able to adopt a more critical attitude toward the actions of the government. The breakdown of the administrative system following the fall of the Safavids left the common people more exposed than before to the arbitrary actions of government officials, and so the *ulama* were increasingly able to play their traditional role as the protectors and refuge of the people against this arbitrary power. Further, as the Qajar shahs opened up the country to foreign concessionaires, and as more and more Persians returned to Iran after completing their higher education in Europe, the *ulama* were able to come forward as the champions of the bazaar merchants against encroachment in the economic sector by foreign entre-preneurs, and as defenders of Islam against the intrusion of foreign and therefore alien and unwanted political philosophies, and against the forces of social change. Trials of strength between the *ulama* and the shahs became inevitable, and commentators on modern Iran usually point to the affair of the Tobacco Concession as marking a turning-point. In 1891 the Muslim activist and reformer Jamal al-Din al-Afghani persuaded the Ithna Ashari *mujtahid* at Samarra to issue a *fatwa* banning the use of tobacco by the faithful. The *ulama* in Iran mobilized the masses in support of this *fatwa*, and in 1892 the shah was forced to rescind the Tobacco Concession. The significance of this victory was not lost upon the *ulama*.

All this, however, has to do with the vexed question of the legitimacy of secular rulers in an Ithna Ashari state. It has to do with the Ithna Ashari doctrinal position that the only legitimate ruler in such a state is the Twelfth Imam, and with the claim of the *mujtahids* that, in the absence of the Twelfth Imam, they, and they alone, have the right to act as his representatives on earth. It says nothing about the question whether Ithna Asharism should be exported to other parts of the Islamic world. The constitutional instruments of 1906–1907 represented an unworkable compromise between the secularists and the *ulama*, and their alliance was of an extremely short duration. The establishment of the Pahlavi dynasty in 1925 ushered in a half century of an attempt, by the state, to secularize government and society. The last Shah, Muhammad Reza Pahlavi, thought that he was on the brink of effecting a separation between 'Church' and 'State', to use Western terminology (see chapter by Menashri). But, as a member of the religious classes wrote in 1966, "the thesis that religion and politics are separate is a fabrication of the colonial powers."[73] On this point, the *ulama* are inexorable. As a result, there is still no consensus in Iran on the question of the system of governance that should be obtained there. Until a consensus is achieved, there is no prospect for peace and stability in that troubled country.

Conclusions

From the argument above, it seems to me that the following general conclusions may be drawn:

First, the Islamic tradition *per se* may be either quietist or activist; to the extent that the Ithna Ashari tradition is part of the overall Islamic tradition, the same may be said about it.

Second, the Islamic world view, which divides the world into Dar al-Islam and Dar al-Harb, reinforced by basic dogmas concerning the superiority of Islam to other religions, concerning *jihad*, etc., makes it inherently likely that Islam will move into an expansionist and missionary mode whenever it has the opportunity to do so.

Specifically, we may conclude:

1. As a result of the circumstances which accompanied its genesis, Shi'ism acquired its basic overtones of opposition, martyrdom and revolt. This fundamental stance of opposition to, and confrontation with, the Sunni caliphs led Ithna Asharis to engage in revolutionary activism during the early centuries of Islam.
2. The death of the fourth *vakil* in 940/1, and his failure to designate a successor, had two important consequences: (a) Ithna Ashari aspirations to achieve political power were postponed until the millennium;

(b) the Ithna Ashari *mujtahids* were acknowledged as the representatives of the Mahdi on earth for the duration of the 'greater occultation' (*ghaybat-e kubra*).

3. The promulgation of Ithna Ashari Shi'ism by the Safavids in 1501 A.D. as the official religion of the state greatly enhanced the power and prestige of the Ithna Ashari religious establishment. The following points should be noted: (a) The Safavid pre-revolutionary *da'wa*, described by Arjomand as "theophanic domination and militant chiliasm,"[74] was superseded after 1501 A.D. by a more 'orthodox' Ithna Ashari ideology; (b) it seems that the *ulama* did *not* attempt to export Ithna Asharism beyond the borders of Iran. The basic reason for this may be that, although Ithna Asharism was the official religion of the Safavid state, the jurists were not the rulers of that state in the way in which they are the rulers of Khomeini's Iran. Even in the period of Safavid decline, when the jurists became increasingly influential in governance, the institution of the monarchy was still an obstacle to their obtaining total control of the machinery of government. The jurists therefore devoted more attention to questions of legitimacy, to discussions of the concept of the 'just ruler', and the like, than they did to the export of Ithna Ashari *da'wa*.

4. Ithna Ashari Shi'ism *did* spread beyond the borders of Iran during the Safavid period and later, most notably in India. However, this process seems to have been the result of factors such as religious persecution, economic opportunities, and the random exploitation of political opportunities by individual Safavid rulers. It was not the result of state policy. Similarly, there is no evidence of any state-sponsored attempt to export Ithna Asharism under Nader Shah or the Qajar monarchs. Neither Nader Shah nor any of the Qajar shahs claimed to be the representative on earth of the Mahdi.

5. It seems, then, that Khomeini, in developing an ideology which sees the world in terms of an apocalyptic struggle between the forces of good and evil, has gone beyond traditional Ithna Ashari messianism. Under his leadership, there seemed to have been a significant shift on the part of Ithna Asharis toward viewing Ithna Asharism as a 'world religion' (see chapter by Menashri). Khomeini claimed to be the leader (*rahbar*) not merely of all Ithna Ashari Shi'is, but of all Muslims. To the best of my knowledge, this is the first time in the fourteen centuries of Islamic history that an Ithna Ashari has made a conscious bid for the leadership of the whole of Dar al-Islam. Nader Shah may have seen himself as leader of Dar al-Islam, but if he did, it would have been in the role of a Sunni leader of a predominantly Sunni Dar al-Islam. Khomeini's deliberate attempts to subvert constitutionally elected, or legitimately established, Muslim governments in other Muslim countries in the Middle East, again seemed to be a *bid'a*.

Notes

1. "Shi'ism offered a way of expression to this nationality that obstinately wanted to survive. Shi'ism made a compact nation of the most diverse people of modern Asia, and lacking other resources the Persian idea was reincarnated in religious form." Eugène Aubin, "Le Chiisme et la nationalité persane," in *Revue du Monde Musulman*, IV/3 (1908), 458.

2. Bernard Lewis, "The Shi'a in Islamic History," in Martin Kramer (ed.), *Shi'ism, Resistance, and Revolution* (Boulder: 1987), 23.

3. V. Minorsky, "Iran: Opposition, Martyrdom and Revolt," in G. E. von Grunebaum (ed.), *Unity and Variety in Muslim Civilization* (Chicago: 1976), 201.

4. See Said Amir Arjomand, *The Shadow of God and the Hidden Imam: Religion, Political Order and Societal Change in Shi'ite Iran from the Beginning to 1890* (Chicago: 1984), *passim*, and especially p. 70: "legalistically and theologically rationalized Shi'ism"; p. 70: "Shi'ite-tinged Sufi extremism"—(a phrase borrowed from A. Bausani, "Religion under the Mongols," in *The Cambridge History of Iran*, Vol. V, 1968, p. 547); "Sufism with a Shi'i Tinge"; p. 160: "millenarian extremism"; p. 105: "Fifteenth century Shi'ite extremism had little in common with Twelver Shi'ism or the doctrine of the Imami sect." This last quotation is repeated verbatim in S. A. Arjomand, "Religious Extremism (*Ghuluww*), Sufism and Sunnism in Safavid Iran: 1501–1722," in *Journal of Asian History*, XV/1 (1981), 1–2, with the exception of the substitution of '*ghuluww*' for 'extremism', and is paraphrased in S. A. Arjomand, "Religion, Political Action and Legitimate Domination in Shi'ite Iran: fourteenth to eighteenth centuries A.D.," in *Archives Européennes de Sociologie*, Tome XX, No. 1 (1979), 39. See also S. A. Arjomand, "Shi'ite Islam and the Revolution in Iran," in *Government and Opposition: A Journal of Comparative Politics*, XVI/3 (1981), p. 295; "The [Safavid] empire was created by the military force of a millenarian warrior order whose members adhered to an *aberrant* variety of Shi'ism" (emphasis added).

5. Arjomand, *Shadow*, 204.

6. According to accepted Ithna Ashari tradition, the Twelve Imams met their end in the following ways:

I. Ali b. Abi Talib	Assassinated by Ibn Muljam, a Kharijite, in 661.
II. Hasan b. Ali	Poisoned by his wife at instigation of the Umayyads in 670/1.
III. Husayn b. Ali	Slain at Karbala in battle with Umayyad troops, 680.
IV. Ali Asghar, Zayn al-Abedin	Poisoned at instigation of the Umayyad Caliph Walid b. Abd al-Malik, 712.
V. Muhammad al-Baqir	Poisoned by the nephew of the Umayyad Caliph Hisham in 732.
VI. Ja'far al-Sadiq	Poisoned on orders of the Abbasid Caliph al-Mansur in 757.
VII. Musa al-Kazim	Put to death on orders of the Abbasid Caliph Harun al-Rashid in 799.
VIII. Ali al-Riza	Poisoned on orders of the Abbasid Caliph al-Ma'mun in 817.
IX. Muhammad Taqi	Poisoned on orders of the Abbasid Caliph al-Mu'tasim in 835.

X. Ali Naqi	"Died in mysterious circumstances." Said to have been poisoned by the Abbasid Caliph al-Mu'tazz in 868.
XI. Hasan al-Askari	Poisoned by the Abbasid Caliph al-Mu'tamid in 873.
XII. Muhammad al-Qa'im	Known as al-Mahdi, the Qa'im, the Hidden Imam, the Hujjah, the 'Lord of the Age', etc. In occultation since 873/4.

Source: Allamah Sayyid Muhammad Husayn Tabataba'i, *Shi'ite Islam* (translated and edited with an introduction and notes by Seyyed Hossein Nasr) Albany: 1975.

7. The text of al-Ma'mun's letter of designation is contained in Patricia Crone and Martin Hinds, *God's Caliph* (Cambridge: 1987), 133–39.

8. *Encyclopaedia of Islam*, new edition, article *Ali al-Rida*, 399–400.

9. Arjomand, *Shadow*, 203–04: "The attempt to subjugate and appropriate political power does not make its appearance until the present century." I think that this view is, to use one of Arjomand's favorite expressions, "untenable."

10. Arjomand, *Shadow*, 266.

11. The Isma'ilis, on the other hand, continued to try to overthrow the Sunni caliph until the middle of the eleventh century. One should not forget the period of intense Isma'ili *da'wa* in Iraq between 1056/7 and 1059. This period of political and religious activism culminated in the attempt by al-Basasiri, the former commander-in-chief of the Buyid ruler of Iraq, al-Malik al-Rahim, to depose the Abbasid Caliph al-Qa'im in favor of the Fatimid Caliph al-Mustansir. The attempt was crushed by the Seljuq Sultan Toghrul Bey (see article "al-Basasiri," in *Encyclopaedia of Islam*, new edition, 1073–75, by M. Canard).

12. Abdulaziz Abdulhussein Sachedina, *The Just Ruler (al-sultan al-adil) in Shi'ite Islam: The Comprehensive Authority of the Jurist in Imamite Jurisprudence* (New York: 1988), 105 ff.

13. Sachedina, 112.

14. Sachedina, 112. Recorded in Muhammad b. al-Hasan al-Hurr al-Amili, *Wasail al-Shi'a ila tahsil masa'il al-shar'iyya*, (20 vols.; Beirut: 1971), XI, 62, hadith No. 11.

15. Sachedina, 112.

16. Norman Calder, *The Structure of Authority in Imami Shi'i Jurisprudence* (University of London, unpublished Ph.D. dissertation, 1980), 156.

17. Roger Savory, "The Safavid State and Polity," in *Iranian Studies*, VII, Nos. 1–2 (Winter-Spring 1974); *Studies on Isfahan*, Part I, 179–212, and Hans Roemer, *Comments*, 213–16.

18. Roger M. Savory, "Some Reflections on Totalitarian Tendencies in the Safavid State," in *Der Islam*, Band 53, Heft 2 (1976), 228.

19. Michel M. Mazzaoui, *The Origins of the Safawids: Ši'ism, Sufism and the Ġulat* (Wiesbaden: 1971), 83.

20. R. M. Savory, "A 15th Century Safavid Propagandist at Harat," in Denis Sinor (ed.), *American Oriental Society Middle West Branch Semi-centennial Volume* (Bloomington: 1969), 189–97.

21. V. Minorsky, "The Poetry of Shah Isma'il I," *Bulletin of the School of Oriental and African Studies*, X/4 (1942), 1006a–1053a; Tourkhan Ganjei, *Il Canzoniere di Šah Isma'il Hatai* (Napoli: 1959). See also Roger M. Savory, *Some Reflections*, 232.

22. Mazzaoui, op. cit., 73.

23. Ibid.

24. British Museum MS. Or. 3248, f. 28b.

25. Id., f. 41b. Emphasis added.

26. See R. M. Savory, *Safavid Propagandist*, 189-97.

27. For some parallels with Russia after the Bolshevik Revolution, see Roger M. Savory, *Some Reflections*, 236.

28. Ghulam Sarwar, *The History of Shah Isma'il Safawi* (Aligarh: 1939), 38 and footnote 18.

29. Ghiyah al-Din b. Humam al-Din Khvandamir, *Habib al-Siyar* (Bombay: lithographed edition, 1836/7), III/4, 34.

30. British Museum MS. Or. No. 3248, ff 73b–74b.

31. See R. M. Savory, "The Consolidation of Safawid Power in Persia," in *Der Islam*, Band 41 (1965), 71–94.

32. My translation of Jean Chardin, *Voyages du Chevalier Chardin* (Amsterdam: 1711), Vol. VI, 249–250. (Emphasis added.)

33. Amin Banani, "The Social and Economic Structure of the Safavid Empire in Its Heyday " (a paper submitted to the Harvard Colloquium on Tradition and Change in the Middle East, December 1967), 26.

34. Space does not permit me to give details of how the Safavid shahs made good this claim. See Roger M. Savory, "The Emergence of the Modern Persian State under the Safavids," in *Iranshenasi* (Journal of Iranian Studies, Faculty of Letters and Humanities, Tehran University), Serial No. 3 (Summer 1971).

35. During the reign of Shah Isma'il II (1576/7), there is an interesting case of a *khalifat al-khulafa* who challenged the assumption that the shah was the *morshed-e kamel*, and claimed that position for himself. See Roger M. Savory, "The Office of *khalifat al-khulafa* under the Safawids," in *Journal of the American Oriental Society*, Vol. 85, No. 4 (October–December 1965), 497–502.

36. R. M. Savory, "The Principal Offices of the Safawid State during the Reign of Tahmasp I (1524–76)," in *Bulletin of the School of Oriental and African Studies*, Vol. XXIV/1 (1961), 81.

37. *Safvat al-Safa*, British Museum MS. Add. 11,745, ff. 811a–b.

38. The reference is to one of the miracles wrought by Moses (see Qur'an, 7:108 and 26:32). The term *yad-e bayda* came to be synonymous with *qodrat* ('power'), the sense in which it is used here.

39. Khurshah b. Qubad al-Husayni, *Tarikh-e Ilchi-ye Nezamshah*, British Museum MS. Add. 23,513, f. 453b.

40. *Habib al-Siyar*, III/4, 113.

41. See *Habib al-Siyar*, III/4, 50; and article "Musha'sha" in *Encyclopaedia of Islam*, first edition, by V. Minorsky.

42. For an obviously Shi'i inscription on the Great Mosque at Gulbarga, built in 1367, see J. N. Hollister, *The Shi'a of India* (London: 1953), 106, and illustration facing p. 106.

43. Hollister, op. cit., 121. The Sultan Ya'qub referred to may possibly be Ya'qub b. Qara Uthman, a prominent Aq Qoyunlu chief who, according to one source, was actually installed by Muhammad Juki, the Timurid prince, as ruler of the Aq Qoyunlu confederacy ca. 1436; Sultan Ya'qub died in 1446 (see John E. Woods, *The Aqquyunlu: Clan, Confederation, Empire* (Minneapolis and Chicago: 1976), 74 and Table 5, 220).

44. Hollister, 117.

45. Hollister, op. cit., 112, 118.

46. Hollister, op. cit., 115–116, 118, 122.

47. The distinctive Safavid headgear with twelve folds or gores commemorating the Twelve Imams; see R. M. Savory, "The Struggle for Supremacy in Persia after the Death of Timur," in *Der Islam*, Band 40/1 (1964), 56.

48. See R. M. Savory, *The Consolidation*, 80–81.

49. Juan R. I. Cole, "Shi'i Clerics in Iraq and Iran 1722–1780: The Akhbari-Usuli Conflict Reconsidered," in *Iranian Studies*, Vol. XVIII, No. 1 (Winter 1985), 8.

50. Keith Hjortshoj, "Shi'i Identity and the Significance of Muharram in Lucknow, India," in Martin Kramer, 294.

51. Hjortshoj, op. cit., 299.

52. Banani, op. cit., 6.

53. *Mahdi-ye Maw'ud*, the translation by Ali Davani of Vol. XII of the *Bihar al-Anvar* of Allama Majlesi (Tehran: Dar al-Kutub al-Islamiyya, 1966), Introduction, 111.

54. L. Lockhart, *Nadir Shah* (London: 1938), 233.

55. Lockhart, 21.

56. Lockhart, 60.

57. Lockhart, 99.

58. Lockhart, 100.

59. Lockhart, 103, records that the poet Qavam al-Din devised the chronogram *al-khayr fi ma vaqa'a*, which gives the numerical value 1736, the correct date for Nader's coronation. The phrase is an Arabic proverb meaning: "What has happened is for the best." Apparently some wits (no doubt anonymously) transposed the first two letters, giving *la* instead of *al-*. The numerical value remained unchanged, but the sense now became: "There is no virtue in what has occurred!"

60. Lockhart, 101.

61. Lockhart, 255.

62. Lockhart, 279–80.

63. Lockhart, 279.

64. John R. Perry, *Karim Khan Zand* (Chicago: 1979), 220.

65. Perry, 220.

66. Perry, 192.

67. Muriel Atkin, *Russia and Iran 1780–1828* (Minneapolis: 1980), 6.

68. Atkin, 34.

69. Atkin, 35.

70. Hamid Algar, *Religion and State in Iran 1785–1906: The Role of the ulama in the Qajar Period* (Berkeley: 1969), 30, 33.

71. Algar, 31. Mirza Abd al-Hasan was, in fact, the *mollabashi*, as mentioned above.

72. Hamid Algar, 34–35.

73. Ali Davani, introduction to *Mahdi-ye Maw'ud*, Davani's translation of Vol. XIII of the *Bihar al-Anvar* of Allama Majlesi, the celebrated Safavid jurist, 111.

74. Arjomand, *Shadow*, 77.

2

Khomeini's Vision:
Nationalism or World Order?

David Menashri

Iran's Islamic revolution presents a new kind of power seizure in the Middle East's modern history. The many coups in this region (as well as in the Third World generally) in the last generation were typically the work of small groups, usually led by army officers, who only *after* their takeover began to mobilize popular support for themselves and their new ideology. The Iranian revolution is a striking exception: it was led primarily by men of religion rather than officers (instead it was directed against the officer class); it enjoyed mass support in advance of takeover (indeed as a prerequisite for it); and its "new" ideology was nothing more than a return to the glorious past of early Islam and to the ideology most familiar to Iranians. More than that: the regime Khomeini set out to overthrow was in some respects more closely akin to other "new" regimes in the Middle East than to the type of rule against which coup leaders had risen elsewhere. True, like other "old regimes" in the region, the shah's was monarchical and pro-Western; but, much like other "new" ones, it had resulted from a military takeover, and it was reformist, modernizing, and secular (to the point of being anti-clerical). And it engaged in nation-state building by drawing on the inspiration of national culture and history (including, indeed emphasizing, pre-Islamic history).

On every single count, Khomeini's ideology prescribed the opposite: the separation of religion and state was to be done away with, spiritual and temporal power to be united in the *velayat-e faqih* ("the rule of the jurisconsult"); and foreign influence and the emulation of foreign models to be halted. Most significantly for the theme of this volume: Khomeini's Islamic ideology ignored the existence of political boundaries within the Muslim community. Nation-building like that of the shah's and of "new" (as well as, for that matter the old) regimes elsewhere in the Middle East was meaningless. The arena of the Islamic revolution was the Islamic world, Islamic unity its quintessential aim.

Tension between these two frameworks of identification has been continuous in the modern Muslim Middle East. Attempts at complete or partial unity of the Muslim world have been unsuccessful, as have been other supra-national movements such as Pan-Africanism, Pan-Slavism or negritude.[1] Despite the attraction of Pan-Islamism, Pan-Turanism, Pan-Turkism and Pan-Arabism, the doctrine of the modern national territorial state prevailed, propagated by leaders such as Mustafa Kemal Atatürk and Reza Shah. By the 1970s, the tendency to abandon supra-territorial concepts in favor of the idea of the territorial nation-state became abundantly evident in the Middle East. Striking examples are the case of Egypt (in the transition from Nasser to Sadat) and Iraq (since the mid-1970s). But Khomeini's revolution sought to move Iran in the opposite direction—from nationalism towards the Islamic *umma*. Ironically, this occurred when it was least expected: in the 1970s the shah seemed successful in fostering national identity and appeared powerful enough to make his own vision a reality. Iran's national identity looked strong and solid. Opposition, if any, was more likely to come from sub-national—ethnic and tribal—groups rather than from supra-national doctrines.

But history flew in the face of likelihood. Ostensibly, then, Khomeini's world view was clear and his ideology coherent, but reality turned out to be different. Once in exile, Khomeini developed his concept of the ideal *hokumat-e Islami* ("Islamic government") concentrating primarily on theological-political questions regarding the *velayat-e faqih*, but did not present a blueprint for (re)unification of the *umma*; neither did he lay down specific guidelines for a new scheme of foreign relations. He seemed simply to disregard the national, religious (Sunnis *vis-à-vis* Shi'is) and ethnic differences (Arabs, Turks, Persians etc.) within the domain of Islam, as well as the fact that Shi'is are no more than a small minority in the Muslim world.[2]

Khomeini's political thought and his ideology underwent considerable changes. This chapter will attempt to analyze his vision of an Islamic order as formulated in his years of exile and his initial concept of "exporting the revolution" and contrast them with his later attitudes. In doing so, it will also seek to offer some tentative explanation for the changes that occurred.

An Oppositionist's Ideology: Toward an Islamic Order

The concept of territorial nationalism (*wataniyya* in Arabic; *mihan-parasti* in Persian) is relatively new in the Middle East. But in the twentieth century, as Khadduri has stressed, "second to Islam, the idea of nationalism has dominated the minds of the Arabs to a greater extent than any other ideology," despite "Islam's tacit or expressed disapproval."[3] Yet problems of national identity continued to occupy a pivotal place in the deliberations of Middle Eastern intellectuals and politicians and foreign scholars.

This was, however, somewhat less true of Iran, an independent state at least since the Safavid period. In its early days, at the turn of the century, the constitutional (and in a way, national) movement had the support of the *ulama* (contrasting oddly with the West where nationalism was secular by nature and spelt the decline of clerical influence). At the same time, in

Iran "the nationalism of much of the liberal constitutional element was inextricably interwoven with devotion to Islam." Both liberal intellectuals and *ulama* seemed to regard nation and religion as indivisible.[4] By and large, early Iranian nationalism "has been concerned less with the problems of *nationhood* than with that of *"freedom."* Only rarely did nineteenth-century Iranian intellectuals refer to such questions as the oneness of the Iranian nation, the constituent elements of its identity and the conflict between Iran's pre-Islamic and Islamic culture. Instead there was a persistent demand for liberal democracy and a constitution, a campaign against corruption and criticism of internal affairs and foreign encroachment. Since there developed no significant intellectual argument over the question of nationalism, Shi'i *ulama* hardly ever felt the necessity to pronounce on it. "When they did, they had no hesitation in denouncing it as an imported heresy undermining Muslim unity."[5] But such attitudes were obscured by the collaboration of the *ulama* with the liberal intellectuals in their common struggles against the monarchy (at the time of the popular movements against the Tobacco Concession, 1891-92; during the Constitutional Revolution, 1905-11; and later over the nationalization of oil, 1951-53).

The challenge only came when the Pahlavis attempted to base nationalism on new ideological foundations, making it synonymous with cultural change and secularism. From then on, nationalism was identified with the shah and his policy, and therefore categorized as hostile to Islam.

In his book *Kashf-e Asrar* ("The Revealing of the Secrets"), written immediately following Reza Shah's abdication, Khomeini still seemed to voice "patriotic" views, and provide a cautious defense of Iranian nationalism. True, he stated that modern states are, by and large, "the products of man's limited ideals," and claimed that unlike the laws in other states, Islamic laws were meant to "remove the borders [between the states] of the world and establish one general state (*yek keshvar-e hamegani*)" which would bring "all people of the world under one flag and law."[6] But this utopian vision, worded in such general terms, can, as Ramazani suggests, hardly prove his "strong" and "categorical" denunciation of the concept of the nation-state at that time.[7] On the contrary, Khomeini even uses some nationalist, or better patriotic-Iranian terminology, for example, when addressing his readers on the concluding page of his book as "dear compatriots" (*ham-mihanan*), "young lovers of Iran" (*Irandust*) and "Iranians who desire glory."[8] Moreover, unlike in the later *velayat-e faqih* (see below), he did not stress Islamic unity in the earlier book. Neither do we find rejection of monarchy and temporal rule which was to become a cornerstone of his *velayat-e faqih* concept.

The earlier book abounds in distinctively Shi'i *motifs*; the later ecumenical Shi'i-Sunni concepts are clearly lacking. On the contrary, *Kashf-e Asrar* attests to the Shi'is' profound hatred of Sunnis and their feeling of superiority over them. Thus the *"fitna* of Karbala," caused by "the Sunnis," was the greatest disaster of Islam.[9] The first caliphs not only usurped the rule rightfully belonging to Ali, but also conspired to annihilate the dynasty of Ali.[10] One chapter of the book is devoted to Abu Bakr's opposition to the

Qur'an (*mokhalefat-e Abu Bakr ba Qur'an*) and another attributes a similar sin to Umar.[11] He speaks of the Umayyid and the Abbasid dynasties as the "worst (*badtarin*) and most usurpatory (*zalemanetarin*) regimes in history" and accuses their caliphs of killing the Imams.[12] Moreover, the references cited by him to argue his points are taken from Shi'i authorities, some of them offensive to Sunnis.

Taking it all in all, Khomeini's views in the 1940s, 1950s and well into the 1960s were in keeping with the attitudes then current among the mainstream *ulama*. The *marja-e taqlid* of that time, Ayatollah Muhammad Husayn Borujerdi, for instance, not only rejected the involvement of the *ulama* in politics but also viewed both the monarchy and Islam fundamental to Iranian nationalism and wrote in defense of nationalist concepts.[13]

By contrast, the radical Islamic concepts voiced by Khomeini from the late 1960s onwards extended far beyond the borders of Iran. They abound in pan-Islamic *motif*s and aim at the realization of Islamic unity (moral, if not political). Being united, Islam would become capable of playing its ordained role in human history. Khomeini considered the Iranian revolution a stage and an instrument in the attainment of Islamic unity and as a model for imitation by other Muslim communities. He declared: "Our movement is for an Islamic goal, not for Iran alone. . . . Iran has [only] been the starting point." Muslims in other countries should come forward and join the Muslim revolution.[14] It should be stressed that Khomeini did not define himself as an Iranian but as a Muslim. The very idea of nationalism now became alien to him, a doctrine opposed to his own, and part of an "imperialist plot" to divide and weaken Islam. Nationalism was no better than tribal solidarity (*asabiyya*).[15] Nationalism, pan-Iranism, pan-Turkism "and such isms, . . . are contrary to Islamic doctrines."[16] He deplored that the Muslim world, in a futile attempt to cure its ills, had embraced foreign ideologies (communism, pan-Arabism, nationalism and others) and proposed that it opt instead for the familiar, indigenous, tried and tested solution of a return to Islam in the fullest sense.

He accused the imperialists of having "divided the Islamic homeland. They have separated the various segments of the Islamic *umma* from each other and artificially created separate nations. . . . Then each of these [nations] was entrusted to one of their servants." He called for the "unity of the Islamic *umma*" and demanded the establishment of a [single] Islamic government "to preserve the disciplined unity of the Muslims."[17] He blamed imperialism for preventing the "liberation of Muslim peoples" and imposing "an atmosphere of despair" on them.[18] Arguing from the same premise, he denied the significance of all ethnic or linguistic minorities and rejected granting them specific rights. "There is no difference between Muslims who speak different languages, for instance, the Arabs or the Persians."[19] In another interview from his Paris exile he said that "Muslims are one family, even if they are subject to different governments and even if they live in regions remote from one another. . . . This is the important and basic point. This is the strategy."[20] Being Shi'i or Sunni "is not the question."[21] The notion of "exporting the revolution" follows naturally.

Khomeini's supra-national philosophy is manifest in the 1979 constitution which closely reflects Khomeini's world view in this and other points. But it also reveals the difficulties of implementing such a vision. According to the constitution, "all Muslims" are "one nation" and the government must exert "continuous efforts" to realize "the political, economic, and cultural unity of the Islamic world" (Article 11). But it also makes the "safeguarding of the independence and integrity of the Iranian territory" the basis of Iran foreign policy (Article 152). It commits Iran to refrain from interfering in the "internal affairs of other nations" yet obliges it to protect "the weak against the arrogant" anywhere (Article 154).

It should be noted in parentheses that Khomeini's views on nationalism were rejected by many *ulama*, mainly those of the rank of *ayatollah ozma*. As in many other fields, the greatest ideological challenge was posed by Kazem Shari'atmadari.[22] His point of departure was an Iranist one, and his ideology lacked pan-Islamic *motifs*. On the contrary, he viewed Islam as the cohesive element of Iranian nationalism and the main instrument in the strengthening of Iran's national unity and sovereignty.[23] As was natural for an Azerbayjani and a liberal, he supported "local rights" (*ekhtiyarat-e dakheli*) for ethnic minorities, thus defying Khomeini, although he agreed with him in objecting to separatism.[24] Another major figure, Ayatollah Mahmud Taleqani pointedly refrained from coming out against Iranian nationalism and failed to support the "exporting of the revolution."[25] None of the important ayatollahs supported the kind of Islamic unity adumbrated by Khomeini with the sole exception of Aytollah Husayn Ali Montazeri who supported exporting the revolution all along.[26]

How can one account for the profound change in Khomeini's national concepts between the 1940s and the 1970s? His thinking on this and other issues in fact represents a revolution in Islam rather than an "Islamic revolution." Although the origins of all his assertions can be found in Iranian-Shi'i thought throughout the ages, and while all are rooted in Islam, none of them had a significant following in the last centuries, at least not among the leading *ulama*. Khomeini not only developed such ideas—hitherto only raised sporadically in marginal circles—into a comprehensive world view but also made the very center of the (Iranian) religious establishment conform to them. While no definite explanation can be given yet, it is possible to assume that they had their roots in a combination of the intellectual trends set out below.

Some radical views go back to the last century. With the inception of the modern national movement in Iran, it was Jamal al-Din al-Afghani who formulated many of the thoughts that Khomeini later made his own. In 1894, a Qajar prince, Abu al-Hasan Mirza (known as Shaykh al-Ra'is) published a tract entitled *Ettehad-e Islam* ("Islamic Unity") which called on Muslims everywhere to halt their decline by placing themselves under the leadership of Abd ul-Hamid, "this enlightened, wise [Ottoman] Sultan, intent on unifying the Muslim world."[27]

Half a century later, Ayatollah Abu al-Qasem Kashani and the *Feda'iyan-e Islam* stressed Islamic solidarity. So did Ayatollah Morteza Motahheri (professor of Islamic philosophy at Tehran University) and one of the founders of *Hoseyniyye Ershad* (a center of religious education and propagation set up in Tehran in 1969). In his influential polemic speeches and writings he denounced the glorification of Iran's pre-Islamic culture, asserting that the Sasanid state was based on social injustice and moral depravity. He also came out against the Arab claim to superiority, arguing that Islam took no notice of ethnic preferences.[28]

If their pan-Islam appears to have been tactical rather than ideological, then this was, after all, typical of all the pan-Islamists in Iran: "their goals are essentially political, and their pan-Islamism appears to be little more than an ineffective propaganda line."[29] Was the case of Khomeini very different? Not really. His struggle, as Mangol Bayat points out, was political and his motives "had little to do with ideological traditions . . . he instituted political innovation in the garb of traditional Islam."[30]

Another possible source of influence was the new generation of lay Shi'i political-religious thinkers (with a western rather than a traditional education) who appeared in Iran in the 1960s. Some of those who had become disappointed with both liberalism and Marxism as a cure for the malady of their country now sought to free Iran from doctrines coming from abroad; inevitably, they turned to Islam. Most influential among them were Jalal Al Ahmad, Ali Shari'ati, Abu al-Hasan Bani Sadr and Mehdi Bazargan. Treatises like Al Ahmad's *Gharbzadegi* ("Weststruckness") or Shari'ati's *Hajj* and *Ummat va-Emamat* undoubtedly encouraged Khomeini in his line and may well have influenced his own thinking. Their call for struggle (*moqavemat*), their criticism of the west and their appeal to Islam to arouse the masses were in keeping with his thinking during his years in Najaf. The pan-Islamic idea was not part of their thinking, but their argument needed only to be taken a step further to arrive at it. One way or another, it is known that Khomeini maintained ties with Iranian intellectuals and encouraged them.[31] It seems to me that they, in turn, encouraged him.

His personal biography may have been yet another factor making for an Islamic, rather than an Iranian, identity. His family had spent a long time at Lucknow in India (his oldest brother became known as the *ayatollah hindi*). He spent a year in Turkey and fourteen years in Iraq. He had contacts all over the Muslim world, mainly among Shi'is.

The general atmosphere in Najaf was also supportive of fostering his radical ideology and his vision of an Islamic order. It was there that radical neo-fundamentalism was first developed to some degree by Ayatollah Muhsin al-Hakim (the *marja-e taqlid* throughout the 1960s, who was, it so appears, a pragmatic activist—see chapter by Baram) and later by Ayatollah Muhammad Baqir al-Sadr.[32] Although further study of the "Najaf atmosphere" is still necessary, the fact that there was a kind of resonance is, I believe, beyond argument.[33] One other point can be made with some certainty: among Iraqi *ulama* there was a greater tendency for ecumenism than elsewhere among Shi'is. Their situation in Iraq compelled them to deal with Shi'i-Sunni relations more frequently and more seriously than did their Iranian coreligionists. For Iranians it was a question of foreign relations, for the Iraqis a basic existential issue right on their door-step.[34]

More strident radical voices, even much before the 1960s, came from the Sunni world. There is, for example, much similarity between the views of Khomeini in the late 1960s and those of Abu al-A'la Mawdudi, Abu al-Hasan Ali Nadwi and Sayyid Qutb, among others, on the national question. Already in the 1930s and 1940s Mawdudi urged his fellow-Muslims to overcome the "diabolical conspiracy" of nationalism. Nationalism was tantamount to having another god next to Allah, contradicting *tawhid*. He blamed imperialism for imposing an atmosphere of "mental slavery" on Muslims, inculcating "cowardly and defeated mentalities" in them, causing them to "nationalize" God and His religion. Nadwi, his disciple, propagated in Lucknow ideas similar to those disseminated by Qutb in the Middle East. According to the latter, any loyalty, other than to *dar al-Islam*—whether to family, race or territory—is "tribalism of the [pre-Islamic] period of ignorance (*asabiyya jahiliyya*)." "God's real chosen people," he argued, "is the Muslim community (*umma*), regardless of the ethnic, racial, or territorial affiliation of its members." Muhammad Eqbal (Pakistan), Muhammad al-Ghazali and Sa'id Ramadan (Egypt), and Muhammad Mahmud al-Sawwaf (Iraq) were other thinkers critical of the nation-state in a manner more or less similar to Khomeini's.[35] Yet it remains a moot point to what degree Khomeini was influenced by them. Sivan argues that Sunni and Shi'i scholars reached such identical conclusions independently. But it seems highly unlikely that Khomeini was not aware of their thinking through his many personal contacts in the Muslim world, through translations into Arabic of Mawdudi's or into Persian of some of Qutb's writings.[36] Eqbal, for instance, was well-known among Iranian intellectuals. (He was one of Shari'ati's heroes). It seems most improbable that these people were unheard-of in Najaf.

But whatever possible intellectual antecedents we can cite, I would still hold that Khomeini's "new" ideology was mainly a response to the realities in Iran such as they emerged since the White Revolution (*Enqelab-e Sefid*) in the early 1960s. Throughout the Pahlavi period, there was a clear correlation between the strength of the shah's overall political position and his policy towards the *ulama*. When he was weak, he accommodated them; when he felt strong, as he did in the 1960s and 1970s, he acted against them.

What is of even greater relevance to our discussion was the shah's campaign of exploiting religious sentiment to reinforce national loyalty. He spoke of the "sanctity" of the homeland (*vatan*), explained his mission in religious terms[37] and made use of Islamic traditions to legitimize his reforms.[38] But at the same time he promoted secularization, worked for separating state and religion, and wanted to restrict clerics to matters of faith and ritual. His vision of The Great Civilization (*tamaddon-e bozorg*) was based on ancient Iranian culture and western science, not on Islam.

As his power grew, the shah's references to Islam became rarer. In proclaiming the White Revolution in 1963, he appealed for loyalty to 'God' (*Khoda*), 'Shah' and 'Homeland' (*mihan*). Twelve years later, when he formed the *Rastakhiz* ("Resurrection") Party, he demanded instead loyalty to the monarchy, the constitution and the White Revolution.[39] God no longer figured in the list. Yet he reaffirmed his faith in Islam[40] and continued to use religious terms, in a manner offensive to the *ulama*, to describe his mission: "I was convinced that God had ordained me to do certain things for the service of my nation. . . . I consider myself merely as an agent of the will of God."[41] And again: "My reign has saved the country, and it has done so because God was on my side."[42] He often repeated the story of how the saints of Islam (Ali and Imam Reza among others) appeared to him in his youth.[43] Such pretensions antagonized the *ulama* just as much as did his emphasis on pre-Islamic history (cf. marking the 2500 anniversary of the monarchy; changing over from the *hijri* to the imperial calendar). The shah had equated the monarchy, nationalism, and the reform "revolution"; therefore, the *ulama* in their opposition to the Shah and his policy anathematized all three.

A Ruler's Ideology: The Islamic Republic

By the nature of things, revolutionary movements, once in power often deviate from their original radical doctrines. The Islamic Revolution was no exception. As long as he headed an opposition movement, Khomeini had depicted a "new Iran" modeled on early Islam. The wholeness of the Islamic *umma*, an ecumenist conception *par excellence*, was the ideal that followed naturally. But, once in power, he knew he could not rule by means of revolutionary slogans—certainly not slogans derived from seventh-century thought. He and his disciples were now called upon to manage, rather than discuss, affairs of state. Soon they compromised with realities, not from any new-found moderation, but from a pragmatism responsive to the exigencies of their situation. The shift was gradual, but clearly felt in all fields. It became evident as early as the winter of 1982, a time when the clerics had just tightened their exclusive grip on power, and it became unmistakably obvious in the autumn of 1984. Whether in domestic or foreign affairs, any modification in the basic line was first given legitimacy by Khomeini himself—whether it was outlined by him or, as was the case with the acceptance of the cease-fire in the Gulf war, he was forced to approve it—and then spelt out in greater detail and more specific terms by the "politicians"—mainly the Majlis Speaker Ali Akbar Hashemi Rafsanjani.[44]

In the early days of the revolution, Khomeini had declared all governments anywhere, and in Muslim countries most particularly, to be illegitimate in principle. The Islamic Republic would ignore governments and deal directly with peoples instead. In 1981 Khomeini still held up isolation as a new ideal for Iran's foreign policy.[45] Gradually the doctrinaire approach was whittled down by realities. In October 1984, he announced that his country wanted "relations with all countries," with the sole exception of the United States, Israel and South Africa. Not to do so, he said then, was "against reason and the Islamic law. We cannot sit idly by saying we have nothing to do with governments," he added.[46]

Though national considerations were alien to Khomeini's own principles and to his theory of foreign relations in general, and within the Muslim world in particular, his regime nonetheless chose to act towards the Arab world from a perception of Iran's national interest. How else is it possible to reconcile his insistence on the irrelevance of borders between Muslim lands (and thus rejecting the demand of the United Arab Emirates for the return of three Gulf islands captured by the shah in 1971), with his demand (until 1988) for the total withdrawal of Iraq from all Iranian territories as one of the conditions of terminating the war? How does his supra-national ideology and his assertion that there was no difference between Muslims anywhere, neither ethnically nor with regard to the Shi'a or Sunna, accord with the article of the 1979 constitution laying down that only a Shi'i of Iranian origin can hold office as president of the Islamic Republic of Iran?[47] How it is possible to explain that one article of the constitution asserts Muslim unity and another lays down that the government must preserve the territorial integrity of Iran? How can one reconcile his abhorrence of national divisions within Islam with his insistence that the Gulf must be called (and therefore be) Persian?[48]

More than that: after the outbreak of the war with Iraq Khomeini himself began to use nationalist-patriotic terminology. In a speech to religious leaders and *Majlis* representatives a week after the war started, for instance, he said that "the honor and the glory of the *mihan* and *din* are dependent on the war." He vowed: "We shall fight the attackers of our beloved homeland (*mihan-e aziz*) until death."[49]

In fact the very name by which the country is now officially called— *Jomhuri-ye Islami-ye Iran*—is a contradiction in terms: its first part befits a government of the *umma*, the second limits it to a small part thereof. Being surrounded by other independent Muslim states which differ from Iran in their ethnic and sectarian affiliation, Khomeini is in an awkward position "for as the Iranian head of state he cannot disavow the idea of the nation-state, but as a revolutionary Islamic leader he cannot make his commitment to the national idea too strong or his commitment to the *umma* too weak."[50] In appealing to Sunnis Khomeini could not use specifically Shi'i language, but had to use more universal, ecumenical terms. But the two languages were incompatible: "In so far as Khomeini chose to emphasize a purely Shi'i ideology, he alienated the Sunni Muslim world. But in so far as he emphasized a universal language, he weakened the appeal of his vision to Iranian Shi'ites."[51]

A broad overview shows that "exporting the revolution" had different meanings during the various phases of the regime's short history, and that it meant different things when addressed to mankind at large, to the Muslim *umma* or to the Shi'i community. Moreover, there were significant differences between more pragmatic elements (headed by Rafsanjani) within the revolutionary establishment and a more doctrinaire group with Hojjat al-Islam Muhammad Musavi Kho'iniha, Ayatollah Ali Meshkini, Ayatollah Montazeri, Hojjat al-Islam Ali Akbar Mohtashami and Mehdi Hashemi most prominent among them. (The latter was executed in September 1987.)

There remained one point on which both trends agreed in principle: it was that while Muslim lands were the primary target for exporting the revolution, eventually it must offer "salvation" to the *mostaz'afin* ("disinherited") of *all* the world (a point at which religious duty fades into social ideology). The idea was powerful enough for Foreign Minister Mir Husayn Musavi to declare, on entering office in August 1981, that one of the "objectives of Iran's foreign policy" were to "carry the message of Iran's Islamic revolution to the [entire] world."[52] Ayatollah Meshkini (the *Imam Jum'a* of Qom) went to the length of saying that the goal of the revolution was "to impose the Qur'an over the entire world."[53] But even then such statements always had a ritual, rather than programmatic, ring to them.

As for the perhaps more practical question of "exporting" the revolution to the Muslim world, the radicals had one advantage: they could point out that the very doctrine of *velayat-e faqih* made it obligatory to do so—whether for the ultimate purpose of the establishment of "the government of the *imam mahdi*" or for the more immediate need of making "the Iranian regional environment safe for Iran's power and for its revolutionary ideology."[54]

But taken all in all, the more radical expressions regarding the "export" of the revolution, typical of the early days, were over time toned down. Khomeini himself, it should be stressed, had consistently refrained from implying any intention to spread the revolution by force. The course of history, he stressed, made the spread of the revolution inevitable and irreversible. Iran need not to "worm its way" into other countries, rather it should walk in "like an invited guest."[55] Until that happened, it was Iran's primary duty to spread the word of Islamic ideology and to make the country's "new realities" known, so as to encourage its being "invited".[56] All his country wanted, he said early in 1984, was to show the Muslims what "correct Islam" really was.[57] By then, the emphasis on "exporting" the revolution had clearly shifted to cultural and ideological themes. As Foreign Minister Ali Akbar Velayati put it: it had nothing to do with "exporting tanks and soldiers."[58]

Even Khomeini's messages to the *hajj* pilgrims, to the participants in the Unity Week, the World Congresses of Friday Imams and the Conferences on Islamic Thought—usually the occasion for voicing radical views regarding the "export of the revolution" and Islamic unity—reveal an implicit recognition of the national affiliation of Muslims of different countries. Over time the plea for unity made room for vaguer appeals for brotherhood (*baradari*), "unity of the word" (*vahdat-e kalam*) and "unity of purpose" (*vahdat-e hadaf*). Khomeini called for solidarity and co-ordination and spoke of the need to "avoid divisions" and to be "in empathy with one another." But he always stopped short of demanding the full unity that his older theories would have required.

Some of Khomeini's associates, however, were less restrained. They continued taking Khomeini's earlier views altogether literally: for many of them "exporting" the revolution was, and still is, a principal goal to be actively and constantly pursued by the Islamic Republic. Some of them continued to think, and speak of him as the Imam for the *umma*—the (spiritual and temporal) leader of the entire Muslim world. The 1984 Congress of Friday Imams resolved to accept Khomeini "as having the necessary qualifications for the *imamate* of Muslims, and we will invite Muslims to follow his call."[59] Again, there may have been something of a ritual in such statements. But that was certainly not the case when it was a matter of referring to Shi'is alone. The claim that Shi'is anywhere must accept Khomeini as their *marja* was a hard-nosed bid for political dominance here and now. Meshkini was obviously speaking for the entire leadership when he spoke of the establishment in Iraq of an Islamic Republic "under the leadership of the Imam of the community, the idol-smasher, Imam Khomeini." Khamene'i for his part stressed:

> The future government of Iraq should be an Islamic and a popular one. The policy of *velayat-e faqih* will be Iraq's future policy, and the leader of the Islamic nation is Imam Khomeini. There is no difference between the two nations of Iran and Iraq in accepting the Imam as the leader, and following the Imam and his line. Government and state officials are limited to international borders, but the Imam is not limited by geographical frontiers.[60]

But—Iraq apart—they too disclaimed any intention to use force to spread the revolution. Khamene'i affirmed in 1984: "We undoubtedly will not give direct aid to [Muslim] movements . . . to help them or to force them to change their regimes. The Islamic Republic has a policy of not supporting such acts, and whatever is said about us to the contrary in this regard is untrue."[61] Musavi stated similarly: "We do not want to export armed revolution to any country. That is a big lie. Our aim is to promote the Islamic revolution through persuasion."[62] It must be remembered in this context that Shi'i doctrine lays down that, until the reappearance of the infallible Imam, the *vali faqih* can only lead a "defensive *jihad*."[63] But then the term "defense" is vague and flexible. The war against Iraq was viewed as a defensive war and some Iranians speak of getting control of the holy cities in Saudi Arabia in order to "defend" Islam.

Despite the gradual shift towards pragmatism in the establishment, appeals for certain types of unified Muslim action continued to be made. This occurred mainly during the *hajj* and the Unity Week or on special occasions such as the Conference on Islamic Thought, the Congresses of Friday Imams and a conference commemorating the anniversary of al-Afghani's death. Some leaders proposed an all-Islamic committee to administer Mecca and Medina,[64] others the formation of an Islamic army,[65] or the creation of an Islamic common market.[66] Others again asked for the formation of an Islamic Court (mainly for the purpose of trying Saddam Husayn), or making Arabic the *lingua franca* of the Muslim world.[67] But, except for the last point, it is difficult to say whether such proposals were made from motives of Islamic unity or of Iranian ("national") interests. Demands to bring Sunnis and Shi'is closer together also continued to be made,[68] but over time they dealt increasingly with relations between the Persian-Shi'i majority and those

Iranian ethnic groups who were Sunnis—that is they had to do with strengthening the Iranian nation-state, not Islamic unity.[69]

Eventually, in a speech during Unity Week in November 1987, President Khamene'i took the entire argument forward to the point of making a distinction between "positive" and "negative" nationalism. He rejected only "extreme nationalism," saying:

> Yes, positive nationalism in which the citizens . . . consider it their duty to defend their country . . . is good. But negative nationalism that denies the nationalism of others and seeks to create a great schism among Muslim brothers is extremely ugly and very wrong.[70]

Even more remarkably, a similar trend was evident in a leaflet distributed among the pilgrims in July 1987. These leaflets habitually displayed radical overtones and might well have been expected to do so again, especially in light of what we now know about the grave disturbances in Mecca shortly afterwards. Hojjat al-Islam Mehdi Karubi—Khomeini's representative for the *hajj*—who wrote the leaflet, presented Khomeini as the "leader of the call" (*ra'id al-da'wa*) for the "unity of the Muslim world" and as the leader who had always appealed to all Muslims to rise "in a united front" (*safa wahida*) against their enemies. But then he went on to make clear that the unity Iran was now calling for "should be based on ideological (*aqa'idiyya*) and emotional (*atifiyya*) foundations [only]." From a self-view as the fountainhead of revolutionary *élan* on the point of sweeping across the Muslim world, Iran's new regime had come round to seeing itself mainly as an exemplar and catalyst.

What has led to this change? It seems to me that the combination of the following factors have joined to produce it:

First: growing internal difficulties. Three sets of problems have preoccupied Iranian leaders—the war with Iraq and Iran's isolation; the prolonged economic downturn and the growing domestic resentment; and the power struggle within the revolutionary establishment. All three have created a sense of disillusionment and have come to pose a challenge to the stability of the regime. While they have not, so far, produced a change in declared policies, they have clearly led to greater pragmatism in the day-to-day conduct of domestic and foreign affairs. The comparative downplaying of "exporting the revolution" is only one aspect of the overall shift.

Second: the initial failure in "exporting" the revolution. When they first came to power, Khomeini and his men firmly expected a chain reaction in virtually all Muslim societies. One of Khomeini's Paris aides told an Arab correspondent: "Be patient . . . we will both see the fate of Saudi rulers six months after our return to Iran."[71] They put their trust in the peoples of Muslim states believing that, emboldened by Iranian example, they would rise against their rulers. This did not happen. In 1985, the Prime Minister made a much more sober assessment, saying:

[Initially] our view regarding exporting the revolution was that the Islamic revolution would spread within a year as a chain reaction. This idea is not altogether unrealistic in the long-run. But it seems that we were wrong in our initial assessments with regard to the fast spread of the revolution.[72]

Having had so little success in exporting its universal ideology Khomeini "turned to devising and exporting a more particularistic Shi'i ideology."[73] But even this did not receive the highest priority. Gradually, Iranian activities among Shi'is abroad became aimed mainly at gaining an advantage in the Gulf war or were linked with other clearly Iranian nationalist interest. (An outstanding exception is Lebanon.) Taking a broad view, there can be no doubt that, as one observer put it, even before the cease-fire Tehran has become "less concerned with fomenting rebellion abroad and more concerned with consolidating its own border."[74]

Iran's decision to accept the cease-fire was in itself the product of the new realities which have made for greater flexibility on revolutionary dogma, in order to save the Islamic regime. In turn, it accelerated these tendencies. It was also the result of the growing power of the more pragmatic elements within the Islamic establishment which by then had proved powerful enough to force their opinion on Khomeini and have him approve the cease-fire. Clearly, the one reason powerful enough to change Khomeini's mind was his concern for the revolution. Linking the two, he said in his message to his followers on 20 July: "God knows," had it not been for this reason, "I would never have agreed." He was ready he said, to drink "the chalice of poison" only "for the sake of the revolution."[75]

Moreover, after the cease-fire, reconstruction became the order of the day. "Reconstruction has became our nation's slogan," said Khamene'i.[76] Such an aim called for greater dogmatic flexibility and for improving ties with the neighboring Muslim states (see below).

Finally, while the cease-fire was, to a degree at least, the product of the pragmatists' gaining the upper hand in the domestic power struggle (demonstrated most significantly by the growing power of Rafsanjani), further changes in that direction were now being expected.

Thus, compromise on the vision of exporting the revolution was not so much the result of the cease-fire, but the product of the circumstances leading to it. Be that as it may, after the cease-fire Tehran proved more flexible in dealing with its Muslim neighbors. Rafsanjani was openly critical of past policies towards some Arab states: "If Iran had demonstrated a little more tactfulness" in its relations with Saudi Arabia and Kuwait, he said late in November 1988, "they would have not supported Iraq."[77] A few days later, he added that his country saw "no obstacles" to expanding relations with the Arab countries of the Gulf.[78] Deputy Foreign Minister Ali Muhammad Besharati spoke of Iran's desire to "turn over a new leaf" in its relations with the Gulf littoral states. He quoted from the Qur'an to support his view that " 'bygones are bygones'; we should think of the future." Referring to Saudi Arabia, he said: "We are prepared to sit down, talk and overcome the great misunderstanding between us." Using arguments, which in themselves were a significant retreat from the old revolutionary slogans, he reminded his listeners that "neighborhood is unchangeable" and that "our holy shrines . . . and our Ka'ba are there. The Prophet is buried in Saudi Arabia. Can we ignore it?"[79] Although the more doctrinaire elements within the establishment still continued to stick to their radical dogma, the statements of the top leadership differed from those made in the early days of the revolution; they reflected a significant change in the tone and contents of Iranian declarations.

While Tehran was now less determined to actively export its revolution (except for Lebanon, which has still remained the 'flag ship'), the cease-fire could have its impact on the willingness of others to import it. First and foremost, this was Khomeini's first failure. Until then the revolution had been presented (and in many ways had been) a success story. Now, there was failure, not only in having to accept the cease-fire, but also in admitting that the many social and economic problems which had initially led to the Islamic revolution, remained unsolved after a decade of revolution and war. Those committed to Khomeini's path may continue supporting their doctrine, but for the larger world of Islam, the balance of achievements and failures of the Islamic regime in Iran is a significant factor in their willingness to import its values and adopt its policies (cf. the Introduction).

Conclusions

In ideological as well as practical terms, one could witness in the first decade of revolutionary Iran considerable deviations from some of the most basic elements in Khomeini's philosophy. Over time, the pragmatic interests of the *state* have clearly gained supremacy over the radical philosophy of the *revolution*. Consequently, significant change could be noticed in the most basic elements of Khomeini's creed. The notion of "exporting the revolution" was no exception.

In fact, Khomeini's policy, like that of other Iranian pan-Islamists in earlier times, was motivated in the main by tactical and pragmatic rather than ideological considerations. Though Khomeini's vision has not been abandoned, its implementation has been subordinated to practical calculations. The initial euphoria and the belief in Iran's capacity to export the revolution has given way to a more realistic view of foreign policy. The expected spontaneous and widespread acceptance of the Iranian revolutionary example has not materialized. This reality and the exigencies of war have compelled Khomeini to change his order of priorities. The export of the revolution had to give way to the consolidation of the revolution in Iran as an attractive example for emulation elsewhere. His theories about Islamic unity of the 1970s are now spread with much greater loyalty by his followers outside the country (i.e. the Hizballah or the Da'wa) than his disciples at home. (See chapters by Kramer and Baram.)

The practical consequence of this change of priorities has been a visible tendency to promote a new form of Iranian territorial identity. As opposed to the regime of the shah which based Iranian nationalism on an essentially secular perception rooted in Iran's pre-Islamic history, Khomeini's perception of Iranian identity sees Islam as the decisive cohesive element. In ideological terms, this still allows for Iran to serve as the nucleus for a large "Islamic order." But in the pursuit of such an order Iran has no choice but to operate within the constraints of *realpolitik*. Its audience is primarily in receptive Shi'i communities, and secondarily, anywhere else the opportunity may arise. This, Khomeini believed, will ultimately lead to the realization of his historical vision.

In this sense the Iranian revolution is not very different form the French, American and (in particular) the Bolshevik revolutions. All initially aspired to export the revolution in one way or another, but all were compelled, sooner or later, to come to terms with reality, though not necessarily to abandon their vision. The intention is certainly not to limit themselves to "Khomeinism in one country," but the ruling clerics have gone a long way from the vision of world (or, at least, Islamic) order that they had formulated when they seized power.

Notes

1. Referring to supra-national movements throughout the world, Smith argued that all such movements have failed, at least partially. The national movements, by contrast, have proved a success story: Anthony Smith, *Theories of Nationalism* (London: 1971), 213–214, 228–229. For a differentiation between types of national movements, see also the same author's, *Nationalism in the Twentieth Century* (Oxford: 1979).

2. Exaggerating greatly, Khomeini claimed in his book *Velayat-e Faqih* that Shi'is constituted 25 per cent of all Muslims, but that still leaves them decidedly in a minority: Ayatollah Ruhollah Khomeini, *Islam and Revolution: Writings and Declarations of Imam Khomeini* (translated and annotated by Hamid Algar; Berkeley: 1981), 138. More balanced estimates put the Shi'is at about 10 per cent of the worldwide Muslim population. See for example, Martin Kramer, "Introduction," in M. Kramer (ed.), *Shi'ism, Resistance and Revolution* (Boulder: 1987), 10 (table).

3. Majid Khadduri, *Political Trends in the Arab World: The Role of Ideas and Ideals in Politics* (Baltimore: 1970), 8.

4. Richard Cottam, *Nationalism in Iran* (Pittsburgh: 1979), 135, 145.

5. Hamid Enayat, *Modern Islamic Political Thought* (London: 1982), 120–122.

6. Ayatollah Ruhollah Khomeini, *Kashf-e Asrar* (Tehran: 1979; first published in 1944), 337.

7. R. K. Ramazani, "Khomeyni's Islam in Iran's Foreign Policy," in Adeed Dawisha (ed.), *Islam in Foreign Policy* (Cambridge: 1985), 17. This was reprinted in Ramazani's book, *Revolutionary Iran: Challenge and Response in the Middle East* (Baltimore: 1986), 20.

8. Khomeini, ibid., 424.

9. Khomeini, ibid., 109.

10. Khomeini, ibid., 285–286.

11. Khomeini, ibid., 144–147 and 147–150 respectively.

12. Khomeini, ibid., 285–286.

13. For Borujerdi's as well as for Ayatollah Muhammad Musavi Behbahani's allusion to the Iranian military as the Army of Islam, see: Shahrough Akhavi, *Religion and*

Politics in Contemporary Iran: Clergy-State Relations in the Pahlavi Period (Albany: 1980), 78.

14. Khomeini's *Islam and Revolution*, 34–35; an interview with *al-Mustaqbal*, 13 January 1979; Radio Tehran, 7 May—DR, 8 May 1979.

15. *Al-Safir*, 18 and 19 January 1979.

16. Radio Tehran, 17 December 1979—SWB, 19 December 1979.

17. Khomeini, *The Islamic Government*, Algar's translation, 48–50, 146–149. Similar views were expressed by Ayatollah Husayn Ali Montazeri in interviews with *Kayhan*, 16 and 18 January 1979.

18. *Le Monde*, 6 May 1978.

19. *Al-Mustaqbal*, 13 January 1979.

20. *Al-Safir*, 18 January 1979.

21. Radio Tehran, 13 February—SWB, 15 February 1979. Yet the 1979 Iranian constitution stipulates that only a Shi'i can become president (see below).

22. For the ideological differences between the two, see my article: "Shi'ite Leadership: in the Shadow of Conflicting Ideologies," *Iranian Studies*, XIII, 1–4 (1980), 119–145.

23. *Ettela'at*, 14 August 1979.

24. Radio Tehran, 30 July–SWB, 1 August 1979.

25. Sayyid Mahmud Taleghani, *Society and Economics in Islam: Writings and Declarations of Ayatullah Sayyid Mahmud Taleghani* (Berkeley: 1982), mainly 86–87; Mangol Bayat, "Mahmud Taleqani and the Iranian revolution," in Martin Kramer (ed.), *Shi'ism, Resistance, and Revolution*, 67–94.

26. *Al-Nahar*, 7 January 1979. (In March 1989, however, Khomeini and his men ceased to view Montazeri as loyal enough to their party and withdrew his nomination as Khomeini's successor.)

27. Shaykh al-Ra'is Qajar, *Ettehad-e Islam* (Bombay: 1894), 74–75, as cited in Enayat, *Political Thought*, 122.

28. See mainly his *Khadamat-e Motaqabel-e Iran va-Islam* (Tehran: 1969/70). Also: Enayat, *Political Thought*, 123–124.

29. Cottam, 153.

30. Bayat, 67.

31. Speaking of young Iranians active in anti-Shah campaigns abroad, Khomeini wrote in *Velayat-e Faqih:* that they ". . . are enjoining the good upon us; they say to us: We have organized Islamic Associations; now help us:" Khomeini, *Islam and Revolution*, 129. For a brief discussion of "Contemporary Shi'i Thought," see Nikki R. Keddie, *Roots of Revolution: An Interpretive History of Modern Iran* (New Haven: 1981). (This section of the book was written by Yann Richard).

32. Many Shi'i fundamentalists spent long periods of time in Najaf in the 1970s. For details see: Marvin Zonis and Daniel Brumberg, "Khomeini, the Islamic Republic of Iran, and the Arab World," *Harvard Middle East Papers*, V (1987).

33. In a paper for the Middle East Studies Association (Boston, 1986), for example, Hrair Dekmejian claimed that the concept of *velayat-e faqih* was in fact originally thought of by Ayatollah Baqir al-Sadr. Others accused Khomeini of plagiarism from Shaykh Muhammad Husayn Kashif al-Ghita. See also chapters by Amazia Baram and Martin Kramer in this volume.

34. Amazia Baram, *National Integration and Exclusiveness in Political Thought and Practice in Iraq under the Ba'th, 1968-1982* (Ph.D. thesis, in Hebrew, submitted to the Hebrew University of Jerusalem, April 1986), see mainly 385, 437–438.

35. James Piscatori, *Islam in a World of Nation-States* (Cambridge: 1986), 101–16; Emanuel Sivan, *Radical Islam: Medieval Theology and Modern Politics* (New Haven: 1985), 15–129.

36. The fact that following its takeover, the Islamic Republic issued a stamp to commemorate Qutb's execution shows that he was well-known among Iranian clerics; certainly even prior to their seizure of power.

37. For his first book he chose the title *Ma'muriyyat Bara-ye Vatanam* ("Mission for my Nation"; though it was translated as "Mission for my Country") and he later claimed to have had a "celestial mission" (*ma'muriyyat-e asemani*).

38. Muhammad Reza Pahlavi, *Enqelab-e Sefid* ("The White Revolution"; Tehran: 1967), 16, 103–106; *Kayhan*, 17 November 1976.

39. *Ettela'at*, 3 March 1975.

40. Mohammad Reza Pahlavi, *Mission for My Country* (London: 1961), 54–58; R. K. Karanjia, *The Mind of a Monarch* (London: 1977); *Kayhan*, 7 November 1976.

41. Muhammad Reza Pahlavi, *Enqelab-e Sefid*, 16.

42. Oriana Fallaci's interview with the Shah, *New Republic*, 1 December 1973, 15–21.

43. Mohammad Reza Pahlavi, *Mission for my Country*, 54-58; *Kayhan*, 7 November 1976; Oriana Fallaci's interview with the Shah, *New Republic*, 1 December 1973, 15–21.

44. For a more comprehensive discussion of the gap between Khomeini's ideology and his policy see my article, "Iran: Doctrine and Reality," in Efraim Karsh (ed.), *The Iran-Iraq War: Impact and Implications* (London: 1989), 42–57; and my book, *Iran: A Decade of War and Revolution* (New York: 1990), mainly the postscript.

45. See, for example, his speech broadcast over Radio Tehran, 3 November— SWB, 5 November 1981. Cf. Menashri, *A Decade of War and Revolution*, 202–203.

46. *Kayhan*, 29 October 1984. For a similar view expressed a year later: *Kayhan-e Hava'i*, 11 November 1985.

47. For the disqualification of a presidential candidate (Jalal al-Din Farsi), in the first presidential campaign (1980), because his father was an Afghan, see: Menashri, *A Decade of War and Revolution*, 120.

48. He even rejected Ayatollah Sadeq Khalkhali's proposal to name it the "Muslim Gulf": *Kayhan*, 29 May 1979. On 5 May 1981, Prime Minister Muhammad Ali Raja'i issued a statement saying that "Persian Gulf" was the "correct historical and original name." He gave instructions for that appellation only to be used in all official documents and speeches: Radio Tehran, 7 May—SWB, 9 May 1981.

49. *Ettela'at*, 29 September 1980.

50. Piscatori, 111.

51. Zonis and Brumberg, 74.

52. *Ettela'at*, 23 August 1981. A few weeks later (as prime minister) he stressed that Iran's struggle would continue, "until the region and the world are rebuilt upon new foundations": *Tehran Journal*, 7 October 1981.

53. *Kayhan*, 19 December 1982.

54. Ramazani, *Revolutionary Iran*, 24–25; idem, "Iran's Islamic Revolution and the Persian Gulf," *Current History*, January 1985, 5–6.

55. *Kayhan*, 24 October 1983.

56. *Kayhan*, 30 September 1982.

57. *Kayhan*, 29 February 1984. Similarly Rafsanjani in: *JI*, 19 July 1984.

58. See words of Ali Akbar Velayati (AFP, 12 January—DR, 13 January 1982) and, Ali Khamene'i (*Tehran Times*, 6 April 1982).

59. Ramazani, *Iran and the Persian Gulf*, 7.

60. SWB, 31 March 1982, as quoted by Shaul Bakhash, *The Reign of the Ayatollahs: Iran and the Islamic Revolution* (New York: 1986), 234.

61. *Ettela'at*, 7 March 1984.

62. Radio Tehran—DR, 30 October 1984.

63. See in this regard Khomeini's message to the 1987 pilgrims: Radio Tehran, 29 July—DR, 30 July 1987.

64. For such suggestions raised by Kho'iniha (aimed at "saving the holy cities" from the "emissaries of the Satan" and the British appointed "illiterate, hireling Beduin") see: *Kayhan*, 24 August, 10 and 15 September 1982. Similar views were expressed by Meshkini (*Kayhan*, 25 September 1982) and Montazeri (ibid., 10 November 1982). The idea was endorsed by an official statement of the Ministry of Foreign Affairs (ibid., 25 September 1982) and the Friday Imams' Congress in 1983 (ibid., 3 January 1983).

65. *Kayhan*, 4 September 1983.

66. See appeals in this regard by Commerce Minister Habibollah Asghar Owladi Mosalman and Foreign Minister Velayati: *Kayhan*, 2 May 1982.

67. This was raised by Meshkini and Ayatollah Muhammad Reza Golpaygani (*Kayhan*, 3 January 1983), and endorsed by the resolutions of the Friday Imams' Congress (ibid., 4 January 1983). An elaborate discussion of the Iranian attempt to advance their ideology through Iranian and international (Islamic) fora, see Martin Kramer's *MECS* chapters for 1982–83, 1983–84.

68. Khomeini offered the "hand of brotherhood" to Sunni Muslims and asked them to view Shi'is as their "cherished brothers": *JI*, 13 September 1980. Montazeri called Sunni *ulama* to study Shi'i *hadith* and *fiqh* sources (*Kayhan*, 4 January 1983; *JI*, 15 December 1984), Ayatollah Shihab al-Din Najafi Mar'ashi and Kho'iniha asked them to study the Shi'a just as they study the four Sunni *madhhabs* (*Kayhan*, 4 January 1983 and 10 December 1984, respectively). Rafsanjani called on *Ashura* mourners to refrain from invoking anti-Sunni sentiment (*JI*, 29 September 1984 and similarly, *Kayhan*, 17 November 1983 and *JI*, 15 December 1984). See also the views of Meshkini (*JI*, 8 December 1984), Ayatollah Abd al-Karim Musavi Ardebili (*Kayhan*, 18 December 1983) and Musavi (*Kayhan*, 20 December 1983).

69. For such appeals, see: Khamene'i in his Friday sermon (*Kayhan*, 1 January 1983); in a meeting with *ulama* from Kurdestan and Azerbayjan (*Ettela'at*, 7 September 1983) and with Sunni *ulama* (*JI*, 12 December 1984); Hojjat al-Islam Muhammad Khatami in meeting with Kurds (*Kayhan*, 1 January 1983) and Ardebili (*JI*, 10 December 1984).

70. Similar expressions occur in his subsequent Friday sermon in Tehran. For both, see Radio Tehran, 6, 8 November—DR, 9, 10 November 1987.

71. *Al-Safir*, 19 January 1979.

72. *Kayhan*, 21 February 1985.

73. Zonis and Brumberg, 74–75.

74. Gary Sick, "Iran's Quest for Superpower Status," *Foreign Affairs*, Spring 1987, 714.

75. *Ettela'at*, 21 July 1988.

76. *Ettela'at*, 8 October; Radio Tehran, 7 October—SWB, 10 October 1988.

77. IRNA (in English), 19 November—SWB, 21 November 1988.

78. Radio Tehran, 29 November—SWB, 1 December 1988.

79. Radio Tehran, 19 November—SWB, 21 November 1988.

3

The Shi'i Praxis:
Domestic Politics and
Foreign Policy in Iran

Farhad Kazemi and Jo-Anne Hart

The Islamic Revolution dramatically reshaped the content and form of Iranian foreign policy. It transformed Iran from a *status quo* regime into one committed to a universalistic religious ideology ready to cause disruption in the Gulf region and beyond. With one major stroke, the founders of the Islamic Republic destroyed Iran's long-standing alliance with the United States and pursued a policy highly antagonistic to a dominant great power. Other alliances in the Middle East and outside were also reshaped and redefined to fit the requirements of Islamic revolutionary ideology and the new regime's perception of its interests and goals. The hostage crisis and the Iran-Iraq war further exacerbated the situation and made Iranian foreign policy both conflictual and more volatile. All of these events occurred during a period of extensive revolutionary change when Ayatollah Ruhollah Khomeini and his followers were determined to create an Islamic government (*hokumat-e Islami*). The Iranian leaders' preoccupation centered on both domestic and foreign affairs, but the lines separating these two aspects of national politics were, for the most part, blurred.

This chapter argues that in order to understand the foreign policy behavior of revolutionary Iran, particular attention must be paid to the interaction of internal and external aspects of its policy. Although interaction between internal and external forces affect all policy-making, it is especially important for Iranian foreign policy behavior since the revolution. Policies have been remarkably successful in answering domestic political needs. Furthermore, rather than being primarily reactive, Iran has managed to exert considerable influence on the course of its external relations. The dynamic relationship between internal and external aspects of Iranian foreign policy can be observed in many different areas. A comprehensive analysis is not possible here. This paper reviews the domestic context of Iranian foreign policy and then presents three different but related cases involving the United States and the Soviet Union to illustrate the nature of the interaction.

The first case discusses a predominantly internal impetus to a major Iranian action: the hostage crisis of 1979–1981. The second case involves an externally imposed situation, the Soviet resumption of arms sale to Iraq, to which Iran responded by a major crackdown on the Tudeh (Communist) Party. The third case reviews the more recent developments in Iran's relations with the US: the covert arms sale to Iran and the reflagging of Kuwaiti tankers. These developments have had important negative consequences for Iran's economic, political, and military position. However, they also delivered some support to the regime from elements in Iran who would not otherwise support the Islamic Republic.

The Domestic Context

The main tenets of Ayatollah Khomeini's world view can be found in his writings and speeches as well as in the analyses of many observers of the Iranian scene. Khomeini's world view, fully accepted by the ruling elite of revolutionary Iran, is concerned with several broad objectives, all of which have direct foreign policy implications. These are:

First, the Islamic Revolution—or more specifically Khomeini's vision of it—must survive and prosper in Iran. The revolution is presented as an attempt to restore authentic cultural traditions to the masses at the expense of alien ideologies. Success and prosperity of the Islamic Revolution is an essential step in acting out God's will on earth. The revolutionary unity must be preserved and its enemies isolated and destroyed. An integral part of the Islamic Revolution is the creation of an Islamic government, in which Shi'i values, as interpreted by the all-powerful jurisconsult and the clerics, reign supreme.

Second, the revolution must be exported to other Muslim countries and eventually to the rest of the Third World. Khomeini saw the revolution not as an Iranian but rather as an Islamic revolution.[1] The purpose of the revolution is to spread the message of Islam to all corners of the world. This is obligatory and essential for all Muslims.[2] (For more details, see chapter by Menashri.)

Third, the exporting of the revolution can be done by uniting the "disinherited" (*mostaz'afin*) against the oppressors (*mostakbarin*). The great powers are identified as the oppressors.

Fourth, Iranian foreign policy must be governed by the maxim of "neither East, nor West, only the Islamic Republic." As Ramazani points out, this is not the same as the idea of non-alignment since in Khomeini's view no state could be "truly" non-aligned.[3] The superpowers' role must, therefore, be rejected and doctrine and practice of "Islamic self-reliance" substituted for it. The United States is designated as the chief external enemy. The Soviet Union is referred to as the "Red Satan," the "Lesser Satan," or the "Other Satan."[4] In a particularly strong denunciation of the superpowers and their allies, Khomeini said:

America is worse than Britain; Britain is worse than America. The Soviet Union is worse than both of them. They are all worse and more unclean than each other! But today it is America that we are concerned with.[5]

Israel, Egypt, and South Africa, among other states, are also frequently and vehemently attacked as lackeys of the United States.[6] Finally, the Iran-Iraq war was declared an "imposed war" and a "crusade of right against wrong." The war must continue, until Saddam Husayn is overthrown. (Both these claims were drastically modified with Iran's acceptance of the cease-fire in July 1988.)

Promoting these objectives has not been easy. Iran has had to reconcile its aggressive foreign policy with the need to pay attention to post-revolutionary domestic priorities. These have had to be undertaken with limited available resources during a period of revolutionary turmoil at home and a long drawn-out foreign war. The problem is exacerbated by the vulnerability to the influence of foreign powers. Whatever the domestic concerns, the Ayatollah's regime has always maintained a visible foreign policy posture. Foreign policy crises and external enemies have been immensely helpful to the regime in maintaining its revolutionary momentum and in keeping the population under control.[7] International confrontation also becomes a yardstick for measuring the revolution's success.

Although the regime has succeeded in eliminating opposition and institutionalizing power, it has done so at a terrible cost. It has alienated an important segment of the professional class and has prompted the exodus of many people whose expertise and services the regime needs. It has also inflicted violence on some targeted groups. The regime's policies have been particularly detrimental to women and certain religious and ethnic minorities such as the Bahais and the Kurds. A high price has been paid for the ruthless cultural revolution and the all-encompassing attempt to Islamicize the polity. Iranian society, always heterogeneous, is now doctrinaire and intolerant. A rigid interpretation of Shi'i-Islamic law rules the day.

There are, of course, those who benefit from the regime and support it. They are members of the Revolutionary Guards or of other military or paramilitary organizations, or belong to the petty bourgeoisie or the clergy, or are simply Islamic zealots; they all see the regime as authentic and rooted in the people. Support is likely to continue as long as the regime provides handsome rewards for their loyalty and monopolizes the means of organized violence.

This does not mean, however, that the ruling elite in Iran is always united in its policy choices. There are, in fact, important divisions among the elite with regard to many policy matters. But it is not easy to point to clearly defined ideological or political groupings. Confronted with similar policy options, the same elite members have sometimes supported different choices or have changed their positions on the same issue. Some may have been "moderate" (or better, pragmatist) on one issue, but radical on another. It is, therefore, not easy to generalize about these divisions. Nevertheless, looking at the elite behavior in a decade of revolution and war one can observe two broad and contrasting views on major domestic policies that have important foreign policy implications.[8] The first view is expressed by those who can be called "economic radicals." They support state intervention in domestic economy, nationalization of foreign trade, drastic land reform laws and other radical measures. The second view is expounded by those who can be labeled "economic conservatives," and who are strongly committed to the ideas of free enterprise and a limited state role in the economy.

These groups have their ideas expressed on a regular basis in two important newspapers, *Jomhuri-ye Islami* and *Resalat*, and can expect the support of powerful clerics and individuals for their respective positions. Khomeini maintained a position that transcended these policy divisions. His sentiments, depending on the circumstances involved, vacillated between one or the other group at any given time.

It is also possible to extrapolate from the domestic policy choices of these two groups their probable foreign policy tendencies. Although this is somewhat speculative, it is reasonable to maintain that the "economic conservatives" have a more positive predisposition towards the United States than the "economic radicals." Their logical preference, all other things being equal, would be for the free enterprise system of the United States as opposed to the state-dominated system of the Soviet Union. Of course, the Iran-Iraq war and the centralized foreign policy decision-making apparatus of the Iranian government has made a full assessment of the above observation difficult.

Important differences on foreign policy, especially on the Iran-Iraq war, did not normally find expression in public policy debates. Iranian foreign policy was formulated by several key decision makers and presented for implementation in a united front. The centralization of power and control of the foreign policy apparatus made it highly unlikely that any major foreign (or domestic) policy could be made without the Ayatollah's knowledge or, at least, tacit approval.

The United States and Iran: The Hostage Crisis

The taking of American diplomats as hostages (on 4 November 1979), and their incarceration for 444 days clearly and dramatically pitted Iran against the United States in a highly offensive act that transgressed international protocols and regulations.[9] Although the taking of hostages was a foreign-policy decision directed at the United States, it also served important internal functions. Ayatollah Khomeini and some of the leading members of the clerical elite were well aware of the potential value of this act in expediting the regime's consolidation of power. It was a highly potent weapon that the clerics could use against their opponents at a critical juncture when they were attempting to gain control over the state apparatus. The prolongation of the hostage crisis allowed the regime to systematically silence the various domestic forces that were not enthusiastic about the idea of an Islamic Republic. In short, the hostage crisis was a watershed event that helped ensure the continuation of clerical rule and eventual imposition of an Islamic theocracy in Iran.

The various internal functions of the hostage crisis for the revolutionary clerics have been discussed by a number of observers.[10] Several points, however, need to be reiterated.

First, the seizure of the American embassy formally ended the tenure of Prime Minister Mehdi Bazargan and his hopes for establishing a liberal nationalist regime that also had some Islamic underpinnings. The taking of hostages was equivalent to a civilian *coup* against the Bazargan cabinet. It discredited his government and showed the limited base of his power. It was a forceful message that also denied any significant role to what has been referred to as "Islamic liberalism" in a future Iranian government.[11]

Second, the hostage crisis allowed the revolutionary clerics to contain and eventually dispose of the left as a viable force in Iranian politics. It is important to note that some of the leftist forces had played a role in the revolution and in the process that eventually led to Khomeini's seizure of power. The left, however, was in a quandary about its assessment of Ayatollah Khomeini and the meaning of the hostage crisis. The nature of the left's internal debate and the issues involved later allowed the anti-leftist clerics to discredit them in the public eye and eventually eliminate them from the political scene. One after another, the leftist forces were isolated and banished. The final act was the closure of the Tudeh Party offices and the arrest and imprisonment of a large number of its members in 1983.

Third, the American embassy documents that were captured during the hostage crisis were used very selectively. Only those documents that could be construed as damaging to potential opponents of the regime were made public and used to isolate or eliminate them. By contrast, much of the information that would have been detrimental to several key clerics was never published. This gave the revolutionary clerics another important weapon.

Fourth, the hostage crisis allowed the revolutionary clerics to gain approval for the proposed constitution that formally established an Islamic republic in Iran.[12] Those opposed to controversial provisions, especially to Article 5 which invested dictatorial powers in the all-powerful jurisconsult (*faqih*), were forced to go along with the authors of the constitution. The embassy seizure and the public frenzy surrounding it were used to push through its final ratification in late 1979.

The hostage crisis illustrates the close relationship between internal and external aspects of Iranian politics and demonstrates how the Ayatollah's regime made effective use of the foreign policy crisis for internal gains. It took full advantage of widespread popular support for the embassy seizure to generate greater zeal and to isolate and banish actual or potential enemies. In a series of calculated acts, well-planned and co-ordinated, it made the crisis an effective lever to take over the state apparatus, and establish a theocratic government.[13]

Soviet-Iranian Relations

The Soviet Union turned against the shah shortly before his fall. Seeing his overthrow as a setback to Washington and an end to the intense military relationship between the US and Iran, the Soviets came to support Khomeini. The new Iranian political forces were perceived as positive by the Soviets because they were anti-American and anti-imperialist.

Moscow hoped the change would signal the emergence of a regime with which it could deal without hostility and, ideally, one which would move toward the Soviet Union. To this end, the Soviets promoted good relations with the Islamic Republic through diplomatic support, considerable assistance for Iran's overland trade, and other economic measures. Consequently, from 1979–1982 relations between Moscow and Tehran were relatively good, particularly in the economic sphere. In 1981, the Islamic Republic's trade with the Soviet Union exceeded that of the shah's. Iranian imports from the Eastern Bloc amounted to 15 per cent of its total imports.[14] Extensive technical and commercial arrangements were in place, including co-operation on hydroelectric projects, a steel mill in Isfahan, and technical training by the Soviets. Iran at first delayed selling natural gas to the Soviets but did sell oil and finally resumed gas sales.

Despite Soviet overtures, the Islamic Republic resisted closer political ties. As part of its firmly held belief in "neither East nor West," Iran refrained from pursuing policies which the Soviets favored, and thus, sources of tension continued to exist between the two states. The Soviets were dismayed by the Islamic Republic's lack of anti-capitalist reforms, and its hostility to leftist groups and certain ethnic minorities. The Iranians also denounced the Soviet invasion of Afghanistan and were often critical of Soviet policies. America's loss in Tehran was, therefore, not Moscow's gain. But overall, until 1982–1983, both the Iranians and the Soviets clearly perceived mutual benefits from accommodation of one another.

The Tudeh Link with the Soviet Union

An important aspect of Soviet-Iranian relations is charted through the course of the well-established close association between the Soviets and the Tudeh Party. At any particular time, the Iranian attitude toward the Tudeh Party is to some degree indicative of Tehran's policy toward the USSR.[15] The Speaker of Parliament, Ali Akbar Hashemi Rafsanjani, has expressed views that are shared by many: he reportedly said that the Tudeh "are inspired abroad; they are practically Russian."[16] And indeed one of Moscow's conduits in pursuing its interests in Iran was through the Tudeh Party. The party loyally follows the Soviet line, and public confessions after the anti-Tudeh crackdown (see below) indicate an extensive dependence on the Soviets. Both the Soviets and the Tudeh Party supported Khomeini's policies following the revolution. The Tudeh provided important backing for the regime during the period of consolidation of power and the crackdown on the *Mojahedin-e Khalq*. This support was significant in carrying the regime through its domestic crisis in 1981.[17] For its docility and support, the Islamic Republic tolerated the Tudeh Party semi-officially for four years.

Soviet-Iran Relations and the Iran-Iraq War

However, the key issue in Soviet-Iranian relations was the Iran-Iraq war. Although there were other points of dispute that separated Iran and the Soviet Union (such as the Soviet invasion of Afghanistan), the war remained a major barrier to a better relationship.

Until 1982, the Soviets were generally supportive of Iran in the war with Iraq. They maintained, however, a long-standing military relationship and an operative Treaty of Friendship with Iraq. Indeed, Iraq expected continued Soviet military support in its war against Iran. But the Soviets were not in favor of Iraq's military campaign and restricted new arms supplies soon after the initial Iraqi invasion of Iran in 1980. They perceived Iran as the key strategic prize in the Gulf region and Iran's primary interest was the non-supply of Soviet arms to Iraq. The USSR sold some arms to Iran and allowed Soviet-manufactured arms and other military equipment to be transferred through Syria, Libya, and North Korea. If the overall context of relations with post-revolutionary Iran required a neutral Soviet role in the Iran-Iraq war, initially that neutrality had a tilt toward Iran.

But relations between Iran and the Soviet Union changed dramatically as a result of the Iranian successes in the war. The tide of warfare had begun to shift in favor of Iran in the Spring of 1982. By July, Iran was on the offensive, ready to cross over into Iraq. The Soviet argument that the war should end did not stop the Iranians. The invasion of Iraqi territory became a major point of conflict between the two countries.

The Soviets decided to resume arms supplies to Iraq and to risk a major deterioration of their relationship with Iran. In the increasingly hostile climate, the Iranians ordered cutbacks of Soviet embassy personnel and eventually lodged serious charges of espionage against Soviet diplomats. Apparently a defecting Soviet intelligence officer had provided key information on Soviet activities in Iran to the British who in turn had relayed them to the Iranian officials. As will be seen, the Tudeh Party bore the brunt of these hostile relations with the official closure of the party and the arrest of its leadership.

From the Soviet perspective, Iran has not been forthcoming despite many attempts by the Soviets to engender closer ties between the two countries. The Soviets had an interest in preventing an embarrassing military defeat of their quasi-ally, Iraq. They were also fearful that the war's continuation could lead to intervention by the United States.

In the spring of 1983, Moscow openly condemned Iran for its failure to negotiate with Iraq. At that time, the Iranian regime had made up its mind to eradicate the Tudeh Party. At first they harassed party activists and expelled Tudeh members from government institutions. Next came the arrest of over a thousand party members. In May, the Tudeh Party was formally banned. The same day, the Islamic Republic expelled eighteen Soviet diplomats as a result of espionage charges stemming from evidence provided by Tudeh Party leaders during their incarceration. Tudeh members belonging to the party's military branch were put on trial (some were later executed), but the political leaders, including Secretary-General Nur al-Din Kiyanuri, have so far (1989) been detained without trial. The crack-down against the Tudeh marked the lowest point in post-revolution Iranian-Soviet relations.

Because the Khomeini regime tends to equate the Tudeh with the Soviet Union, the dramatic banning of the party indicates that the Tudeh was punished in retaliation for Soviet aid to the Iraqis. Some analysts draw an explicit connection between these events. For example, Shahram Chubin maintains that "the episode had little to do with the Tudeh as such but with Tehran's anger at renewed Soviet support for Iraq."[18] The case, however, is more complex. It resulted from the interplay of both external forces— the Iranian refusal to cut back its war aims and the Soviet decision to resupply Iraq—as well as several domestic factors, especially the consolidation of power by the Islamic Republic. This domestic factor cannot be ignored. By consolidating his political power, Khomeini was able to gradually install supporters of the Islamic Republic in the major state institutions: the army, judiciary, and bureaucracy. The more Khomeini supplanted his opposition, the easier it was for the Islamic Republic to turn against the Tudeh Party and finally crush it in 1983.

Although 1983 was the nadir of Iranian relations with the Soviet Union, neither state wished to permanently alienate the other. Lines of communication remained open and economic relations continued to prosper. By 1983 Soviet trade with Iran, excluding military supplies, outpaced that with Iraq.[19] The Soviet deputy foreign minister visited Tehran in the summer of 1987 and signed an agreement to co-operate on various large-scale economic projects, including oil pipelines, a railroad, and co-operation in the areas of steel and energy. While direct Soviet arms sales to Iran remained suspended, the flow of Eastern Bloc arms has increased since mid-1986.[20] But in March 1988, in the context of the escalated "war of the cities" thousands attacked the Soviet embassy in Tehran and denounced the Soviets for their role in supplying long-range missiles to Iraq.

This pattern of relations indicates both Tehran's pragmatism and Soviet flexibility. Iran did not permanently cut ties with Moscow and has been able to separate (at least to its own satisfaction) political from economic relations. Furthermore, it continued to acquire military supplies from the Soviet bloc. Although the signs point to a possible further warming of relations, important problems remain. Until the cease-fire, the war and its immediate aftermath continued to be a source of contention between the Soviet Union and Iran.

US-Iranian Relations: Arms Sales and Reflagging

From the Iranian perspective, the 1985–86 arms deal with the US must be viewed in the crucial context of the intense difficulty Iran had in acquiring weapons, ammunition, and spare parts during the course of the war with Iraq. Most important, whether for the war effort or for the post-war rebuilding of their armed strength, were weapons and equipment of US manufacture—the backbone of the Iranian military is American-equipped. With the fall of the shah, the US had begun to cancel arms contracts and shipments. Then, with the taking of the hostages and the collapse of American-Iranian relations, Iran faced an embargo on American weapons and spare parts. Military purchases from the US dropped dramatically: from about $2.6 billion in 1979 to $14 million the next year.[21]

When the war with Iraq began in 1980, Iran proved remarkably resourceful in obtaining arms on the international market by exploiting nearly any avenue. Iran dealt with at least 41 countries,[22] at a cost of between $2–3 billion each year.[23] Suppliers included the superpowers, Eastern bloc states, several Western European countries (among them Britain, France, Portugal, Sweden and Spain), Israel, Brazil, South Korea, Singapore, Vietnam, and Syria. In the last three years of the war, North Korea and China also became important sources of arms.

The diversity of suppliers and types of supplies has created problems for Iran on a number of levels. Due to the intended Western embargo, Iran has been forced to buy many of its weapons illegally, paying cash at highly inflated prices. Iran is estimated to have paid as much as three times the regular price of a TOW missile in its transactions with the US. Deliveries have involved frequent and costly delays. An important negative aspect of this unsteady and hodge-podge purchase of arms supplies is the fact that some of these Iranian purchases are not compatible with American-made equipment. The Iranian military has been forced to absorb unfamiliar equipment and weapons.

But, however expensive, unsatisfactory, insecure and inadequate supplies were, arms acquisition was of paramount importance to political leaders in Iran, both in terms of sustaining the war effort and of the role the war had come to play in domestic politics. In the face of various obstacles, the Iranian leaders were therefore determined to pursue all available options. It is in this context, then, that Iran negotiated arms purchases from the US.

In 1985 the US took a series of decisions which led eventually to the covert sale of weapons to Iran. The episode is important not only as a dramatic phase of American-Iranian relations, but because the Iranians appear to have exerted control over the process and because of its consequences in the Gulf. Iran got (at least partly) what it wanted from the arms deal, the Americans did not. Partly at least as a result from the ensuing scandal in the US, the American military extended protection to Kuwaiti tankers. The US reflagging almost tripled the American military presence in the Gulf area and created an external dynamic that affected Iranian internal politics.

US covert arms sales to Iran took place in 1985 and 1986. More than 2,000 TOW anti-tank missiles, 235 Hawk anti-aircraft missiles, and extensive spare parts were sold to Iran. These involved six separate shipments, the value of which is still difficult to ascertain but is thought to be about $64 million. Direct US TOW and Hawk transfers are estimated at approximately $30 million, and the addition of parts as well as Israeli sales significantly increased the overall value of the arrangement.[24]

The idea of an American initiative toward Iran began as early as the end of 1984. The reorientation was grounded in the broad goal of establishing some useful contact with Iran in order to pursue long-term interests in the area, as well as in a specific immediate objective of gaining the release of American hostages in Lebanon. Members of the administration, particularly the National Security Council (NSC), began to believe that with proper inducements the Iranians could bring pressure to bear on the release of the seven American hostages being held there. The hostage issue was increasingly viewed as a political problem for the president, engaging the attention of his close political advisors.

The Israelis also supported and encouraged the idea of improved US-Iranian relations and specifically the arms sales. The US had long been aware that the Israelis were shipping arms to Iran.[25] Israeli arms dealers had a network of contacts in Iran which allowed them to act as the middlemen of the covert American arms sales. The Israeli director-general of the foreign ministry, David Kimche, met with Michael Ledeen, an NSC consultant, and many of the major private arms dealers involved in the operation. These include a Saudi, Adnan Khashoggi, an Iranian, Manuchehr Qorbanifar, and two Israelis, Al Schwimmer and Yaacov Nimrodi, among others. The US covert arms deal was a result of these negotiations.

The details of the deliveries as well as the domestic complications eventually stemming from them have been spelt out in a detailed Congressional report,[26] and in the Tower Commission Report[27] and need not be repeated here.

The Reagan Administration has made efforts to describe the Iranians with whom they dealt as a special group of "moderates" in order to justify the long-term value of the arms deal policy. There was indeed a group within the Iranian leadership, with Rafsanjani at its head, who worked for the purchase of US arms. Whether this was done from their assessment of Iranian war-time need, from an acknowledgment of the superiority of US-made equipment, or from ulterior motives of bringing the two countries closer again is still a moot point. As far back as July 1984, Rafsanjani had stated publicly that Iran would not object to buying US spare parts, preferably through a third party, but if need be, directly. After the first deliveries, but before the deal became public knowledge, he said it was "not a shame" to buy American arms.[28] It was also true that there was a group of hardliners opposing Rafsanjani's approach. Many American policy-makers mistakenly believed that those who benefited from the arms sale in Iran would eventually tilt towards the US after Khomeini's departure from the scene. It was not, after all, possible for a major undertaking such as the arms sales to be conducted in Iran without Khomeini's knowledge and approval. Rafsanjani's spectacular rise in the establishment after the disclosure of the arms deal bears witness to the fact that he had not incurred Khomeini's disfavor.

The subsequent turn of events proved that the US assessment was indeed inaccurate. The Iranians were able to manipulate the situation to serve their purposes. The Congressional Report's summary is revealing on this point.

> The lesson to Iran was unmistakable: All US positions and principles were negotiable, and breaches by Iran went unpunished. Whatever Iran did, the US could be brought back to the arms bargaining table by the promise of another hostage.[29]

The Iranians emerged from the covert arms deal the initial winners by gaining access to weapons they required. The number of hostages in captivity was not diminished and the US was ultimately severely embarrassed both internationally and at home. The final effect, however, significantly impinged on Iran's position in the war. The US reflagging venture was a consequence of the covert sales to Iran and of the ensuing damage to US credibility in the region. This was a situation to which Iran had to respond for domestic purposes.

The problem created by the American reflagging efforts interrupted a relatively pragmatic phase in Iranian foreign policy—an often overlooked consequence of these events. Ramazani outlines this pragmatism beginning in early 1983 when Iran was distancing itself from terrorist acts and trying to overcome its status as a pariah state. Iran successfully expanded its relations with the West as Western Europe became Iran's leading trade partner. Rafsanjani visited Japan and China and spoke of an emergent third bloc. Within the region, the Saudi Prince Sa'ud visited Tehran, and Iran developed closer economic and political relations with Turkey and Pakistan. This shift in foreign policy parallels a consolidation of the Islamic Republic's domestic power and a greater awareness of Iran's political and economic problems.[30] There is little doubt that the increased US tilt toward Iraq and the American militarization of the Gulf was detrimental to Iranian interests and in fact disrupted the direction of their foreign relations.

Politics of US Military Actions in the Gulf

In March 1987, the US decided to extend military protection to Kuwaiti tankers which were endangered in the Gulf tanker war. It did so by reflagging eleven Kuwaiti ships with US flags thus technically qualifying them for American military escort. In undertaking this mission, the stated motivation of the US was to guarantee the free passage of oil through the Gulf and to facilitate an end to the Iran-Iraq war. The primary drive behind the US move, however, was to counter the damage to its credibility following the Iran arms deal and to prevent the Soviet Union from expanding its role in the area. The Reagan Administration became interested in the Kuwaiti request only after it learned that the Kuwaitis had negotiated an agreement by which the Soviets would lease three Kuwaiti tankers. The US pursued reflagging as a way to outbid the Soviet offer.

No specific Iranian action triggered the American military operation; indeed the changed dynamics of the Gulf war were imposed on Iran. For domestic political reasons, Iran had no choice but to respond to the American challenge. The dynamics of the Iranian response however, eventually helped create a situation where Iran had to abandon its war effort. Although the Reagan Administration intended to mount the reflagging mission without any increase in American naval forces in the Gulf, it became necessary to nearly triple those forces. The military presence provoked a response from Iran. By July 1987 Iran began mining Gulf shipping lanes and a year-long series of US-Iranian military encounters ensued.

Within a month of the initial tanker escort, the US Navy had fired missiles at Iranian aircraft on two separate occasions. In September, an Iranian ship, presumed to be laying mines in the Gulf, was attacked by the US. Shortly thereafter, the US sank three Iranian speedboats that had fired on American helicopters. The major event in the fall was the attack on two Iranian offshore oil drilling platforms which were used as bases for Iranian gunboats. Gulf mining resumed in the following spring when the US frigate *Roberts* was damaged. The US retaliated by sinking or damaging six Iranian naval vessels, two oil platforms, and attacking two Iranian fighter jets. The culminating event in the confrontation was in July 1988 when the US cruiser, *Vincennes*, mistakenly shot down an Iranian airliner and 290 civilians were killed.

The American military action clearly played an important role in Iran's decision to accept the cease-fire (18 July 1988). Also significant was the Soviet contribution to the Iraqi ability to wage the demoralizing missile war against Iranian cities that spring. Indeed, pressures from the superpowers were explicitly cited by Iranian leaders, including Khomeini and Rafsanjani, when they explained the cease-fire. However the US role should be seen as part of a larger convergence of factors—the military defeats on the ground and the paralysis of the Iranian military, the severe economic and political war-time strains, the Iraqi use of frightening chemical weapons, and the intense international isolation—which taken together forced the Islamic regime to forsake the war in order to preserve its survival.

The US reaction to events in the Gulf reflect a persistent tension between regionalism and globalism in American foreign policy. The reflagging betrays the prominence of an East-West framework, or global perspective, in the American assessment of a regional conflict. It is consistently difficult for the US to maintain a circumscribed evaluation of regional conflicts. In the Gulf war, the superpowers had maintained a reasonable distance from direct involvement. However, the US transformed a regional conflict by treating it as a global issue with strong East-West implications.

The reflagging case was one where the US confused the desire to exert influence with the capacity and efficacy of force. Military involvement in such a regional conflict always risks unintended consequences. In this case, the US mission was surely not designed to indefinitely commit an almost tripled naval force to an unpredictable Gulf war. The fact that the US involvement did not escalate further before a cease-fire was affected, does not diminish the initial risks inherent in the *ad hoc* American policy. It would be a mistake to overly credit the US military role in the eventual cease-fire.

Containment of the Soviet Union is inherently linked to the military policy in the Gulf. The focus of US planning is defense against a possible Soviet military attack in the region—specifically against a Soviet invasion of Iran. The key military question to which the US addresses itself in the Gulf is how a Soviet advance could be stopped. This clearly reinforces the propensity to interpret regional events in East-West terms and obscures salient regional factors and their relevance to American interests. It is a pattern which Iran must be certain to consider in the future.

Conclusions

The preceding discussion highlights the multi-faceted character of Iranian foreign policy under the Islamic Republic. Iran has both responded to and initiated major events in its external environment in a way which has reflected the dynamics of politics within the country. Khomeini and his followers had relentlessly pursued the idea of establishing a viable Islamic government and securing its future. This goal has been the primary focus of Iran's domestic politics and foreign policy behavior.

Foreign policy events have been routinely used by the Khomeini regime to further the internal needs of the Islamic Republic. Iran on the whole has been fairly successful in manipulating foreign relations to suit its domestic purposes. The actual developments, however, have had a varied impact on the country. The hostage crisis helped consolidate Khomeini's internal power, but in contrast the US reflagging interrupted the direction of Iran's foreign policy and constituted a major problem for the regime. In the end it was the failure in foreign affairs—the inability to win the war—which threatened the viability of the Islamic regime.

In the case of the Soviet Union, the principal Iranian concern was arms supplies to Iraq. When Soviet support to Iraq increased, Iran retaliated by containing Soviet diplomatic activities in the country and by eliminating the Tudeh party as a factor in domestic politics.

It is important to place Iran's relations with the superpowers in perspective. The Soviet Union has managed to maintain, and even improve, its options with Iran, despite the deterioration of their political relations after 1983. In 1989, the Soviet foreign minister visited Tehran and met with key Iranian leaders including Ayatollah Khomeini. Also, in June, Rafsanjani headed an Iranian delegation to Moscow. The US, however, is not in a similar position and has, for the present, foreclosed its options with Iran. But the Iranian acceptance of the cease-fire and the considerations leading to it, may facilitate a future attempt to bridge the gap between Tehran and Washington.

Notes

1. Farhang Rajaee, *Islamic Values and World View: Khomeini on Man, the State and International Politics* (Lanham, MD: 1983), 82.

2. R. K. Ramazani, *Revolutionary Iran: Challenge and Response in the Middle East* (Baltimore: 1988), 24.

3. Ibid., 21.

4. David Menashri, "The American-Israeli-Iranian Triangle," *New Outlook*, 30 (1987), 11; Ramazani, 22.

5. Ruhollah Khomeini, *Islam and Revolution: Writings and Declarations of Imam Khomeini* (Berkeley: 1981), 185.

6. Richard Cottam, "Iran's Perceptions of the Superpowers," in Barry Rosen (ed.), *Iran since the Revolution* (New York: 1985).

7. Sepehr Zabih, *Iran since the Revolution* (Baltimore: 1982), 168.

8. Shahrough Akhavi, "Institutionalizing the New Order in Iran," *Current History*, 1987, 55.

9. Warren Christopher et al., *American Hostages in Iran: The Conduct of a Crisis* (New Haven: 1975); Gary Sick, *All Fall Down: America's Tragic Encounter with Iran* (New York: 1985).

10. Farhad Kazemi, "The Iranian Revolution: Seven Years Later," *Middle East Insight*, V (1987), 14–15; Zabih, *Iran since the Revolution*, 42 ff.

11. H. E. Chehabi, "State and Society in Islamic Liberalism," *State, Culture, and Society*, I (1985), 85–101.

12. Shaul Bakhash, *The Reign of the Ayatollahs* (New York: 1984), 71–91.

13. For details see: David Menashri, "The Islamic Revolution in Iran: The Consolidation Phase," *Orient*, IV/84, 499–515.

14. Muriel Atkin, "The Islamic Republic and the Soviet Union," in Eric Houglund and Nikki Keddie (eds.), *The Iranian Revolution and the Islamic Republic* (Syracuse: 1986), 195.

15. Shahram Chubin, *The Iran-Iraq War* (Office of Net Assessments, Department of Defense, 1986), 187.

16. Chubin, ibid., 187; Sepehr Zabih, *The Left in Contemporary Iran* (Stanford: 1986), chapters two and three.

17. Zabih, *The Left*, 37.

18. Chubin, *The Iran-Iraq War*, 171.

19. Atkin, 195.

20. Anthony Cordesman, *The Iran-Iraq War and Western Security: 1984–87* (London: 1987), 33. See also Shahram Chubin and Charles Tripp, *Iran and Iraq at War* (Boulder: 1988); Majid Khadduri, *The Gulf War: The Origins and Implications of the Iraq-Iran Conflict* (New York: 1988).

21. Cordesman, 26.

22. *New York Times*, 11 April 1987.

23. Cordesman, 32.

24. Ibid., 58.

25. Ibid., 77.

26. US House of Representatives, Select Committee to Investigate Covert Arm Transaction to Iran, *Iran-Contra Affair* (Washington, D.C.: Government Printing Office, 1987), *passim*.

27. *Tower Commission Report* (New York: 1987), 41.

28. For this and a more detailed discussion of "Tehran and the American Arms," see Chapter 9 in David Menashri's *Iran: A Decade of War and Revolution* (New York: 1990), 374–85.

29. *Congressional Report*, 170.

30. For details, see Ramazani.

4

Iran and the Persian Gulf States

Shahram Chubin

Any discussion of Islamic Iran's foreign policy must start with the centrality of the struggle with Iraq since 1980. Indeed nearly eight years of hostilities have made the war and the revolution merge in historical consciousness and in Iranian myth. How its outcome will affect the future of the regime, indeed the revolution itself, cannot yet be assessed in the present situation of no-peace/no-war. Undoubtedly the post-war situation is a critical concern for Islamic Iran.

What needs emphasis at the outset is the degree to which the war with Iraq conditioned and constrained the Islamic Republic.

Without the war, revolutionary Iran, brimming with self-confidence and vitality, would have publicly proved a heady mixture of activism and implicit role-model for its neighbors. Combining a strong dose of messianic impulses and universal claims as a model at least for all Muslims, Iran could have been a formidable force for change in Middle Eastern politics in the 1980s. As it is, it has played something of a role like that, but not quite in the way that might have been expected. Nevertheless, two propositions seem arguable from the vantage point of 1989: first, that the war has weakened whatever hold Iran might otherwise have had on other Muslim states; and second, that the conflict has indeed contributed to the transformation of Middle Eastern politics by shifting Arab priorities and alignments throughout the entire decade.

Iran's relations with the Gulf states, like its foreign policy in general, may be divided into two periods—1979–1984 and 1984–1988—corresponding with its overall capabilities and dynamism.

The first period was characterized by militant enthusiasm moved along by force and intimidation. The second period, by contrast, has seen a greater emphasis on Iran's own situation stemming from the stalemate in the war and Iran's need to escape from a form of self-inflicted isolation. The second period was not uniform; in 1987 Iran, as we shall see, reverted to a policy of intimidation against the Gulf states, but this occurred for specific reasons rather than from the indifference and confidence of the period before 1984.

Perhaps more accurately we might subdivide Islamic Iran's relations with the Gulf states into periods of:

(1) claims, threats and pressures, 1979–1984;
(2) cultivation, dialogue and fence-mending, 1984–1986;
(3) crises, estrangement and return to a balance, 1987–1988.

It was precisely the nature and the tone of Iran's claims *vis-à-vis* its immediate Arab neighbors of the Gulf that (alongside other reasons) caused one of them to embark on what it saw as a preventive war against its revolutionary neighbor. At the very least we can infer from the deafening silence of the other Arab states of the Persian Gulf that they shared a similar view of Islamic Iran as a menace to the region. Just when it was no longer being perceived as an obvious military danger, Iran seemed to have been transformed almost overnight into a more sinister and altogether more insidious threat. For its part, revolutionary Iran saw its neighbors not as independent nation states but as parts of the Islamic world for which the "Islamic republic" and "Islamic revolution" had duties in mind which included what others would call "intervention."

The Islamic world which Iran invoked as a constituency served several functions for Iran. It provided, of course, a source of legitimacy and validation of Iran's broader claims for its revolutions, but at the same time it enabled Iran to transcend the limitations inherent in either Iranian nationalism or Shi'i sectarianism. Iran's claim to a major, if not defining, role in the world of Islam as a whole was doubtless sincere. But it was also fortuitously convenient as it enabled Shi'i Iran to escape from the limitations and constraints of sectarianism, nationalism, culture and geography. Iran's Islamic-centered world view thus envisioned a central role for Iran in what was traditionally referred to as Middle Eastern politics.

The claim of universal applicability of Iran's Islamic revolution for the world of Islam, and the traditional proselytizing accompanying it, that was characteristic of other revolutions as well, served to encourage malcontents abroad, Islamic and otherwise. In 1979 Islam with Iran as its standard-bearer appeared irresistible and irrepressible, an incipient tidal-wave. At the very least Iran's revolutionary example galvanized the Muslim world, giving notice of the unparalleled capacity of Islam to serve as a mobilizing force and act as a catalyst for a revived and militant message.

Inevitably, the revolution was to have its most direct impact on Iran's immediate neighbors. Proximity made them particularly sensitive to any major changes in its power and policies. On the Islamic dimension, too, they were most closely affected, for in addition to communities of Iranian nationals they contained large communities of Shi'i who, whatever the protestations emanating from Qom, were bound to be a factor in Iran's foreign concerns.

Insofar as Iran's appeal is primarily to the Shi'is (a proposition which, as we have seen, Iran denies as unduly limiting) the most numerous communities of cosectarians inhabit not the Arab world but rather the Indian sub-continent: India, Pakistan and Afghanistan. In the Arab world, Shi'is constitute no more than 15 out of approximately 180 millions. However, of these 15 million, the majority live near Iran; in Iraq and Bahrain they constitute a majority, 8 of 15 million and 230,000 of a total of 415,000 respectively. In Kuwait (if non-citizens are included) they comprise 60 per cent; in the Eastern Province of Saudi Arabia they number some 300–400,000; and in Lebanon they are the largest of its various groupings.

In brief, the Gulf states constituted a natural area of Iranian revolutionary activism due both to the realities of proximity and power, and to the nature of Islamic Iran's primary appeal and natural constituency.

It was therefore without any hesitation that, on the morrow of the revolution, Iran's new leaders proclaimed the right and duty to pass on the Islamic "credentials" of other states, and in the first instance that of its neighbors. Time and again the threat of revolution and holy wrath was invoked against them. It was often unclear, to be sure, whether these were rhetorical devices and flourishes or statements of government policy, but Iran's smaller neighbors were understandably disconcerted. Listening to Iran's appeal to Islam as the sole yardstick for judging other states, its neighbors remained suspicious that Iran retained some specifically national and chauvinist goals that had little to do with Islam and a great deal with power and ambition.

Lending credence to this was Iran's apparent vendetta against Iraq: its determination to overthrow the Ba'th regime in Baghdad as a prelude for creating a Shi'i-dominated Islamic republic in its own image. Furthermore, the amirs of the Gulf states noted that Khomeini in his pronouncements appeared to cast doubt on the compatibility of monarchy and true Islam. Iran's tendency to ignore or slight the conventions of modern diplomacy such as respect for sovereignty and non-intervention, did nothing to reassure the smaller Gulf states. It must have been with something approaching relief that these states watched propaganda campaigns and border clashes between Iran and Iraq in 1979–1980 flare up into a full-fledged war. Nor can there be any doubt about the similarity of view among these states in seeing Iran as the principal menace in the region, and to their perception of Saddam Husayn's Iraq as the principal pillar for their defence. If they did not actually help Iraq in the initial period, they colluded with it and sympathized in its attempt to rid the region of "this turbulent priest."

These views were reinforced when the tide of war changed in mid-1982, and when Iran decided to carry the war into Iraqi territory as a first stage towards changing the face of the Gulf. Ruhollah Khomeini's statements at that time left no room for doubt about this intention.[1]

By 1984 after repeated costly frontal offensives had remained inconclusive, the war had turned into a stalemate. By intemperate rhetoric and policies, Iran succeeded in alienating both superpowers and most of the regional states simultaneously—a rare achievement. No longer anticipating a spontaneous revolution among Iraq's Shi'i population, Iran, in early 1984, began to shell Basra. In the same year, more aware now of the costs of rhetorical excess (and following a clash with the Saudi air force) Iran sought a dialogue with the other Gulf states. Mutual visits by the Saudi and Iranian foreign ministers in the course of the next year contributed towards a "clearing of the air."[2]

Insofar as words were capable of giving reassurance, these renewed contacts served their purpose by at least ostensibly reducing the overt alignment of the Gulf States with Iraq. Indicative of this was cautious and moderate language of the Gulf Co-operation Council (GCC) summit statement in Muscat in December 1985.

However, there were inherent limitations to this process of normalization. For Iran had not changed its ultimate goals in the war, or indeed its foreign policy, but merely modified its tactics. At the same time it persisted in its dual policies of regularizing formal relations while cultivating sub- and trans-state actors and groups, be they Iraqi dissidents, Iranian nationals abroad, or indigenous militants (whether Shi'i or not). Iran was suspected of direct involvement in the attempts at a *coup d'état* in Bahrain in 1981 and in Kuwait in 1983. For this reason, there were lingering suspicions among the Gulf States when Iran attempted to reassure them after 1984.

This was particularly true of Kuwait, which became the target for a campaign of intimidation from the Islamic Jihad which most states took to be a very thinly disguised instrument of the Islamic Republic of Iran. Kuwait was singled out both for its determination to continue its support for Iraq in the war, and to prosecute the terrorists apprehended in connection with the bombings of the US and French embassies in December 1983. The diplomacy of reassurance launched by Iran in 1984–1986 thus did not extend to Kuwait. Bomb attacks on Kuwaiti public buildings and an attempt on the life of the amir occurred in mid-1985. Kuwait was particularly concerned at signs that as the war went on, sabotage and terrorism were no longer the monopoly of foreigners, but became instruments of some of the indigenous Shi'i and other dissidents. Because of this new internal threat, the authorities launched a harsh campaign of expulsion of Iranian and other Shi'is who were resident in, but not citizens of, Kuwait. Inevitably, this further soured relations with Iran.

In February 1986, Iran's success in occupying Fao put Kuwait under even greater pressure. Greater Iranian confidence generated by military achievements was mirrored by increased frustration on the part of the Gulf states and particularly Kuwait. Thus confidence and exasperation on the one hand, and renewed fears of an Iranian military victory on the other, combined to plunge relations between the two shores of the Gulf to a new low. Reflecting this were the communiqués now issuing forth from the GCC; no longer did these try to be even-handed as had been the case in December 1985, but, in the wake of Fao, reverted to direct criticism of Iran.

The limits to Iran's ability to reassure the Gulf States, to separate its conflict with Iraq from its relations with the other littoral states, stemmed as much from Iraq's war needs as from the Gulf States' own intrinsic suspicions of Iran's universal pretensions. It served Iraq's interests to play the role of protector of the smaller Gulf States in the face of the Islamic hurricane emanating from Iran, to "Arabise" the conflict and to depict itself as the Arabs' last hope. (No matter that Ba'thist Iraq had earlier been the primary threat to these states' security; it had been superseded by a new and infinitely more serious threat from revolutionary Islamic Iran.) As a token of the shared perception of the threat from Iran, the Gulf States had by 1987 provided Iraq with funds amounting to perhaps $50bn—ostensibly as loans. Iran did not see this as a sign of total disinterestedness in the war.

More significant in embroiling the other Gulf states directly in the war was Iraq's strategy of widening the war, hoping to internationalize it, i.e. to bring pressure to bear on the international community to in turn pressure Iran to end the war. To this end, Iraq had in 1983 declared a "total exclusion zone" around Iran's principal oil export terminal, and from 1984 had begun serious air attacks on tankers serving Iran's ports. By 1985 Iraqi air attacks on Kharq had become intensive and in 1986 a sustained period of bombing of Iranian facilities and tankers began to bite into Iran's oil exports and revenues. At the same time Iraq's acquisition of long-range bombers and improved missiles enabled Iraq to range as far south as the Straits of Hormuz to interdict the shuttle tankers that Iran had organized to escape from Iraq's earlier attacks. In response, Iran initiated a strategy of striking at tankers serving the Gulf States. (For there were of course no tankers serving Iraq which had lost access to the Gulf's waters at the start of the war.) Iran's calculation behind its strategy of holding these states hostage to Iraq's good behavior was simple: as paymasters and *de facto* allies of Iraq, they were presumably in a position to prevail upon Baghdad to desist from the expansion of the war and to recognize the costs associated with that course of action. At the same time, Iran's policy of responding in kind to Iraqi attacks put the international community on notice that Iran was determined to prosecute the war "until victory" and refuse to be intimidated. While the triangular interaction between Iraqi air attacks on Iranian targets and Iranian retaliation against Gulf States objectives was not always self-evident to the casual observer, their logic was clear enough to the governments concerned.

Equally clear but apparently less acceptable was Iran's policy of singling out, and denouncing, Kuwait for its assistance to Iraq, and concentrating retaliatory attacks on tankers serving that state. Iranian attacks on Kuwaiti shipping combined with bombings and threats against the amirate throughout the late 1986 led that state to end the period of limited parliamentary democracy, and to turn to the superpowers for assistance. As we have suggested, Iran's particular concentration on Kuwait arose from the latter's proximity to Iraq. This meant that it was under pressure from Iraq to allow goods destined for it to be unloaded in Kuwait and to be transshipped to its beleaguered neighbor. The fact that some of these cargoes included arms and other war material meant that Kuwait (and some other Gulf states) were more actively involved in Iraq's war effort than mere financial aid would have implied. The financing, supply and transshipment of arms could not be considered as genuinely neutral conduct in the war and could hardly be construed as a friendly act towards Iran. This was doubly true of the occasional use of Gulf States' airfields (suspected by Iran) as staging posts for Iraqi aircraft engaged in long-range bombing missions. As a result of Iraq's stepped-up bombing of Iran's oil installations and Iran's inevitable responses, the "tanker war" intensified in late 1986. During that year, there were more attacks on shipping than in any previous twelve-month period between 1980–1985.

The upshot of this development and of Kuwait's appeal to the superpowers was the internationalization of the war. The immediate precipitants of the US decision to "reflag" eleven Kuwaiti tankers and to offer them the appropriate protection need not concern us here in detail. Suffice it to say that as a result of commitments to the Gulf States, guilt-feelings over Irangate, and of rivalry with the USSR, the US decision to enter the Gulf war, soon led to an even broader internationalization of the war. More saliently for our purposes, it was neither conceived of, nor interpreted as, a neutral or disinterested measure.

The presence of what became a multi-national naval force (with the eventual participation of five European states) was presented as a measure to protect international shipping. In reality, the entanglement of outside powers, ostensibly on a mission of assuring freedom of navigation, was anything but neutral. For it was designed not to end the "tanker war" by stopping Iraq's air attacks, but to inhibit Iran's retaliatory measures. Iran for its part saw this presence as part of a broader conspiracy aimed at buttressing Iraq and depriving Iran of victory.

Under the threat of an unprecedented degree of superpower co-operation in the Security Council on mandatory measures to bring the war to an end, Iran reacted in 1987 with an uncustomary lack of caution which increased the stakes all round:

1) Despite a clear and concrete interest in the flow of oil through the Gulf, Iran's position became encapsulated by the phrase "either all shipping is safe or none is," implying that if Iran's oil exports were in jeopardy, Iran would put all exports through the Gulf at risk.

2) Once outside powers were invited into the Persian Gulf, both Persian *amour propre* and revolutionary self-interest were threatened. Iran's 'natural' preponderance was inevitably diluted by this infusion of foreign power which up to now, at least in the rhetoric of the region, was deemed to be illegitimate and undesirable. Iran's response to what it saw—correctly—as an unfriendly presence, was to seek to increase the general insecurity, to underline how counter-productive such a presence was, and perhaps thus to convince Kuwait to rescind the invitation.

3) A related component of this strategy was to increase the pressure on the other Gulf States, in particular Saudi Arabia, to inhibit any greater co-operation between them and the US and to heighten the rhetoric of confrontation with the US—without, to be sure, seeking an outright confrontation.

4) A further element in Iran's response was typical of the Islamic Republic: the willingness to confront—at least rhetorically—all the evils of the world,

led by the Great Satan (at the cost of diverting some effort from more pressing concerns). This mindset led to a series of acts in mid- to late 1987 intended to punch holes in the US defense umbrella over Kuwait.

It was this perception that led Iran to undertake a number of acts that many observers considered as proof of lack of moderation. For example it was with the intention of increasing general insecurity that Iran started to mine the Gulf's waters, not so much to interfere with shipping but to make Kuwait and its foreign allies see the futility of their naval presence. In the event, being caught red-handed (in September 1987), Iran came to appear to many outside states as the embodiment of fanatical forces that needed to be contained. So did the Mecca episode of late July when Iran's leaders decided to punish Saudi Arabia for its assistance to Iraq and co-operation with US forces to the area, by encouraging political demonstrations meant to embarrass the Saudi authorities. Saudi over-reaction, and the unpredict-ability of mass demonstrations, led to a result neither sought nor anticipated by the Iranian authorities. Again, what had seemed to Iran a reasonable response, backfired against it, increasing the general apprehension about its aims and even its rationality. Yet if one studied Iran's reaction to two incidents in 1987—a US attack on Iranian ships in late September, and the destruction of two oil platforms in October—such doubts would surely have evaporated. Iran responded neither by confronting the US directly, nor did it let itself be cowed. Instead, it shifted its attacks to probing the ambiguities of the US commitment to Kuwait, especially to Kuwait's territorial waters not covered by the tanker leasing agreement. Iran still singled out Kuwait for especial pressure but sought to do so without confronting the US. By the end of the year, Iran had also shifted its stance of defiance to a more differentiated policy of selective accommodation with the Gulf States. This reflected Tehran's recognition that it had lost control of events in the preceding twelve months by playing into the hands of Iraq. The latter had managed to internationalize the war and to accelerate a polarization between Arabs and Iranians which it was Iran's interest to avoid. The failure of the Gulf states to sever diplomatic relations after the events at Mecca, and the subsequent failure of the Arab summit conference in Amman in November 1987 to do anything more than verbally condemn Iran were cold comfort for Iran in its four-year search for a better relationship with the Gulf States.

An Iranian TV commentary struck the precise note of mixed irritation and superiority felt by Iran:

> If this conference is Arab and sincere, it must view the aggressive colonialist war imposed on the Islamic revolution fairly and justly and not from a bigoted tribal perspective.[3]

It was a consistent theme of Iran that its war against Iraq was a war of Islam against blasphemy, not a clash of nationalisms or a contest between two sects within Islam. President Khamene'i put this clearly:

Everyone must be extremely careful today. If expressions of nationalism are intended to create barriers between Muslim brothers, cause separations among them and threaten their fraternity, then this is 100% forbidden. There are no Arabs and non-Arabs in Islam.[4]

True, there was an element of national pride in its reaction to the entry of foreign military forces into the Gulf, not unlike that existing in Pahlevi Iran. Iran's efforts to undermine the confidence of the Gulf States in the protection this connection would afford them were understandable from the standpoint of traditional *realpolitik*. Hence Ali Akbar Rafsanjani's warning:

The ignorant and reactionary Arab countries who invited them [i.e. foreign forces] have tied their fate to a tiny hair which is connected to them and which can be torn off at any moment.[5]

Nevertheless, Iran's concrete demands from the Gulf States were neither excessive nor unreasonable. Often articulated, their gist was that they should remain genuinely neutral. Rafsanjani put it in the form of "three options" the US and the Gulf States had for restoring peace in the Gulf:

1) To stop or hinder Iraqi attacks against Iranian tankers;
2) to designate Iraq the aggressor in the war;
3) to cease all military and financial assistance to Iraq and adopt true neutrality.[6]

On a later occasion, he put the case for neutrality in even clearer terms: "We do not want anything from you except that you stay neutral. Do not give [Iraq] oil, airspace, pipelines, roads and ports so that they can make the Persian Gulf insecure. Don't give them intelligence and switch your propaganda to the side of neutrality. If you do so you will have a good neighbor to the north, who will be your friend and has the readiness to forgive you for your sins. But this Saddam's sins are such that he cannot be forgiven; he must be punished."[7]

Given the degree of actual support provided by Kuwait and Saudi Arabia to Iraq—subsidies, oil outlets, transshipment of goods including arms, access to bases, intelligence, diplomatic support etc.—Iran's demands could scarcely be considered excessive or unreasonable. Indeed, to be fair, Iran's restraint in the face of such patently non-neutral behavior could only be called formidable. Also, Iran's conduct of the war or, if you will, its interests, did not altogether threaten the Gulf States' interests. For example, unlike Iraq, Iran had no interest in extending the war to the Gulf's waters or in threatening the shipping of others except as retaliation for Iraqi attacks. It was not Iran but Iraq that sought to escalate the war by projecting it into other parts of the region, and by stepping up attacks against civilian targets. Even the internationalization of the war which threatened an escalation of hostilities in the region was not Iran's doing.

If Iran had got rather a raw deal in its relations with these states, this was not simply due to a bad press. Iran's repeated offers of good relations with the other Gulf States, of the kind it already had with the United Arab Emirates and to some extent with Oman, were not necessarily disbelieved. It was simply that as long as revolutionary Iran continued the war with Iraq, Tehran's interests and those of its southern neighbors were bound to be incompatible.

The dilemma for Iran, simply stated, was to separate these states from Iraq, without modifying its own war aims; how to reassure them without renouncing its intention to defeat Iraq. The more pressure Iran brought to bear on them with a view to detaching them from the Iraqi camp, the greater was their fear of Iran's threat to them; on the other hand, the less Iran did to seek their neutrality, the more they contributed to its adversary's war effort. A result of this basic and inescapable dilemma, Iran's many diplomatic reassurances were relatively worthless. As we have seen in the transition from the period of contact and dialogue (1984–1986) to the subsequent one of crisis and estrangement, the dynamics of war can itself be a catalyst for further deterioration. Hence Iran's success at Fao led to greater fear on the part of the GCC. The same process was also capable of working in the reverse: the greater the frustration of Iran over the course of war, the greater was its tendency to take it out (so to speak) on Iraq's allies and paymasters.

From the perspective of the Gulf States too, there were serious constraints on the degree to which relations with Iran was capable of improving. "Normalization," however desirable in theory, could imply that they approved of, or were indifferent to, Iran's clearly expressed war aims. Despite their lack of trust of Ba'thist Iraq, there was little question that the Gulf states saw Iraq as the lesser evil. Moreover, they had grounds for remaining skeptical of Iran's attempts at reassurance:

1) Iran had not renounced its ultimate war aims.
2) An Iranian military success could at any time undo whatever moderation existed in Tehran with regard to the other Gulf States.
3) Revolutionary Iran conducted a two-tack diplomacy, part classical state-to-state, part revolutionary through shady transnational groupings, often engaged in subversion and intimidation, but always formally unacknowledged or at least deniable. The experience of Kuwait was not reassuring in this regard, having suffered more than twelve attacks, (admittedly small scale) in 1987 alone.
4) There also remained doubts about Iran's future orientation. It was known that power in Tehran was divided between groups of varying outlook and there could be no certainty that the hard-liners would not ultimately win out.

Under these conditions, the Gulf States have risked Iran's ire and remained committed, by and large, to Iraq. This commitment stemmed from necessity rather than free choice or affection, reflecting the needs of the moment. But as the unwillingness of the Gulf states to break completely with Iraq had shown, they did not wish to sever all contacts with Iran, and did not despair of an eventual improvement of relations. The basic structure of Persian Gulf politics militates against a permanent polarization; the smaller states' interests are best served by a rough balance of the three larger states: Iran, Iraq and Saudi Arabia. This may well be as true of the post-war as of the war-time situation.

In the meantime, the threat from Iran was too direct, too vivid, to be disregarded. And although there was no reason to doubt Rafsanjani's comment to a West German journalist that Iran had no especial interest in fomenting revolution abroad and did not consider Kuwait as particularly "ripe,"[8] there were equally no reasons to doubt that Iran had been active, clandestinely, in the politics of that state.

While Saudi Arabia admitted in January 1988 that throughout the 1987 crisis over Mecca (see chapter by Goldberg), as well as later on, Saudi diplomatic dialogue with Tehran had continued, Kuwait was more cautious. Its prime minister and foreign minister argued that before a genuine dialogue could be conducted between the GCC and Iran, the latter should stop meddling in the domestic affairs of the GCC states and pledge not to take hostile actions against them.[9]

There are grounds for arguing that the relationship between Iran and the Gulf States was relatively stable, given the fact that the region had experienced a long bloody war, without complete polarization between Iran and the Arabs. One could also argue that Iran no longer laid claim to the universal pretensions that were the original reason for driving the Gulf States into Iraq's arms. And to some extent it was true that there had been a learning process on the part of Iran, which had discovered the costs of indifference to the interests of others. But this conclusion would be insufficient by itself. As long as the war lasted there was a chance that it would end in an Iranian victory, or in an apocalyptical spasm catalyzed by a desperate or merely vengeful Iraq, by missiles, chemical weapons etc. which could lead to an Iranian response. Given these circumstances, one has to qualify the relationship between Iran and the Gulf States as relatively stable, moving between the twin poles of outright hostility and real friendship, but characterized by a wariness on both sides.

It bears emphasis however that the evolution toward pragmatism in Iran's policies and claims was not a spontaneous one, but stemmed from the war-time experience of hardship and adversity. In this sense, the war was the primary conditioner of Iran's foreign policy in general and especially towards the Gulf States. But speaking more broadly, the prime determinant was Iran's being bogged down in a stalemate. The momentum and *élan* of its masses was seen to evaporate, its revolution was becoming demystified. The domestic model of the revolution looked no longer alluring, no more brilliant. Gone was the sense of standing at the edge of new dawn, the sense of inevitable, irreversible victory, the exhilaration of martyrdom, the glorification of the collective will, and the refusal to count costs. As the war became banalized, so did the revolution and with it Iran's claims.

However, the principal contribution of Iran to Middle East politics, *viz.* the concretization of the Islamic message, the implicit support for Islamic fundamentalism in general, had already been made when the Islamic Republic was set up in 1979. The fact that since mid-1982—the high point of Iran's power and influence in the region—there has been a steady erosion of that influence and power does not change the fact that Islam or, if you will, Islamic fundamentalism has entered into the mainstream of Middle Eastern politics, whatever the ultimate fate of the experiment in Iran.

Iran's decision to accept the Security Council resolution 598 a year after its initial proposal resulted in the cease-fire of August 1988. Iran's acceptance of the reality that the war could not be won and was in danger of being dramatically lost, reflected the comprehensive defeat of the war strategy of Iran under Ayatollah Khomeini. There was little disguising the scope or nature of the defeat, and the Iranian leader made little attempt to do so. War was followed by an unstable cease-fire. Negotiations for a comprehensive settlement alternately in Geneva and New York foundered on the unwillingness of either Iran and Iraq to compromise. Iran, perhaps understandably, did not wish to further broadcast its humiliation by giving up national territory. Iraq in turn had no stomach for facing its own people without tangible—i.e. territorial—gains from the war. More than a year after the "negotiations" had begun, there had been signally little progress, even in dealing with the release of prisoners of war.

The cease-fire remained unstable not because of the likelihood of an early resumption of hostilities, but because the occupation of some 1,000 sq. kms. of Iranian territory by Iraqi troops. If prolonged, this would serve as an irritant in relations which in time, could become a national *irredenta*, causing further rounds of fighting when Iran had recovered its military capabilities. The fragile cease-fire also served to freeze Iran's relations with the Arab states. The latter remained unwilling to break ranks with Iraq until peace was relatively assured. In the absence of progress in negotiations, the Gulf states had to plan for the possibility of renewed war and position themselves accordingly. Thus the natural balance—or equidistance—between Iran and Iraq that most of these states would have preferred, could not be re-established while Iran constituted a continuing threat to their security.

That the Saudis continued to feel uneasy about Iran was reflected in their refusal to resume relations with Iran (severed in April 1988) and its continuing insistence that because of temporary repairs and infrastructure problems Iran would have to limit the number of pilgrims sent on the *hajj*. A quota reflecting population size allowed Iran some 45,000 pilgrims for 1988 and again in 1989. Iran, interpreting this as a political decision, refused in both years to accept such restrictions and relations remained strained. Ayatollah Khomeini's attempt to revive the flagging revolution by using Salman Rushdie's book as an Islamic issue and condemning its author to death for blasphemy and apostasy, was not without significance for the Gulf states. Without taking radically different positions, they subtly disassociated themselves from the kind of political "grandstanding" that they suspected was Khomeini's aim.

It remained unclear at the time of writing (June 1989) whether Ayatollah Khomeini's death on 3 June would change Iran's policies toward its neighbors. Despite Khomeini's last admonitions to his successors in his will to continue to show hostility to Saudi Arabia (as well as Jordan and Morocco), it is unlikely that these instructions will be followed. Without explicitly repudiating his legacy, his successors are likely to do so in practice and seek to mend fences in the Gulf and further afield. It is indicative of the scale of regional disruption and animosity left behind by Khomeini's decade in Iran that one cannot imagine an early restoration of trust between the two shores of the Persian Gulf. In this respect as in so many other areas, Khomeini has taken his country backward at a breathtaking speed. Yet in the final analysis, most of the missiles he hurled have turned out to be boomerangs for an unfortunate Iran rather than threats to his neighbors.

Notes

1. So it was inevitable that the newly formed Gulf Co-operation Council (May 1981), organized by Saudi Arabia, reflected a general sympathy for Iraq and ranged itself fairly squarely against Iran.

2. For a detailed discussion, see Shahram Chubin and Charles Tripp, *Iran and Iraq at War* (London: 1988), Chapter 9 (especially pp. 162–170).

3. Tehran television in response to the Amman conference, 9 November—DR, 11 November 1987.

4. Radio Tehran, 6 November—DR, 7 November 1987.

5. Excerpt from Rafsanjani's Friday sermon, Radio Tehran, 15 January—DR, 18 January 1988.

6. Radio Tehran, 23 October—DR, 27 October 1987. See also, *Le Monde*, 25–26 October 1987.

7. Excerpts from Rafsanjani's Friday sermon, Radio Tehran, 15 January—DR, 18 January 1988.

8. See *Die Welt*, 10 August—DR, 11 August 1987.

9. Kuwaiti News Agency (in English), 22 March—DR, 24 March 1988.

5

Khomeini's Iran
as Seen Through Bank Notes

Peter Chelkowski

The study of the iconography of bank notes and postage stamps of countries with authoritarian governments can be quite revealing. Emmanuel Sivan puts it succinctly: "Both are a monopoly—i.e., a sovereign attribute of the state as well as an efficient iconographic propaganda vehicle thereof. They can tell us something about the official discourse of the state, the one for which it attempts to ensure ideological hegemony."[1]

During the Pahlavi reign, both stamps and bank notes glorified twenty-five centuries of Persian achievements and contributions to world civilization. The emphasis was on pre-Islamic architecture and art, and on modern industrial complexes, gigantic dams, and means of transportation. A portrait of the monarch was featured prominently on both stamps and notes. On the bank notes, the monarch is usually shown dressed in a gala military uniform. Next to the portrait are the national emblems of the Lion and the Sun, under the Pahlavi crown. The symbolic animals which formerly decorated Achaemenid (550–330 B.C.) palaces and Sasanid (224–651 A.D.) silverware form another motif. Sometimes, as in Persepolis, the royal hero is shown killing a ferocious dragon, symbolizing the victory of good over evil. On other bank notes Furuhar, the winged image of the god Ahura Mazda, is dramatically spread-eagled across the surface. Often the reverse (back) sides of the bank notes are resplendent with architectural *motif*s, especially the ruins of the palaces of Darius or Xerxes, the columns of the Apadana hall at Persepolis, and the friezes of tribute bearers, fighting animals, and Darius on the throne from Persepolis.[2] Another *motif* from antiquity is the tomb of the founder of the Persian Empire, Cyrus the Great. A mediaeval *motif* on the reverse side of notes is the palaces of Shah Abbas in Isfahan, while famous bridges, one from the Sasanid and one from the Safavid (1501–1722) periods, are featured on the backs of other notes. The magnificent snow-covered peak of Mount Demavand, associated with many national legends, graces the back of still another bill.

During the reign of Reza Shah, modern achievements, such as the Trans-Iranian railway, the seaport of Bandar Pahlavi, and the National Bank building, are shown on the reverse side. In the reign of his son, Muhammad Reza Shah, the number of pictures of industrial plants, irrigation works and civic compounds increased. The most striking designs of this particular era are the immense Karaj Dam near Tehran, the Mehrabad Airport in Tehran, the oil refinery at Abadan, and the modern triumphant Shahyad Gate to the city of Tehran, built to mark 2500 years of the Persian Empire.

The filigree of the bank notes also drew inspiration from the pre-Islamic art of Iran. The lofty fluted columns, the animal-shaped capitals, the "immortal guards" standing at attention and the rosette ornaments from the friezes of Persepolis are all features that fit well into the border decoration. From 1971 onward, the portrait of the shah covered more space on the obverse (front) side of the note. In the portrait, he looks relaxed, very assertive and confident. It appears on bank notes of all denominations issued in and after 1971, until the Islamic Revolution. For the filigree of these bank notes, the artists drew inspiration from the masterpieces of the Iranian arabesque decorative tradition. This, the fifth and, as it turned out, the last series of Muhammad Reza Pahlavi bank notes, is very refined and artistically appealing.[3]

After the revolution, the same currency had to be used until new bank notes and coins could be issued. To obliterate the portrait of the shah and to use up old stocks of postage stamps was not very difficult.[4] But to efface the portrait of the monarch on a bank note required far more work, since the watermark with a profile of the shah also had to be blotted out. The doctored bank notes from the old stock came out in three stages: (1) with the portrait of the shah obliterated; (2) with both the portrait and the watermark obliterated; (3) with the portrait of the shah removed and replaced with a picture of the mausoleum of Imam Reza in Meshhed, and the watermark on both sides of the bank notes blotted out with a dark colored seal. On this seal, the words, "The Islamic Republic of Iran" are spelled out in fine calligraphy.

As soon as the Central Bank of the Islamic Republic of Iran was ready to print new notes, the authorities and graphic artists joined forces to make certain that the new bills would carry the message of the new Islamic order loud and clear! Emmanuel Sivan writes: "Nowhere in the Arab world have the last six decades produced a phenomenon like that which occurred in revolutionary Iran, where the whole pre-Islamic past, so vaunted under the shah, suddenly disappeared from postal and monetary iconography."[5] Each bank note of the Islamic Republic utilizes the symbols of the new political mythology to carry messages on two levels: one appeals to the visual sense, the other to religious sensibility.

In order to show graphically the departure from the glorification of pre-Islamic Iran and the pro-Western ideology of the shahs and the transition to the traditional Islamic attitude of Ayatollah Ruhollah Khomeini, it is convenient to compare the imperial one-hundred-rial bank notes with the same note issued by the Islamic Republic (see both illustrations below). The last Pahlavi bank note was printed in 1976 on the occasion of the Golden

Jubilee of the dynasty. This hundred-rial note was as common in Iran in the late 1970s as the one-dollar bill in the United States. Portraits of both Pahlavi rulers, father and son, appear on it. Muhammad Reza is also visible in the water mark. The modern building of the National (*Melli*) Bank of Iran is in the middle foreground. The cornerstone of this bank, done in the neo-Achaemenid style with *motifs* taken from Persepolis, was laid by Reza Shah himself in 1934.

On the reverse side, the Pahlavi crown is in the center, surrounded by two circles of twenty-five small dots (one for each year of the Pahlavi dynasty). The bold inscription, "The Fiftieth Year of the Pahlavi Reign" and the date 2535 (1976/7, according to the new imperial calendar) links the Pahlavi rule to that of Cyrus the Great, the founder of the Persian Empire. (The Shi'i clerics objected to the imperial calendar: any computation not taking the year 622 as year one was considered a deviation by them. It must be added, however, that the dating of Iranian bank notes has always been erratic. More often than not, they were not dated.)

By contrast, the hundred-rial bill issued by the Central Bank of the Islamic Republic of Iran could serve as a symbolic monument to the political changes brought about by the revolution. It was printed in the same lavender color and in almost the same size as the former royal bill. The portrait of the two Pahlavi monarchs was replaced by a bust of Ayatollah Seyyed Hasan Modarres with a formidable beard. He is shown wearing the Shi'i clerical garb and turban. Under the name of the Ayatollah appears his famous pronouncement: "Our religion is identical with our politics—our politics is identical with our religion." Modarres (born near Isfahan in 1871) was a famous Islamic scholar, teacher, preacher, and politician. Repeatedly elected deputy to the *Majlis*, he was the charismatic leader of the clerical opposition to Reza Shah. He objected to the latter's authoritarian rule and to his reform programs. In foreign policy, he was an advocate of a "neutral balance" between the USSR and Great Britain, a policy now championed by the Islamic Republic under the slogan: "Neither the East nor the West." In 1927, Reza Shah blocked the re-election of Modarres and sent him to internal exile in the eastern province of Khorasan, where he died nine years later in suspicious circumstances.

On the reverse side of the new bank note is a picture of a modern building, formerly the Senate building but now designated "The Islamic Consultative Assembly." The symbolic implication of this iconography can hardly be missed: Modarres has removed from the bank note the portraits of those who removed him from office, just as the Islamic Assembly has replaced the old parliament. (Modarres is also honored by a postage stamp: his portrait appears in a series of stamps showing the "Forerunners of the Revolutionary Movement.")

The watermark of the new 100-rial bill is a calligraphic arrangement of the word "Allah" in the shape of a tulip. The tulip in the Iranian culture symbolizes love and sacrifice.[6] It has been made an official emblem of the Islamic Republic of Iran. In addition to the ingenious calligraphic form, it

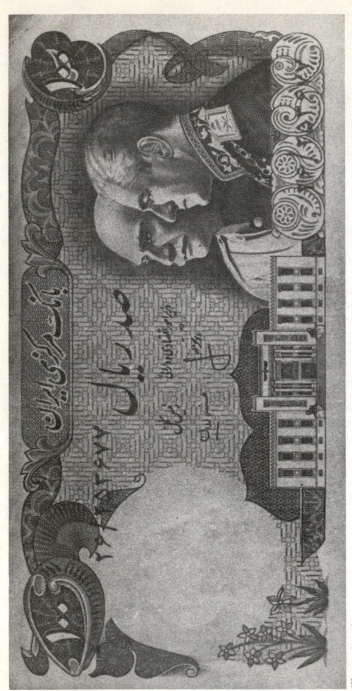

Illustration 1

Illustration 2

is written in such a way that it encompasses the Muslim profession of faith: "There is no God but God."All bank notes issued by the Islamic Republic of Iran carry this watermark. On the 100-rial bank note, it is framed by the contours of a *mihrab.*

A different tradition is called to mind by the five-hundred-rial note. In the mediaeval Islamic state, there were two major indicators of the seat of power. A coin was struck in the name of the ruler for all to see. But of greater significance was to have the name of the ruler mentioned in the *khutba* during the Friday congregational prayer. From the early history of Islam, rulers often acted as *khatibs*, the spokesmen-preachers of the Friday sermons. In this fashion, important pronouncements were made, orders were given, enemies were cursed, and views of politics and other issues of general interest were disseminated. The Pahlavi monarchs were almost oblivious of this tradition, relying instead on the modern media. Ayatollah Khomeini, on the other hand, employed and exploited the *khutba* extremely skillfully. He knew and appreciated the importance of the oral message in the Iranian culture. The network of mosques in Iran used *khutba*s as the powerful extension to the modern media during the revolution. As for the modern media, Khomeini used them masterfully as well. It may also be said that the Islamic Revolution in its final phase was dialed in by the means of the international telephone and the pre-recorded cassettes which in turn were used as *khutba* material. In the Islamic Republic of Iran, the traditional and modern media complement each other. Soon after his return to Iran, Ayatollah Khomeini called for the reinstitution on a regular basis of the *khutba* at Friday communal prayers, and urged the faithful to participate in these prayers. Thus, though radio, television, and the newspapers are the mouth-pieces of the Islamic government, major political pronouncements and condemnations are made at Friday communal prayers throughout the country, often making local Friday prayer leaders more powerful than the provincial governors. The huge open spaces of the campus of Tehran University have become the central prayer grounds for the government. Here on the first Friday of Ramadan in 1979, the very gifted orator Ayatollah Mahmud Taleqani told the congregation that it was the Prophet Muhammad's intention that Friday communal prayer should be devoted to worship and politics. Every Friday, free-fare buses bring thousands of people to Tehran University.[7] Here they pray together, listen to the keynote speeches, and become mobilized and excited together.

The new five-hundred-rial bank note (see the illustration below) portrays the leader of the congregation standing in front of rows of people of all ages and all classes, as clearly indicated by their apparel. It is even more revealing because a Sunni of Turcoman appearance, with characteristically folded arms, is in the front row. Here is a political statement to show that another sect is joining the communal prayers, thus conveying the regime's claim to the leadership of the entire Muslim world. This claim is at the bottom of the theory of "exporting" the revolution. Tribal people are shown along with villagers, city dwellers, military and clerics. Beneath the prayer

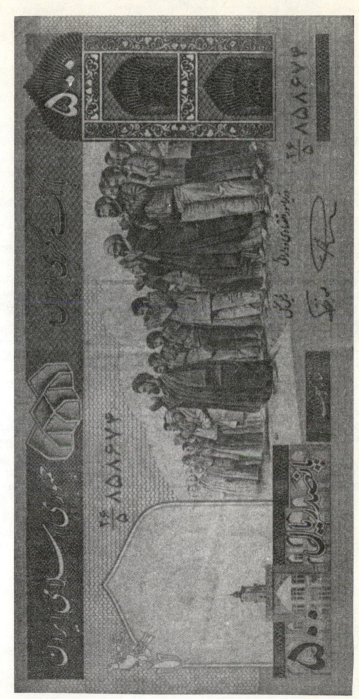

Illustration 3

carpet of the leader of the congregation is written in Persian: "the Friday prayer." In the lower left corner of the bank note there is a picture of the famous theological seminary in Qom at which Ayatollah Khomeini taught. Above it, a watermark appears within an arch of the niche. On the reverse side, the main gates to the grounds of Tehran University are shown. These gates had witnessed many bloody encounters during the revolution, and now thousands of people pass through them every Friday to participate in the communal prayer.

Ever since the French Revolution, a very common visual image of "revolution" in the Western mind has been that of make-shift barricades behind which the insufficiently armed citizenry hide from the onslaught of the well-equipped forces of the rulers. Similarly, the visual image of the Iranian revolution of 1978–1979 has been a massive column of people moving through a town. Thousands of marchers in formation hold their fists above their heads, shout, and carry banners emblazoned with religious and political slogans. To some extent, the symbolism of the political march merges into the image of the Muharram processions commemorating the suffering and death at Karbala of the Imam Husayn, grandson of the Prophet Muhammad.[8] The participants weep, wail, and flagellate themselves. Elias Canetti, writes of the processions that "the pain which the participants inflict on themselves is the pain of Husayn, which by being exhibited, becomes the pain of the whole community."[9]

In addition to self-mortifiers, the cursers (*tabarra'iyan*) move around in columns and curse the enemies of Husayn and his father Ali. They also curse those who oppose the current "just" leaders of the community. They profess their loyalty to their leaders and extol their virtues. These old-established Muharram processions then served as prototypes for the massive revolutionary marches in Tehran and other Iranian towns during the recent revolution. The logistics and passion of the Muharram processions were converted into well-organized revolutionary marching columns,[10] the network of mosques, *Hoseyniyye*s and *tekiyye*s (places for stationary Husayn rituals) were converted from traditional assembly places into rallying grounds. The highly-motivated crowds form columns which eventually link up with marchers from other districts in a tightly-knit river of humanity flowing along the main artery of the town.

The pictorial representation of this phenomenon appears on the five-thousand-rial bill. The marchers, with raised, clenched fists, stretch into infinity on the horizon. The front of the column is marching into the warm rays of a symbolic sun. Men and veiled women from all walks of life are led by clerics holding portraits of Khomeini and banners inscribed: "Independence, Freedom, Islamic Republic,"[11] and: "We are your soldiers, (O) Khomeini." These are the very slogans people carried in the revolutionary marches immediately preceding and following the advent of Khomeini.

Unlike on the pre-revolutionary bank notes, the rulers' portrait does not appear directly on the notes of the Islamic Republic.[12] This is a clever symbolic manipulation to suggest that Khomeini has not imposed his rule but is the "chosen" representative of the people who carry his portrait out of love and devotion. The same is true of the postage stamps, since only those who have been "martyred" are honored with stamps. There is no stamp with a portrait of Khomeini, but there is a stamp dedicated to his son Mustafa who died (in 1977) under strange circumstances while in exile in Iraq.[13]

On the reverse side of the five-thousand-rial bank note, there is a picture of the shrine-mosque in Qom. This is a tomb of Fateme, the sister of the eighth Imam, Ali Reza. Qom is the second-most important Shi'i pilgrimage site within the borders of present-day Iran and the country's most important theological center. The main Shi'i pilgrimage site in Iran, the shrine of Imam Ali Reza in Meshhed, is honored on the reverse of the ten-thousand-rial bank note. The obverse side of this note (see illustration) has the same design as on the five-thousand-rial bill. The only difference is that the five-thousand-rial is in cranberry color and the ten-thousand-rial in grey-blue. It is rather unusual to have the same graphic design on bank notes of different denomination. Clearly this was done because the marching scene is such a graphic reflection of Khomeini's *Weltanschauung*.

The poster of Khomeini appears also on the two-thousand-rial note (see illustration). This bill commemorates the reconquest by Iranian troops of Khorramshahr, the major port city of the Persian Gulf, in May 1982. The groups of combatants represent the three components of the Iranian armed forces, i.e., the Revolutionary Guards (*pasdaran-e enqelab*), the Volunteers of the Mobilization Forces (*basij*) and the regular armed forces. A portrait of Khomeini is held in front of them. The combatants can be recognized by the uniforms they wear. One young man from the *basij* wears a head bandana on which is written in red, "O Husayn"—thus invoking the "Prince of Martyrs." From the letters which are visible on the two banners held by the combatants, one can deduce that the verses written on them are in Arabic and therefore carry a religious connotation.

In the background there is the battered mosque of Khorramshahr. The flag of the Islamic Republic of Iran is flying from the left minaret. From the parapet of the roof of the mosque hangs a white banner on which is written, "At the dawn of victory, we regret the absence of the martyrs." At the time, victory over the Iraqis at Khorramshahr looked like the dawn of total victory in the then twenty-month-long war. It was to last another six years, but the recapture of Khorramshahr did erase the humiliating stigma of Iran's initial defeat and marked a turning point for the Iranian forces as they moved from the defensive to the offensive. It was greeted with festivities all over Iran. A postage stamp was issued to honor the occasion. The graphic design on the bank note conveys the impression that the victorious combatants are engaged in a holy war. This is further underlined by the drawing on the reverse side of the bank note, which depicts the Ka'ba in Mecca. This holiest of the holies for the Muslims is the subject of many posters and stamps issued annually for the Islamic "Unity Week," observed concurrently with the birthday of the Prophet Muhammad. The

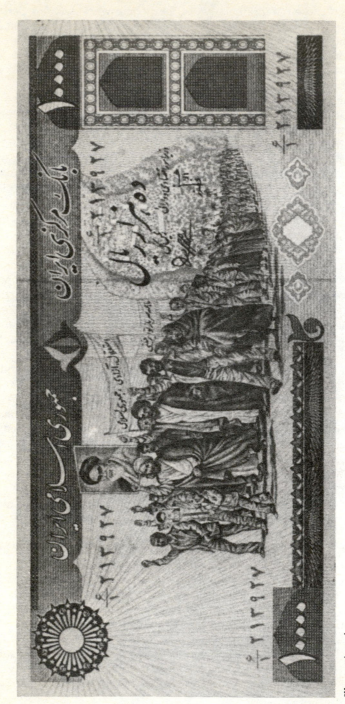

Illustration 4

Illustration 5

indirect message behind these designs is to depict the Islamic Republic of Iran as a unifying force for all Muslims, thereby once again preaching the "export of the revolution."

The third most important place for the Muslims, after Mecca and Medina, is Jerusalem, the direction of the first *qibla* and the scene of Muhammad's Night Journey and Ascent to Heaven (Qur'an, Sura xvii.1). During the month of Ramadan in 1979, Khomeini asked the Friday preachers to stress unity among Muslims, proclaiming the last Friday of Ramadan "Jerusalem Day." Every year since then, special stamps and posters have been printed for the occasion. Most of them feature the Dome of the Rock as the centerpiece. A bank note displaying the Dome of the Rock has also been issued. However, the one-thousand-rial note with the picture of the Dome of the Rock had to be recalled, since the graphic artist or the calligrapher mistakenly labelled it "Al-Aqsa Mosque." The one-thousand-rial notes now in circulation have had the erroneous label removed but the proper name of the shrine has not been inserted.[14]

On the obverse side of the one-thousand-rial bank note is a picture of Madrase-ye Feyziyye in Qom. This famous *madrase*, a pride of the Center of Religious Learning in Qom, is located in one of the four courtyards of the shrine of Fateme (depicted on the five-thousand-rial bank note). For the last forty years, the Feyziyye seminary has been tied to the name of Ayatollah Khomeini. It was there that Khomeini delivered a series of anti-shah and anti-American sermons which precipitated the uprising of June 1963. This is now regarded as the beginning of the revolutionary movement which brought about the Islamic Revolution and Khomeini's return to Iran from exile. Graphically, the events of 1963 are most often depicted with the help of the Feyziyye building. Sometimes the sun in the shape of the emblem of the Islamic Republic is rising from behind the *madrase*. Sometimes the courtyard in front of the *madrase* is turned into a river of blood. Or, as on the bank note, just a picture of the *madrase* is shown. The one-thousand-rial bank note is rather unusual in that it shows edifices on both sides of the bill; usually the front of a bill depicts a story and the back a building.

The two-hundred-rial bank note is another exception which proves that there are no strict rules regarding the graphic arrangements of bank notes printed by the Islamic Republic of Iran, as long as the message comes across. It has a building on the front and the story on the back. The building is that of the Friday mosque in Yazd. The story is devoted to the *jehad-e sazandegi* or "construction *jihad*." For this *jihad*, established under a 1979 decree of Imam Khomeini, volunteers are recruited from various walks of life—unskilled workers, engineers, technicians, and paramedics. The original goal was to improve the welfare and health of villagers and small-town dwellers. In 1982, the volunteer organization was converted into a government ministry and its activities spread far beyond its original aims. They even came to include the construction of frontline defenses in the war with Iraq. Many trench and bunker builders from the *jihad* have died under enemy fire. It does not differ greatly from the three "corps" of the "White Revolution"

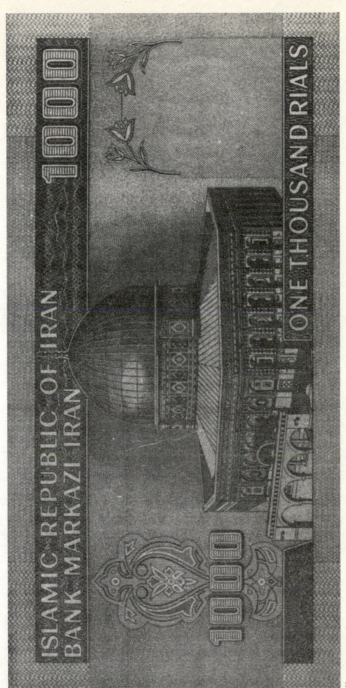

Illustration 6

Illustration 7

established by the shah (particularly from the Development Corps—*sepah-e abadani*). It is the Islamic ideological aspect that sets it apart from the shah's corps. The one-hundred-rial bill issued in 1971 shows the literacy, development and public health corps. On the fifty-rial note issued the same year, the shah is seen distributing property deeds to the farmers under the aegis of the land reform.

On the current two-hundred-rial note, above the sign *Jehad-e Sazandegi*, we see men with shovels building a gravel road through barren terrain. A tractor driven by a man is next to the workers, while in the distance at the foot of gently rolling hills a village is visible. The fact that the mosque of Yazd is depicted on the obverse side of the bill underlines not only the Islamic dimension of the *Jehad-e Sazandegi* but also its concern for the people living in the remote parts of the country. Yazd is situated on the edge of the Great Desert and the villages surrounding it must cope with the harsh environment.

In conclusion, the bank notes of the Islamic Republic of Iran, in addition to their currency function, are a public means of demonstrating that Islam dominates the economy just as it dominates the political scene. It is a daily reminder to the general public of the pre-eminent role played by Islam in their entire life. The famous statement by Ayatollah Modarres: "Our religion is identical with our politics—our politics is identical with our religion," is quoted only once on the bank notes, but it is implicit in them all.[15]

Notes

1. Emmanuel Sivan, "The Arab Nation-State: In Search of a Usable Past," *Middle East Review*, Spring 1987, 21.

2. As a general rule, the obverse sides of the bank notes are inscribed in Persian and the reverse sides in Latin alphabet transliteration. However, there are exceptions. The bank notes issued during the reign of Reza Shah in 1933 and 1936 were inscribed in Persian on both sides. So were the notes issued under Muhammad Reza in 1945 and 1947. The reverse side of the bank notes issued in 1938 is inscribed in French. The bank notes issued by the Islamic Republic of Iran have their reverse side inscribed in English. This is very interesting, in view of the fact that America is considered by the government of the Islamic Republic as its main enemy.

From 1864 until 1926, modern banking in Iran was in the hands of foreign banks. In 1926, *Bank-e Melli* (National Bank of Iran), was established. In 1960 a Monetary and Banking Act was passed, establishing the *Bank-e Markazi* (The Central Bank of Iran). This bank acts as a repository for government accounts; transacts all government business; represents Iran in international monetary organizations; maintains a balance of foreign payments; issues bank notes; controls gold and foreign exchange transactions; and sells government-issued bonds.

3. *Majmu'e-ye Eskenasha-ye Montasher Shode Dar Dowran-e Panjah Sal-e Shahanshahi-ye Dudeman-e Pahlavi* (Tehran: Bank-e Melli, 1976).

4. Peter Chelkowski, "Stamps of Blood," *American Philatelist*, June 1987, 556.

5. Sivan, op. cit., 23.

6. The tulip as the symbolic *motif* is commonly employed by the Islamic Republic of Iran. On coins of one, two and five rials the tulips form a wreath around the coin. On the coin of twenty rials issued for the commemoration of the second

Illustration 8

anniversary of the revolution, the two tulips symbolizing two years of the Islamic rule in Iran cover half of the big coin surface (1 1/4 inch across.) A twenty rial coin struck for the third anniversary of the Islamic revolution features three intertwined tulips in an arabesque in the center of the coin. Around the tulip arabesque a fine calligraphy reads: "The twenty second of Bahman, one thousand three hundred and sixty, the third anniversary of the victory of blood over the sword." Originally it was the 8th of September 1978 (17th of Shahrivar) that was called by Khomeini "the victory of blood over the sword."

7. The campus of Tehran University is in the shape of an inverted letter U. The buildings of various colleges are situated on the arms of the U. Between the arms there is a huge open space which has been used for various purposes, such as sport events, revolutionary rallies, and lately the Friday prayers.

8. See Peter Chelkowski, "Shia Muslim Processional Performances," *The Drama Review*, Vol. 29, No. 3, Fall 1985.

9. Elias Canetti, *Crowds and Power* (New York: 1978), 150.

10. Peter Chelkowski, "Iran: Mourning Becomes Revolution," *Asia* (New York), May/June 1980.

11. The same slogan appears on a fifty-rial coin issued in 1983. It features a topographic map of Iran, surrounded by the words: *Esteqlal; Azadi; Jomhuri-ye Islami.*

12. However, the portrait of Khomeini appears on countless posters, some of gigantic size. Such posters are carried in marches and cover the inside and outside walls of Iranian towns and even villages. Some of the huge portraits of Khomeini are painted directly on the walls. The posters and the wall paintings are supposed to be a spontaneous act of the people.

13. Chelkowski, "Stamps of Blood," 566.

14. The Dome of the Rock appears also on the one-rial coin. This very coin was issued in 1980/81 to commemorate Khomeini's proclamation of the International Day of Jerusalem to be observed every year on the last Friday of Ramadan. That is why on the same side of the coin it is written "Ramadan al-Mubarak—1400." On the other side of the coin under the number 1 it is written in Arabic: "Yawm al-Quds"— the day of Jerusalem. On either side of the number 1, a string of tulips appear. This coin is in yellow metal imitating gold.

15. The only thing that has escaped those who are in charge of the art of persuasion in the Islamic Republic of Iran is the original meaning of the name of the currency they are using. Rials means royal. It was the name of a Spanish coin from the end of the 15th century. The coin was very popular in the Near East and North Africa. Some countries adopted its name for their currencies. Reza Shah adopted it for the name of the imperial currency.

PART 2

Arab Shi'i Communities:
Emulation and Subversion

6

Redeeming Jerusalem:
The Pan-Islamic Premise
of Hizballah*

Martin Kramer

Hizballah—the "Party of God"—is a movement of Shi'i Muslims who wish to restore Islam to a place of pre-eminence in the political, social, and economic order of the Muslim world. Hizballah began as a movement of social and political protest, arising out of the breakdown of the Lebanese state and the messianic expectations which the Islamic Revolution in Iran stirred among Lebanon's Shi'is. In order to survive and compete in the Lebanese arena, Hizballah established an armed militia and a covert branch. The means at its disposal have been mixed with consummate skill to advance Hizballah's declared aim of Islamic revolution.[1]

That aim has the support of the Islamic Republic of Iran, which has made a major material, political, and emotional investment in Hizballah.[2] The role of Iranian support and guidance in Hizballah's growth is obvious, although the precise linkages still constitute secret history. That history, if it is ever written, is likely to be a bewildering one, because many Iranian agencies are at work in Hizballah: the Revolutionary Guards, the foreign ministry, the Martyrs' Foundation, the ministry of Islamic guidance, the ministry of intelligence and internal security, the personal representatives of Imam Khomeini, Ayatollah Husayn Ali Montazeri, and others. But if the details remain obscure, the general conclusion is inescapable: there is a great deal of co-ordination between Iran and Hizballah.

At any one time between 1982 and 1989, there were several hundred Iranian Revolutionary Guards (*Pasdaran*) in the Biqa Valley, where they provided regular military training to the militiamen of Hizballah. Iran co-ordinated the political activities of Hizballah through a governing Lebanon Council (*Majlis Lubnan*) which brought together the movement's men of

---

*The author wishes to thank The Harry Frank Guggenheim Foundation for its support of this research.

thought and action, and Iranian officials also conducted formal and informal consultations with figures in Hizballah at all levels, in Lebanon, Syria, and Iran. The financial and social assistance provided to Lebanese Shi'is is also a matter of public record. Iran opened pharmacies, clinics, and hospitals in parts of Lebanon, and planned to establish agricultural co-operatives and schools.[3] It is unlikely that Hizballah could have achieved its present standing without the consistent backing of Iran. According to one Shi'i cleric in Hizballah, the gains made so far by the movement would have taken fifty years to achieve had it not been for Iran's support.[4]

But there are other factions in Lebanon that enjoy the support of external states, and material and political dependence does not distinguish Hizballah from its rivals. What is striking and distinctive about Hizballah is its cultural deference to Iran's Islamic symbols, its spiritual deference to Iran's Islamic authority, and its ideological deference to Iran's Islamic vision. Members of Hizballah take much more than money and arms from Iran: they borrow the content and trappings of a new identity, and an allegiance to the Imam Khomeini and his Islamic revolution. So thoroughly have they integrated their sense of purpose with Iran's mission that they do not see themselves as a Lebanese movement at all, but as the extension of a worldwide Islamic movement under the guidance of the Imam Khomeini, for the creation of one great Islamic state. Hizballah's premise is not only Islamic but pan-Islamic.

A noted historian of Iran has defined pan-Islam as a nineteenth-century "proto-nationalism"—a form of Muslim resistance to the high imperialism of the late nineteenth century that disappeared in the twentieth, when new linguistic and territorial nationalisms staked a more compelling claim. Pan-Islam was "an important phase in preparing minds and spirits for local nationalisms," but "died as a serious political force after the Turks themselves took the step, profoundly shocking to many of their Muslim brethren, of abolishing the caliphate in 1924."[5] A noted historian of Turkey has written that "the pan-Islamic hallucination" was "in reality a drive for freedom and independence in almost every Muslim country," and "found its reward not in a unification of believers around the caliph but in Western-supported nationalist movements."[6] Nineteenth-century pan-Islam did prepare the way for parochial nationalisms, as a form of primary resistance to the encroachments of the imperial West. Yet, in Hizballah, pan-Islam has reappeared unexpectedly in a late twentieth-century guise, as a "post-nationalist" protest against the prevailing state order in the Islamic world and the values of the parochial nationalisms that supposedly displaced it. The timing of this reappearance is a challenge to the argument that the nation and the state have finally become the legitimate focus of allegiance in the Arab world, and that modern Islam has resigned itself to the inevitability of the nation-state.

Not only does Hizballah's pan-Islamic premise defy consensus. The vast sweep of Hizballah's pan-Islamic nationalism seems to defy reality, for it is out of all proportion to the resources of the movement and its patrons. The movement thrives amidst the despair of the southern suburbs of Beirut, whose inhabitants, while battling world powers on behalf of all Islam, must also struggle for their daily bread. While professing allegiance to Khomeini, Hizballah's members are bound up in a complex web of other allegiances— to family, neighborhood, patrons, and individual men of religion—that are very much rooted in the small realities of Lebanon. Many are caught in the middle ground between the movement's pan-Islamic nationalism and the fragments of prior loyalties—Shi'i, Lebanese, and Arab—that each Hizballahi brings with him.

Yet pan-Islam has emerged as the most widely accepted theme of political discourse in Hizballah. The embrace by Hizballah's adherents of a pan-Islamic identity is one of the most radical effects of Iran's revolution in the wider Muslim world. And the hold it has acquired upon Shi'is in cosmopolitan, multi-confessional Lebanon must be counted one of the wonders of the revolution. There is no doubt that Hizballah's pan-Islamic premise is "non-conformist,"[7] and that it is not widely shared in the Arab world, even among Shi'is. But a decade ago it had few adherents, and its very appearance, first in Iran and later in Lebanon, has been a striking deviation from the path beaten by the West.

This deviation has yet to run its course. The end of the Iran-Iraq war and internal developments in Iran may undermine Iran's commitment to Hizballah and the movement's pan-Islamic premise. The evidence assembled here is specific to a phase of Hizballah's development between 1982 and 1988, coinciding with a phase of the Iranian revolution. But whatever the future holds for Hizballah, its championing of pan-Islam in the early 1980s has been an omen that collective identities in parts of the Muslim world remain volatile. The idea of a unitary Islamic state under the guidance of a divinely-inspired leader—a nineteenth-century "hallucination"—has inspired a mass movement even as the twentieth century draws to a close. Its message perhaps is that while the faith yet survives, so too must the vision of a united Islam.

This chapter does not propose to explore all the dimensions of Hizballah's intimate relationship with Iran, but to touch on the three principal realms of Hizballah's deference to Iran. The first is the symbolic realm—the external trappings of Hizballah that serve as vivid evidence for the movement's acculturation to Iranian norms. The second is the realm of authority, centered upon the domineering figure of the Imam Khomeini. The third is the realm of ideological vision, where the influence of Islamic Iran upon Hizballah finds formulation in pan-Islamic doctrine.

The methodological assumption is that the symbols, the allegiances, and ideals that serve Hizballah are a window into its world, and not some form of Shi'i or Lebanese dissimulation behind which lies a hidden agenda. Hizballah employs dissimulation in the operational sphere, in order to confuse its enemies. But when Hizballah flies the Iranian flag at a demonstration in the Biqa Valley or plasters the southern suburbs of Beirut with posters of Khomeini, it is speaking directly to its own following. While such acts include rhetorical elements, they are not simply rhetorical devices devoid of all meaning. They may be interpreted and contextualized, but cannot be dismissed.

Points of Origin

For the sake of order, it is worth dwelling in brief upon the history of Islamic Iran's penetration of the Lebanese Shi'i community. The process is rooted in the now-vanished world of the Shi'i academies of Iraq. A generation of young scholars, educated in the shrine cities of Najaf and Karbala in the 1960s and 1970s, came under the powerful influence of radical theories of Islamic government and economics first formulated by Iraqi Shi'i thinkers. Najaf in particular was the site of great intellectual ferment during those two decades, a ferment fueled by the fears of the Shi'i clerics that their Islamic values and religious autonomy were threatened by westernizing influences. Their response was to elaborate a theory of an Islamic state which could offer a satisfying alternative to the rival doctrines of nationalism and communism that had made inroads even in Najaf. These clerics thought, lectured, and wrote on such subjects as Islamic government, Islamic economics, and the ideal Islamic state. Concepts of Islamic government reached their furthest refinement after the arrival in 1965 of Ayatollah Ruhollah Khomeini, who spent fourteen years of exile in Najaf and there formulated his intellectual case for Islamic government. The principles of Islamic economics reached their fullest articulation at about the same time in the teachings of an Iraqi Shi'i theoretician, Ayatollah Muhammad Baqir al-Sadr.[8]

At the time of formulation, these ideas were so remote from implementation that they could only be described as theoretical. This was particularly true of the denial of western principles of nationality and the affirmation of the possibility and viability of a unitary and universal Islamic state. An aversion to Arab and Persian nationalism came readily to classrooms where Arabic- and Persian-speakers sat together in the study of sacred texts. The bonds forged in this brotherhood found a natural expression in the assumption that Islam transcended all other boundaries of personal and collective identity, and could serve as the basis of a pan-Islamic movement.

The Arab-Persian symbiosis of the Shi'i academies of Iraq laid the foundations for the emergence of Hizballah. Upon their return to Lebanon, young Shi'i scholars schooled in Najaf indoctrinated their followers with the same ideas they themselves had imbibed during their student days. For the most part, these clerics remained aloof from the Amal movement, which was then under the leadership of the Iranian-born Imam Musa al-Sadr. Sadr also had extensive connections with the world of Shi'i scholarship in Najaf, and gave his moral support to the idea of an Islamic state in Iran and Iraq. But as the pre-eminent leader of the Shi'i community in Lebanon, Sadr did not call for revolution in Lebanon, but demanded the reform of Lebanon's confessional system along more equitable lines.[9]

In contrast, many of the Najaf-schooled clerics were convinced of the moral obligation to champion the idea of an Islamic or pan-Islamic state, even if its implementation in Lebanon seemed remote. They preached their doctrine to relatively small numbers of Shi'i followers, whose ranks were suddenly swollen by the triumph of the Islamic movement in Iran in 1979. That revolution fired the imaginations of the Najaf-schooled clerics, who saw their former classmates elevated to positions of the highest authority in a state devoted to the implementation of the ideals of their youth. When Iranian emissaries arrived in Lebanon following the Iranian revolution, their meetings with these Shi'i clerics were not first encounters; they were reunions.

It is all the more paradoxical that the first efforts to build bridges between Islamic Iran and Lebanon were not made through the agency of the Najaf-educated clerics. Several of Islamic Iran's leading lay figures had spent periods of exile in Lebanon in the ranks of Palestinian organizations. After Iran's revolution in 1979, some of them sought to enter the Lebanese arena through the agency of the Palestine Liberation Organization, which invited and anticipated Iranian assistance.[10] The idea of sending an Islamic expeditionary force to Lebanon at Palestinian invitation was the brainchild of Hojjat al-Islam Muhammad Montazeri, son of the Ayatollah Husayn Ali Montazeri. The younger Montazeri, known for his unstable and volatile personality, had spent some time in Lebanon with Palestinian groups prior to the Iranian revolution. Following the revolution's success, he began to recruit volunteers for an expeditionary force of 1,000 Revolutionary Guards who would be sent to Lebanon, and whose ranks were eventually intended to be expanded to 10,000. The Lebanese government grew very apprehensive about the possible arrival of these volunteers, and even planned to close Beirut's airport should a flight of volunteers arrive. In the end, the younger Montazeri led a group of a few hundred Iranians to Damascus, in the hope that the Syrian government would permit their passage to Lebanon. But Syrian President Hafiz al-Asad deemed their presence an unwanted complication, and assured Lebanese President Elias Sarkis that the Iranian volunteers would not be permitted to cross into Lebanon. When Iraq invaded Iran a few months later, the Iranians departed for that other battlefront, which provided a seemingly inexhaustible outlet for the zeal of would-be martyrs.

The initiative of 1979 proved to be a false start. But although the volunteers failed to arrive (cf. chapter by Olmert), delegations of Iranian clerics became a frequent sight in the Shi'i-populated areas of Lebanon after 1979, and Lebanese Shi'is visited Iran in growing numbers. Iranian emissaries began to seek out Lebanese Shi'i partners who would translate and transmit Islamic Iran's message, and faithfully implement the program of the Imam Khomeini for the redemption of Islam from the grip of the "world-devourers." At first, Iran did not attempt to establish a separate framework for its supporters, but sought closer ties with existing organizations, such as the Supreme Islamic Shi'i Council (SISC) and the Amal movement (which opened an office in Tehran). The Iranian embassy in Beirut also conducted its own activities in the Shi'i southern suburbs of the city, organizing meetings and demonstrations and subsidizing various Lebanese Shi'i publications.

The attempt to work solely through the established institutions of the Shi'i community did not succeed. These institutions were not malleable, and their leaders remained jealous of their independence. While they were prepared to make ritual obeisance to Khomeini, theirs were essentially Lebanese institutions, and they viewed the Shi'i predicament as a Lebanese problem which could only be resolved through the reform of the Lebanese state. In taking this stand, they essentially dismissed the Iranian doctrines of Islamic revolution, government, and unity as irrelevant to the complex confessional situation of Lebanon. The head of the SISC, Shaykh Muhammad Mahdi Shams al-Din, argued as late as 1983 that "the Shi'i Muslims in Lebanon have always been Lebanese first . . . every sect in Lebanon at some time in its history has resorted to calling for help from an outside foreign power—with the exception of the Shi'i Muslims, who have always been loyal and sincere to Lebanon. Lebanon is their native land. When dealing with matters concerning Lebanon, their premises are always purely Lebanese."[11] It was Iran's intention to undermine this claim by building a following loyal not to Lebanon but to Islam as defined and led by the Imam Khomeini.

To do so, Iranian emissaries had to identify and encourage Lebanese Shi'is who did not share a fundamental commitment to the Lebanese state. Iran eventually found them among the Najaf-educated clerics. In addition to their past clandestine membership in Islamic political groups operating against the Iraqi regime, some of them appeared openly as leaders of the Lebanese Muslim Students' Union. This organization, based in the Arab University of Beirut, brought together a number of Shi'i youths who shared a devotion to the idea of Islamic rule in Lebanon. The Lebanese Muslim Students' Union may properly be called the precursor of Hizballah. On the pages of its periodical, *al-Muntalaq*, there is much evidence for Iran's early efforts at building influence among those Lebanese Shi'i clerics and laymen who were already partisans of an Islamic state in Lebanon. Once Iran's clerics began to operate through Lebanon's Najaf-educated scholars, their effectiveness grew and their message gained resonance. Elsewhere in the Muslim world, Iran's spokesmen had to provide a double translation of Iran's revolutionary message. Not only did they have to translate from Persian to Arabic; they had to substitute a bland all-Islamic ecumenism for the evocative symbols of Shi'ism. But in Lebanon, Iran found a large Shi'i community which fully understood the nuanced symbolism of Iran's revolution and the particular emphasis on the seventh-century martyrdom of the Imam Husayn as a paradigm of political action.[12] Among the Najaf-schooled clerics, Iran found spokesmen adept at translating Khomeini's message into eloquent Arabic and arguing its relevance to the predicament of Lebanon.

In 1982, after Israel invaded Lebanon, Iran sought to demonstrate solidarity with the Palestinians, the Syrians, and Lebanon's Shi'is in the fight against Israeli occupation. This it again proposed to do by sending Iranian volunteers through Syria into Lebanon, where they would battle Israeli forces. The context of this proposal differed decisively from that of the failed initiative of 1979. The collapse of all central authority in Lebanon meant that the Lebanese government's protests counted for naught in Damascus, and Syria was free to make its own calculation.[13] A small Iranian contingent thus reached the Biqa Valley and, beginning in October 1982, established itself there. They were joined by a group of Lebanese Shi'is who had abandoned the Amal movement during the summer to create their own Islamic Amal. A leading spokesman of Hizballah later claimed that the arrival of the Revolutionary Guards in 1982 was "the basic factor in changing the course of Lebanese and Middle Eastern history, for it dashed the American, Israeli, and Maronite plans."[14]

Almost immediately upon their arrival in the Biqa Valley, the Iranians began the systematic recruitment of Lebanese Shi'is to their flag. By a brilliant combination of ideological indoctrination and material inducement, the Iranians created a sizeable constituency among Lebanese Shi'is, and this following took the name of Hizballah, derived from the Qur'anic verse: "And verily the party of God is sure to triumph." As its logo, Hizballah chose a raised arm bearing an automatic rifle against the background of a globe; below the logo appeared the motto: "The Islamic Revolution in Lebanon." The movement rapidly gained momentum, and soon spread to the other major areas of Shi'i population, in the southern suburbs of Beirut and the villages and towns of southern Lebanon. Hizballah's message had great appeal for that part of the Shi'i community that had despaired of the Lebanese state. The Islamic movement, claimed Hizballah, would rid Lebanon of foreign intruders, end confessional strife, establish a regime of social justice, and set the stage for the liberation of Jerusalem. Within a year of its creation, Hizballah was a going concern, led by eloquent Lebanese Shi'is who commanded an armed militia and a highly effective clandestine branch.

The Symbolic World of Hizballah

Hizballah's style sets the scene for any analysis of the substance of its message. Judging simply from appearances, the untrained eye might have difficulty distinguishing between a demonstration by Hizballah in Beirut or the Biqa Valley, and a similar one in Tehran. Highly ritualized, from the order of procession to the burning of the American flag, they are essentially a re-enactment of Tehran street demonstrations. In matters of dress and personal appearance, the influence of Iranian example upon the rank and file in Hizballah is also obvious. But the imitation also extends to visual symbols. Hizballah does have its own symbol, which makes no explicit reference to Iran (although its artistic lines are clearly inspired by Iranian models). The accompanying symbols, however, are overwhelmingly Iranian.[15]

Thus, Khomeini's portrait dominates the symbolic world of Hizballah. Khomeini appears on the masthead of Hizballah's own weekly newspaper, *al-Ahd* (in the place occupied by a portrait of the Imam Musa al-Sadr in the newspaper of the rival Amal movement). Khomeini's portrait is prominently displayed at all events sponsored by Hizballah. And on the anniversary of Iran's revolution, little girls dressed in chadors distribute pictures of

Khomeini to passing motorists.[16] Often Khomeini's visage is accompanied by portraits of leading figures in Iranian martyrology such as Ayatollah Motahheri, as well as portraits of living leaders, such as Ayatollah Montazeri. There are also portraits of Lebanese Shi'i martyrs, especially Shaykh Raghib Harb,[17] and also of the missing Imam Musa al-Sadr. The indulgence in this kind of iconography, as well as its artistic style, is highly reminiscent of current Iranian models, and probably owes its origins to examples imported by the Iranian Revolutionary Guards in the Biqa Valley. The flag borne by Hizballah is the Iranian flag, regarded by its bearers as the "flag of Islam."[18]

The vocabulary of slogans is similarly borrowed from Islamic Iran, and so too are the rhetorical devices of many of Hizballah's spokesmen. Even before Hizballah had its own publications and radio station, Iranian materials in Arabic enjoyed a wide circulation in Lebanon. What resounded in Iran often resounded just as well in the Shi'i community of Lebanon. The name Hizballah, although itself taken from a verse in the Qur'an, is nonetheless a borrowing from the political vocabulary of post-revolutionary Iran, where it connotes the populist and sometimes violent vigilante groups that championed the "line of the Imam" against would-be compromisers. Similarly, Hizballah has adopted all of the principle catchwords of Iran's revolutionary rhetoric. The Muslims (and the other oppressed peoples of the world) are the "disinherited," the *mustad'afun* of the Qur'an; the United States and the Soviet Union represent "world arrogance," *al-istikbar al-alami*, which is one hostile bloc pitted against the *mustad'afun*. These themes are evident not only in Hizballah's official programmatic statement,[19] but in the daily exhortations of its clerics. And they are echoed at the lowest level of Hizballah's discourse: in the last wills and testaments of Hizballah's militiamen, which are published regularly in Hizballah's weekly newspaper and clearly owe their form and content to the tens of thousands of Iranian examples published during the Gulf war.[20] The movement demonstrates, dresses, speaks and writes almost exclusively in the revolutionary parameters set by the Islamic Republic of Iran.

The richness of Hizballah's symbolic world is difficult to appreciate from the outside. An ostensibly simple symbol—a ring worn by Hizballahis, from leading clerics to airline hijackers—may be laden with symbolic meanings that are not immediately apparent. Often it speaks of a past visit to Iran; but does it imply more, representing membership or authority? What are the social and cultural implications of the use by Hizballahis in the Biqa Valley of Persian salutations? It is on this level of minutiae that many members of Hizballah experience personal transformation and mental escape from the confines of one sect in a small state of many sects. Identification with the vastness of Islamic revolution may find its most satisfying expression in dress or speech that identify the Hizballahi with an Islamic state, leader, cause, or cultural legacy much greater than his own, much as the Maronite in East Beirut adopts dress and speech that demonstrate affiliation with the West. While East Beirut vainly seeks to emulate Paris, the southern suburbs seek to recreate Tehran. Beirut cannot be either, yet momentary illusions are created day by day through the discriminating use of symbols.

The Duty to Obey

Once it has been determined that Islamic Iran established Hizballah, funds Hizballah, and provides Hizballah with everything from portraits of Khomeini to tried and tested slogans, it remains to be demonstrated that Hizballah sees itself primarily as an instrument of Islamic Iran. The Lebanese client is famous (or notorious) for his willingness to take everything but orders from his patron. It is for this reason that the insistence upon obedience and discipline has become Iran's principal preoccupation in its relationship with Hizballah.

The fullest programmatic statement issued by Hizballah is its "open letter" to the "disinherited of Lebanon and the world," dated 16 February 1985. By issuing a statement of aims in the form of an "open letter," Iran's closest collaborators in Hizballah hoped to enforce a modicum of ideological discipline and assure that Hizballah spoke with one voice. The "open letter" includes a straightforward declaration of allegiance to Iran and Khomeini:

> We are sons of the nation of Hizballah, whose vanguard God made victorious in Iran, and who re-established the nucleus of a central Islamic state in the world. We abide by the orders of the sole wise and just command of the supreme jurisconsult who meets the qualifications, and who is presently incarnate in the Imam and guide, the Great Ayatollah Khomeini, may his authority be perpetuated—enabler of the revolution of the Muslims and harbinger of their glorious renaissance.[21]

While the front cover of the letter carries a portrait of a "martyred" Lebanese Shi'i cleric, the back is illustrated with a portrait of Khomeini. This is Hizballah's fundamental pledge of obedience to Khomeini, who is named elsewhere in the open letter as "the leader" (*al-qa'id*), in imitation of the Persian designation of Khomeini as "leader" (*rahbar*) of the Islamic revolution.[22]

The political theory to which Hizballah subscribes is the principle of government by the just jurisconsult, *al-wali al-faqih*. This is the same theory made famous by the Imam Khomeini as the doctrine of *velayat-e faqih* in his well-known tract on Islamic Government, and it is the theory enshrined in the 1979 constitution of the Islamic Republic of Iran. Its fundamental assumptions are Shi'i, in that it emphasizes the passage of authority to the just jurisconsult in the absence of the Twelfth Imam. According to the leading clerics in Hizballah, the authority of *al-wali al-faqih* knows no limits. As Sayyid Hasan Nasrallah explained, "the *faqih* is the guardian during the absence [of the Twelfth Imam], and the extent of his authority is wider than that of any other person. . . . We must obey *al-wali al-faqih*; disagreement with him is not permitted. The guardianship of the *faqih* is like the guardianship of the Prophet Muhammad and of the infallible Imam. . . . When *al-wali al-faqih* orders that someone be obeyed, such obedience is obligatory."[23]

For Sayyid Ibrahim al-Amin, the most important distinguishing feature of Hizballah is the tie between the people and the just jurisconsult (*al-faqih al-adil*); Hizballah carries out the decisions issued by the just jurisconsult. That jurisconsult need not be Lebanese, for it is the geography of Islam, and not of Lebanon, which defines the arena of Hizballah's activity. "We do not derive our political decision-making from anyone but the jurisconsult (*al-faqih*). The jurisconsult is not defined by geography but by Islamic law." And so no barriers separate the faithful in Lebanon from the faithful in Iran: "We in Lebanon do not consider ourselves as separate from the revolution in Iran, especially on the question of Jerusalem. We consider ourselves—and pray to God that we will become—part of the army which the Imam wishes to create in order to liberate Jerusalem. We obey his orders because we do not believe in geography but in change." "God willing," declares Ibrahim al-Amin, "we will live up to our allegiance (*mubaya'a*) to the Imam."[24] Sayyid Hasan Nasrallah ascribes to Khomeini the qualities of a true Imam: descended from the Prophet Muhammad, he embodies the link with the Imam Husayn and the Prophets; he is the fulfillment of a divine promise; he stands at the point where the past, the present, and the future of the nation (*umma*) of Islam meet; to hear him speak is to hear Islam itself.[25]

Given Hizballah's certainty that the Imam Khomeini is divinely guided, ideological discipline is largely self-enforced. Yet there are times when contradictions emerge between the duty to obey and other ideological principles, and Hizballah must sometimes be reminded of its duty to accept Khomeini's superior judgment. This does not occur often or openly, but when it does, a certain tension is introduced into Iran's relationship with Hizballah—a tension that plays upon doubts which remain at the very back of the minds in Hizballah.

One of these doubts is particularly potent, for it touches on Lebanese Shi'i faith in the Imam Musa al-Sadr, the man who may best be described as the community's patron saint. The prevalent opinion among the Shi'is of Lebanon is that Libya's Mu'ammar al-Qadhdhafi is responsible for the fate of Sadr, who disappeared in 1978 while on a trip to Libya. On this account, the Amal movement is deeply hostile to Libya, and it seems probable that many in Hizballah are also convinced of Libya's guilt in the Sadr affair. Yet Islamic Iran maintains a co-operative relationship with Libya, through which both have sought to break out of an isolation imposed by the United States. For the Amal movement, this has represented a serious point of disagreement with Iran. Amal's spiritual leader, the Ja'fari Mufti Shaykh Abd al-Amir Qabalan, once told Iran's chargé d'affaires in Beirut that "if the Imam Khomeini does not return the Imam Musa al-Sadr to us, his way is different from ours, and his God is different from our God."[26] For some in Hizballah as well, Iranian support for Libya has created a distressing conflict between their duty to the missing Imam Sadr and the living Imam Khomeini. This becomes a burning issue once a year, when both Amal and Hizballah mark the anniversary of Sadr's disappearance. On these occasions, speakers at Amal's rallies, and especially at the great gathering in Tyre, usually condemn Libya and demand that Libya return Sadr to his flock, if indeed he is alive.

Some in Hizballah have resolved their dilemma by refusing to believe that Khomeini has sanctioned close political ties with Libya. Such ties, they believe, must have been established against his will. For Hizballah, this belief has serious implications, for it suggests that the guidance offered to Hizballah by Iran may not always have the sanction of the Imam Khomeini. Hizballah's Shaykh Hasan Tarad went to great lengths to dispel all such doubts, in a speech in a Beirut *husayniyya*. Iran's decision to establish strategic relations with Libya, he explained, was based on Libya's important role in the regional political balance. "The great Imam Khomeini is the Islamic Republic and the Islamic Republic is the Imam. A decision like this decision could only be the Imam Khomeini's, taken at his instruction and under his supervision." Khomeini was to the Imam Sadr as "a father to his son and a teacher to his disciple," and so Khomeini would leave no stone unturned in his quest to discover Sadr's fate. But Iran was isolated politically, economically, and militarily, and Khomeini had determined that there was no choice but to take a positive stand toward Libya (and Syria). His primary consideration was his "solicitude for Islam and the defense of the general interest." And Shaykh Tarad reminded his listeners that the Imam Khomeini, "the absolute leader of the Islamic nation," is "the absolute authority (*mujtahid mutlaq*) for legal rulings, who solves any problem. Just as he is an authority for legal rulings, so he is an authority in all affairs."[27]

In practical terms, this constituted an admonition that members of Hizballah desist from criticizing Libya, even while calling for the return of the Imam Sadr. And indeed, in Hizballah's own rallies marking the event, no mention is made of Libya. Sadr's disappearance is attributed only to "the division of Islamic ranks." On one such occasion, Shaykh Hasan Nasrallah squarely placed Sadr in a subordinate place to Khomeini in Hizballah's eschatology: "Sayyid Musa al-Sadr was a foretoken of the revolution; the Islamic revolution then achieved a great victory, and the sun of the Imam Khomeini rose in the East. We live in the warmth of that sun; and were it ever to be concealed from us, the Imam would lead us back to it."[28] It is rare that Hizballah needs to be reminded so forcefully of its duty to submit to the superior judgment of the Imam Khomeini. The need to do so in this instance reflected the depth of Lebanese Shi'i resentment over the disappearance of the Imam Sadr.

Indeed, so important is the sanction of the Imam Khomeini that it is sometimes inferred rather than known. Such was the case in the suicide bombing attacks against Hizballah's adversaries in Lebanon, and in the kidnapping of foreigners. Both of these methods became subjects of some discussion within Hizballah, because they involved complicated problems of Islamic law.[29] The Imam Khomeini did not issue any explicit ruling in favor of the suicide bombings, because Iran disavowed any involvement in them. Considerable outside speculation focused on the possible role of

Hizballah's own clerics in sanctioning the attacks. But Hizballah could not salute such operations if the Imam Khomeini was known to be indifferent to them. After the bombings ceased, Sayyid Ibrahim al-Amin made this assurance:

> Those who blew up the [US] Marines headquarters and the Israeli military governor in Tyre did not martyr themselves in accord with a decision by a political party or movement. They martyred themselves because the Imam Khomeini permitted them to do so. They saw nothing before them but God, and they defeated Israel and America for God. It was the Imam of the Nation [Khomeini] who showed them this path and instilled this spirit in them.[30]

In the case of the foreign hostages, Iran again has been most cautious to disavow any direct involvement in their detention, and so Khomeini has issued no formal opinion on the legality of seizing innocents. Once again, however, it has been Sayyid Ibrahim al-Amin who has claimed that these operations enjoy Khomeini's sanction. Amin pointed out that Khomeini's silence over the seizure of the American Embassy in Tehran constituted tacit approval: "The Imam neither protested this action nor said it was wrong." Since Khomeini has remained silent about hostage-holding in Lebanon, this must also be read as tacit approval.[31] For Hizballah, reading the will of Khomeini sometimes poses problems (as it does in Iran itself); but no one doubts the absolute authority of that will, and every effort has been made to fathom its myriad expressions.

Another test of Hizballah's faith involved the arms-for-hostages dealings between Iran and the United States. Once again, certain persons in Hizballah could not believe that the secret contacts between the United States and Islamic Iran enjoyed the sanction of Khomeini. "The Islamic revolution asserts rejection of America and the refusal to deal with it," Husayn al-Musawi, the leader of Islamic Amal, said when asked about his attitude to Amal leader Nabih Birri. He said: "Nabih deals with the Americans."[32] Word that Islamic Iran itself had dealt with the Americans again raised the question of whether the actions of the Islamic Republic were in full accord with the will of the Imam Khomeini. Shaykh Isma'il Khaliq, Ayatollah Montazeri's representative in Beirut, did not think so, for it was he who reportedly informed a Lebanese news magazine of Robert McFarlane's secret mission to Tehran.[33]

In treating these revelations, Hizballah's own newspaper simply repeated the denials and rationalizations made by the leading Iranian figures in the episode. It carried the full text of the speech by Majlis Speaker Ali Akbar Hashemi Rafsanjani, who explained that the contacts had Khomeini's sanction.[34] The newspaper also reminded the rank and file in Hizballah of Iran's need for spare parts, and the importance of diplomatic as well as military victories for the triumph of the Islamic cause.[35] But all this seemed too ingenuous for the clerics of Hizballah. They were prepared to justify dealing with Libya, and no one had to remind them of the importance of seeking Syrian favor, however distasteful these two alliances might be. But none of them was prepared to make the same argument in favor of dealing with the United States, the "root of all vice," and none of them did. Hizballah's clerics, by their total avoidance of the arms-for-hostages episode in their speeches and interviews, indicated their silent horror and the conviction that perhaps the Imam Khomeini did not know all that Iranian officials did in his name after all. They were obviously relieved that the initiative collapsed, and positively celebrated the political deterioration in the Gulf during the summer of 1987.[36]

The duty to obey is not always easy to bear, but is nonetheless bearable because of a conviction that the Imam Khomeini is divinely guided. The dependence of Hizballah on the charismatic authority of the Imam Khomeini is absolute, and the question of the Iranian succession has become a matter of the utmost interest in Hizballah. Montazeri was recognized by Hizballah as Khomeini's designated successor (*khalifa*), and gained an elevated standing in Hizballah because of the active role played in promoting Iranian involvement in Lebanon. When disagreements appeared in Hizballah, apparently over the issue of which Iranian persons and agencies represented the will of Khomeini, it was Ayatollah Montazeri who issued a decisive appeal for unity.[37] Fidelity to the Imam has had the same effect of deterring conflict in Hizballah as it has had in Iran. But members of Hizballah tended to align with their Iranian patrons over the devolution of Khomeini's authority and are likely to do so again now that he is dead. Should confusion develop as to the locus of spiritual and political authority in Iran, it is bound to be reflected in the ranks of Hizballah.

The Vision of Pan-Islam

If Khomeini's authority as the just jurisconsult knows no limits, then any frontier that artificially impedes the exercise of that authority is illegitimate. Hizballah therefore operates in Lebanon only as a branch of a larger Hizballah. That larger movement is composed of all downtrodden Muslims who struggle under the supreme guidance of Imam Khomeini against the injustices of imperialism and colonialism, throughout the world of Islam. According to Husayn al-Musawi, the aspirations of Hizballah in Lebanon are "an extension of the aspirations of adherents of Hizballah throughout the Islamic world." "Some say we are Muslim Lebanese," he observes. "No! We are Muslims of the world and we have close links with other Muslims of the world."[38] "We announce to the world," says a lesser cleric, "that the Islamic Republic is our mother, our religion, our Mecca, our blood, our arteries."[39] Hizballah's struggle, says an editorial in the movement's newspaper, "is an inseparable part of the overall Islamic strategy in the great and comprehensive confrontation with the aggression of Zionists, Crusaders, and world arrogance." Hizballah is simply a "forward position" of this struggle, which is being conducted simultaneously on many fronts.[40] "We are all brothers and fighting for the same cause," according to Sayyid Abbas al-Musawi. "Any attempt to separate us from our Iranian brothers or from Muslims in general is a crime."[41]

The corollary is that Iran as a state with its own interests does not exist for Hizballah. According to Sayyid Ibrahim al-Amin, "the strategy in which the Muslims of Lebanon are fighting with the revolution in Iran is not on behalf of the state of Iran; it is on behalf of Islam, which first burst forth in Iran."[42] That outbreak is of fundamentally eschatological significance for Hizballah; as Sayyid Hasan Nasrallah declares, "the divine state of justice realized on part of this earth will not remain confined within its geographic borders, and is the dawn which will lead to the appearance of the Mahdi, who will create the state of Islam on earth." Indeed, human history may be divided into two eras: that which preceded the Islamic revolution in Iran, and that which will follow it.[43] But the fact that this revolution began in Iran is of no significance, since it is destined to sweep across all of the artificial frontiers which divide Islam. Hizballah's clerics infrequently call the Islamic Republic of Iran by its official name, since this connotes the distinct existence of Iran as a state. In Hizballah's lexicon, the Islamic Republic of Iran is Iran of Islam, *Iran al-Islam*, which suggests that Iran is simply the province of that greater Islamic entity which even now is taking form.

The logical extension of this premise is that the principles of Arab or Persian nationalism, which divide the Muslim community along artificial lines, are utterly bankrupt. "We follow God and his religion of Islam, not Persia or the Arab nation," says Husayn al-Musawi. "If nationality and race obstruct Islamic links, then they are unacceptable."[44] Again, this is not the belief of a handful of ideologists, but has filtered down to the lower ranks of the movement, as in the remarks of a shaykh in a village mosque in South Lebanon, on the occasion of a visit by the chargé d'affaires of Iran's Beirut embassy (in 1986):

> There is no Arab brotherhood or nationalist brotherhood here, because the Arabs have given us no aid despite the continuation of the crisis here for ten years. . . . The most unifying link is Islam. . . . Is it not Islam which has brought brother [Mahmud] Nurani [the Iranian chargé d'affaires] to us? Where are the Arabs? Why does the Persian come, but not the Arab? This demonstrates that the true tie between one man and another is that of thought and belief. We have no solidarity or common denominator with any being who does not believe in God and His Prophet.[45]

Hizballah holds that the ties of Islamic belief are the only ties which truly bind, and they bind without distinction of origin, nationality, race, language, or sect. "The Arabs"—those who see themselves first and foremost as Arabs—are a subject of Hizballah's derision. "The Arabs for a long time have wanted peace with Israel," says Shaykh Subhi al-Tufayli,[46] and a headline in Hizballah's newspaper proclaims the same.[47] Far from representing the vanguard of Islam, "the Arabs" are responsible for its corruption; until Iran's Islamic revolution, "the Islamic nation (*umma*) was a stiff corpse."[48]

All believing Muslims must work together to implement what Sayyid Ibrahim al-Amin calls "the one Islamic world plan," the aim of which is the creation of a "great Islamic state" which will unite the entire region.[49]

This plan will proceed in four stages: confrontation with Israel; the toppling of the Lebanese regime; the liberation of Lebanon from any form of political or military intervention by the Great Powers; and the establishment of Islam as the basis of rule "until the Muslims of Lebanon join with the Muslims throughout the world in this age, to implement the single Islamic plan, and so become the centralized, single nation (*umma*) willed by God, who decreed that 'your nation will be one'."[50]

Hizballah therefore does not simply seek to establish an Islamic republic in Lebanon: "We do not believe that it would be natural for an Islamic state to arise in Lebanon outside the plan," says Ibrahim al-Amin. "We wish Lebanon to be a part of the plan."[51] The establishment of an Islamic state in Lebanon "is not our demand," says Husayn al-Musawi. The aim is rather to create an "all-encompassing Islamic state" which will include Lebanon.[52] "We do not work or think within the borders of Lebanon," declares Shaykh Subhi al-Tufayli, "this little geometric box, which is one of the legacies of imperialism."[53] According to Ibrahim al-Amin, Lebanon's agony will end only "when the final Middle East map is drawn. We seek almighty God's help in drawing this map as soon as possible, with the blood of the martyrs and the strength of those who wage the *jihad*."[54] This messianic notion that a "final" map of the entire region is now being drawn in blood sets the struggle of Hizballah in a larger pan-Islamic context for its adherents.

The strategy of an Islamic republic in Lebanon is therefore predicated upon Lebanon's inclusion in a larger Islamic state, which itself requires the success of Islamic revolution in adjacent lands. In this sense, Hizballah's strategy must be as grand as Lebanon is small. And until Iran's setbacks in the Gulf war and the cease-fire of 1988, Hizballah's spokesmen made victory in the Gulf war a prior condition for the realization of this vision. Husayn al-Musawi stated that "as long as the banners of Islam do not wave over Baghdad and an Islamic government is not established in that land, the establishment of Islamic rule in Lebanon is not likely."[55] His statement reflected the widespread conviction in Hizballah that the movement could not achieve its aims independently: Lebanon was an isolated island surrounded by forces hostile to the idea of an Islamic republic. Even were an Islamic republic established there, it would not be viable so long as Hizballah was not contiguous with the larger movement's consolidated base in Iran. Hizballah's spokesmen therefore emphasized regional victory over victory in Lebanon. In thought and deed, Hizballah accorded priority to the war between Iran and Iraq—struggle between "Truth and Falsehood"—on the assumption that an Iranian victory in the Gulf war would set the stage for Hizballah's own inevitable triumph in Lebanon.

This is what Husayn al-Musawi meant when he declared that "no person, Lebanese or Iranian, believes that what happened in Tehran can also occur in Beirut," and concluded that "it is not proper now to present a plan for the formation of an Islamic republic."[56] That would be premature, said Abbas al-Musawi, because the overall "program of expansion" had been "delayed" by the Gulf war.[57] Still, the ultimate triumph of Islam in this contest was not in doubt. Hizballah's newspaper offered exhaustive coverage of the innumerable Iranian offensives in the Gulf war, assuring readers that the victory of "the Islamic forces" was "only a matter of time."[58] For Hizballah, the Iranian claim that the Gulf war was the first step toward the liberation of Jerusalem was not a rhetorical one, but reflected the inevitable chronology of events according to the larger plan. Hizballah argued that until the successful conclusion of the Gulf war, Iran's Revolutionary Guards in Lebanon were under orders not to engage Israel directly. As Husayn al-Musawi explained, "they are far from their supply routes." But once victory was achieved in the Gulf, those routes would be shortened and the Revolutionary Guards would "be the vanguard of the holy struggle which will liberate Jerusalem. The road to Palestine will be open."[59] "Saddam will fall," declared Sayyid Ibrahim al-Amin during Iran's drive against Basra early in 1987: "We must ready ourselves to become soldiers in the Army of Jerusalem."[60]

In the minds of those who elaborated this vision, there was nothing fantastic about this expectation. No one had believed that an Islamic state could be created against the will of the United States and the Soviet Union in Iran, yet it was done. No one had believed that a few dedicated Muslims could have driven the Americans, French, and Israelis from the heart of Lebanon, yet they did. Hizballah attributed these successes to the divinely-inspired and virtually infallible guidance of the Imam Khomeini.

Yet that same obligation to obey led Hizballah to endorse what had been unthinkable: a cease-fire with Iraq.[61] Khomeini's decision to accept United Nations Resolution 598 must have had a demoralizing effect upon Hizballah, which had viewed an Iranian victory as an essential condition for Hizballah's own success. An article in *al-Muntalaq*, explaining Khomeini's decision, put forward two basic arguments: one suggested that even though the cease-fire spelled the end of the war, martyrdom in the path of God had constituted a spiritual victory despite the military setbacks; the other suggested that the cease-fire was no more than an attempt to buy time and regroup, in accord with the precedents set by the Prophet Muhammad in the first wars of Islam.[62]

These arguments could do little to soften the blow, and Hizballah felt none of the relief sensed by many Iranians following Khomeini's cease-fire decision. So long as the war raged and Iran promised to incorporate Hizballah in a larger Islamic strategy, Hizballah's cause did not seem quite so fantastic. The cease-fire deflated the illusion and demonstrated Hizballah's far greater dependence on a pan-Islamic premise for its sense of purpose. Islamic Iran, as a sovereign state ruling over a large land mass and a population of some fifty million, might choose to abandon the dissemination of its revolutionary message and settle for Islam in one country. But the equivalent for Hizballah would be to settle for Islam in a few Beirut neighborhoods and outlying towns, surrounded on all sides by enemies. While the promotion of a "great Islamic state" might have always been a "hallucination" for the Iranians, it represented an absolute necessity for Hizballah.

And so despite the defeat in the Gulf war, Hizballah has not abandoned its pan-Islamic assumption that the movement cannot hope to succeed unless Islam triumphs in adjacent lands. Since the cease-fire, the Gulf war has been replaced in Hizballah's discourse by events in Palestine, described by its spokesmen as the "Islamic *intifada*." The rallies organized by Hizballah are now devoted to solidarity with the *intifada*, which is interpreted as a sign that the liberation of Jerusalem is not a distant dream after all.[63] Islam may have retreated in the Gulf, but it is advancing in Palestine itself, even under the Israeli occupation. The outbreak of the *intifada* and the prominent role of Islam in the Palestinian uprising (greatly exaggerated in Hizballah's presentation) has allowed the movement's thinkers to sustain their fundamental pan-Islamic vision despite the setback in the Gulf. Instead of reformulating their program in narrowly Lebanese terms, Hizballah's spokesmen are engaged in a process of reformulating a pan-Islamic strategy that discounts the Gulf and fixes upon Palestine.

This is all the more incongruous at a moment when Hizballah is investing the better part of its military energies in a battle against Amal. In most respects, this is a typically Lebanese struggle between militia groups over the control of turf. Yet Hizballah refuses to understand the conflict in narrowly Lebanese terms: it is conceived by Hizballah's spokesmen not as part of the struggle for Lebanon, but as a chapter in the struggle to liberate Jerusalem. Hizballah is committed to that liberation, Amal is not, and so Hizballah's struggle in Beirut's alleyways is really a battle for the redemption of Jerusalem. Hizballah continues to refuse to legitimate its struggle against Amal in Lebanese terms, as though Lebanon itself were not a prize worth the fight.

This pan-Islamic perspective, even on the street battles of Beirut, invests profound purpose in every act of Hizballah. By embracing the broadest perspective, Hizballahis fight their little wars not as resentful men and women from one aggrieved sect in a small state populated by many sects; they fight as Muslims of the world, the vanguard of a worldwide struggle, men and women who have transcended the narrow limits of confessional identity imposed upon them by the Lebanese state and the "world arrogance" of imperialism. Without a pan-Islamic premise, Hizballah would be reduced to the sorry dimensions of a Lebanese militia—not soldiers in the "Army of Jerusalem," but the wayward bandits of Islam.

A Lebanese Face of Hizballah

In this sea of subservience to Iran, there is an island of resistance represented by one influential Lebanese Shi'i cleric closely identified with Hizballah. The views of Ayatollah Sayyid Muhammad Husayn Fadlallah constitute a balancing act between Hizballah's Iranian patrons and its Lebanese clients. He provides a counter-point to Hizballah's pan-Islamic premise, and so represents a source of unresolved tension in the movement.

Fadlallah owes his political ascent in Lebanon to his supposed influence over Hizballah. He is the most senior Shi'i cleric affiliated with Hizballah, and is unquestionably the most articulate and subtle advocate of Islamic rule in Lebanon. Fadlallah was born in Najaf in 1935, but his father hailed from a village in southern Lebanon. In Najaf, Fadlallah studied under the leading theoreticians of Islamic government and economics, but he also felt the moderating influence of another teacher, the Imam Abu al-Qasem Kho'i, renowned for his apolitical devotion to scholarship. Fadlallah arrived in Beirut in 1966, and there began a promising career in preaching, teaching, writing, and communal work. He also became involved in the activities of the Lebanese Muslim Students' Union, and the idea of an Islamic state figured prominently in his preaching after Iran's revolution. Following the Israeli invasion in 1982, he turned his pulpit into a platform for criticism of foreign intervention in Lebanon and appeals for the implementation of Islamic law.[64]

Fadlallah is a man of no small ambition who claims a following not only in Hizballah but in Amal and even among Shi'is outside Lebanon. He aspires to be Lebanon's great persuader, a man of religion who stands above the mire of Lebanese militia politics, and to whom all will eventually turn for mediation. He does not wish to disqualify himself from a future role that might establish his authority far beyond the confines of Hizballah. Fadlallah therefore has no interest in being singled out as the leader, spiritual or otherwise, of Hizballah. He has repeatedly declared that were he the leader of Hizballah, he would "have enough courage to own up to that fact. It is simply not so." This allows him to affirm that "I am not responsible for the behavior of any armed or unarmed group."[65] Fadlallah avers that he has a following within Hizballah, but he rejects even the label of "spiritual guide" of the movement.[66]

Yet for all that, Fadlallah stands atop the informal hierarchy of clerics associated with Hizballah. He is senior to them all in his learning and status. They sometimes turn to him for guidance, and he is a regular fixture at Hizballah's rallies. Many who are devoted first and foremost to Fadlallah fill the ranks of Hizballah, and adherents of Hizballah fill his mosque in the Bi'r al-Abid quarter of Beirut. Hizballah uses his mosque for gatherings, and it may be Hizballah that guarantees Fadlallah's personal security against would-be assassins. Fadlallah's speeches and lectures figure prominently in Hizballah's newspaper, alongside the statements by clerics who openly identify with Hizballah. There are ties of mutual dependence among Hizballah's clerics, their Iranian guides, and Fadlallah, and a sense of shared purpose binds them. But for all that, Fadlallah has his own agenda, and it can never be assumed that his own positions represent any significant body of opinion within the movement. Fadlallah may well be excluded from the inner circles of consultation in Hizballah. Of his many independent stands, the most important for the purpose of comparison are his approaches to the authority of the Imam Khomeini, the significance for Lebanon of the Islamic revolution in Iran, and the strategy of Islamic unity.

Fadlallah's attitude toward Khomeini is one of respect and admiration. "The Imam Khomeini represents an authority. He is a great and inspiring

Islamic leader, and, as such, we hold him in high esteem, and believe that he represents a mature and inspiring Islamic leadership."[67] Yet by this abstract and formalistic profession of admiration, Fadlallah dissents from the absolute allegiance offered by the clerics of Hizballah: Khomeini represents "an authority" but not the sole or absolute authority for Muslims everywhere. He is "inspiring" but not divinely-inspired. Once asked what most impressed him about Khomeini, Fadlallah did not cite the Imam's perfect judgement, but the fact that "he accepts no compromises with regard to himself or others."[68] While an admirable and perhaps even rare trait, this adherence to principle is not in itself a guarantee of infallibility. It is indeed rare for Fadlallah even to mention Khomeini unless specifically asked for an opinion by an interviewer. Unlike Hizballah's clerics, professions of allegiance to the Imam are not part of his repertoire.

More significantly, in the flood of words generated by Fadlallah there is no elaboration of the theory of rule by the just jurisconsult, the very bedrock of Hizballah's doctrine. This omission is not careless. Fadlallah remains to this day the general representative (*wakil amm*) of his former teacher, the elderly Imam Kho'i, who still resides in Najaf. In this capacity, Fadlallah continues to administer philanthropic institutions on Kho'i's behalf in Beirut. Prior to the Iranian revolution, the Imam Kho'i was widely regarded in Lebanon as the personal "source of authority" for most Lebanese Shi'is, and Fadlallah originally owed his standing and influence to his position as Kho'i's representative. Fadlallah must have sided with his teacher when Kho'i and Khomeini both taught in Najaf and Khomeini first began to theorize on the guardianship of the just jurisconsult. Kho'i claimed that no such guardianship existed, a stand which prompted Khomeini to deliver his famous series of lectures on Islamic government.[69] Fadlallah's present disinclination to proclaim the validity of Khomeini's theory is in harmony with his own intellectual origins and his continuing allegiance to his teacher.

Fadlallah admires but does not adore, and his attitude toward Islamic Iran has been one of respect mitigated by criticism. The regional significance of the Islamic revolution is not lost on him: he regards it as an "earthquake." But for Fadlallah, it is not an eschatological event above history, and it is subject to critical analysis. The Islamic revolution in Iran, despite the guidance of the Imam Khomeini, still represents no more than "an attempt to apply Islam. It makes mistakes, but it has the courage to admit its mistakes. It is trying to apply Islam to all aspects of life, but I do not think that it is 100 per cent successful yet because the changing of society requires time."[70] This view is doubtless held by others in Hizballah, but no one else dares pronounce it openly. Fadlallah is also bold in declaring his allegiance to his own conscience before all else. "I am not an agent for anybody's policy," Fadlallah once declared in response to a question concerning his relationship with Iran. "I am simply trying to implement my policy, which is based on Islam and which complements all the Islamic world's forces."[71] Fadlallah regards Iran as the "solid base" of the world Islamic movement, and he "adheres to Iran's line," but he asserts that "we are not agents of Iran, as the media try to depict us. We do not owe allegiance to Iran in the full sense of the word." Fadlallah has gone so far as to claim that "we have the freedom to have our own views on special Lebanese affairs when speaking to Iranian brothers and others. We have our own views even in international issues, methods of political work, and lines of political thought."[72]

For Fadlallah, the implications of the Islamic revolution in Iran for Lebanon are not necessarily revolutionary, and Hizballah's official slogan of "Islamic revolution in Lebanon" is not his. In Iran, there was "a population composed of Muslims only, which accepts the line of Islam, and a regime that had become an obstacle in the way of Islamic rule. The only solution was to fight this regime." But such conditions do not obtain in Lebanon, and revolution may not be the solution there. "Sometimes there are obstacles that a revolution cannot eliminate."[73] It is Fadlallah's view that the rule of Islam in Lebanon will be achieved later rather than sooner, given the certain opposition of other religious communities in Lebanon and their powerful foreign supporters. That opposition cannot be reduced solely through intimidation and violence, but must be eroded gradually through a campaign of persuasion. Once that campaign has succeeded, Islam can be made to prevail through democratic means. Instead of arguing for the divine obligation of obedience to *al-wali al-faqih*, Fadlallah argues for rule by the majority.

And so it was Fadlallah who prevailed upon the drafters of Hizballah's "open letter" to include a passage declaring that Hizballah sought to "allow all of our people to decide their fate and choose the form of government they want with complete freedom."[74] For the drafters of the "open letter," the will of the majority was of no consequence when weighed against the will of the divinely-guided Imam. But Fadlallah made freedom to choose a matter of principle, and it is only this passage that gives the "open letter" the faint ring of a document of compromise. On the basis of this achievement, Fadlallah declared three months later that "Iranian decision-making officials" now "believe that the Lebanese problem should be solved through democracy or democracy of the majority because Lebanon can bear no more suffering."[75] In fact, Fadlallah's position created much resentment among certain Iranians and some of the clerics in Hizballah, valued his oratory but did not always sympathize with the mind behind the mouth. They tried to consign him for a time to a purgatory of their own making, by not inviting him to Iran and by according him only marginal coverage in Hizballah's media.[76] But these forms of pressure had no effect upon Fadlallah's standing, and were eventually abandoned.

Fadlallah's position regarding Lebanon has implications for his view of the regional situation, which Hizballah views strictly through the ideological prism of pan-Islam. Fadlallah also speaks of Islamic unity, but not in the categories employed by the clerics of Hizballah. He does not refer to the near or eventual establishment of a "great Islamic state," even when he affirms the essential unity of the nation (*umma*) of Islam.[77] Neither does he refer to the "overall Islamic strategy" within which Hizballah claims to operate. The "export of the revolution" is understood by Fadlallah as a process limited by the power of the "exporting" state and the real circumstances of the "importing" countries. "We believe in exporting the revolution, but there is a difference between exporting the revolution as 'one unit' and exporting it as 'parts'. We believe that the nature of the actual circumstances necessitates its export as 'parts', since only this will bring us actual results."[78] The first of these "parts" is certainly not the establishment of a "great Islamic state."

For Fadlallah, the unity of Islam is not so much a process of political amalgamation as it is a process of sectarian reconciliation, especially between Shi'is and Sunnis. Because Fadlallah is aware of the tensions produced by this internal division in Islam, a tension which is acutely felt in Beirut and other parts of Lebanon, he has cleansed his rhetoric of nearly all Shi'i symbolism, with its heavy reliance upon the representative drama of Karbala. Often it is impossible to determine from the texts of these remarks that their author is a Shi'i. This is not the case for the other clerics in Hizballah or for the Hizballah-controlled media. Even while they proclaim the essential unity of Islam, they make as wide a use of Shi'i symbolism as Iran does, as though they expect not to be read or heard by Sunnis at all.

Fadlallah also understands the liberation of Jerusalem in an idiosyncratic manner. It has been argued that when Hizballah speaks of liberating Jerusalem, its hidden aim is to mobilize support for the seizure of power in Lebanon and the establishment of an Islamic state in Lebanon. In this view, the "rhetorical insistence on liberation comes second in the order of priorities of the Islamic movement," and the liberation of South Lebanon "is considered second to an essential goal, the establishment of an Islamic state. In that, the Islamic groups are not different from any other of the groups of the Lebanese civil wars scene."[79] This assertion is demonstrably false for Hizballah as a whole, but precisely explains Fadlallah's own use of the theme of liberation. Fadlallah has asserted that Israel's elimination cannot be achieved in "one, two, or ten years," but that "we must persecute Israel for one hundred years if necessary."[80] One day, says Fadlallah, Jerusalem will be returned, but "in this connection we think of great periods of time."[81] When Fadlallah preaches Jerusalem's liberation, it is to mobilize a movement to liberate Lebanon for Islam.

And so Fadlallah represents an independent line. Were the young clerics of Hizballah—Ibrahim al-Amin, Subhi al-Tufayli, Hasan Nasrallah, Abbas al-Musawi, Hasan Tarad—capable of mobilizing sufficient support on their own, the movement's Iranian guides might have dispensed with Fadlallah's services and perhaps even conducted a campaign to discredit him. Instead, Hizballah courts Fadlallah. Fadlallah does inspire genuine confidence in some powerful Iranians, such as Ali Akbar Hashemi Rafsanjani. But the supporters of Montazeri and some of the younger clerics in Hizballah have suspected Fadlallah of insufficient zeal for Khomeini.

The Persistence of Pan-Islam

Throughout its modern history, pan-Islam has evoked both apprehension and skepticism in the West. "Pan-Islamism was a fashionable bogy in the same way and at the same time as the Yellow Peril was," writes Maxime Rodinson of the late nineteenth century. "Any anti-imperialistic demonstration, even when it sprang from purely local feelings, was attributed to pan-Islamism. The very word suggested an attempt at domination, an ideology of aggression, a conspiracy on a world-wide scale."[82] But after the collapse of the Ottoman Empire, pan-Islam was dismissed as a species of bluff, deemed "ineffective" by Arnold Toynbee in a memorable passage in *A Study of History*.[83] The inability to penetrate the worlds in which pan-Islam has had some meaning—from the religious orders of the nineteenth century to Islamic Jihad in our own time—accentuates a tendency to over- or underestimate pan-Islam.

If the measure of pan-Islam's effect is its capacity to bedevil the West, then Iranian-inspired pan-Islam in the 1980s must be counted a triumph. But if the measure of pan-Islam's effect is its capacity to reconcile fundamental differences within Islam, then Iran's pan-Islam has clearly failed, as evidenced by sectarian interpretations of the Iran-Iraq war, the revival in the 1980s of vicious Sunni-Shi'i polemics, and the bloodshed during the pilgrimage of 1987.[84] Yet perhaps there are effects that are still hidden from view, working their way into the personal and collective identities of Muslims. On that level, it is not yet possible to know the consequences of Iran's pan-Islamic message.

Nevertheless, it is not too early to pronounce that Hizballah's growth in the 1980s has demonstrated that pan-Islam is not congenitally ineffective or anachronistic. Despite the apparent contradictions of the pan-Islamic premise, Iran and Hizballah have together inspired desperate men and women to act with pure zeal and purpose. The strong Iranian and Shi'i orientation of this pan-Islam has been its most serious limitation, and Hizballah remains the only mass movement outside Iran's frontiers to draw direct inspiration from the Imam Khomeini. But by its example, Hizballah has revived pan-Islam as a tenable set of assumptions about the real world. Pan-Islam worked for Iran in Lebanon because Lebanon was itself unworkable. Elsewhere in the Muslim world, similar kinds of unravelling may be underway. There are already signs that other Muslim movements, while rejecting the specifically Shi'i and Iranian content of Islamic Iran's message, are reintegrating a pan-Islamic premise in their expanding vision of the possible. This ultimately may prove to be the most far-reaching consequence of the heroic era in the short history of Hizballah.

Notes

Hizballah's weekly newspaper, *al-Ahd,* carries only the Islamic date. For the sake of precision, it has been cited here by issue number; the converted date appears in parentheses.

1. A growing secondary literature is devoted to Hizballah. The most extensive discussions are provided by Martin Kramer, "The Moral Logic of Hizballah," in Walter Reich (ed.), *The Psychology of Terrorism: Behaviors, World-Views, States of Mind* (Washington: The Wilson Center, forthcoming); French translation, "La morale du Hizbollah et sa logique," *Maghreb-Machrek* (Paris), no. 119 (January–February–March 1988), 39–59, with postscript by Jean Leca, 60–64; and Shimon Shapira, "The Origins of Hizballah," *The Jerusalem Quarterly*, 46 (Spring 1988), 115–30. For a brief description of the movement in the context of Lebanon's other Islamic movements, see Marius Deeb, *Militant Islamic Movements in Lebanon: Origins, Social Basis, and Ideology*, Occasional Papers Series of the Center for Contemporary Arab Studies, Georgetown University (Washington: November 1986), 12–19. Hizballah's relationship to Amal is briefly considered by Augustus Richard Norton, *Amal and the Shi'a: Struggle for the Soul of Lebanon* (Austin: 1987), 99–106. Cf. journalistic accounts of Hizballah in books by Robin Wright, *Sacred Rage* (New York: 1985); and Amir Taheri, *Holy Terror* (London: 1987).

2. For a partial analysis of Islamic Iran's policy toward Lebanon, see R. K. Ramazani, *Revolutionary Iran: Challenge and Response in the Middle East* (Baltimore: 1986), 175–95. The activities of Islamic Iran in Lebanon are also covered in the present author's essays in the *Middle East Contemporary Survey*, commencing with volume 8 (1983–84).

3. The fullest account of this assistance is the interview with the General Director of the Beirut office of the Martyrs' Foundation, *al-Ahd*, no. 135 (23 January 1987).

4. Speech by Shaykh Ali Yasin, *al-Ahd*, no. 88 (28 February 1986).

5. Nikki Keddie, "Pan-Islam as Proto-Nationalism," *Journal of Modern History*, vol. 41, no. 1 (March 1969), 27.

6. Niyazi Berkes, *The Development of Secularism in Turkey* (Montreal: 1964), 270.

7. See James P. Piscatori, *Islam in a World of Nation-States* (Cambridge: 1986), 114–15.

8. On the intellectual climate in this period in the Shi'i shrine cities, see Hanna Batatu, "Shi'i Organizations in Iraq: al-Da'wah al-Islamiyya and al-Mujahidin," in Juan R. I. Cole and Nikki R. Keddie (eds.), *Shi'ism and Social Protest* (New Haven: 1986), 179–200; Pierre Martin, "Le clergé chiite en Irak hier et aujourd'hui," *Maghreb-Machrek* (Paris), no. 115 (January–February–March 1987), 41–51; Chibli Mallat, "Aux origines de la guerre Iran-Irak: l'axe Najaf-Téhéran," *Les Cahiers de l'Orient* (Paris), no. 3 (3d trimester, 1986), 119–36; idem, "Religious Militancy in Contemporary Iraq: Muhammad Baqer as-Sadr and the Sunni-Shia Paradigm," *Third World Quarterly* (London), X/2 (April 1988), 683–98; and Amazia Baram's chapter in this volume.

9. For an assessment of Sadr and his legacy, see Fouad Ajami, *The Vanished Imam: Musa al Sadr and the Shia of Lebanon* (Ithaca: 1986).

10. Early co-operation between the Palestine Liberation Organization and Khomeini is documented in the booklet *al-Imam al-Khomeini wal-qadiyya al-filastiniyya* (n.p., April 1979). This includes such texts as Yasir Arafat's letters to Khomeini, and Khomeini's statements in support of the Palestinian cause.

11. *Al-Mustaqbal*, 5 March 1983.

12. The sharing of these symbols is considered by Yves Gonzalez-Quijano, "Les interprétations d'un rite: célébrations de la 'Achoura au Liban," *Maghreb-Machrek*, no. 115 (January–February–March 1987), 5–28.

13. For Syria's considerations, see Olmert's chapter in this volume.

14. Speech by Sayyid Ibrahim al-Amin, *al-Ahd*, no. 133 (9 January 1987). Sayyid Ibrahim al-Amin, Hizballah's official spokesman, is the most prominent cleric openly identified with Hizballah in the Lebanese capital.

15. This comparative perspective relies in part upon William L. Hanaway, Jr., "The Symbolism of Persian Revolutionary Posters," in Barry M. Rosen (ed.), *Iran since the Revolution* (New York: 1985), pp. 31–50, 150–72; cf. the report on an Islamic art and portraiture exhibit in *al-Ahd*, no. 87 (2 February 1986).

16. Photograph in *al-Ahd*, no. 34 (15 February 1985).

17. Shaykh Raghib Harb was born in 1952 in the village of Jibshit in South Lebanon. He spent four years as a student in Najaf until deported by the Iraqi authorities, and returned to his village where he gained a following and a reputation for outspoken militancy. At the time of the Israeli invasion, he was in Iran, but he returned to South Lebanon and was detained by Israeli authorities in the spring of 1983. Protests prompted his release. Later that year he returned to Iran, but in February 1984 unidentified assassins shot him dead near his village. Hizballah claimed that his murder was the work of Israeli agents, and Shaykh Raghib Harb immediately became the central figure in Hizballah's expanding martyrology, known as *shaykh al-shuhada*, "shaykh of the martyrs." Hizballah observes the anniversary of his death through demonstrations and the paying of homage to his widow, and he is even commemorated by an Iranian postage stamp. See *al-Ahd*, no. 34 (15 February 1985), which includes recollections and many photographs; and no. 88 (28 February 1986), with biographical details and more photographs.

18. See the photographs of field units of the Hizballah-sponsored Islamic Resistance carrying Iranian flags, *al-Ahd*, nos. 131 (26 December 1986), 132 (2 January 1987), 133 (9 January 1987). For a photograph of the use of the Iranian flag to drape the coffin of a "martyred" fighter, see *al-Ahd*, no. 155 (12 June 1987).

19. See Hizballah's "open letter" to the "disinherited of Lebanon and the world," which constitutes the movement's manifesto. The letter first appeared as a pamphlet entitled *Nass al-risala al-maftuha allati wajjahaha Hizballah ila al-mustad'afin fi Lubnan wal-alam* (n.p. [Beirut], 26 Jumada II 1405/16 February 1985) (henceforth: *al-Risala al-maftuha*). An English translation appears in Norton, *Amal and the Shi'a*, 167–87.

20. The Iranian examples have been studied systematically by Werner Schmucker, "Iranische Märtyrertestamente," *Die Welt des Islams*, vol. 27, no. 4 (1987), 185–249.

21. *Al-Risala al-maftuha*, 6.

22. The well-known revolutionary slogan in Persian declares that "God is great, Khomeini is leader" (*Allahu akbar, Khomeini rahbar*); the Arabic equivalent proclaims that "God is one, Khomeini is leader" (*Allahu wahid, Khomeini qa'id*).

23. *Al-Ahd*, no. 148 (24 April 1987). This theory is fully elaborated in a seven-part series on the theory of Islamic rule by Hizballah's newspaper; see *al-Ahd*, nos. 124—130 (7, 14, 21, 28 November; 5, 12, 19 December 1986). Nasrallah is one of the most prominent clerics from South Lebanon in Hizballah.

24. *Al-Harakat al-Islamiyya fi Lubnan* (Beirut: 1984), 150–51.

25. Speech by Sayyid Hasan Nasrallah, *al-Ahd*, no. 85 (7 February 1986).

26. According to Sadiq al-Musawi, *Tehran Times*, 30 July 1981.

27. *Al-Ahd*, no. 63 (6 September 1985).

28. *Al-Ahd*, no. 115 (5 September 1986).

29. For the debate over both issues, see Kramer, "The Moral Logic of Hizballah."

30. *Al-Ahd*, no. 135 (23 January 1987). It would certainly seem that the families of those who achieved "martyrdom" in this fashion have been assured that their "martyrs" died with the sanction of Khomeini. In the home of the parents of the youth who destroyed the Israeli military facility in Tyre (Ahmad Qusayr), there hangs a plaque presented by an official representative of Iran, bearing an inscription, the face of Khomeini, and the symbol of the Islamic Republic of Iran. A photograph appears in *al-Ahd*, no. 125 (14 November 1986).

31. Speech by Ibrahim al-Amin, quoted by UPI, 30 June 1987.

32. *Al-Nahar al-Arabi wal-Duwali*, 28 October–3 November 1985. Musawi, a school teacher in his forties, is the only prominent spokesman of Hizballah who is not a cleric. His Islamic Amal is subsumed organizationally in Hizballah, although it apparently remains under his personal authority.

33. The involvement of Shaykh Isma'il Khaliq in bringing the news to the Beirut magazine *al-Shira* is discussed in *al-Dustur*, 22 December 1986.

34. *Al-Ahd*, no. 126 (21 November 1986).

35. Editorial in *al-Ahd*, no. 125 (14 November 1986).

36. See especially *al-Ahd*, nos. 161, 162 (24, 31 July 1987).

37. Text of appeal (and reproduction of the handwritten text with seal), *al-Ahd*, no. 123 (31 November 1986).

38. *Kayhan*, 27, 29 July 1986.

39. *Al-Ahd*, no. 146 (10 April 1987).

40. *Al-Ahd*, no. 89 (7 March 1986).

41. *Le Révue du Liban,*, 27 July–3 August 1985. Shaykh Abbas al-Musawi spent eight years in Najaf before coming to the Biqa Valley in 1978 in order to teach in a local academy which he helped to found.

42. *Al-Ahd*, no. 97 (2 May 1986).

43. *Al-Ahd*, no. 85 (7 February 1986).

44. *Al-Nahar al-Arabi wal-Duwali*, 10–16 June 1985.

45. *Al-Ahd*, no. 88 (28 February 1986).

46. *Al-Ahd*, no. 115 (5 September 1986). Shaykh Subhi al-Tufayli, Hizballah's most prominent cleric in the Biqa Valley, spent nine years studying in Najaf, and a brief time in Qom.

47. *Al-Ahd*, no. 153 (29 May 1987).

48. *Al-Ahd*, no. 115 (5 September 1986).

49. *Al-Harakat al-Islamiyya fi Lubnan*, 148.

50. *Al-Ahd*, no. 128 (5 December 1986).

51. *Al-Harakat al-Islamiyya fi Lubnan*, 148, 160-63.

52. *Al-Harakat al-Islamiyya fi Lubnan*, 226-27.

53. *Al-Ahd*, no. 146 (10 April 1987).

54. *Kayhan*, 19 October 1985.

55. *Kayhan*, 27 July 1986.

56. *Kayhan*, 27 July 1986.

57. *La Révue du Liban*, 27 July–3 August 1985.

58. See especially the coverage of the drive on Basra, *al-Ahd*, no. 135 (23 January 1987).

59. *Al-Nahar al-Arabi wal-Duwali*, 10–16 June 1985.

60. *Al-Ahd*, no. 135 (23 January 1987).

61. Text of Hizballah statement on Iran's acceptance of United Nations Resolution 598, *al-Nahar*, 22 July 1988.

62. *Al-Muntalaq*, no. 46 (September 1988), pp. 58–70.

63. For accounts of such demonstrations, see *al-Ahd*, no. 195 (18 March 1988).

64. For a fuller biographical account, see Martin Kramer, "Muhammad Husayn Fadlallah," *Orient*, vol. 26, no. 2 (June 1985), 147–49. Some of Fadlallah's theoretical writings, mostly from the 1970s, have been examined in two articles by Olivier Carré: "Quelques mots-clefs de Muhammad Husayn Fadlallâh," *Révue française de science politique*, vol. 37, no. 4 (August 1987), 478–501; and "La 'révolution islamique' selon Muhammad Husayn Fadlallâh," *Orient*, vol. 29, no. 1 (March 1988), 68–84.

65. *Monday Morning*, 15–21 October 1984; *al-Nahar*, 3 October 1984.

66. *Al-Ittihad al-Usbu'i,* 30 January 1986.

67. *Monday Morning,* 15–21 October 1984.

68. *Der Spiegel,* 1 April 1985.

69. Gregory Rose, "*Velayat-e Faqih* and the Recovery of Islamic Identity in the Thought of Ayatollah Khomeini," in Nikki R. Keddie (ed.), *Religion and Politics in Iran* (New Haven: 1983), 177.

70. *Monday Morning,* 15–21 October 1984.

71. *Le Quotidien de Paris,* 23 September 1986.

72. Radio Monte Carlo, 13 May 1988; quoted in DR, 20 May 1988.

73. *Middle East Insight,* June–July 1985.

74. *Al-Risala al-maftuha,* 15.

75. *Al-Hawadith,* 24 May 1985.

76. See for example the minimal coverage given to his remarks on the seventh anniversary of the revolution, *al-Ahd,* no. 85 (7 February 1986).

77. E.g. interview with Fadlallah on Iranian television; text in *al-Ahd,* no. 152 (22 May 1987).

78. *Al-Ahd,* no. 125 (14 November 1986).

79. Chibli Mallat, *Shi'i Thought from the South of Lebanon* (Oxford: 1988), 36–37.

80. *Monday Morning,* 14 September 1986.

81. *Der Spiegel,* 1 April 1985.

82. Maxime Rodinson, "The Western Image and Western Studies of Islam," in Joseph Schacht (ed.), *The Legacy of Islam* (2d ed.; Oxford: 1974), 53.

83. See Arnold J. Toynbee, "The Ineffectiveness of Pan-Islamism," in *A Study of History,* vol. 7 (London: 1954), 692–95.

84. See Martin Kramer, "Tragedy in Mecca," *Orbis* (Philadelphia), vol. 32, no. 2 (Spring 1988), 231–47.

7

The Impact of Khomeini's Revolution on the Radical Shi'i Movement of Iraq*

Amazia Baram

Nowhere in the Islamic world did the success of Khomeini's revolution in Iran have such an immediate and profound impact as among the Shi'a of Iraq. According to the various radical Shi'i opposition organizations, and judging by the extreme reactions of the Ba'th regime, it galvanized large segments of the Shi'i population of Iraq and posed a significant threat to the regime's stability, or so it seemed to the regime at the time. But just over a year later, the regime was still very much there, while the radical Shi'i opposition was a shambles.

This chapter attempts to show that as long as the radical Shi'i movement in Iraq developed its ideology and the *modus operandi* of its institutions according to the constraints of the local environment, it had some modest but tangible organizational successes, alongside various setbacks. On the ideological level, the radical elements within the "Circle of Learning" (*al-hawza al-ilmiyya*) of Najaf even managed, between 1958 and 1979, to radiate their intellectual influence outside Iraq. But when they tried to imitate Khomeini's victorious revolution in Iran and to follow his directives uncritically, they played straight into the hands of the Ba'th regime and thus lost any chance they might have had to rescue their movement from disaster.

The Formative Years: 1958–1968 (Organizational Aspects)

The decline of religious Shi'i life in Iraq since the 1940s is well-known today. The number of students in the theological schools of Najaf and Karbala declined; so did their income. A general atmosphere of secularism

---

*This chapter was written during my stay as a Fellow at St. Antony's College, Oxford, and at the Woodrow Wilson Center for Scholars, the Smithsonian Institution, Washington D.C., 1988–89.

spread in southern Iraq, Communist influence spread and was substantially augmented after Abd al-Karim Qasim's advent to power in 1958.[1]

The response of the more activist elements among the teachers and students of religion in the holy cities became apparent on a number of levels: within a few years, two clandestine political parties were established; at least one circle of radical *ulama* was formed in Najaf, and a number of cultural, educational and philanthropic organizations sprang up.

The first political organization, the Islamic Da'wa party, was reportedly established back in 1958. According to most sources that deal with its genesis (including Da'wa sources), the leading figure among the founders was Muhammad Baqir al-Sadr (1933 or 1935–1980), a young and ingenious *mujtahid* who had become prominent among the radical (or politically active) *ulama* of Najaf in the 1950s. Sadr was also an important link between the activist circle of Najaf and a number of Lebanese and Iraqi students of religion there. Some of these eventually ended up in Lebanon where they established educational, cultural and charitable organizations intended to spread Najaf-style activist ideas. Others established a twin Lebanese Da'wa party that sought guidance from Najaf. For our study it is important to point out that following Sadr's execution in Iraq in 1980, the Lebanese Da'wa ceased to exist as an independent body; it merged with Amal and later with Hizballah.[2]

According to its own sources, as early as 1963 the Da'wa already numbered "thousands" of members. This seems inflated, but even the recruiting of a few hundred would have been a meaningful achievement. According to outside sources, it was at first a small cultural and educational movement. Only after 1968 did it become a decidedly political and military organization. In its early phase, at least, Ayatollah Muhsin al-Hakim and his family were somehow connected with the party's revivalist Islamic activities.[3]

A short while after the formation of the Da'wa, another Shi'i movement was established in Karbala by Ayatollah Hasan Mahdi al-Shirazi and his brother Ayatollah Muhammad al-Husayni al-Shirazi, and their two nephews Muhammad Taqi and Hadi al-Mudarrisi. The new grouping, *Munazzamat al-Amal al-Islami* (The Organization of Islamic Action, Amal for short) regarded Da'wa as too "soft," but in practice there was no real difference between their *modus operandi*.[4]

A third movement, the Islamic Movement of Iraq, was reportedly established later, in the early 1970s, in Kazimayn, by the descendants of the famous *mujtahid* who rose against the British in 1920, Muhammad Mahdi al-Kazimi al-Khorasani al-Khalisi.[5]

An organization of a different kind, tenuously connected with the Da'wa, was *Jama'at al-Ulama* (sometimes with the addition: *al-mujahidin*,) formed in Najaf sometime between 1958 and 1960. It also included a few *ulama* in other parts of Iraq but all were closely connected with Najaf. Muhammad Baqir al-Sadr was too young to be a full member of the group, but contributed articles to its magazine *al-Adwa* ("The Lights") and is said by his followers to have been the ideological moving force behind that group.[6]

Finally, during the 1960s Grand Mujtahid Muhsin al-Hakim and his followers established a variety of charitable, educational and cultural institutions that increased their political and ideological weight.

Muhammad Baqir al-Sadr's Intellectual Contribution

Of no less importance than the organizational developments were the writings of Sadr and, to a lesser extent, those of other activist *ulama* like Ayatollah Muhammad al-Husayni al-Shirazi and his brother Hasan, in combating western secularizing influence and arousing the Islamic conscience of the younger generation. In 1959, Sadr issued his *Falsafatuna* ("Our Philosophy"). By Sadr's own testimony, the book was aimed primarily at Iraq's secular, Marxist-inclined youth. In other words, the book is clearly an immediate response to a specific Iraqi problem: the Communist tide under Qasim, and is an effort to fight the enemy with his own tools.[7]

Sadr's second book with the same aim in mind, *Iqtisaduna* ("Our Economics"), was issued in Beirut in 1961. In it, Sadr presents a critique of both capitalism and socialism and tries to prove the superiority of the Islamic social system. He develops an approach to Islamic social justice that was new, even revolutionary, in 1960 in the Shi'i world, particularly in relation to land ownership.[8] The *shari'a*, Sadr states, enforces "an objective limitation on freedom" by instructing believers to obey the *shar'i* "rulers" (*ulu al-amr*). Where the *shari'a* is specific, it is the ruler's duty to act according to its instructions. However, in certain areas of economic activity it does not provide specific rules, and leaves a "free (or empty) zone" (or: "a discretionary zone") (*mintaqat al-faragh*). With regard to them, the ruler must be guided by the Islamic ideals of social justice. In traditional Islam, Sadr continues, "he who worked the land, invested in it efforts and redeemed it, has more right to it than others." This is so because in Islam "work is the basis for acquiring rights and private ownerships."[9] Yet today, with modern tools to work the land, one person can cultivate vast areas. If the traditional principle is adhered to "blindly," it will "rock social justice and [harm] the interests of the community." Thus, in this "free zone," it is the duty of the ruler to intervene in order to "prevent by compulsion" cultivation on a large-scale by a single individual.[10]

This theory was new in Shi'i religious circles and had many points in common with the thought of Ayatollah Mahmud Taleqani, who published his work *Islam va-malekiyyat* ("Islam and Ownership") in Tehran about the time Sadr's *Iqtisaduna* appeared. Both give the government wide-ranging discretionary powers, and both fully legitimize land reform to the extent that it is necessary to establish elementary social justice.[11] Given the closeness of the Shi'i establishments in Iraq and Iran, it is possible that Taleqani and Sadr were acquainted with, and possibly influenced by, each other's views. Yet each responded, with marked originality, to challenges in his own society. Furthermore, Sadr's book is clearly a continuation of his *Falsafatuna*, and forms an integral part of the much broader activity of the Iraqi *marja'iyya* aimed at combating Marxism. By providing an Islamic legitimization for land reform and by producing an overall theory of Islamic social justice, Sadr offered an Islamic alternative to those Shi'i youngsters who had turned to Marxism or to Ba'thi or Nasserist "Arab socialism" as a protest against the reactionary social approach of the *marja'iyya*. That Sadr's *Iqtisaduna* is far from being an uncritical imitation of the political thought of the Iranian *marja'iyya* is further demonstrated by the fact that both he and Taleqani soon proved to be exceptional figures, far from representing the general view of their class. In 1962 and 1963, the Iranian *marja'iyya* conducted a major battle against the shah's "White Revolution"—a reform program that included agrarian reform. Even earlier, the grand *mujtahid* Husayn Borujerdi, explicitly objected to land reform on the grounds that it was contrary to Islam.[12]

Even after the establishment of the Islamic Republic, many *ulama*, including leading *mujtahid*s such as Muhammad Reza Golpaygani and Sadeq Ruhani, objected to land reform as un-Islamic. In 1979–80, a fairly radical Agrarian Reform law was vetoed by the Council of Guardians. It was Sadr's posthumous vindication that the leaders of the Iranian land reform lobby drew mainly on his theory when they sought to legitimize their demands.[13]

In Iraq, however, Sadr's death at the hands of the Ba'th regime in April 1980 left the Shi'i activists without a guide, whether in the field of social theory or in other areas. (That will be discussed below.)

In his *Iqtisaduna* and *Falsafatuna*, Sadr contributed to the solution of another major Iraqi problem, namely the Sunni-Shi'i rift. In both books he is careful to deal only with issues of concern to both communities. This approach of upholding Islam as a whole is also apparent in a number of his books written in the 1960s and 1970s, some of which were published posthumously.[14] But it ought to be stressed that until his last message (see below) Sadr was not truly ecumenical; he never explicitly called for co-operation between the Sunna and the Shi'a based on mutual recognition of their legitimacy. Rather, he implied the existence of a wide workable common denominator between the two, mainly in the socio-economic sphere. In doing so, he showed respect for some Sunni sensitivities. And in two of his last three messages he turned to "the Iraqi people" as a whole.[15]

This quasi-ecumenical style was necessary especially in conditions then obtaining in Iraq. In the first place, to combat Communist, Ba'thi and Nasserite ideologies, Sadr had to turn to the Sunnis as well: to despair of winning them over to an Islamic society would have been a fatal mistake in a society that consists of close to 50 per cent Sunnis (Arabs and Kurds) and that has been traditionally ruled by Sunnis. Secondly, as pointed out above, many of Sadr's books were aimed at secular youths. He must have been aware that young Shi'is turned to Communism or Ba'thism in large measure because these movements offered them Sunni-Shi'i equality and a chance to integrate as equals in modern Iraqi society. (As is well-known, young Shi'is achieved great prominence in the ranks of both the Communist and the Ba'th parties during the 1950s and 1960s. Adopting a blatant and offensive anti-Sunni style would have been counter-productive. Young Shi'is on the point of turning secular would have regarded such an approach as anachronistic bigotry.)

A similar approach is apparent in some writings of at least one other leader of the activist trend within the Iraqi *marja'iyya*, Muhammad al-Husayni al-Shirazi. Indeed, such an ecumenical tendency was not new in Iraq; in the anti-British revolt of 1920, for example, Sunni-Shi'i co-operation was significant, as both sides realized that for them to have any chance of success they needed to co-operate. In a few cases, in 1919–1920, Sunnis and Shi'is held joint political meetings and prayers in Sunni or Shi'i mosques. Sunni-Shi'i ecumenism, which to Khomeini and other Iranian activists is essentially a matter of foreign policy necessitated by their commitment to export the Islamic Revolution, was to the Iraqi activists an urgent issue of home policy.

In the last months of his life, in his third and last message (in late 1979 or early 1980) Sadr became explicitly ecumenical; he turned to both sects saying: "I am with you, O my Sunni brother and son, as I am with you, O my Shi'i brother and son; I am with you to the extent that you are with Islam." He assured both "the sons of Ali and Husayn" and "the sons of Abu Bakr and Umar," that "the battle is not between the Shi'a and a Sunni rule," but rather between all true Muslims on the one side and a rule that is neither Sunni nor Shi'i on the other. This rule is an anti-Islamic dictatorship, and as such it is anti-Sunni as well as anti-Shi'i. Sunni rule, he explains, can be (in fact is) acceptable to the Shi'a, as long as it is truly Islamic; Ali himself, he points out, "raised his sword in its defense" when he fought under Abu Bakr against the apostates. Like him, Sadr promised "we shall all fight . . . under the Islamic banner" whether Sunni or Shi'i.[16]

It is true that in the writings of some modern Shi'i ecumenical *ulama* one may find a degree of legitimization of two of the first three caliphs whom Shi'is traditionally regard as "base, ignorant despots" who robbed Ali of his right to the caliphate.[17] Yet Sadr's legitimization for power-sharing and even for Sunni supremacy go much further; in fact: further than any writings of the Twelver Shi'a that the present author has seen. But Sadr's legacy is not that simple. Just as one can trace ecumenical tendencies in his writings so one can trace Shi'i particularism, with occasional anti-Sunni salvos occurring already in his first book and culminating in two of his last ones.

Sadr's first book *Fadak fi al-Tarikh* ("Fadak in History") was published when Sadr was not yet twenty. As Sadr's biographer and follower understood it, the book treated the highly emotional issue of the struggle between Fatima al-Zahra, the Prophet's daughter who became Ali's wife and the mother of the Imams Hasan and Husayn, and Abu Bakr and Umar, the first two caliphs, "who robbed her of her right" to the estate of Fadak. Even though Sadr was careful to treat the first two caliphs with respect the book is nothing but an attempt to prove how totally wrong they were.[18] Throughout his life, except in his aforementioned last message, when referring to a personality revered by the Sunna and criticized by the Shi'a, Sadr always treated them in a manner proper on the face of it, but, at the same time, he set out to expose them according to Shi'a tradition as dishonest and, on occasion, ignorant.

Sadr's legacy further complicates the issue of Sunni-Shi'i relations by invoking the principle of the political rule of the Shi'i Imam. As early as 1966, some four years before Khomeini published his *Islamic Government*, Sadr paved the way for Khomeini's assertion of "the rule of the jurisconsult" by arguing that the Imams were as much temporal political rulers and, at least potentially, military leaders as they were jurists and teachers.[19] The difference between the two, however, was, that while in Khomeini's thought the contemporary *faqih* enjoys a status identical to that of the Imam, and thus is the only person to be trusted with the ultimate political power,[20] Sadr was satisfied with giving a historical account, and left his listeners and readers to apply their conclusions to the contemporary scene. This difference is meaningful in terms of Sunni-shi'i relations because Khomeini left his audience in no doubt that the contemporary jurist-ruler was indeed a Shi'i *mujtahid*. In 1979, however, Sadr allowed himself to be swept off his feet by Khomeini's victorious revolution. In a reply to a group of Lebanese Shi'i *ulama* (some of them Najaf-educated) who asked him for a legal ruling on the Iranian draft constitution, he wrote:

> After the era of occultation [of the twelfth Imam] the Imamate was extended to the *marja'iyya*, [just] as the Imamate was, for its part, an extension of the Prophecy. . . . The *marja'iyya* is the legitimate [*shar'i*] deputy-general of the Imam. Accordingly, he [is] . . . the supreme representative of the state and the supreme commander of the army.[21]

Unlike Khomeini, Sadr did not even use the more general term *faqih* applicable to Sunni as well as to Shi'i *ulama*. Thus, towards the end of his life, Sadr augmented the dichotomy between the two poles of his theory: he drove Sunni-Shi'i ecumenism further than he had ever done before and, at the same time, created an unsurmountable obstacle in the way of Sunni-Shi'i co-operation by implying that the *whole* Muslim community should accept the rule of a Shi'i *marja*.

Here, too, Sadr's death left his followers and disciples (and *all* the radical Iraqi Shi'i opposition movements regard themselves as his followers) in disarray, and placed them at a clear disadvantage in their confrontation with the Ba'th which did its best to project a clear-cut ecumenical image.

1958–1978: Cautious Activism

As long as Abd al-Karim Qasim was in power, an important feature of the *modus operandi* of the Da'wa Islamic Party and of Hakim was that for all their relentless struggle against the Communist party, they kept a line open in the direction of Qasim. Even when they criticized Qasim, they took care not to burn their bridges. As a rule they blamed the Communists for the secularizing policies of Qasim's government and treated Qasim himself as an errant son who should not be despaired of. In an interview with *al-*

Hayat, for example, Hakim turned to Qasim very respectfully and asked him whether, "now, that the Communists were out of the way, would he abolish the secular personal status law which he had introduced." Qasim reciprocated by visiting him at his bedside when the chief *marja* was hospitalized and they were photographed chatting amiably. Years later, a moderate Shi'i opposition magazine spoke of this gesture as "heartwarming."[22]

Under Abd al-Salam Arif and his brother Abd al-Rahman, Shi'i religious circles, were critical of their socialist measures, which they considered un-Islamic. They also complained of the brothers' "official [Sunni] sectarianism" which they claimed, was occasionally translated into arrests of *ulama* and plans "to strike at the followers of the Prophet's family" (namely: at the Shi'a). However, according to these very reports, conflicts were settled through dialogue and non-violent protests, and no large-scale confrontations were reported between the Arifs and Shi'i circles.

It may be assumed that, the *marja'iyya* was keenly aware that the only feasible alternatives to Arif's religiously-inclined Sunni-cum-socialist regime were the Communists or the Ba'th secularists whom they detested. Their opposition to the Arif brothers' socialist and pan-Arab policies found expression under Abd al-Rahman, the second and less bright of the two, but at no point did it reach acute proportions. Furthermore, there is some evidence that Hakim was ready for limited co-operation with the Arifs.[23]

After the Ba'th coup of 1968, things changed: the first large-scale confrontation between the new regime and the *marja'iyya* of Najaf and Karbala occurred in the second half of 1969. In addition to the old, deeply-rooted mutual animosity between the Ba'th secularists and the *marja'iyya*, there were more immediate reasons for the confrontation. In the first place, the new regime was wary of the growing influence of the activist Shi'i circles in Najaf and Karbala, and it became clear that it intended to control education and other aspects of life. More specifically, an Iraqi-Iranian confrontation over the Shatt al-Arab had erupted in the spring of 1969 which aroused the regime's fear of a pro-Iranian fifth column there. The *marja'iyya*, for their part, complained of the new socialist measures adopted by the regime, and of the government's actual or alleged plan to license the sale of alcoholic drinks and to open places of entertainment in Najaf and Karbala. Government repression led to protests by the *ulama* and further complaints that the Ba'th was aiming at the destruction of the center of Islamic learning. There were a number of tribal uprisings in the south and at least one major clash between demonstrators and the security forces in Najaf that led to bloodshed. According to the usually well-informed Lebanese press there were many arrests, deportations and a few dead. Centers of Islamic culture and learning were closed down and many *ulama* fled the country.[24]

During this confrontation the *marja'iyya*, led chiefly by Hakim, made essentially defensive and fairly limited demands, namely that the regime should not interfere with the Shi'i centers of learning in Najaf and Karbala and should refrain from further socialist steps in the south. In doing so, the religious leaders refused to be drawn into a dangerous vortex by the masses who shouted during the demonstrations, *"maku wali illa Ali wa-nurid qa'id Ja'fari"* ("there is no ruler but Ali and we want a Shi'i leader").[25]

Another sign of the *marja'iyya's modus operandi* in 1969 was that they did not hesitate to swallow their pride and turn for help to the Pope, to Bertrand Russell, to Jean-Paul Sartre, to the secretary-general of the UN and to the Sunni Shaykh al-Azhar in Cairo. The fact that many *ulama* fled the country before the regime could lay its hands on them is further evidence of their down-to-earth approach: realizing that the regime possessed all the means of suppression, they avoided a frontal collision. Among those who sneaked out of Iraq were Ayatollah Muhammad al-Husayni al-Shirazi and, more surprisingly, Muhammad Baqir al-Sadr. The arrest of the former's brother, Hasan (who, in turn, fled the country as soon as he was released and went to Lebanon where he was assassinated in 1980) and the search for Mahdi al-Hakim gave them ample warning. Sadr's biographer insists that his "journey" to Lebanon was merely in pursuit of his duty, as he engaged in secret propaganda there in support of the *marja'iyya* of the holy cities.[26] Indeed, his activities there were so secret that he did not come to the notice of the Lebanese press and was allowed soon afterwards to return to Najaf without any reprisals. Whatever the precise reason for his stay in Lebanon, it is quite obvious that Sadr, Shirazi and Hakim, as well as seven other senior *mujtahid*s and 1,000 students of religion decided to act wisely rather than heroically and keep at a safe distance until the storm subsided.[27] The same decision was reflected in the flat denial by the *marja'iyya* that Hakim had at any time issued a *fatwa* against the "infidel atheist Ba'th government" who "desecrated the rules of our monotheistic religion."[28]

By contrast, in 1979–1980, under the influence of Khomeini's revolution, the political demands of the *marja'iyya* and its delegitimization of the regime were to be substantially radicalized and, in fact, came to leave no room for any accommodation.

But that time had not yet come. The 1969 confrontation abated after both sides realized that an accommodation was necessary. It started with an appeal by Muhsin al-Hakim to President Ahmad Hasan al-Bakr to release Ayatollah Hasan al-Shirazi, and with an open letter from the *marja'iyya* of the two holy cities to the president, listing their grievances.[29] At first, the regime responded with further acts of repression. Yet by late September, after a crisis with Lebanon that was pushed by its Shi'is to intervene on behalf of the Iraqi Shi'a, the regime allowed a delegation of Lebanese journalists, Sunni *ulama* and seven Shi'i *mujtahid*s to visit southern Iraq and to see for themselves that the holy places were suffering no undue repression.[30]

While tension between the two leaderships persisted throughout the seventies, it was sufficiently defused to allow for President Bakr's conspicuous participation in the funeral of Muhsin al-Hakim and for lavish praises by the Iraqi official press to the deceased *alim*. The Iraqi authorities also took a few other conciliatory steps.[31]

All these gestures, although unlikely to fool a seasoned political observer, could be made because the lines of communication between the most senior *mujtahid*s and the government were never completely severed. All this does not mean that Hakim was a quietist.[32] From the fact that he and his sons worked hand in hand with the most influential of the activist *ulama*, Muhammad Baqir al-Sadr, and from the description in the Lebanese press of the *modus operandi* of the Shi'a under him during the crisis of 1969, he emerges as a tough leader. His vigorous political and media campaign presented the Ba'th regime in a bad light in the Arab world and set Iraq and Lebanon on a collision course. (Iraq needed Lebanese ports for its imports and did not wish to push that country into Syria's sphere of influence). Hakim's policy was totally different, for example, from that of Ayatollah Ali Kashif al-Ghita, who headed a government-sponsored mission to Lebanon sent out to refute all anti-Ba'th accusations.

Despite his caution, Hakim was admired by Shi'i radicals, both during his lifetime and with the hindsight of the 1980s.[33] Indeed, the best-known of the radical *ulama*, Ayatollah Muhammad Baqir al-Sadr, took upon himself to edit an important study of his in a gesture of respect and appreciation.[34] In fact, Hakim was a pragmatic activist who very ably managed a crisis not entirely of his own making. Mindful of the limitations of his community and his class, he sparred expertly with a hostile, agitated, insecure, and thus trigger-happy Sunni regime.

The term "quietist" might suit much better another Ayatollah who was present at the time in Najaf as a political exile: Ruhollah Khomeini. Throughout the period of tension, the Lebanese press mentioned many names of senior and less senior *mujtahid*s who were in one way or another involved in the confrontation with the regime. Many of these were of Iranian origin, some had Iranian nationality. Khomeini's name was not mentioned once. In fact, when the 1969 conflict had only just subsided, Khomeini even gave an interview to the Iraqi government newspaper on the symbolic occasion of the Imam Husayn's birthday in which he supported the Ba'th policy of not participating in the Rabat Islamic conference. His inherent radicalism could, however, be gleaned from his vehement opposition to the repair of the Aqsa mosque in Jerusalem after the 1969 fire there, because "the ashes of the ancient mosque should remain in front of the eyes of all Muslims to remind them of the crimes of Zionism in 'Islamic [as distinct from Arab] Palestine'."[35] But this radicalism was not aimed against the Ba'th. No doubt, his position was vulnerable; as a prominent political exile from Iran, his stay in Iraq depended on the goodwill of the Ba'th. But then, some Shi'i activists, Arab and Iranian, risked not only deportation but their lives in 1969 and after; and, indeed, a few were executed (see below).

The tension between the regime and the Shi'i religious establishment abated, comparatively speaking, in the next few years. From time to time, new eruptions were sparked off by a variety of factors that are often difficult to trace. One such eruption occurred in 1970; another in late 1971 and early 1972 resulted from renewed tension with Iran. The regime deported scores of thousands of Iraqis of Iranian origin, sparking off demonstrations in the holy cities that resulted in many casualties.[36]

The next confrontation occurred in 1974, when the *Ashura* processions turned into "angry political protests." Apparently the Da'wa was responsible for the riots, at least in part.[37] Whether this was so or not, the regime cracked down on them. Sadr was arrested for a brief period and five Da'wa leaders were executed.[38] According to an Iranian report, these executions were accompanied by arrests and deportations of students of religion and the closure of religious institutions.[39]

At this new moment of crisis, Sadr proved that his political radicalism was matched by very cautious tactics: he safely distanced himself from the Da'wa by issuing a *fatwa* forbidding *ulama* from joining any "party organization."[40]

February 1977 saw the largest Shi'i uprising since 1969. As in most cases such as this, it occurred on an important religious occasion, the fortieth day after the *Ashura*.[41] As far as can be judged by the existing evidence, this event was not initiated either by Sadr or by the Da'wa. And although it was clear that a confrontation between the Shi'a and the authorities was looming in the offing, not even one *mujtahid* is mentioned by the opposition sources as responsible. Rather, the impression given in the detailed description of the event is that it erupted from the grass roots of the Shi'i religious community.

According to opposition sources the regime tried to persuade the leaders of the annual processions from Najaf to Karbala held in memory of Husayn, not to march that year. The leaders, whom the sources do not describe as *mujtahid*s, refused to co-operate and the processions left Najaf as scheduled. Despite a few serious incidents between the marchers and the security forces on the way, they reached Karbala on the third day. Throughout the march, the crowd shouted anti-Ba'thi slogans. (Government sources never admitted an attempt to prevent the processions, but admitted that people in the crowd attacked police stations and shouted hostile slogans.) In Karbala, many were arrested and no one was eventually allowed to enter Husayn's tomb; the authorities claimed that a Syrian agent had planted a bomb there and they sealed the place off, explaining that this was done to protect the public. Of particular interest to our study is the role played by Sadr in this incident. The most detailed opposition source reports that on the second night of the march, before it entered Karbala, the marchers were approached by Muhammad Baqir al-Hakim (son of the late chief *marja* and the future alternate head of The Supreme Council of the Islamic Revolution in Iraq [SCIRI, with its seat in Tehran]) whom Sadr had instructed to come there from Najaf. He was to persuade them to refrain from shouting provocative slogans and keep to traditional and harmless ones like, "*abadan wallah, ma nansa Husayna, ya Husayn ya Husyan*," ("By God, we shall never forget our Husayn, O Husayn! O Husayn!"). The marchers promised Sadr that they would abide by his request. All this was meant to deny the regime "a pretext . . . to disperse the procession with arms."[42]

In the writings of the Da'wa itself, even though they take great pride in the events of February 1977, calling it "the first Islamic revolution" that preceded the one in Iran, they did not claim responsibility for the events nor did they report any new Da'wa martyrs as a result of the 1977 riots.[43]

The Shi'i Revolution

The next major clash between the Shi'i religious circles and the Ba'th government occurred, for the first time in the history of the radical movement, as a result of an event that happened far away. According to the opposition's own account, demonstrations started in Najaf outside al-Hadra mosque on the first Friday after Khomeini's return to Tehran in February 1979. This time the demonstration was openly supported by Grand Ayatollah Muhammad Baqir al-Sadr and it was dispersed forthwith by the internal security forces: if it is true that two of the three most senior internal security figures, Brigadier-General Dr. Fadil al-Barrak and Interior Minister Sa'dun Shakir, were present, then this is a clear indication of the regime's deep concern. Possibly, their presence was meant to convey a hint to the religious circles.

According to Shi'i sources, Najaf youngsters started to pass out leaflets, apparently printed by *al-Da'wa*, and to write graffiti on the walls in the style of *"na'am lil-Islam, la li-Aflaq wa-Saddam"* ("Yes to Islam, no to Aflaq and Saddam") and to put up posters showing Khomeini's picture. For the first time there were also reports about Shi'i opposition activity in al-Thawra (later Saddam City)—the poor Shi'i quarter of Baghdad. Opposition sources reported that the public started looking for "an Iraqi Khomeini" and found him in Sadr.[44] Sadr reportedly issued clear-cut instructions to the public, through "scores" of his disciples whom he dispatched to "all parts of Iraq" (in fact, only to the south) to "lead there the Islamic revolutionary upsurge."[45] According to other sources his role was less direct, though he intentionally served as an inspiration to the revolutionaries.[46] Al-Da'wa reported that their leaders were in constant touch with him.[47] Be this as it may, all the opposition sources agree that Sadr supported the Iranian Revolution and expressed his wish for it to spread.[48] According to opposition sources, a wave of religious sentiment swept through Iraq. The number of girls wearing *hijab* in high schools and universities increased markedly and mosque attendance increased, apparently including worshippers who were Ba'th party members.[49]

Despite some conflicting versions, the dramatic and crucial events of mid-1979 through April 1980 as seen by the opposition (the Ba'th never published its own version and there are very few independent reports) may be reconstructed at least in their general outlines. And since the opposition's are the accounts that reveal its own mistakes most glaringly, there is no reason to doubt their general story, even if some details may be inaccurate.

Following riots in February and March 1979, the next two months were quiet because the public was effectively terrorized by the regime. Sadr started to re-think his tactics, and toward the end of May he decided to leave Iraq. When Khomeini learned of this, he hastened to send him a message informing him: "I do not regard it as appropriate that you leave Najaf . . . and I am worried about it." Sadr was quick to respond. In a meek message dated 1 June 1979, he did not deny that he intended to leave Iraq, but assured Khomeini that his "paternal interest" in Najaf was well received and that his "directive" (*tawjih*) (*sic!*) gave him (Sadr) "spiritual encouragement."[50]

This seems to have been the point of no return. From early June onwards, Sadr behaved as though possessed. The day he replied to Khomeini, Sadr gave the last of a series of lectures to his students in Najaf. In that lecture he said: "My father did not live any longer than I have lived now. My brother did not live any longer than I have lived. By now I have had my full share of life. It is [therefore] most logical that I should die at the age at which my father . . . [and] brother died."[51] On 12 June, Sadr sent a telegram to the "Arabs living in Iran" calling upon them to support Khomeini and Islam (and, by implication, to reject Ba'thism and Arabism as a political creed). The next day he was arrested, either because of this telegram or because of his call for a general strike in protest against the recent mass arrests. These had been the Ba'th response to the renewed demonstrations sparked by the news of Sadr's correspondence with Khomeini and his decision to stay in Najaf.[52] (Apparently, Sadr himself saw to it that they became public knowledge.)

But Sadr had given the regime a few more good reasons to arrest him. According to Shi'i opposition sources, when he realized that the brutal suppression of the demonstrations by the regime "made the Iraqi individual think twice before starting any anti-government demonstration" rendering street demonstrations "almost impossible," and after he accepted Khomeini's instructions to stay in Najaf, he "decided to break through the barrier of fear." He issued a *fatwa* forbidding Muslims to be members of the Ba'th party; he announced his "total support" for Khomeini's revolution, and in another *fatwa* promised immunity for shedding the blood of "the headless arrows of the regime" (that is, in the first place, the regime's security forces but possibly Ba'this in general). Moreover, he gave permission to disregard *shar'i* rules if this was necessary in order to purchase arms or engage in other *jihad* activities. Finally, Sadr instructed his followers to encourage popular delegations to come to him from the various parts of Iraq to express their support. At that point when, as the Da'wa itself put it, "the barrier of fear started to crumble, and people started to demonstrate again," Sadr was arrested. This, in turn, provoked mass demonstrations in al-Thawra and Kazimayn quarters of Baghdad, as well as in Diyala and the Shi'i south. These events coincided with Ali's birthday, giving the demonstrations a special impetus. When the government realized the extent of the demonstrations, it released Sadr the same day. Khomeini immediately added fuel to the flames by sending Sadr a message of total support.

Sadr apparently perceived his release as a sign of weakness on the part of the government, and therefore encouraged the masses to continue the demonstrations. Indeed, a day later his sister, Bint al-Huda, led a women's demonstration to Ali's tomb in Najaf. Other demonstrations erupted in Kufa, al-Thawra, Kazimayn, Samarra and Diyala. This led to severe clashes with the security forces which occupied parts of Najaf, Karbala and Kazimayn. Opposition sources reported "tens of thousands" of arrests.[53]

This time the authorities chose to put Sadr under house arrest in Najaf where he remained under guard until his execution in Baghdad in April 1980. His house arrest did not prevent him from reasserting, in a telephone conversation, his support for Khomeini, speaking of him as a "lighthouse of Islam" and as the guardian of the "monotheistic religion." On 16 June 1979 Sadr, clearly following Khomeini's example, recorded his first taped message to the Iraqi people. He accused the regime of imposing its rule on the Iraqi people "by force of iron and fire," yet his message, a combination of protest, warning and appeal, stopped short of an explicit call for the overthrow of Saddam Husayn.

His second message, recorded on 6 July 1979, sounded a very different note. In it Sadr branded the regime as "bloody murderers" and "despots" who, panicking at the sound of the people's growl, arrested, tortured and executed "tens of thousands" of Iraqis, starting with the *ulama*. He accused it of forcing the Iraqi people to comply with "Aflaq and other agents of the [Christian] mission and imperialism" rather than keep faith with Muhammad and Ali. The duty of every Muslim in Iraq, he went on, was to do his utmost, including giving his life, to rid Iraq of the Ba'thi "nightmare." He concluded: "I have decided on martyrdom, and this may be the last you hear from me. The gates of heaven have already opened to greet the [ascending] columns of martyrs!"[54]

Sadr's third message was recorded some time between mid-July 1979 and early April 1980. It called upon all sons of the Iraqi people, "Arabs and Kurds, Sunnis and Shi'is" to unite against "the ruling despots . . . [who] desecrate Islam, Ali and Umar alike" and to build a "noble, free Iraq, where Islamic justice will abound and human dignity will reign."[55]

By recording and sending out his last two messages he courted death: a message like this, if published or intercepted by the Ba'th, was sufficient to bring about his execution. His choice of a martyrdom was obviously more than rhetoric. Sporadic demonstrations and armed attacks on party and government installations continued through 1979 and 1980. When Saddam Husayn became president in July 1979, the government changed its tactics. The first step was a law enacted by the Revolutionary Command Council (RCC) on 31 March 1980 decreeing the death penalty for everyone who had at any time belonged to the Da'wa party or had helped in disseminating its ideas.[56] At the beginning of April, two students died when a hand grenade was tossed at Tariq Aziz, the Christian member of the RCC and deputy prime minister. Another grenade exploded at their funeral on 5 April, and another student was killed. The same day, Sadr and his sister were brought from Najaf to Baghdad, jailed for a day or two and then executed, apparently on the basis of the new law.[57] Within a short time, several hundred of Sadr's followers were executed as well.[58] In addition, between February 1979 and April 1980 about 10,000 people had been arrested.[59] In April and May 1980, tens of thousands of Iranian citizens and Iraqis of Iranian origin were deported to Iran. According to the authorities, "every Iranian family whose unfaithfulness towards the revolution and the homeland was proven was deported even if they carried Iraqi citizenship"[60]

Three years later, on 20 May 1983, 130 members of Hakim's family were arrested and six of them, three of Muhammad Baqir al-Hakim's brothers and three of his nephews, were executed as a reprisal against his activities in Tehran as heads of the SCIRI. A fourth brother was sent to Tehran with a written demand addressed to Hakim to stop all anti-Ba'thi activities.[61]

The most convincing sign that the backbone of the radical Shi'i movement had been broken as a result of Saddam Husayn's ruthless measures was that while Sadr's arrest had led to disorder and mass demonstrations, his execution, a year later, triggered no mass protests, either in Baghdad or in the south. The Shi'i opposition press had nothing to report and Khomeini expressed his distress at the lack of reaction (which seems to have shocked him more than the actual execution). In a message to the Iraqi people, he said:

> It is not surprising that the late Sadr and his wronged sister gained martyrdom but it is surprising that the Muslim nations, especially the noble nation of Iraq and the tribes of the Tigris and the Euphrates and the brave university youth and the other dear youth of Iraq accept these great calamities, which are inflicted upon Islam and upon the family of the prophet [Sadr was a *sayyid*] . . . with indifference, and thus give the chance to the damned Ba'th party to martyr their glories one after the other.[62]

When the late Ayatollah Hakim's sons and grandsons were executed in 1983, there were reports in the Shi'i press about demonstrations in Iran, in London, in Kuwait, in Bahrain, in Beirut and even in Nabatiyya, under the Israeli occupation, but not in Iraq.

Another indication of the collapse of the opposition was the fact that from mid-1980 onwards reports in *Al-Da'wa Chronicle* on demonstrations and civil disorders in Iraq were becoming more and more infrequent. (The last reported mass demonstrations in Najaf, Karbala, al-Thawra, Kut and Samarra took place between April and July 1981.)

There is no better way of learning about the situation as it looked to the radical Shi'a themselves than from the conclusion that the Da'wa drew from the events of 1979–1980:

> The uprising was successful but coming to think of it we realized that hastiness and the lack of short-term and long-term goals caused some people to hesitate as to what attitude to assume regarding this uprising. People did not know what the Imam [Sadr] had wanted from these delegations he received and what the aim had been. Moreover, no plans were drawn up with a view to counter the various reactions that the authorities . . . were likely to have. Furthermore no actions were planned as alternatives . . . panic and lack of

preparation were evident . . . the probabilities of the Imam's arrest [were not] studied carefully before it happened.[63]

Four years later, the party admitted that the confrontation with the regime in 1979–80 taxed the party so heavily ("tens of thousands of its members" being lost) that it had been completely disoriented. At long last it understood that "there are differences between conditions in Iraq and Iran. The formula that worked in Iran would not have the same effect in Iraq."[64] Muhammad Baqir al-Hakim, the spokesman of SCIRI, admitted that the call-up of Shi'i youngsters to the army, no less than the brutal suppression, totally prevented mass demonstrations in Iraq.[65] The party drew the conclusion that in the future the only means of action should be covert activity by small underground groups.[66]

Conclusions

For twenty years before the advent of Khomeini, radical Shi'i activists worked patiently and successfully resisted the temptation of a head-on clash with the regime. In these twenty years they made some progress. It is not easy to assess the numerical strength of the various radical movements or how far the activist message spread. But there are some indications. The Da'wa reported in 1984, as we have seen, that it lost "tens of thousands" of members. The mass arrests were tangible indication that the regime's assessment, too, was of a membership of thousands.

As for the spreading of the message, it is noteworthy that Sadr's *Iqtisaduna* went into 14 editions (the last in 1981) attesting to an undiminished and wide readership. Intellectual contributions of a similar kind also came from others in Sadr's circle in Najaf, as well as from Kazimayn and Karbala, and from Najaf-educated *ulama* in Lebanon. And Sadr's thought influenced the Iranian *marja'iyya*. Another conduit were the cultural and welfare institutions that sprang up in the holy cities of Iraq.

The arrests of thousands (if not tens of thousands) of Shi'i activists and the execution of hundreds hit the opposition cadres very hard and the deportation of hundreds of thousands of Iraqis of Iranian stock or of people who were suspected of pro-Khomeini sympathies denied the movement an important reservoir of public support.

Could Shi'i radicals have anticipated such harshness on the part of the regime? The answer to that question must be in the affirmative. The Shi'i radicals had ample proof of the extreme measures that were adopted by the regime when it was seriously threatened: The mass arrests and the closure of religious institutions in 1969, the mass deportations of 1971–72, five executions in 1974, the use of tanks to block marchers (and, according to one source, the actual use of tank fire to put down a tribal uprising in February 1977), and (according to the opposition) the arrest of 15,000 people, the torture to death or the execution of over 50 Shi'i activists in February and March 1977—all these should have been resounding warnings.[67]

Even if opposition accounts are exaggerated, independent reports and those of the government itself sufficed to convey the severity applied by the Ba'th regime when dealing with Shi'i uprisings. By then the Iraqi people had had ample proof that the regime treated even its own members with extreme harshness when they were suspected of plotting. The Shi'i opposition should have been aware that the Ba'th regime would stop at nothing when it comes to its very survival and Sadr's and Khomeini's words show that they knew this. The *modus operandi* of the oppostion is therefore more readily explained in terms of a mistaken evaluation of their chances to topple the regime rather than the regime's likely reaction to an attempt to do so.

This misjudgment which the Shi'i opposition had not made between 1958 and 1979 resulted, as may be concluded from the Da'wa's own accounts, from the intoxicating influence of Khomeini's revolution on the Iraqi Shi'is and from Khomeini's instructions. In practically every opposition magazine dealing with the events of 1979–80, it emerges that a near-messianic atmosphere took hold of the Shi'i areas of Iraq in early 1979. This led directly to major clashes between troops and opposition activists, with heavy casualties for the latter. But by May 1979, it was clear to the Shi'is that government coercion had brought mass demonstrations to a standstill and that the tactics which had brought Khomeini to power in Iran, had failed in Iraq. Hindsight taught the Shi'i radicals that "there are differences between the conditions in Iraq and Iran." By this they presumably meant the essentially Sunni character of the regime's elite and therefore its immunity (in comparison with that of the shah) to Shi'i pressures from within as well as to the criticism of Western public opinion.

Due to the failure of the mass demonstrations to topple the regime, Sadr seems to have concluded that there was a need to return to the old pattern of long-term underground work. Apart from his understandable wish to stay alive, his decision to escape from Iraq seems to have been intended to spare the radical movement the double setback of the death of the most important *marja* and further repression in response to further demonstrations. To follow a living *mujtahid* was a cardinal Shi'i rule. Even the most influential writings of a deceased *mujtahid* cannot take the place of a living one. However, all these considerations were waived when Sadr deferred to Khomeini. When he decided to stay Sadr must have realized that he had signed his own death warrant. This is borne out by his reference to his end being close, made soon after he received Khomeini's letter. It seems that Sadr decided to turn his death into a turning point in the Shi'i struggle. Remembering that his arrest alone had started major demonstrations in a number of Shi'i areas, he may have expected that his death would play havoc with the whole south and with al-Thawra quarter and give a new momentum to the Islamic Revolution in Iraq. Again, he and his followers grossly miscalculated. The regime's response severely handicapped the revolutionary cadres and Sadr's death deprived the radical movement of the only figure capable of holding together whatever was left of it.

The behavior of the Shi'i opposition in 1979–80 contributed towards the regime's decision to crack down on them as hard as it did, and made it easier for Saddam Husayn and his close circle to convince their party of the need to adopt the harshest counter-measures. In the same way it may have helped Saddam Husayn to convince the Iraqi public, or those who were undecided, that Iraq was indeed faced with the danger of splitting into three "statelets" (*duwaylat*): one Sunni, one Shi'i and one Kurdish.[68]

But Sadr miscalculated also in another sphere, that of ideology. In a moment of enthusiasm he gave his unreserved support to Khomeini's particular political system, yet at the same time he called for Sunni-Shi'i co-operation on the basis of complete equality. By doing so he left behind a riddle that only a living *mujtahid* could have solved. True enough, co-operation between Sunni and Shi'i religious radicals was, in 1980, a vision for the distant future, if only because of the almost complete absence of Sunni religious radicals in Iraq. But to despair of it, as the radical movement did after Sadr's death, was a serious mistake for any movement intending to conduct "the battle between Islam and *kufr*"—"a message that cannot be measured by time alone."[69] This was particularly evident in view of the efforts the Ba'th regime had been making since the mid-1970s to integrate young, secular Shi'is into the party as well as the state apparatus and the officers' corps (even though it had no more than partial success) and in a high-profile endeavor since 1968 to integrate Shi'i symbols into the Iraqi national pantheon. It was the secularist Ba'th rather than the religious Shi'i (or Sunni) activists who showed the greatest flexibility in bridging the Sunni-Shi'i divide, at least on the ideological and symbolic levels.[70]

Postscript

Beginning in the early 1980s, the center of operational and political Shi'i opposition activity moved to Tehran, with some Iraqi-Shi'i presence also in Syria and some political and cultural activity being maintained by the Shi'i diaspora in London.

According to the opposition sources, more than 10,000 Iraqi youngsters, members of the various opposition groups, were fighting alongside the Iranian army against "the Ba'th mercenaries." There are also many reports from opposition sources of sabotage activities in Baghdad, Iraqi Kurdistan and southern Iraq. If read uncritically, they create the impression of a lively, effective and a fairly large movement (or coalition of movements) working harmoniously with its host countries, and particularly with Iran. A more critical look, however, reveals grave problems. In the first place, even though the Da'wa is still central and SCIRI very conspicuous, the Shi'i opposition consists today of a large number of splinter groups (at least fifteen rather than two or three as in the past) and there is much evidence of political differences and rivalry between them and even within some of them, including the Da'wa. Secondly, it seems that relations with Iran are far from harmonious, and there are signs of resentment in the various movements at their lack of independence in the Iranian diaspora. But most importantly, to judge by independent reports of opposition activities inside Iraq, the movements have hardly been able to re-start grass root activities after the crash of 1979–80. In fact, all the existing evidence points to the expatriate movements being cut off from the main body of the Shi'i population inside Iraq. Following Iran's acceptance of the cease-fire in the war with Iraq, Shi'i opposition hopes, expressed so often, to return to Baghdad behind Khomeini's bayonets, have evaporated, and even guerrilla activity from the Iranian border seems to be seriously hampered since then. In short, the Shi'i opposition is likely to be in the wilderness for a long time.

SCIRI attempts to show a bold front, announcing that "our people's cause and its struggle against the Aflaqi regime existed before it attacked the Iranian-Islamic Republic and it will not end with the end of the war." It promised: "We shall continue to exercise our natural right and our Islamic and human duty. . . . The end of the fighting will not affect our legitimate right to continue our resistance and *jihad* until the *kafir* regime is toppled."[71]

At the same time, however, even the main opposition organ admitted in late 1988: "We are in dire need for plans of action and . . . brave initiatives . . . inside Iraq, . . . [because people say:] this is the enemy, and this is the arena, but where is my weapon and where is my position?"[72]

The answers to these questions are not easy, and thus it seems that the expatriates in Iran may be stranded in exile for a long time.

Notes

1. Uriel Dann, *Iraq under Qassem* (Jerusalem: 1969), 110–13, 125–26, 144, 234–93; Hanna Batatu, *The Old Social Classes and the Revolutionary Movements of Iraq* (Princeton: 1978), 858, 891–7, 950–53; Batatu, "Iraq's Underground Shi'a Movements," *MEJ*, Vol. 35, No. 4 (Autumn 1981), 578–94; Batatu, the same article updated, "Shi'i Organizations in Iraq: al-Da'wa al-Islamiyya and al-Mujahidun," in Juan Cole and Nikkie Keddie (eds.), *Shi'ism and Social Protest* (New Haven: 1986), 139–200.

2. Shimon Shapira, "The Origins of Hizballah," *The Jerusalem Quarterly*, 46 (Spring 1988), 115–125. Until his death in 1970, Ayatollah Hakim, combining economic resources and a charismatic personality, exerted the greatest influence on the Lebanese Shi'a among Najaf-based *ulama*.

3. *Al-Da'wa Chronicle*, No. 4 (August 1980), 6. An interview with Mahdi al-Hakim, *Impact International*, 25 April–8 May 1980, 550.

4. *Al-Massar*, 28 October 1987; *al-Nashra*, No. 5 (December 1983), 23–5, quoted in *JPRS*, 10 October 1984; *Jeune Afrique*, 25 January 1984; *al-Mukhtar al-Islami*, 17 June 1981.

5. Interview, Europe, July 1982. For al-Khalisi's role in the 1920 revolt see Ali al-Wardi, *Lamahat Ijtima'iyya min Tarikh al-Iraq al-Hadith* (Baghdad: 1976), 201–231.

6. A. Najaf, *Al-Shahed al-Shahid* [The Witness, the Martyr] (Tehran: 1981), 12, 27, 45; also *al-Shira*, 1 August 1986. On *Jama'at al-Ulama* see also Chibli Mallat, "Religious Militancy in Contemporary Iraq: Muhammad Baqir al-Sadr and the Sunni-Shi'a Paradigm," *Third World Quarterly*, April 1988, 716.

7. A. Najaf, 15; and see the 12th edition (Beirut: 1982), cover; and also 7–9.

8. While Sadr's political importance is recognized by all, his intellectual originality is a more controversial issue; see Batatu, *Underground*, 580; *Shi'i Organizations*, 182.

9. This view was, and still is controversial in radical Shi'i circles. See, for example, Homa Katouzian, "Shi'ism and Islamic Economics: Sadr and Bani Sadr," in Nikki R. Keddie (ed.), *Religion and Politics in Iran* (New Haven: 1983), 148, for Ayatollah Motahheri's views as set forth in Iran in 1980.

10. Sadr, *Iqtisaduna* (Beirut: 1981), 721–28, 302. See also Sadr, *Ikhtarna Laka* ["A Choice for you"] (Beirut: 1975), 118–122.

11. Land reform and nationalization were sanctioned at the same time among Sunnis by the leader of the *Ikhwan* in Syria, Mustafa al-Siba'i, but the two Shi'i thinkers leave the ruler much greater room for judgment. For an analysis of Siba'i's work see Hamid Enayat, "Islam and Socialism in Egypt," *MES*, IV (January 1968), 161– 63. For Taleqani's theory and more on Sadr's, see the analysis by Shaul Bakhash, *The Reign of the Ayatollahs* (New York: 1984), 166 ff.

12. See Azar Tabari, "The Role of the Clergy in Modern Iranian Politics," in Keddie, *Religion and Politics*, 66-72. Khomeini, too, issued a *fatwa* against land reform: Bakhash, 203.

13. Bakhash, 201–209.

14. For example, *Al-Madrasa al-Islamiyya* ("The Islamic School"), issued in 1962; *al-Bank al-la-Ribawi fi al-Islam* ("The Non-Usurious Bank in Islam"), published in the early 1970s; *al-Usus al-Mantiqiyya lil-Istiqra* ("The Logical Foundations of Induction"), published in the early 1970s; *Sura an Iqtisad al-Mujtama al-Islami* ("A Picture of the Economics of Islamic Society") (Beirut: 1979); *Khutut Tafsiliyya an Iqtisad al-Mujtama al-Islami* ("Detailed Features of the Economics of the Islamic Society") (Beirut: 1979).

15. See A. Najaf, 127–33; Harakat al-Mujahidin fi al-Iraq, *al-Qa'id al-Shahid Yuhaddidu Ma'alim al-Thawra al-Islamiyya fi al-Iraq* ("The Martyred Leader Defines the Characteristics of the Islamic Revolution in Iraq") (Tehran: n.d.).

16. A. Najaf, 135–38; *Al-Qa'id al-Shahid.*

17. Cited from Etan Kohlberg, "The Evolution of the Shi'a," *Jerusalem Quarterly*, No. 27 (Spring 1983), 115. For ecumenical expressions, see, for example, the Iraqi Ayatollah Muhammad Hasan Al Yasin, *Al-Imam Ali b. Abi Talib . . . sira wa-tarikh* (Beirut: 1978), 43–48. Also Shaykh Haydar al-Mirjani of Najaf, as quoted by Mallat, 703.

18. A. Najaf, 8; and see the issue of *Fadak* in Tehran, 1983.

19. See his *Buhuth Islamiyya* (Beirut: 1975), 57–70; al-Fayyad, 23-26. As for Khomeini, at least until 1963, he "defended constitutional monarchy." (See William Millward as quoted by N. R. Keddie, "Iran: Change in Islam, Islam in Change," in *IJMES*, Vol. XI, No. 4 (July 1980), 541. Cf. above chapter by David Menashri.

20. See, for example, Gregory Rose, "Velayat-e Faqih and the Recovery of Islamic Identity in the Thought of Ayatollah Khomeini," in Keddie, *Religion and Politics*, 177.

21. *Lamha Tamhidiyya an Mashru Dustur al-Jumhuriyya al-Islamiyya* ("A Preliminary Glance at the Draft Constitution of the Islamic Republic") (Beirut: February 1979), 13, 20. For a more detailed study of Sadr's theory of the Imam's rule which he developed since 1966 see my *National Integration and Exclusiveness in Political Thought and Practice in Iraq under the Ba'th, 1968–1982* (Hebrew University of Jerusalem, April 1986), 432–438.

22. *Al-Tayyar al-Jadid*, 20 July 1987.

23. See *Al-Jumhuriyya*, 8, 10 May 1964; *al-Thawra*, 27 March 1968.

24. For example, *Middle East News Agency*, from Baghdad, 7, 11 June; *al-Nahar*, 24 June, 5 July, 26 September; *al-Hayat*, 2, 11, 22, 23, 26, 27 June, 12 July, 2 August; *Nida al-Watan*, 21 July 1969.

25. A. Najaf, 27.

26. A. Najaf, 14–15.

27. *Al-Hayat*, 2 July; *al-Safa*, 19 July 1969.

28. This alleged or real *fatwa* was quoted by the Iranian broadcasting station of Ahvaz. The denial came in Lebanon within a few hours. See *al-Hayat*, 30 June, 1 July 1969.

29. *Al-Hayat*, 23, 27 June, 11, 12 July; *al-Nahar*, 5 July; *Nida al-Watan*, 21 July 1969.

30. *Al-Nahar*, 26 September 1969.

31. *Al-Jumhuriyya*, 7, 8, 12 November 1969, 23 June 1970.

32. The shah apparently regarded him as a quietist: in 1961 he implied that he wanted to see him replace the deceased chief *mujtahid* Borujerdi. Indeed, Hakim did not intervene in Iranian politics. But in the Iraqi context his behavior was radically different.

33. For example: A. Najaf, 11, 13, 26. *Al-Ahd*, 20 November 1987.

34. See Sadr's footnotes to Hakim's *Minhaj al-Salihin* (Beirut: 1980).

35. *Al-Jumhuriyya*, 23 October 1969.

36. See for example, *Reuter* from Tehran, 1 February 1972; and from New York, 4 January 1972. *Al-Da'wa Chronicle*, No. 10 (February 1981), 9.

37. Batatu, *Underground*, 590; H. R. Dekmejian, *Islam in Revolution: Fundamentalism in the Arab World* (Syracuse: 1985), 130, 218, quoting *al-Jihad* (the *Da'wa* weekly, Tehran), 14 March 1983.

38. *The Guardian*, 16 December 1974; *Imam*, April–May 1982, 56–61; A. Najaf, 29.

39. *Saddam Husayn Warith al-Shah*, (Tehran: 1981), 47–48.

40. *Al-Shira*, 1 August 1986; *al-Massar*, 28 October 1987, 13.

41. See *al-Jumhuriyya*, 8, 11, 12 February 1977.

42. For the opposition's version, see *al-Shahada*, 22 November 1983; *Saddam Husayn, Warith al-Shah*, 48–49; according to the latter there were some 200,000 people in the procession. See also *al-Da'wa Chronicle*, No. 10 (February 1981), 9. For the government version see *al-Jumhuriyya*, 8, 11, 12 February 1977.

43. For example: A. Najaf, 51; *al-Da'wa Chronicle*, No. 22 (February 1982), 4. Muhammad Baqir al-Hakim who had some connection with the *Da'wa* was arrested and later released.

44. *Liwa al-Sadr*, 9 February 1983, 5–7, 10; *Imam*, Vol. 2, No. 3–4 (April-May 1982), 59–60.

45. *Imam*, ibid.; A. Najaf, 58–59.

46. *Al-Da'wa Chronicle*, No. 3 (July 1980), p. 3; *Saddam Husayn, Warith al-Shah*, 51.

47. *Al-Da'wa Chronicle*, No. 37 (May 1983), 1, 8.

48. A. Najaf, 55; and see also in Sadr's *Lamha Tamhidiyya*, (Beirut: 1979), 15.

49. *Liwa al-Sadr*, 9 February 1983. Indeed, in the resolutions of the Ninth Regional Congress of the Ba'th convened in June 1982, the party severely criticized many of its members for having started to pay excessive tribute to religion.

50. A. Najaf, 63–4; *Imam*, April–May 1982, 61. And see the two following notes.

51. A. Najaf, 62.

52. *AP*, from Tehran, 14 June 1979; *Imam*, ibid.; A. Najaf, 131–2.

53. Hizb al-Da'wa al-Islamiyya, *Istishhad al-Imam . . . Sadr* ("The Martyrdom of the Imam . . . Sadr") (Beirut: 1981), 38–39; A. Najaf, 56–65; *al-Da'wa Chronicle*, No. 37 (May 1983), 1, 3; *al-Mukhtar al-Islami*, ibid., 75; *Imam*, ibid., 60–61; *al-Ahram*, 5 August 1979. According to *Imam*, Sadr's sister led a women's demonstration in Najaf

on the day of Sadr's arrest and they were joined by students of the Najaf theology school.

54. A. Najaf, 131–2; *al-Qa'id al-Shahid,*, 11–13.

55. A. Najaf, 135–138; *al-Qa'id al-Shahid,* 14–19; *Al-Da'wa Chronicle,* No. 3 (July 1980).

56. *Alif-Ba,* 9 April 1980. See also a later law to the same effect, *al-Waqa'i al-Iraqiyya,* 2 January 1984, 3.

57. *Al-Da'wa Chronicle,* No. 10 (February 1981), 9; *Imam,* ibid., 61; *al-Thawra,* 5, 6 April; *The Dawn of the Islamic Revolution, Echo of Islam* (Tehran: 1982), 57; *Impact International,* 25 April–8 May 1980, 5–6.

58. Tariq Aziz in *NYT,* 11 January 1981. Also, ibid., 3 April 1984. According to opposition sources, thousands of activists were murdered. For example, A. Najaf, 63–4. Amnesty International reported at least 520 executions from 1978 to 1980, and particularly in 1980. *Report and Recommendations . . . to the Government of . . . Iraq,* 22–28 January 1983, 21. Official admission, 39.

59. *Amnesty International News Release,* London, 10 March, 12 June 1980. According to the opposition, there were "tens of thousands" of detainees. For example, A. Najaf, ibid.; and *Imam* (April–May 1982, 60–61) claims that 20,000 were arrested.

60. *Alif-Ba,* 16 April 1980, 15. The opposition claimed that 40,000 were deported in this period (A. Najaf, ibid.). Many more were exiled later: an Iranian source estimated their total number at 500,000 Arabs and 40,000 Kurds, see *Tehran Times,* 28 February 1989.

61. *Al-Da'wa Chronicle,* No. 38 (June 1983), 8; No. 39 (July 1983), 3; No. 37 (May 1983), 1; No. 40 (August 1983), 8. *Sawt al-Iraq,* September 1983, 4; *al-Nahar,* 25 June 1983. For official confirmation of the executions from Baghdad, see Tariq Aziz to *Reuter* in Kuwait, 20 July 1983.

62. *Arab Press Service,* Vol. 13, No. 19 (November, 1980), 5–12.

63. *Al-Da'wa Chronicle,* No. 3 (July 1980), 4.

64. *Al-Da'wa Chronicle,* No. 49 (May 1984), 6–7.

65. *Imam,* III, 1 (January 1983), 30; and admission of Saddam Husayn's success in deterring people from demonstrating, *al-Da'wa Chronicle,* No. 16 (August 1981), 4.

66. *Al-Da'wa Chronicle,* No. 3 (July 1980), 4.

67. For all these, see: Hizb al-Da'wa, *Istishhad al-Imam,* 37; *al-Shahada,* 22 November 1983. And see reports of "widespread torture" by *Amnesty International Mission . . . January 1983,* 2–7.

68. For the first hint in this direction see Saddam Husayn's speech enumerating the reasons for the cancellation of the Iraqi-Iranian agreement of March 1975, *al-Jumhuriyya,* 18 September 1980. In later speeches he was much more explicit.

69. *Istishhad al-Imam,* 42.

70. For details see A. Baram, "The Ruling Political Elite in Ba'thi Iraq, 1968–1986; The Changing Features of Collective Profile," *IJMES,* XXI/4 (November 1989), 447–494.

71. *Al-Jihad,* 25 July 1988.

72. *Liwa al-Sadr,* 27 November 1988.

PART 3

The Sunni-Arab Heartland: Inspiration, Suspicion, and Confrontation

8

Saudi Arabia and the Iranian Revolution: The Religious Dimension

Jacob Goldberg

If we think of the Islamic Revolution as sending out concentric circles of ripples into the Muslim world, the Gulf falls into the innermost of the circles, with Saudi Arabia as its second closest segment (after Iraq). The strategic implications of this configuration have attracted much attention;[1] less so the religious dimension which is at the center of this chapter. Yet it was clear from the outset that the Saudi claim to "represent Islam," and the ultimate Iranian goal of exporting its own "authentic" brand of Islam would set the two countries on a collision course. The confrontation became all the more marked as both sides shared—strange as this may look—one premise: that religion and politics are inseparable. Islamic themes and symbols thus became central in the struggle to advance one's own position and undermine the other's.

In its drive for a leading role in the Islamic world, Tehran perceived Saudi Arabia as its main rival. That the presence of a considerable Shi'i minority there made the Saudi Kingdom an excellent target for exporting the revolution became a secondary consideration; primacy was given to the goal of replacing the Saudis as a predominant Islamic force. Hence Iran's aim was to weaken the House of Saud; to undermine its primary source of legitimacy—Islam; and to challenge its status of "Guardian of the Holy Places."

The first part of this chapter explores Iran's arguments and modes of operation in its "Islamic" struggle against the Saudi Kingdom; the second analyzes Saudi responses to the dangers and challenges posed by Iran.

Iran's Islamic Challenge to Saudi Arabia

Iran's claim to be the sole authority to speak on behalf of Islam inevitably challenged the traditional Saudi bid for Muslim primacy. Iranian leaders were determined to demonstrate that their Islam—revolutionary, radical, indeed messianic—was of a completely different nature from that of the Saudis. They claimed for the Islamic Revolution a much broader social, political and religious significance representing the yearnings of all Muslims for genuine freedom and progress.

It soon became clear that it was revolutionary Iran's policy to carry its message directly to the Muslim masses whom it claimed to represent, while simply bypassing governments. Khomeini depicted the Saudi regime as oppressive and as the ally of other oppressive Muslim governments. Naturally, then, Tehran expected the Muslim masses—and primarily those in the Arabian Peninsula—to be more receptive to Iran's revolutionary message than to their respective governments. It appealed to the Saudi people to "take control of your state in your own hands" and let it be understood that any popular Muslim movement directed against an oppressive regime would have Iranian support.[2]

A recurring *motif* was that "monarchy and Islam are mutually exclusive." Khomeini explained that Kingship was alien to Islam and an explicit deviation from its tenets. Hence, he spoke of the Islam of Saudi Arabia as "false Islam," or "American Islam."[3]

It was Ayatollah Husayn Ali Montazeri who, in 1985, took these charges one step further, calling into question that the Saudis, as followers of the Wahhabi movement, were Muslims at all. "Wahhabism was originally founded by mercenaries affiliated to foreigners, and its chief objective was to create factionalism and division between the world's Muslims. . . . This sect did not have any faith in Islam or the Qur'an, and Shi'is and Sunnis loathe this sect and the things that they do. The aim of this sect is to eliminate the history of Islam." A year later, he depicted the Saudis as "a minority sect completely isolated among Muslims, which is still bent on imposing its divergent notions on others."[4] Such attacks grew harsher after the Mecca incident of July 1987 (see below). Iran's Interior Minister Ali Akbar Mohtashami charged that the Saudi leaders had "supported the pioneers of paganism and apostasy." The Speaker of the Majlis, Ali Akbar Hashemi Rafsanjani, promised to avenge the martyrs by "purging the holy shrines of the wicked Wahhabis and by uprooting them from the region." Finally, Khomeini himself denounced the Royal Family, saying: "Mecca is now in the hands of a group of infidels who are grossly unaware of what they should do."[5] The implication was very clear: The Saudis were no more than a small, isolated sect; by contrast it was Iran which represented authentic Islam.

A second major argument was to draw an analogy between the Pahlavi dynasty and the Saudi Royal Family. The shah was not alone in having been installed and maintained by imperialism, said Ayatollah Montazeri; "British colonialists had put an illiterate Bedouin in power in Arabia, and now his discredited family, who are unfamiliar with Islam, control the Holy Cities." Saudi Arabia, a spokesman said, was playing "the same criminal role played by the Shah as an American station and outpost and bridgehead for Western imperialism."[6] Like the shah, the Saudi regime was squandering the resources of the country—properly belonging to the people. It had adopted the shah's "corrupted, hypocrite, secular, Western way of life." "The ostentatious display of wealth and conspicuous consumption by Royal Family members, and the evolution of a corrupt, Western consumer culture" all pointed to the failure of the Saudis to uphold the standards of Islamic morality and exposed the hypocrisy in "their commitment to an austere and ascetic Islam."[7] Iranian broadcasts mentioned the "$50 million private aircraft and the $20 million yacht" King Khalid had purchased and spoke of the "gambling habits of the Commander of the Faithful, Crown Prince Fahd." The Royal Family was "robbing the people's funds and spending them on gambling, drinking and shameless dancing and orgies." They referred to Fahd as "the new shah." No wonder, said Iranian spokesmen, that "many Saudis questioned aloud why they should be bound by a strict religious code of law enforced by the Royal Family, while the Family itself was at liberty to violate the law."[8]

The analogy between the shah and the House of Saud carried greater meaning: its ultimate point was the inevitable fate at the end of the road. As Iran was finally free of the shah, so the sacred places would be liberated from "the claws of Satan," and from "the reactionary, deceitful, filthy Saudi regime."[9]

A third major target were specific Saudi policies which, Iran argued, were an antithesis to Islam. For instance, Khomeini declared that the 1981 Fahd Plan for an Arab-Israeli settlement was a deviation from Islam and "whoever supports it is a traitor to Islam." Later, the Fez summit conference was condemned for passing a resolution "aimed at the recognition of Israel," something "totally rejected by Islam."[10] Even more vehement attacks were reserved for Saudi support of Iraq in the war against Iran. Iranian spokesmen condemned the "reactionary, deceitful, filthy Saudi regime" for "fighting Islam in the robe of Islam." How could a regime pretending to speak on behalf of Islam "support the Ba'thists, who do not believe in religion, in their war against the Islamic revolution in Iran?"[11] Other attacks on the Islamic credentials of the Kingdom centered on the sanctity of Mecca and Medina. The Iranian media accused the Royal Family of letting American-piloted AWACS planes fly over "the two holy mosques and other holy places in Mecca and Medina, thereby violating their sacredness."[12]

A fourth target of Iranian criticism was the Saudi religious establishment. Underlying the attacks was the Iranian effort to undermine the prestige and image of the "Wahhabi *ulama*" by portraying them as "political tools" in the hands of the House of Saud. The occasion for the sharpest attack was provided by Shaykh Abd al-Aziz Ibn Baz, Chairman of the Council of *ifta*, and the highest religious authority in Saudi Arabia. In a *fatwa* he issued in November 1981 regarding the widespread practice of celebrating the Prophet Muhammad's birthday, Ibn Baz ruled that "God has not decreed for us any birthday celebrations, either for the Prophet or for anyone else"; he urged all Muslims to abandon this "heretical innovation." Instructing all Iranians to observe the Prophet's birthday, Khomeini retorted that "this *mulla* [i.e.

Ibn Baz] was a lackey of the Saudi Arabian court who wants to implement the King's wishes; therefore, he stands against Muslims and makes such remarks: Is it blasphemy to respect the apostle of God? Does this *mulla* understand the meaning of blasphemy?" Shaykh Ibn Baz, he concluded, was "extremely ignorant of Islam."[13]

Another opportunity was provided by the controversy in Saudi Arabia regarding the right of women to drive cars. Officially asked to provide a ruling, Ibn Baz stated that "Islamic law banned women drivers since allowing them to drive is fraught with depravity, including being bare-faced, being alone with strangers, and running the risk of falling into incalculable sins." Khomeini quickly contested the *fatwa*, proclaiming that there was no religious objection to women driving so long as they observed all religious duties, including that of covering their faces."[14] All this was part of a wider Iranian campaign against Saudi *ulama*, whom the Iranian media frequently described as "preachers" (*wu'az*) and "court clerics" (*ulama al-balat*).

But polemics were not enough: they needed to be turned into practical policies. Soon after the revolution, the Iranian leadership realized that it needed an inter-Islamic mechanism to disseminate its revolutionary message. There was a need for Islamic organizations in which other Muslims could demonstrate their identification with the Islamic revolution and endow it with a much broader basis of Islamic support. However, the existing inter-Islamic bodies were either dominated or influenced by Iran's principal rival—Saudi Arabia. Chief among them were the Islamic Conference Organization (ICO) and the Muslim World League (MWL), both based in Saudi Arabia. The first Iranian goal was therefore to discredit them. President Ali Khamene'i referred to the ICO as a "reactionary tool of Western imperialism" and attacked it as well as other Islamic organizations for having fallen into "the hands of the same powers which themselves were the source of discord among Muslims and the obstacle in the way of their unity." The Iranian media portrayed the MWL as the subversive instrument of the House of Saud, consisting of "lackeys with connections to US schemes."[15]

Having been discredited, the existing organizations needed to be replaced. Already in 1980 Iran began to argue in favor of another Islamic framework which, rather than representing governments would represent the Muslim masses, especially those oppressed by tyranny. Consequently, in November 1980, delegates of five Islamic "liberation movements," including a Saudi one, met in Tehran to co-ordinate their efforts in fighting oppression. In 1983, Iran sponsored the First Conference on Islamic Thought, held in Tehran and attended by some 300 guests from 80 countries. A second such conference followed in 1984. Also in 1983, Iran organized the First World Congress of Friday Imams, a group of functionaries perceived as crucial if Iran was to successfully disseminate its message among the masses. About 130 prayer leaders participated in the first conference, 500 in the second. The meetings hailed Khomeini as leader of all Muslims, praised the achievements of Islamic Iran, and attacked the MWL and the ICO.[16] In addition, Iran began to seek other ways to expand its influence at Saudi Arabia's expense by calling for the formation of such new organizations as an "Islamic Front for Palestine Liberation," an "Islamic News Agency," and an "Islamic Common Market."[17]

Important as these conferences and schemes were, it was the annual pilgrimage to Mecca and Medina on which Iranian revolutionary theory focused as the principal means of spreading Iran's Islamic message among the oppressed and disinherited. In this view, the pilgrimage constituted the most authentic demonstration of Muslim unity and, as such, the most promising conduit for exporting Iran's revolutionary Islamic call. The *hajj* thus became a microcosm of the Saudi-Iranian confrontation.

As the first pilgrimage after the revolution was approaching, the new Iranian leaders advanced their old argument that the *hajj* was a political event no less than a religious occasion. Indeed, during the pilgrimage seasons of 1979, Iranian pilgrims organized demonstrations against the Saudi regime and in support of Khomeini and spread political propaganda among various Saudi groups. The same was done in 1980. Demonstrators, shouting "God is great, Khomeini is [the] leader," called for the overthrow of the Saudi regime because of its deviation from genuine Islam. The Saudi authorities found leaflets and brochures containing "subversive Iranian propaganda which had nothing to do with the aims of the pilgrimage," as well as photographs of Khomeini.[18]

Prior to the 1981 *hajj*, Ayatollah Khomeini himself blamed the Saudi regime, stating that while the "pilgrimage should promote unity among Muslims," some "so-called leaders of Islamic countries" used the *hajj* to impede unity. Despite Saudi warnings, Iranian pilgrims organized political demonstrations and carried Iranian flags and portraits of Khomeini; the Saudi security units had to break into the Grand Mosque and use tear gas to disperse demonstrators, and arrested many Iranians.[19]

That the 1982 pilgrimage would be even more unsettling than that of 1981 could be foretold by the appointment of Hojjat al-Islam Muhammad Musavi Kho'iniha—mentor of the students who had seized the US Embassy in 1979—as Khomeini's representative and supervisor of the Iranian pilgrims. This time the Iranians conducted "unity marches" during which portraits of Khomeini appeared and slogans offensive to the Royal Family were shouted repeatedly. Iranian sources said that the Saudis used water cannons and tear gas and tortured Iranian pilgrims. Among the many arrested was Kho'iniha himself. When the Saudis invoked "an agreement" they had with Iran which the latter had violated, Iran's deputy foreign minister stated that the Saudi interpretation of the agreement was based on "a misconception and misunderstanding."[20]

Soon the matter was taken a step further and Iranian officials proclaimed Saudi Arabia unfit to control the Holy Cities. Ayatollah Montazeri and Ayatollah Ali Meshkini demanded that Mecca and Medina be administered by "an international Muslim Council," and the Second World Congress of Friday Imams endorsed this demand.[21] Speaker Rafsanjani, who had originally disavowed the scheme, changed his mind after the Mecca incident of July

1987; he now vowed to "avenge the martyrs by purging the holy shrines and freeing them from the mischievous and wicked Wahhabis." Khomeini, too, stated that by their "brutal behavior" and "aggression in the House of God," the Saudis had forfeited the right, and indeed had demonstrated their inability, to rule over the holy places "which belong to all Muslims."[22]

Another area in which Iran posed a religious challenge to Saudi Arabia had to do with the large Shi'i minority in the Eastern Province (Hasa), in close proximity to Iran. Soon after the revolution, leading Iranian clerics, notably Ayatollahs Sadeq Khalkhali and Sadeq Ruhani, singled out Hasa (and Bahrain) as areas where "Shi'i brothers" were being persecuted and, hence, needed help. In the summer of 1979 leaflets began circulating in Hasa calling on the Shi'is not to co-operate with the Royal Family. Also circulating were cassette recordings of Khomeini's religious sermons with strong political anti-Saudi overtones.[23] It is against this background that one has to assess the two waves of demonstrations and violence that erupted in late November 1979 and early February 1980 in Hasa. These disturbances were undoubtedly rooted in the political and economic disenfranchisement of the Shi'i population. But active Shi'i resistance was sparked by the Iranian revolution and the propaganda emanating from Tehran. This was the first real political challenge posed by the Hasa Shi'is since the establishment of Saudi Arabia, and it was no coincidence that it surfaced just ten months after the revolution in Iran.[24]

The new regime in Tehran viewed the 300,000-strong Shi'i community in Saudi Arabia not only as an ideal conduit for the export of the revolution but also as a direct subversive instrument which could be used to undermine Saudi authority. The fact that the entire Shi'i population was concentrated in the most crucial part of the Kingdom—the oil region—made the Shi'is all the more valuable to Iran and exacerbated the challenge they posed to the Saudi regime. The danger was not confined to Shi'is: there was also the snowball effect that their resistance could have on other, still dormant opposition groups in the Kingdom.

In order to effectively activate the Saudi Shi'is and other potentially revolutionary groups, mass communication was critical. The principal medium Iran employed *vis-à-vis* Saudi Arabia was Radio Tehran's daily Arabic-language program. After the outbreak of the Iran-Iraq war, Tehran's Arabic transmissions were expanded to 17 hours a day. Most of the announcements addressed to Saudi Arabia were made in the name of a body calling itself "The Revolutionary Islamic Organization of the Arabian Peninsula," and the recurring theme was the call to "all oppressed Muslims to rise, [and] overthrow the corrupted, secular, deviationist Saudi family."[25]

The Saudi Response

Initially, as the Shah was overthrown and the Iranian clerics gradually consolidated their position, Saudi spokesmen were at pains to dispel any notion that they feared the new Iran. Instead, they went to great lengths in stressing the common Islamic factor. Thus, in a telegram of congratulations to Khomeini, King Khalid expressed satisfaction that the republic was "based on firm Islamic foundations"; Prince Abdallah asserted that from now on Islam would be the basis "of our relations and common interests." Other Saudi leaders expressed "relief that Islam and not heavy armaments" would underlie their dialogue and that this would remove previous "causes of frictions and tensions."[26]

However, it took the Royal Family but a short time to realize that the Islamic Revolution constituted probably the most severe challenge to the Saudi Arabian Kingdom in the twentieth century—a challenge to its very existence and security, to its social and religious cohesiveness, and, most of all, to its Islamic legitimacy.

The most immediate Saudi anxiety was that the revolutionary Iranian syndrome might be emulated in Saudi Arabia. Feeding such anxiety were forecasts made at the time that "the Saudis are next" and that "the revolutionary Islamic wave which swept Iran will inevitably engulf Saudi Arabia too."[27] The parallel drawn by Tehran between the shah and the Saudi Family heightened this anxiety, the more so as the similarities could not be denied: both royal regimes were conservative and pro-Western, ruling oil-rich Muslim countries caught in the middle of rapid modernization and socio-economic transformation. The Royal Family, then, needed to demonstrate that the revolutionary syndrome was not applicable to Saudi Arabia; to refute the analogy with the shah; and prove that the differences outweighed the similarities. How this was done will be shown presently.

But first we must note that the similarities were palpable enough to add their weight to the ongoing Saudi debate over the speed of modernization. The overthrow of the shah turned this from a somewhat academic exercise into an actual problem with alarming implications; Saudis began to fear that there was a nexus between modernization and instability. The Iranian revolution, so close to home, highlighted the risks inherent in rapid modernization and social change. On the one hand, Shaykh Ibn Baz declared that "Western-style economic development is a threat to Islamic values and the serene Muslim way of life."[28] Others argued that the pace had to be kept both to build a firm economic infrastructure and to meet rising popular expectations for a higher standard of living. The Saudi leadership was thus confronted even more sharply than before with the necessity to reconcile modernization with the maintenance of the traditional way of life. Furthermore, Saudi Arabia's own religious or fundamentalist circles were increasingly resentful of the erosion of traditional Saudi-Wahhabi values. Many of them were mindful of the gap between the official puritanical Islamic posture and the changing, often secular, daily realities, including the personal conduct of many senior princes. Against the background of such frustrations, could not the Iranian Revolution serve as an inspiring model? Was not the attack on the Grand Mosque in November 1979 a step in this direction?

With such questions in the air, the necessity to refute the Shah-Saud analogy became all the more peremptory. As Iran had questioned Saudi legitimacy on religious grounds, it was on religious apologetics that the Saudis placed the primary emphasis. They stressed that the Kingdom was genuinely Islamic and expressly rejected the separation of state and religion, and that the Royal Family had always ruled with Islam rather than against it, as the Pahlavi dynasty had done. Both the government and the House of Saud had consistently identified themselves as inherently Muslim and as dedicated to the service of Islam, its ideals, its laws and its final authority in human affairs. Was it a coincidence that Saudi Arabia was the only Muslim country to have no secular constitution but only the *shari'a* as its law? The shah's regime, by contrast, had distanced itself and the country from anything Islamic and the ideals it put forward were antithetical to Islam, thereby alienating many sectors of Iranian society. "Unlike the shah," stated Fahd, "we adhere faithfully to our constitution, the holy Qur'an, whose law is being carried out in letter and spirit."[29] To drive the point home, the regime adopted, in 1984, a new national hymn which was more Islamic in content and style. And in 1986, King Fahd ordered that the honorific "His Majesty" be dropped and replaced by "Servant of the Two Sacred Shrines" (of Mecca and Medina).

More importantly, Saudi leaders insisted that there had never been a conflict between the religious and political leaders: the House of Saud had always been at pains to keep close ties with the *ulama*, and to consult them on all major issues. In addition to links of kinship, the religious establishment had a vested interest in the perpetuation of Saudi rule under which they wielded a measure of power and influence they were unlikely to obtain under another regime. In Iran, in contradistinction, the shah's policy had put him on a collision course with the religious establishment. Alienated and antagonized, they felt that their long-held status, rights and privileges, as well as the Islamic character of the society, were all in jeopardy. Consequently, unlike the Saudi *ulama*, the Iranian clerics endeavored to overthrow the regime.

To substantiate such arguments, the Saudis began showing even greater deference toward the Wahhabi *ulama*, and to insist on a stricter, public enforcement of the austere and restrictive Wahhabi code of law and morality. Thus, in 1981 there was a crackdown on the employment of women, on the publication of pictures of women and on mixed bathing. Bowing to pressure from the *ulama*, the authorities imposed a ban on all religious services other than Islamic ones, even at compounds of foreigners. Hotel swimming pools, beauty parlors and women's hairdressing salons were closed. Drug smuggling was made a capital offence by a law anchored in the *shari'a* through a special *fatwa*. A campaign against cigarette smoking was started.[30] On the whole, much more power was granted to the "Committee for the Commendation of Virtue and the Condemnation of Vice" (known as the "religious police") in charge of enforcing a strict observance of Islam in public places. Also, more publicity was given to harsh punishments against all kinds of criminals.

Saudi spokesmen extended their arguments to areas not directly connected with Islam. Power in the Kingdom, they asserted, was not in the hands of one man, as was the case in Iran; rather, it was divided among a considerable number of princes who acted from mutual interest and strove for consensus. Moreover, unlike the Pahlavis, the House of Saud had roots in the Arabian Peninsula going back almost three centuries and had always maintained the Muslim tradition of direct access to the throne. Furthermore, in distinction from Iran where only a small fraction of the population benefited from the oil boom, Saudi wealth was more widely and equitably spread, reaching all levels of society. Consequently, the kind of a broadly-based movement which had sprung up in Iran was unlikely to occur in Saudi Arabia.[31]

But defensive argument was not enough; Saudi spokesmen and the Saudi media took the offense. They accused the "corrupt clique in Tehran" of having made Iran into a "slaughterhouse," to the point of setting up special gallows for hanging children. One Saudi commentator declared that the history of Islam offered "no parallel" to the "ferociousness, meanness and rancour" of Iran's present rulers who were "a disgrace to Islam," had, in fact, "nothing to do with Islam." Other commentators described the "butchers of Iran" as a "misguided and ignorant band representing the agents of Satan in Tehran and acting like mentally-retarded persons with all attributes of an insane fascist regime."[32]

Moreover, the Saudi leadership tried to convey the message that rather than exporting Islam, Iran was exporting terrorism and imperialism. Prince Na'if stated that the Iranians had "become the terrorists of the Gulf, working to destabilize the Gulf states." Khomeini's aim was "dominating the Arab side of the Gulf." To implement these designs, Iran was establishing "training camps where adolescent deviationists are being trained." Other Saudi commentators and editorialists compared Khomeini's ideology with that of the Third Reich in the sense that both "the Nazis and Khomeini" sought "to realize ideological and political plans outside their own territories." They predicted that Khomeini's fate would be like Hitler's and that the collapse of his revolutionary ideology was "imminent."[33]

Another target of Saudi criticism was the sale of Israeli weapons to Tehran: "Iran is body and soul in the same trench with Israel confronting Arab countries; Israel has found a good friend and ally in Khomeini who plays the role of Israel's surrogate in the Gulf."[34]

Finally, Saudi leaders started to refer to Iran by its former name of Persia in order to show up the nationalist aspirations underlying Khomeini's particular designs in Iranian policy, as opposed to the Islamic message Tehran claimed to espouse. In particular, they referred to the Iran-Iraq war as an "Arab-Persian conflict" in which "we Arabs can neither accept an Iraqi defeat, nor remain neutral."[35]

After the Mecca incident of July 1987, which the Saudis regarded as Iran's most severe provocation yet, they adopted unusually harsh language. Referring to Iran's leaders as "criminal gangs" and "barbarians," and to Khomeini personally as "Satan," Saudi spokesmen vowed to "try and demolish them politically and Islamically." Saudi attacks focused on Khomeini personally in a round of unprecedented newspaper cartoons and denunciations. Specifically, they made much of a wristwatch worn by Iranians, the face of which was inscribed with "the call of Khomeini"—a sacrilegious wordplay, the Saudis charged, on "the call of Allah."[36]

Such bluntness, however, characterized Saudi response only when the Royal Family felt directly provoked by Iranian behavior and statements. Otherwise, the Saudis sought to disseminate their brand of Islam by utilizing two principal frameworks: the Muslim World League and the Islamic Conference Organization. The first had its own periodicals, a publishing house and special agencies, and operated through hundreds of *imam*s and missionaries all over the world. It organized periodic conferences and financed Islamic centers, educational projects, published editions of the Qur'an, drawing on its annual government allocation of 100 million Saudi rials. The second, with its triannual summit meetings, was designed to boost the Saudis' self-esteem and bolster their international image.

Another step to demonstrate Saudi Arabia's Islamic leadership was the establishment of a $1 billion investment company—*Dar al-Mal al-Islami*—whose purpose was "to provide opportunities to Muslims to perform their transactions in accordance with the rulings of the *shari'a*."[37] Yet another was the creation of an annual award named after the late King Faysal—the "Faysal Prize for Service to Islam." In 1982 King Khalid received the prize, and in 1984 it went to King Fahd "for his commendable efforts to unite the Islamic community." In other years it went to foreign Muslim figures who either had Saudi ties or preached themes which could advance "Saudi Islam."[38]

The peak of Khomeini's challenge to Saudi Arabia was his vision of the pilgrimage and his relentless determination to politicize it. The Saudi regime faced therefore the recurring dilemma of how to treat the Iranian pilgrims. To deter Iranian participants by obstruction or to put a restricted quota on them would have been counter-productive, because it would have been interpreted as contravening Saudi guardianship of the Holy Places. At first, therefore, Riyadh issued the usual warnings against political activity during the pilgrimage and sought to arrive at some understanding with the Iranian authorities to ensure a tranquil *hajj*. In 1981, King Khalid requested Khomeini to instruct Iranian pilgrims to abstain from any acts which might disturb peace, but Khomeini turned him down.[39] After the clashes and incidents between Iranian pilgrims and Saudi security forces during the 1979, 1980 and 1981 pilgrimage seasons, the Saudis tried again in 1982 to arrive at an understanding with Tehran, asking the Iranian government to take direct responsibility for the conduct of its pilgrims. This turned out to be playing into Khomeini's hands. His personal representative, Kho'iniha, gave the Iranian pilgrims equivocal instructions. Eventually, the pilgrimage ended with Kho'iniha's arrest in Mecca.

It was not until 1983 that the two protagonists reached a certain compromise: there would be no hostile propaganda by either country against the other during the pilgrimage, nor were there to be calls for mass marches which had triggered riots and clashes in the past. Pilgrims would not be allowed to import printed matter of a political nature, and were not to initiate "spontaneous demonstrations." But Khomeini's representative would be allowed to organize two pilgrim rallies, one in Medina, the other in Mecca. Only slogans against the US, USSR and Israel would be permitted there. Also, the number of Iranian pilgrims was to be allowed to rise to 150,000, making them the largest single foreign pilgrim contingent. The compromise, made possible for reasons to be discussed below, ensured relatively uneventful pilgrimage seasons in 1984, 1985 and 1986. The visit of Saudi Foreign Minister, Sa'ud al-Faysal, to Tehran in 1985 provided an opportunity to discuss the *hajj* issue in the broader context of Saudi-Iranian relations and to reaffirm the understanding.[40]

But then came the most turbulent pilgrimage of 1987, which ended in the worst clash ever with Iranian pilgrims causing, according to Saudi sources, the death of 400 people—275 Iranians, 85 Saudi security personnel, and 42 pilgrims of various nationalities. With diametrically-opposed versions emanating from Tehran and Riyadh, it is still impossible to ascertain what precisely triggered the eruption of violence. What is certain is that the previous understanding was blown to pieces and that the Saudi authorities were adamant in their determination to prevent such Iranian excesses in the future: "We have been tolerating a lot from the Iranians when they conducted political demonstrations in Mecca. Unfortunately, they did not appreciate our gestures, and misconstrued our behavior as weakness. Under no circumstances will we accept the recurrence of these incidents."[41]

Indeed, the 1988 pilgrimage represented a turning point in Saudi policy toward Iran's participation in the *hajj*. The Royal Family felt that its inability to fully control the provocative behavior of 150,000 Iranian pilgrims was a major source of embarrassment for the Kingdom's status of Guardian of the Holy Shrines. Saudi anxieties were further heightened by Khomeini's statements in early 1988 promising to send even more pilgrims and to wage "even more vehement demonstrations with more vigor and enthusiasm" than in 1987. The Saudi leadership refused to go along with Iran sending over 150,000 pilgrims whereas the second largest group, of more populous Egypt, did not exceed 60,000. Consequently, Riyadh decided to limit the number of Iranian pilgrims to a manageable level. Unwilling, however, to portray the decision as aimed only against Iran and seeking to confer a stamp of all-Islamic legitimacy upon their policy, the Saudis decided to act through the Islamic Conference Organization. At its meeting in Amman in late March 1988, the ICO passed a general quota system of one pilgrim per 1,000 people from *each* Muslim country. Iran, thus, was allocated a quota of 45,000. Khomeini immediately rejected the quota and vowed to ignore it; but eventually he decided to boycott the pilgrimage altogether. The overall Saudi objective was achieved: the absence of Iranian pilgrims assured order and tranquility and, for the first time in a decade, the *hajj* passed without any demonstrations or clashes.[42] Similarly in 1989, no Iranian delegation took part in the *hajj*.

To the extent that the Iranian Revolution had a direct impact on Saudi Arabia's own population, the regime was primarily concerned with the

Shi'is, and all the more so in the aftermath of the riots of November 1979 and February 1980. It was obvious that the Iranian Revolution had sparked the disturbances. But the Saudis were also aware that the outburst reflected deeply-rooted Shi'i grievances arising from their perception of being second-class citizens suffering from social and economic discrimination.

The Royal Family, then, decided to devise a long-term policy and began to apply a stick-and-carrot approach. On the one hand, security forces put down the disturbances violently and swiftly, arresting many of the Shi'i leaders. But on the other hand, immediately after suppressing the second round of riots, the government launched a comprehensive plan aimed at improving the standard of living of the Shi'is in Hasa. This included an electricity project; schools for boys and girls; hospitals and clinics; better street paving and lighting; water, sewage and draining projects; youth welfare; telephone services, and other projects.

It seemed that the desire to mend fences was mutual; unrest in Hasa subsided, and there were no further riots. The Saudis, admittedly, managed to overcome the Iranian challenge in Hasa by a constant flow of money and attention to the Shi'is. But this, in itself, does not sufficiently account for the Iranian failure. It must be remembered that the Hasa Shi'is did not have close ties with the Shi'i clerics in Iran, nor did they have the clerical tradition of neo-fundamentalism or modern reformism to support an indigenous activist movement. Moreover, they became increasingly disillusioned by the turmoil that continued to convulse Iran. Detached from Shi'i centers in Iran, intimidated by the Saudi stick and tempted by the Saudi carrot, the Shi'is in Hasa did not assimilate Iran's Shi'i revolutionary ideology. The tranquility in Hasa, then, has been the result of a combination of Saudi success and Iranian failure.[43]

Finally, the revolution in Iran forced the Saudi regime to reassess its attitude toward the rapid pace of modernization that Saudi society was going through. Of particular concern was the impact that social and economic change had on the stability of the Royal Family, the problem being whether to let the process continue, slow it down, or limit its scope. It was Fahd, when still Crown Prince, who defined the Saudi response: "We want to see the development of our country, but a development based on our heritage, values and beliefs; we refuse to see progress at the expense of our heritage and moral fibre." And in 1983 he stated that "Islam accepts modern accomplishments and urges their pursuit."[44]

The conceptual response to the challenge was provided by the attempt to draw a clear line between Western culture and civilization and Western technology. While the former was rejected, the latter was seen as acceptable and legitimate since it was bound to strengthen and consolidate Islamic society and improve the lives of Muslims. But making such a distinction in theory was one thing; translating it into practical terms was something else. For in reality the two were very often inter-related and inseparable. In the absence, however, of a long-term solution to this basic dilemma and unwilling to slow the pace of modernization, the regime sought to minimize and mitigate its potentially disruptive consequences. This required walking a tightrope between the necessities of industrial development and the traditional, religious values and lifestyle.

But in order to do so, the regime had to distance itself from many negative aspects and undesirable social phenomena which either became identified with modernization or were its byproducts. The Royal Family began to show more awareness of the criticism directed at the way of life of its princes. In an obvious attempt to disarm criticism and cleanse the air of charges of corruption and misbehavior, the regime announced a series of stringent measures regarding the involvement of princes in business deals. Also, Fahd vowed to curb the flamboyant way of life of Royal Family members and other wealthy Saudis: "This is a disease that needs to be cured, perhaps by attaching a set of rules to Saudi passports to remind travellers [going abroad] that they belong to a Muslim country with traditions and principles which it is our duty to uphold and preserve." In addition, efforts were made to enforce anti-corruption laws which would outlaw payment of excessive commissions and limit the roles of middlemen. With similar aims in mind, the regime sought to limit contact between Westerners and Saudi youth as a means of preventing "decadent Western information" from circulating among Saudis. For that purpose, the Royal Family restricted the number of Saudis permitted to travel abroad and discouraged young Saudis at home from mixing with foreign residents. Finally, the leadership continuously sought to hold down the number of foreign workers, viewing them as an element which endangers "the traditional Saudi way of life."[45]

Conclusions

The multi-faceted challenge posed by the Iranian revolution presented Saudi Arabia with the gravest danger it had faced in the twentieth century. It embodied all the elements which the other two severe challenges—that of the Hashimites and that of Nasserism—had contained, but it had one major additional dimension: religious challenge, both ideological and practical, to the very legitimacy of Saudi rule. That this came in the form of an "export-oriented" revolution exacerbated the challenge. Though the Saudi leadership displayed a clear overall preference for cultivating "normal" relations and playing down the conflict, the religious issue frequently created severe frictions between the two countries.

Even at times of tension, however, the Saudi Royal Family consistently sought to keep its options open and maintain a dialogue with Tehran, hoping that political realities would eventually compel the Iranian regime to modify its hostile attitude. Indeed, whenever some modicum of reconciliation seemed to evolve between the two states, it was the result of *political* considerations which had nothing to do with the *religious* confrontation between them. On the Saudi side, such rare periods of *rapprochement* reflected more than just goodwill and desire to avoid a confrontation with Khomeini; they were also aimed at dissuading Iran from prolonging the war against Iraq. This was, for instance, the reason underlying King Fahd's personal invitation to Rafsanjani to visit Mecca during the pilgrimage of September 1984, a visit vetoed by Khomeini.[46]

On the Iranian side, attempts at *rapprochement* with Riyadh can be accounted for by three separate sets of reasons. First, the Iranian leaders were interested in drawing Saudi Arabia away from Baghdad, so as to weaken Iraq's war effort. Secondly, internal rivalries in Tehran affected the course of Saudi-Iranian relations, with Rafsanjani's camp opting for a more conciliatory attitude towards Riyadh, against the wishes of Montazeri. Thirdly, a Saudi-Iranian semi-*rapprochement* in 1985 and 1986 was part of the American-Iranian abortive deal also known as "Irangate." It manifested itself by quiet pilgrimage seasons, exchange of visits by senior ministers from both sides and a general relaxation in the propaganda war between the two countries.[47]

On the whole, changing Iranian attitudes towards Saudi Arabia reflected fluctuating priorities in Tehran: the initial centrality of the goal of exporting the revolution *versus* what was described as "the normalization of Iran's foreign policy." Indeed, the magnitude of the challenge Iran posed to Saudi Arabia was primarily a function of *Iranian* considerations and priorities. This exposes a salient feature in the pattern of relations: In their religious-Islamic confrontation, it was always Iran which held the initiative, while the Saudis merely reacted.

In the Saudi-Iranian struggle to capture the support of the Muslim world, it was inevitable that the weaknesses and vulnerabilities of each side be exhibited. If the ICO was thought of as the main instrument in the Saudi plan, then the ICO's summits exposed some of the basic Saudi weakness: the Organization's lack of political unity. This was conspicuous in the summits' inability to cope with any major conflict involving Muslim countries: the Soviet invasion of Afghanistan, the Iraq-Iran war, the Western Sahara conflict and the Lebanese crisis. In the aftermath of the conferences, the weaknesses appeared to weigh more heavily than Saudi initial aspirations and successes.

But in the final account, they were balanced by Tehran's failure to create alternative all-Islamic institutions which would serve as an effective sounding board for its message. If Iran has so far been unable to turn its challenge into concrete achievements, that was not so much due to Saudi success as to Iranian shortcomings.

Notes

1. For a study of these issues, see Shahram Chubin's "Iran and its Neighbours," *Conflict Studies*, No. 204 (1987), and his chapter in this volume.

2. IRNA, 15 October—SWB, 16 October 1981.

3. *Al-Shahid*, 25 November 1981.

4. Radio Tehran, 1 December—SWB, 3 December 1985; R. Tehran, 9 September—SWB, 10 September 1986.

5. *NYT*, 3, 9 and 25 August 1987.

6. Radio Tehran, 10 October—SWB, 12 October 1982; Radio Tehran, 6 March—DR, 8 March 1980. See also Marvin Zonis and Daniel Brumberg, "Shi'ism as Interpreted by Khomeini: An Ideology of Revolutionary Violence," in Martin Kramer (ed.), *Shi'ism, Resistance, and Revolution* (Boulder: 1987), 51.

7. Radio Tehran, 6 March—DR, 8 March 1980; *NYT*, 25 February 1980.

8. Radio Tehran (in Arabic), 8 March—SWB, 11 March 1980; *NYT*, 25 August 1987; *Crescent International*, 16-31 January 1984; *al-Hawadith*, 9 November 1979.

9. Radio Tehran, 10 October—SWB, 12 October 1982; Radio Tehran, 4 October—SWB, 7 October 1980.

10. *Al-Shahid*, 23 September and 25 November; Radio Tehran, 6 September—DR, 8 September 1981; Radio Tehran, 4 September—SWB, 7 September 1982.

11. Radio Tehran, 4 October—SWB, 7 October 1980.

12. Radio Tehran, 7 November—DR, 9 November 1981.

13. Saudi Press Agency (SPA), 21 November—SWB, 24 November; *Akhbar al-Alam al-Islami*, 23 November; Radio Tehran, 16 December—SWB, 17 December 1981.

14. *Al-Jazira*, 28 December; *Kayhan al-Arabi*, 30 December 1981.

15. IRNA, 6 May—DR, 7 May; *Tehran Times*, 7 May; *Crescent International*, 16-31 January 1984; Radio Tehran, 1 August—DR, 1 August; Radio Tehran (in Arabic), 4 August—DR, 7 August 1985.

16. For details on the conferences, see Martin Kramer, "The Muslim Consensus Undone," *MECS*, 1981–82, 290–1; "The Divided House of Islam," *MECS*, 1982–83, 239–40; and "Muslim Statecraft and Subversion," *MECS*, 1983–84, 168.

17. Radio Tehran, 24 August—SWB, 28 August; IRNA, 4 October—SWB, 6 October 1981; *Kayhan al-Arabi*, 1 and 2 May 1982.

18. Radio Tehran, 28 September—DR, 1 October 1979; *Akhir Sa'a*, 7 May; SPA, 9 October—SWB, 11 October 1980.

19. *Daily Telegraph*, 25 September; IRNA, 4 October—DR, 5 October; Radio Tehran (in Arabic), 5 October—DR, 6 October; for the Saudi version, see *Ukaz*, 5 August; *al-Riyad*, 1 September; *al-Jazira*, 1 October; Radio Riyadh, 19 October—DR, 20 October 1981.

20. Radio Riyadh, 10 September—SWB, 13 September; Radio Tehran, 16 September—DR, 18 September; Radio Tehran, 15 September—DR, 16 September 1982; Radio Tehran, 24 September—DR, 24 September; IRNA, 24 September—DR, 27 September 1982.

21. Radio Tehran, 10 October—SWB, 12 October 1982; IRNA, 8 July—SWB, 10 July; text of resolutions is in *Kayhan al-Arabi*, 3 January, and *Tehran Times*, 4 January 1983; Radio Tehran, 10 July—DR, 11 July 1984.

22. *NYT*, 3 and 6 August; IRNA, 2 August—DR, 4 August 1987.

23. MENA, 20 January 1980; *Financial Times*, 12 March; for a discussion of the disturbances, see Jacob Goldberg, "The Saudi Arabian Kingdom," *MECS*, 1979–80, 688–90.

24. For an extensive analysis of the Shi'i problem in Saudi Arabia, see Jacob Goldberg, "The Shi'i Minority in Saudi Arabia," in Juan Cole and Nikki Keddie (eds.), *Shi'ism and Social Protest* (New Haven: 1986), 230–46.

25. See for example Radio Tehran (in Arabic), 8 and 14 March—SWB, 10 and 17 March 1980, respectively.

26. Saudi News Agency, 2 April—DR, 3 April; Gulf News Agency, 21 April—DR, 25 April; Na'if's interview with *al-Hawadith*, 22 June 1979.

27. *Newsweek*, 12 February 1979.

28. Interview with the *NYT*, 25 March 1981.

29. *Newsweek*, 28 January 1979; *Al-Riyad*, 23 February 1980.

30. Accounts by eye witnesses, quoted in *The Observer*, 12 August 1979; Radio Riyadh, 10 March—SWB, 12 March 1987.

31. *Arabian News*, 17 January 1979; *Al-Hawadith*, 23 February.

32. Radio Riyadh, 8 November—DR, 9 November; Radio Riyadh, 17, 18 November—SWB, 19, 20 November 1981, respectively.

33. *The Times*, 21 December 1981; *al-Madina*, 12 February; *al-Siyasa*, 28 March; *al-Madina*, 12 February; *al-Riyad*, 2 May 1982.

34. *Ukaz*, 2 December 1981; *al-Jazira*, 5 January, 28 May; Radio Riyadh, 27 May—DR, 29 May 1982.

35. *al-Sharq al-Awsat*, 24 September; *Ukaz*, 26 September; Iraqi News Agency, 25 September—DR, 27 September 1980.

36. On the Saudi reaction to the Mecca incident, see Radio Riyadh, 31 July—DR, 2 August; *al-Riyad* and *al-Jazira*, 5 August; and the *NYT*, 25, 26, 29 August 1987.

37. On the DMI, see for example, *Eight Days*, 7 November 1981.

38. *Al-Sharq al-Awsat*, 9 December 1983.

39. Radio Tehran, 10 October—DR, 13 October 1981.

40. For details on the pilgrimages, see Martin Kramer, *MECS*, 1981–82, 301–3; *MECS*, 1982–83, 250–1; *MECS*, 1983–84, 175–6; and *MECS*, 1986, 149–51.

41. *NYT*, 26 August 1987.

42. Iranian Television, 6 February—DR, 8 February; *IHT*, 25 March; IRNA, 11 April—DR, 12 April; Radio Riyadh, 19 April—DR, 20 April; *NYT, FT*, 17 June 1988.

43. On the Saudi policy towards the Shi'is, see Jacob Goldberg, "The Shi'i Minority in Saudi Arabia," op. cit., 230–46. On the Iranian failure, see Marvin Zonis and Daniel Brumberg, "Khomeini, The Islamic Republic of Iran, and the Arab World," *Harvard Middle East Papers*, V (1987), 50–54.

44. *Al-Jazira*, 12 December 1978; Riyadh Television, 7 June—SWB, 21 June; *al-Sharq al-Awsat*, 8 June 1983.

45. Interview with *al-Hawadith*, 11 January; Interview and article, *IHT*, 24 April and 8 May 1980; *al-Bilad*, 7 May; *al-Madina*, 18 May 1983; *The Observer*, 28 March 1979; *Washington Post*, 30 August 1980.

46. Radio Tehran, 15 July—DR, 16 July; *al-Siyasa*, 22 July; *Saudi Arabia Newsletter*, 23 July 1984.

47. For details, see Jacob Goldberg's "The Saudi Arabian Kingdom," *MECS*, 1984–85, 598, 605–6; and *MECS*, 1986, 562–563.

9

Iranian-Syrian Relations: Between Islam and Realpolitik

Yosef Olmert

"Both the challenge of Revolutionary Iran and the response of other Middle Eastern states to Iran's challenge are multidimensional," wrote Professor Ramazani in his authoritative book on Islamic Iran's foreign policy and its regional repercussions. Therefore, he went on, "an exclusive emphasis on the military, ideological, or political [and, one might add, the economical] aspects of these phenomena will not adequately explain them."[1] This general observation is particularly true in the case of the Iranian-Syrian relationship.

Both Iran and Syria have regimes that profess a particular ideology. Both tend to formulate and present their foreign policy in terms conforming with their official ideologies. In the case of Iran, this is the supra-national Islamic revolution; and, in the case of Syria, secular, socialist-oriented pan-Arabism.

These two seem to be irreconcilable. Nonetheless, Iran and Syria found some common ground with regard to a variety of regional issues, most notably, during the Iran-Iraq war and certain phases of the Lebanese crisis. They have also developed extensive economic ties. Yet their political interests, though similar, are not identical.

Consequently, Iranian-Syrian relations in the past ten years have been characterized by co-operation amid strain and competition. Their relations have been determined by the combined effects of closely-related interests on the one hand, and the need to address contradictory ideological visions on the other.

The Formative Setting:
From Clandestine to Official Connections

Throughout the 1960s and 1970s, the hostility between the Ba'th regimes in Syria and the shah's regime in Iran was a constant feature of Middle Eastern politics. Iran was pro-West, Syria pro-Soviet; Iran had diversified relationships with Israel, Syria was Israel's self-professed arch-enemy; Syria regarded the oil-rich Iranian province of Khuzestan as "Arabistan";[2] Iran was friendly with some Arab countries which were hostile to Syria (in the mid-1970s

Iran, Saudi-Arabia and Egypt formed a pro-Western axis which was resented by Damascus); Sadat's peace initiative, backed by the shah, was vehemently opposed by Syria.[3]

Under these circumstances, it was natural that the Syrian Ba'th supported the emerging movement of Ayatollah Ruhollah Khomeini.[4] The old adage: "The enemy of my enemy is my friend," proved apt once again. This was particularly true of Khomeini's movement which badly needed the support of a state as strong and important as Syria. Hafiz al-Asad for his part had other considerations closer to home: domestic, Lebanese and regional interests.

In the mid-1970s, the earlier relative stability of the Asad regime was challenged by the Syrian Muslim Brethren. Their movement focused on the non-Islamic character of the regime and forced it to search out Muslim allies. One such ally was the up-and-coming leader of the Shi'i community in Lebanon, Musa al-Sadr. In 1973, Sadr implicitly granted the Alawids recognition as Shi'i Muslims.[5] Sadr was also one of the early supporters of Khomeini. His good relations with Syria facilitated the establishment of co-operation between Damascus and Khomeini's movement.

But the emerging Syrian-Lebanese, Shi'i-Khomeini axis did not solve Asad's problems with his domestic Muslim opposition. It was a Shi'i-inspired alliance, while the Muslim Brethren of Syria claimed to represent the political and religious aspirations of the Sunni Muslim majority in Syria.[6] Nevertheless, the new axis enabled the Ba'th regime to enhance its Muslim profile.

Beyond that, the new axis had important ramifications with regard to the Lebanese situation. Musa al-Sadr sought an alliance with Syria because he wanted to enlist Syria's support in the Shi'i bid to improve their lot in Lebanon. Asad, for his part, viewed the Shi'is as a potential ally in Syria's effort to consolidate its position of dominance in Lebanese politics,[7] and most of the Shi'is were indeed pro-Syrian, even after the disappearance of Musa al-Sadr, in Libya, in late August 1978.[8]

In the regional context, the Syrian regime was at a low ebb in the late 1970s. The Egyptian-Israeli *rapprochement* was particularly detrimental to Syria's regional position. Syria's relations with the Palestine Liberation Organization (PLO) grew tense. Also, the Syrian-Jordanian alliance of the mid-1970s faltered towards the end of the decade.[9] Syria's response was the creation of the "Arab Front of Steadfastness and Resistance."[10] However, this alliance with remote countries such as South Yemen, Libya and Algeria, could not redress the strategic balance in the Middle East, which had swung against Syria. Asad tried to reverse this trend by initiating, in October 1978, a reconciliation with the rival Ba'th regime in Baghdad. But, by June 1979, the two countries were again hostile to each other and Syria's regional standing suffered another major blow.[11] The new Islamic Republic in Iran was anti-West, anti-Egypt, anti-Iraq and anti-Israel and, generally-speaking, posed a challenge to conservative Arab regimes. An alliance with it, therefore, presented Syria with a realistic chance to tilt the regional balance of power in its favor. Besides, Iran was bound to exercise considerable influence over Lebanon's Shi'is, Damascus' most trustworthy allies in Lebanon. Good relations between Syria and Iran, could, therefore, ensure Damascus the ongoing support of Lebanon's Shi'is. Syria's support for the new regime in Tehran was, therefore, a foregone conclusion. The question was how Khomeini, now that he was in power, would view his relationship with Syria. Could the clandestine connections of pre-revolutionary days evolve into a full-fledged public alliance? Officially the foreign policy of the revolutionary regime in its early days focused on two themes: anti-imperialism and Muslim solidarity.[12] On the face of it, that left not much common ground between the Islamic Republic and Syria. On the first point, while Iran strongly denounced the Soviet invasion of Afghanistan as an act of imperialism, Syria supported it.[13] On the second point, even while the Syrian regime extended diplomatic support to the Islamic Republic, the Syrian Muslim Brethren greeted the Islamic Revolution as the "revolution of all Islamic movements in the world,"[14] emphasizing the total Islamic solidarity between them and Iran. (The fact that their attitude would later change does not detract from the impact of their initial reaction.)

In fact, there were two different trends of thought in Tehran with regard to Syria: one wished to support the Islamic opposition in Syria; the other argued that in the present phase of the Islamic Revolution, Iran should have government-level relations with Syria, Libya and Algeria. The second option eventually became policy because, it was argued, the surrounding world was like a "filthy swamp," and Iran therefore, needed "some stepping stones in this contaminated swamp." One such "stepping stone" could be a temporary alliance with Syria. It was necessary because the Islamic Republic needed allies, yet was bound to be temporary, because Syria was a secular state. This was the argumentation used by pro-Iranian groups outside Iran, trying to justify the developing relations between Iran and Syria. They added that the early history of Islam recorded that the Prophet himself had sent messages to, or negotiated with, non-Islamic leaders.[15] The Iranian regime itself did not resort to such apologetics. Rather, it praised Syria and condemned the Muslim Brethren as "gangs carrying out the Camp David conspiracy."[16]

Expediency won out here, as it did in other aspects of Iran's foreign policy. Ideology, however, continued to dictate policy in all cases where it was unlikely to be in conflict with the regime's interests. Thus it maintained its claim to ideological purity, even in the case of its developing relationships with secular Syria: it praised Syria's firm stand against the "enemies" of Islam (Egypt, the USA and Israel—all engaged in the "Camp David conspiracy") as sufficient reason for allying itself with Damascus. Soon official Iranian support for Syria paid off: Syria gave Iran its unqualified support over the issue of the American hostages.[17]

Iran and Syria in the Gulf War: A Strained Alliance

The Gulf war gave the Syrian-Iranian relationship a strong boost. Wartime co-operation became a multi-dimensional effort.

Right from the start, Iran encouraged Syria to apply military pressure against Iraq in order to increase the latter's sense of insecurity and tie down as many Iraqi troops as possible along the Iraqi-Syrian border. The Syrians responded positively, particularly in the early stage of the war.[18] There have also been occasional reports that Syria supplied Iran with Soviet arms and that it mediated in an arms-for-oil deal between Iran and North Korea.[19] On the whole, however, Syrian military assistance to Iran was sporadic and negligible. This was so for several reasons: first, the Syrian army is Soviet-equipped, while the Iranian army has American-made equipment. Consequently, Iran has had to buy arms from its own, and Syria's, worst enemies—the US and Israel—much to the consternation of Syria. Second, Syria's own security situation has required the constant presence of nearly all the Syrian army on the Golan Heights opposite Israel, in Lebanon and in the Syrian interior, leaving only a few troops to be deployed along the Syrian-Iraqi border. Third, threatening another Arab country by concentrating troops on its borders was bound to place a heavy political onus on Damascus in its relations with the Arab world.

From the Syrian standpoint, therefore, it seemed more effective and less damaging, politically, to exert indirect pressure against Iraq by encouraging subversive elements in Iraq and inflicting damage on Iraqi interests in Lebanon. Some Iranian volunteers came to Lebanon, late in 1979 and early 1980, and fought briefly on the side of the Palestinians in South Lebanon.[20] On 15 December 1981, the Iraqi Embassy in Beirut was completely demolished. The ambassador was among the 30 victims. The attack was orchestrated by the Syrian and Iranian intelligence services.[21] Between 1980 and 1982 Syria also encouraged the Shi'i militia, Amal, to intensify its military pressure against pro-Iraqi elements in Lebanon.[22]

In Iraq itself, the circumstances of the war have encouraged anti-government elements, particularly Kurdish groups, and parties, to resume their struggle against the Iraqi regime. Both Iran and Syria were quick to seize upon the opportunity to undermine the Iraqi regime by coming to the aid of the Kurds. There was more than a bit of historical irony in Syria and Iran assisting Iraqi Kurds, considering Islamic Iran's ongoing battle with the Iranian Kurds, and the complete negation by Syrian Ba'thists of Kurdish national aspirations in Syria itself.[23] However, enmity of Iraq proved enough of a common denominator between Iraqi Kurds, Iran and Syria. In May 1981, it was reported that weapons were supplied to Kurdish insurgents in northern Iraq, particularly to the Kurdish faction led by Jalal Talabani.[24] In April-May 1982, Kurdish insurgents stepped up their anti-Iraqi activities.[25] It was probably no coincidence that the trouble occurred at a time when Iraq's military position was at a low ebb. The two Kurdish groups which received substantial Syrian support were the Patriotic Union of Kurdistan (PUK—Talabani's faction) and the Kurdish Democratic Party (KDP), which also had Iranian backing.[26]

The impact of the Iranian-Syrian-Kurdish co-operation was particularly noticeable in 1983, when Iranian front-line pressure against Iraq was heaviest in the Kurdish areas of northern Iraq, where the Iranian military effort was actively supported by the KDP. The PUK, on the other hand, started a slow process of *rapprochement* with Iraq and, in December 1983, a cease-fire agreement was signed. The PUK was subsequently expelled from the ranks of the Syrian-backed anti-Iraqi coalition, known as the Patriotic National and Democratic Front (PNDF).[27] Anti-Iraqi Kurdish activities, instigated by both Iran and Syria, continued intermittently and climaxed again, in late 1987 and early 1988, when Iran launched an offensive in the Kurdish regions of northern Iraq.[28]

Economic co-operation started in March 1982 when Syria's Foreign Minister (later Vice-President) Abd al-Halim Khaddam visited Tehran and signed a barter deal of far-reaching importance. Iran agreed to supply Syria with 174,000 barrels per day of crude oil for one year, starting on 1 April 1982, in exchange for phosphates, textiles, glass, barley and other foodstuffs.[29] Part of the payment would take the form of Syria supplying tourist services to visiting Iranians.[30]

The timing was crucial, coming as it did in the aftermath of the massacre at Hamah.[31] It is safe to assume that the agreement was in the making for quite some time before its actual signing. However, one is tempted to speculate that the Syrian regime was now eager to sign quickly, ensuring that Tehran would not voice any criticism of the mass killings of innocent Muslim believers. In fact, the Iranian regime did refrain from making any official criticism; only unofficial publications condemned the atrocities at Hamah.[32] Following the oil agreement, Syria decided, on 8 April, to close its border with Iraq and to cut off the passage of Iraqi oil via Syria through the pipelines to the Mediterranean.[33]

The exact details regarding Syria's payment for the oil, were not made public. However, it was reported that some of the oil was charged at prices below market price, some was paid for under the barter deal, and the rest was supplied as a grant.[34]

The closure of the Syrian pipeline caused considerable damage to Iraq, mainly because of the need to construct new pipelines and expand the existing one through Turkey. The agreement with Iran freed Syria from its dependence on Iraqi oil and clearly signaled the widening of bilateral relations into a full-fledged strategic alliance against Iraq. However, it was soon to cause friction between the two partners because Syria's dependence on Iraqi oil was now simply being replaced by dependence on Iranian oil. The fact that Syria had to negotiate a yearly deal for the supply of oil from Iran made Syria vulnerable to Iranian pressures.[35]

The Political Liabilities of Co-operation

The difficulties of the Iranian-Syrian economic co-operation, mentioned above, are illustrative of wider difficulties. While Syria was happy to play the role of a spoiler of Iraq's war effort, the political management of co-operation with Iran became increasingly difficult. It was subject to built-in constraints reflecting not only the basic contradictions of the Iranian-Syrian relationship, but also added difficulties caused by the dynamics of the war and related regional developments. The course of the war strained Syria's position for a variety of reasons: first, Syria is part of the inter-Arab system and its regional policy is not predicated on its hostility towards Iraq alone, but also on wider inter-Arab considerations; second, the war brought about a realignment in inter-Arab politics which worked to the disadvantage of Syria's regional interests; third, Syria was not an active player in the war, therefore its ability to influence its course was limited; fourth, Syria's economic dependence on Iran grew significantly during the war (see above), thereby further weakening its ability to influence Iran's policy.

Syria's ideological justification of its anti-Iraq policy focused on the argument that the Gulf war, launched by Iraq, detracted attention from the Arab-Israeli conflict. Therefore, Syrian support for Iran against Iraq was in the best interests of the Arab struggle against Israel. Iraq's "defection" from the Arab front against Israel was particularly injurious to Arab interests because Iraq had an impressive military potential[36] capable of being used against Israel and of ensuring "strategic parity" between the Arabs and Israel. Moreover, Iran's Islamic regime had been on the point of mobilizing its resources against Israel but was prevented from doing so by the Iraqi attack. Thus, instead of creating an effective "eastern front" composed of Iran, Iraq and Syria, the Arabs in general, and Syria in particular, became increasingly vulnerable to Israeli pressures. This was amply demonstrated in December 1981, when Israel decided to extend its jurisdiction and administration over the Golan Heights.[37] Later that month, Asad set out on a tour of the Gulf States and Saudi Arabia. A Syrian commentator said that Damascus was now giving first priority to the need to bolster Arab solidarity in the struggle against Israel.[38] But "Arab solidarity" against Israel was hard to come by when Syria prevented this very "solidarity" from being formed against Iran. It was President Saddam Husayn of Iraq who reminded his Syrian rival that Iraq had been "stabbed in the back" by Syria.[39]

Saudi Arabia and the Gulf states were less straightforward in their criticism of Syria but there was no doubt that the Arab world resented Syria's support of Iran. Syria was to pay a heavy political penalty for this support as the war in Lebanon, in the summer of 1982, was to show, dramatically. During that war, the Arab world was remarkably passive. This was so because Arab attention was primarily focused on the Gulf war and also because many Arab countries were not unduly distressed by Syria's humiliation.[40] In fact, the only external support which Syria received during the crisis was from Iran (see below). Developments in the inter-Arab system caused, in no small part, by the Gulf war made matters worse for Syria. This was evidenced at the Arab summit conference in Amman in November 1987, when a large number of Arab states decided to resume diplomatic relations with Egypt. Egypt's siding with Iraq and the Gulf states in the war had a great deal to do with this.[41]

Syria responded to the political conditions in the Arab world in a number of ways: it tried to play the role of a *mediator* holding the balance between

Iran and the Gulf states; it occasionally participated in Arab and Islamic conferences even though anti-Iranian resolutions were on the agenda; it involved itself in reconciliation attempts with Iraq; on occasion, it has tried to lower the public profile of its relations with Iran.

Syria first endeavored to perform the role of mediator in the fall of 1981, at a time when two front-line events sent nervous tremors up and down the Gulf: they were the relief of Abadan by Iranian troops and the bombing of Kuwaiti oil installations by the Iranian air force.[42] Soon afterwards, Asad promised to support Kuwait if it was attacked.[43] Syrian sources also indicated that Asad wished to contact Iran about the war, in an attempt to end it.[44] However, Iran's foreign minister, Ali Akbar Velayati, denied that there had been any Syrian mediation between Iran and Iraq.[45] In May 1982, when Iranian forces went over to the offensive, Syria tried to allay the fears of the Gulf states by assuring them that Iran's aim was the overthrow of Saddam Husayn rather than territorial aggrandizement. Damascus, too, the Syrians stated, was opposed to Arab territory being conquered.[46] In May 1984, when the war escalated, Syria made it clear once more that it was opposed to aggression against non-combatant Gulf states.[47] Shortly afterwards, Iran and Syria's foreign ministers stated that they had developed "a complete understanding on the need to avoid expanding the area of the Iraq-Iran war, and on preventing the involvement of any Gulf state in the war."[48] Syria repeated this call on other occasions, especially when Iranian military gains caused anxiety throughout the Gulf states. Such was the case when the Iranians occupied Fao, early in 1986, and, again, when Iran launched its offensive against Basra, towards the end of 1986 and early 1987.[49] Following the events in Mecca in July 1987 (see chapter by Goldberg), Asad personally conveyed his regrets over the incidents to the "custodian of the two holy mosques, His Majesty King Fahd."[50]

Syria boycotted the Amman conference in November 1980 where anti-Iranian resolutions were eventually adopted.[51] It sent a low-ranking delegation to the first Fez summit in November 1981,[52] but Asad himself attended the second Fez summit, in September 1982, a fact attributable, by and large, to Syria's predicament following the Lebanese war. Syria's handling of the anti-Iranian resolution which was adopted was indicative of its delicate position as the main Arab backer of Iran. Asad did not object to the anti-Iranian resolution at the conference, itself,[53] but the official Syrian conference report omitted all reference to it and Syria's information minister, Ahmad Iskandar Ahmad went to Tehran to reassure the leaders there that Syria remained a friend.[54] In August 1985, Syria again boycotted an Arab summit (in Casablanca).[55] By that time, its regional position seemed stronger than in September 1982, mainly due to the near-completion of Israel's withdrawal from Lebanon. But it participated in the Islamic Conference in Kuwait in February 1987, in defiance of an Iranian boycott plea.[56] Syria also participated in the Arab summits in Amman in November 1987, in Algiers in June 1988 and in Casablanca in June 1989. The Amman conference adopted a strongly-worded, anti-Iranian resolution and Asad did not object.[57] But the Syrians hastened to make another effort to allay Iranian fears regarding a change in their position. Official Syrian commentaries emphasized that thanks to Syria's firm stand the summit did not call for a complete break of diplomatic relations between the Arab states and Iran. They also emphasized that Syria was in full solidarity with Iran in its struggle against the American naval presence in the Gulf.[58]

As for a Syrian-Iraqi *rapprochement*, there were numerous reports to that effect during the war, but none proved correct. However, the frequent reports were not necessarily detrimental to Syria since they attested to a wide range of opinions *vis-à-vis* Iran, on the one hand, and the Gulf states, on the other. In June 1983, it was reported that the USSR had made strenuous efforts to bring about a reconciliation between Syria and Iraq. Unconfirmed reports spoke of a secret meeting, in Moscow, between the Syrian and Iraqi foreign ministers.[59] However, nothing further transpired. In May-June 1986, following Iran's suspension of deliveries of oil to Syria in October of the preceding year, there was another attempt at reconciliation, through Jordanian and Saudi mediation. In retaliation against the Iranian step, Asad led Jordan and Saudi Arabia to understand that he was interested in a dialogue with Iraq. Following a meeting between security officers of Syria and Iraq, the foreign ministers were supposed to meet, in June 1986, but the meeting did not materialize. The Iraqis claimed that Syria had demanded an immediate union of the two countries as a pre-condition.[60] The real reason for Syria's change of heart was Iran's decision to resume its oil deliveries and to tone down its demand for Syria to service its debt to Iran.[61] Despite the setbacks, Syrian-Iraqi contacts continued and reached a climax in late April 1987, when presidents Asad and Saddam Husayn met in Jordan, for the first time in eight years, under the auspices of King Husayn of Jordan. But this meeting did not bring about a breakthrough either.[62] The two rival presidents then met again at the Amman summit in November 1987,[63] together with six other Arab leaders. Again, no dramatic improvement in Syrian-Iraqi relations ensued.[64]

Overall, Syria sought to keep its ties with Iran in a state of low public visibility. This is born out by an examination of the intensive exchange of visits by high ranking officials and political leaders: the frequency of visits by Iranians to Damascus is rather higher than that of Syrians to Tehran. This discrepancy is highlighted by the fact that Iran's President Ali Khamene'i paid a visit to Syria, Libya and Algeria, early in September 1984,[65] but Asad failed to reciprocate. A pro-Iranian source claimed that Khomeini was determined not to meet Asad.[66] This version was intended to serve the Islamic Republic in its propaganda war against Muslim adversaries, such as Syria's own Muslim Brethren. However, it seems likely that Asad deliberately avoided a visit in Tehran for fear of further straining his position in the Arab system. This version gains credibility as Iranian sources had reported on various occasions that an invitation to visit Tehran had been extended to Asad.[67]

Iran, Syria, and the Lebanese Shi'a: A Clash of Visions

The Iranian policy of "exporting the revolution" to every corner of the Muslim world has been particularly relevant in the case of Lebanon. Lebanon has a large Shi'i, mostly underprivileged, population which, in the late 1970s, was in the midst of a revolutionary change.[68] The lack of a strong central government facilitated Iran's penetration. Iran also sought to influence Lebanon's large Sunni population by arguing that Iran's revolution formed the vanguard of a wider Muslim one and that it, alone, expressed the genuine aspirations of all Muslims—Shi'is and Sunnis alike. Lebanon's proximity to Israel enabled the Iranian regime to claim a part in the holy war (*jihad*) against Israel, the "avowed enemy of all Muslims." In sum, Iran's policy towards Lebanon, has largely been determined by its Islamic vision.

Syria, for its part, has quite a different vision of Lebanon. From the Syrian standpoint, its presence in Lebanon is a fulfillment of a historical right. Syria perceives its huge investment in Lebanon as crucial to its own political stability, its ability to determine Palestinian politics and its overall standing in the pan-Arab system. It is precisely for these reasons that Syria has continuously tried to localize the Lebanese crisis. This has meant a persistent effort to contain local Lebanese factions as well as preventing external actors from interfering there.[69]

In the case of the PLO (which is beyond the scope of this chapter) as well as in the case of Iran, this effort has failed. Basically Iran and Syria have conflicting visions with regard to Lebanon. Nonetheless, over the last nine years, spells of co-operation have outnumbered periods of friction and dissent. This has been so for three main reasons: first, Syria has continuously viewed the Shi'i community in Lebanon as a key element in its bid to dominate Lebanese politics; second, Iran, having no border with Lebanon, needs the co-operation of Syria in order to maintain an effective presence there; and third, at most times both have managed to close ranks against common enemies in Lebanon.

Iranian-Syrian relations in Lebanon have passed through three stages: 1) 1979–1982 (years of co-operation on a small-scale) 2) 1982–1985 (years of joint struggle against Israel and the US); 3) 1985 to the present (years of growing friction).

1979–1982

During these years, Iran's impact in Lebanon was insignificant, although some senior revolutionaries, such as Mustafa Chamran, stayed in Lebanon prior to the revolution.[70] Amal, the main Shi'i organization, was led by disciples of Imam Musa al-Sadr such as Nabih Birri who realized that the "Khomeinization" of Lebanon would mean the demise of the state as a pluralistic entity based on inter-communal dialogue and compromise. Some religious leaders, most notably Shaykh Muhammad Mahdi Shams al-Din, acting head of the Supreme Islamic Shi'i Council (SISC)—"acting" because the vanished Imam, Musa al-Sadr is still considered chairman—called upon

Amal to adopt a more religion-oriented position. Others went a step further: as early as 1981, some Amal activists tried to turn it into an Iranian-led group, even at the expense of the basic loyalty of Amal to the idea of a Lebanese state. When their line was censured by the leadership, some of them—led by a school teacher, Husayn al-Musawi—broke away from Amal, in the summer of 1982, and established a new movement: Islamic Amal.[71] Still, at this early stage, the strict pro-Iranian elements in the Shi'i community were outnumbered by the mainstream Amal. The latter was pro-Syrian. Iran was waiting in the wings, looking for an opportune moment to enter into the Lebanese arena in force. That moment came, in June 1982, with Israel's invasion of Lebanon.

1982–1985

On the second day of the Israeli invasion, a high-ranking Iranian military and political delegation arrived in Damascus. It included the commander of the Islamic Army's Ground Forces, Colonel Sayyad Shirazi, who stated that they had come to plan "a religious war (*jihad*) against Israel."[72] Soon afterwards, several hundred Iranians on their way to Lebanon marched through the streets of Damascus, chanting: "After Baghdad: Beirut and Jerusalem."[73]

The anti-Israeli zeal of the Iranians was not in tune with the sentiments of their co-religionists in Lebanon, such as they were during the initial stages of the Israeli presence in Lebanon. Since the beginning of the invasion, Amal had made it clear that it was not ready to take part in the confrontation with Israel. There were public denunciations of the invasion, but the Shi'i leadership did not call upon the population to rise against the Israeli occupation.[74]

The immediate impact of the evacuation of the PLO from West Beirut was a consolidation of Amal's position there, since it remained armed and well-organized. As for the Iranian volunteers, their entry into Lebanon and their concentration in Ba'albak in the northern Biqa valley, was soon to cause problems. On 22 November 1982 (Lebanon's Independence Day), an estimated 300 armed Iranians attacked Lebanese army barracks in the city. Leaflets attacking Birri and Shams al-Din were distributed in the area. Not all the Shi'is of the Biqa were content with the Iranian presence and a local organization called the Biqa Grouping came out against it.[75] So did the SISC in Beirut.[76] Nevertheless, Iranian reinforcements arrived in the Biqa and the Guards set up a radio station there.[77] Early in March 1983, the Iranians and their local Shi'i allies again attacked the Lebanese army barracks in Ba'albak.[78]

By that time, there were already 1,500 Iranian Revolutionary Guards in the Biqa where they co-operated with local pro-Iranian Shi'i factions: Islamic Amal, led by Husayn al-Musawi, and Hizballah (the "Party of God"), led by Abbas al-Musawi and Shaykh Subhi al-Tufayli. The Iranian contingent included *ulama* who engaged in religious indoctrination.[79] All this could not have taken place without the active co-operation of the Syrian authorities in the Biqa. The Biqa was strategic and vital to the Syrian presence in Lebanon because of its proximity to Damascus. From the perspective of Syrian policy in Lebanon, letting Iranian forces into it was, therefore, an aberration. However, given the immediate constraints of the Israeli invasion, Syria was ready to admit them. Since then, Iranian-Syrian relations in the Biqa have developed along two contradictory lines: on the one hand, operational co-operation against common enemies; on the other, Iranian attempts to turn the Biqa into a miniature model of an Islamic Republic, much to the dismay of the Syrians.

Iran's ambassador in Damascus, Hojjat al-Islam Ali Akbar Mohtashami, co-ordinated Iranian activities in Lebanon and Syria. His Syrian counterpart was Brigadier Ghazi Kan'an, head of Syrian intelligence in Lebanon. In the early months of 1983, pro-Iranian elements infiltrated Beirut with active Syrian support.[80] The effects of this move became manifest on 18 April 1983 when a bomb blast at the US Embassy in Beirut killed at least forty-eight people. A Shi'i organization calling itself *al-Jihad al-Islami* (apparently the code name of Musawi's group) claimed responsibility.[81] The pro-Iranians revealed their most effective weapon: their willingness to go to any length to further their interests. They proved this again, on 23 October 1983, when bomb attacks on the US and French contingents in Beirut claimed the lives of nearly 300 people. Again *al-Amal al-Islami* was reported to have been behind the attack.[82] A certain Iranian, code-named Abu Muslih, who had reached the Biqa a year earlier, was responsible for the bombings. He could not have worked effectively without Syrian help. It is of significance that Husayn Shaykh al-Islam, Iran's deputy foreign minister, visited Damascus a few days before the April bombing, and again, a few days before the October attacks. His other jobs were chief of the Revolutionary Guards and supervisor of secret cells outside Iran. It was apparently he who, in close co-ordination with the Syrian government, gave Musawi the final order for the bombings to be carried out.[83]

The success of the Iranians further radicalized their Lebanese Shi'i supporters. One of them, speaking at a Biqa ceremony marking the fifth anniversary of the Iranian revolution, declared that "we shall continue the struggle until the Jumayyil Government is toppled . . . we shall not stop fighting until an Islamic government, led by the Imam of the *umma* [Khomeini] is established."[84] In Beirut, the leading light of the pro-Iranians was Shaykh Muhammad Husayn Fadlallah, who visited Iran in late January 1984, met Khomeini and Khamene'i and hailed the former as "leader of the world's Muslims, the only person to confront the infidels with all his power and might."[85] (But see chapter by Kramer on Fadlallah's reservations towards Iran.) In taking such a stand, he and other Shi'i clerics moved beyond Amal's and Syria's ideological orbit. However, in 1983–1984, Amal, the pro-Iranian Shi'is, Iran and Syria were all engaged in fighting external enemies. Their own divisions were, therefore, relegated to the background. In February 1984, Amal scored its biggest victory, occupying West Beirut. About that time, the foreign units, grouped together in the Multi-National Force, left

Beirut under the impact of the battering they had suffered at the hands of Lebanese Shi'is and their external backers. Soon afterwards, president Amin Jumayyil found himself constrained to go to Damascus and there, succumbing to Syria's pressures, abrogated the 17 May 1983 agreement with Israel.[86]

There remained for Syria, Iran and their Lebanese Shi'i surrogates to deal with the Israeli presence in southern Lebanon. In the Lebanese Shi'i southern heartland of Jabal Amil, Iran's influence was not decisive, in 1983–1984, but the Islamic Republic was not without friends there. One of them, Shaykh Raghib Harb from the village of Jibshit, visited Iran in December 1983, where he declared that "my house in Lebanon is the embassy of the Islamic Republic of Iran."[87] (Shortly before, Lebanon had severed diplomatic relations with Iran.) In February 1984, Harb was shot dead by unidentified gunmen near his village.[88]

The dominant Shi'i force in southern Lebanon was Amal. In a major shift of policy, it moved from its initial passive support of Israel's presence in the south to one of active hostility. The shift occurred in spring of 1984, immediately after the Amal takeover of West Beirut and a number of factors contributed to it; a) Israel's insistence on a dominant role for the mainly Christian South Lebanon Army (SLA); b) Syrian pressures to which Amal had to be amenable, in view of Syria's crucial support during the battle for Beirut; c) the feeling of many Shi'is that since Israel was losing the battle for Lebanon, an Israeli withdrawal was just a matter of time—a feeling which was reinforced by Israel's withdrawal from the Shuf Mountains in September 1983.[89] Another important factor was the negative influence of Shi'i extremists, including the Iranian Revolutionary Guards. From the spring of 1984 until mid-1985, the Shi'is, backed mainly by Syria and Iran, launched a persistent struggle against Israel. In May-June 1985, the IDF pulled out of most of southern Lebanon, confining itself to a small area known as the Security Zone.[90]

Israel lost, but who won? The successful Iranian-Syrian coalition was soon to come under new pressures fathered by its own success.

1985–1989

During this period, Syria made vigorous efforts to establish a *pax Syriana* in Lebanon. These came to a head with the so-called, Damascus Agreement to solve the Lebanese crisis, signed on 28 December 1985 by Walid Junblat, leader of the Druze Progressive Socialist party; Nabih Birri, leader of Amal; and Elie Hubayka, chairman of the mainly Maronite Lebanese Forces.[91] The agreement contained nothing likely to attract the support of Shi'i fundamentalists in Lebanon and their Iranian mentors. However, it was not their objections which undermined the agreement and rendered it ineffective, only three weeks after its being signed. The main culprits were dissident Maronites who, with the help of President Jumayyil, removed Hubayka from his position. Without any credible Maronite partner, the agreement became meaningless. Since then Syria has not managed to force the Lebanese factions to come to terms. This failure has served to highlight the realities of Syria's position in the battered country: Damascus was successful in precipitating the Israeli and American withdrawals from Lebanon, in putting effective pressure on Yasir Arafat's PLO, and in establishing a local coalition to fight its Lebanese enemies. But in the matter of finding a positive formula to settle things in Lebanon, Syria turned out to be powerless.

Iranian-Syrian relations, in these years, however, have underlined this state of affairs. Iran intensified and diversified its activities in Lebanon in a number of ways. First, it increased its support of Hizballah, in its competition with Amal for the hearts and minds of the Shi'i community. The Shi'i militants came forward with a comprehensive message which touched the social, economic, spiritual and political aspirations of the average Shi'i. What made it all the more attractive was the fact that Iran proved capable, despite its own economic problems, to channel substantial funds to Lebanon. The exact amount is hard to come by, but it is safe to assume that payments were in the range of $80m per year. Consequently, both Hizballah's political and military strength has grown considerably. It is estimated that Hizballah has 4,000 fighters, of which 2,500 are in the Biqa, 1,000 in Beirut and 500 in the south. There has been a gradual shift from small clandestine units to large, semi-regular military formations.[92] Second, Iran and Hizballah together intensified their campaign against Arab and Western individuals and institutions.[93] This was particularly damaging to Syria's interests for three reasons: a) it proved how precarious Syria's hold over Lebanon continued to be; b) it happened at a time when Syria was trying to improve its international image which had suffered considerably following revelations that Syria was involved in terrorist operations in Europe in 1986;[94] c) Iran managed to use the hostage situation as a leverage against western countries, as was exemplified in the Irangate scandal. It is of significance, that the first leaks about the American-Iranian-Israeli arms-for-hostages deal appeared in a pro-Syrian weekly in Beirut.[95] Third, Hizballah has stepped up its attacks against the SLA and the Israeli forces in the "Security Zone." These have not necessarily been contrary to Syria's interests. However, due to the sensitivity of the Israeli-Lebanese border situation, Syria prefers to be in complete control of anti-Israeli activities in order not to be drawn, at the wrong time, into a dispute with Israel, in and over Lebanon. Such a confrontation might result from uncontrolled Hizballah activities. Fourth, Iran intervened diplomatically in the "war of the camps," in late 1986, between Amal and the anti-Syrian Arafat loyalists in the PLO.[96] It mediated a cease-fire which Hizballah was supposed to observe as well. The latter had argued that Amal's war against the Palestinians pitted Muslim against Muslim, whereas the true effort of all Muslims should be the "liberation of Jerusalem."[97] This was a challenge not only to Amal but also to their Syrian patrons who were reminded by Shaykh Fadlallah that Arab nationalism was less important than Islam.[98] Fifth, Iran extended its support to segments of the Sunni community, most notably the Tawhid Movement in Tripoli, led by Shaykh Sa'id Sha'ban, an avowed enemy of Syria.[99]

The chaotic situation in West Beirut, coming as it did shortly after the kidnapping of the British mediator Terry Waite by pro-Iranian terrorists,[100] finally goaded Syria into action. On 23 February 1987, a few thousand soldiers of Syrian elite units took over West Beirut. There was no report that there had been any prior consultation between Syria and Iran but it was reported that Syria had consulted the US.[101] During the fighting, the Syrian units clashed with Hizballah fighters. Twenty-three members of Hizballah were killed. According to Shaykh Fadlallah's account, "not one shot was fired at the Syrians. It was a cold-blooded massacre." Some 50,000 persons attended the funeral of the victims. There was a chorus of denunciations in Iran itself, which decried the Syrian official account according to which the Hizballah fighters had provoked the Syrian soldiers.[102]

Be that as it may, the killings have left their mark on Iranian-Syrian-Lebanese Shi'i relations, as did the subsequent kidnapping of the American journalist, Charles Glass, by pro-Iranian activists and his release, later on, due to Syrian pressures.[103]

Renewed tension erupted a few months later, from February to May 1988, between Amal and Hizballah, over the control of the Shi'i regions in Lebanon. Amal won the battle in southern Lebanon but the fundamentalists won the day in South Beirut. Under these circumstances, Syria, fearing that its position in Beirut and elsewhere in Lebanon might be in jeopardy, decided to intervene militarily in order to prevent the defeat of Amal. However, even then the Syrians were at pains to prevent an all-out confrontation with Iran. This was so for two reasons: first, they did not wish further to destabilize Lebanon, especially in a year of presidential elections; second, Syria realized that a confrontation with Iran over Lebanon might well lead to a complete rupture. If a break occurred, it would be to Syria's disadvantage at a time when Iraq's standing in the Gulf War was improving and when the Gulf States were under less pressure than before. The Arab world was, therefore, unlikely to come forward with economic assistance to replace Iranian aid at this particular juncture. Iran, on the other hand, felt that an accommodation with Syria over South Beirut, in which Hizballah could save much of its newly-acquired gains there, was preferable. The alternative, viz. an all-out confrontation with Syria, implied risking Hizballah's very presence in Beirut and might spell the loss to Iran of a considerable financial and political investment (not to mention the loss of face). A compromise was therefore found, according to which Syria took it upon itself to police the southern suburbs of Beirut in agreement with Hizballah. Yet this compromise did not signal any meaningful strategic *rapprochement* between the two parties whose ideological and political visions regarding Lebanon's future remain poles apart.

Conclusions

The Iranian-Syrian alliance has so far lasted ten years, no mean feat in a region as volatile as the Middle East.

The initial driving force for both was their respective isolation in the regional context of the late 1970s. Setting out to overcome it, they also managed to inflict severe blows on some of their adversaries. This has been particularly true in the case of Lebanon, less so in the case of the Gulf War.

However, Iran and Syria seem to be unable to share the spoils in Lebanon. For all their common interests, there remains the underlying clash between Syria's ambition to gain local hegemony and Iran's Islamic aspirations. In the case of the Gulf war, there seemed to be a clash between Syria's enmity towards Iraq and its desire to close ranks—at one time or another—with the rest of the Arab world. It is one thing for Syria to try to bring down Saddam Husayn's regime in co-operation with Iran, and another to do so in face of a united Arab world. At any rate, the end of the Gulf war removed an important reason for the Iranian-Syrian alliance.

Therefore, in light of the cumulative experience of recent years revealing the growing cracks in Iranian-Syrian relations, the question is whether the two countries can manage their differences as well as they managed their efforts against common enemies. This may well prove very difficult. The Gulf war cease-fire is bound to make it even more so.

Notes

1. R. K. Ramazani, *Revolutionary Iran: Challenge and Response in the Middle East* (Baltimore: 1986), 3.

2. Ibid., 176.

3. On Iran's foreign policy and its co-operation with pro-western Arab states, see R. K. Ramazani, "Emerging Patterns of Regional Relations in Iranian Foreign Policy," *Orbis*, XIX (Winter 1975), 1043–69.

4. J. Alpher, "The Khomeyni International," *The Washington Quarterly*, III (1980), 58–63.

5. M. Kramer, "Syria's Alawis and Shi'ism," in M. Kramer (ed.), *Shi'ism, Resistance and Revolution* (Boulder: 1987), 247–49.

6. On the Syrian Muslim Brethren, see H. Batatu, "The Muslim Brethren," *Merip Report*, 110 (November-December 1982), 12–20; T. Mayer, "The Islamic Opposition in Syria, 1961-1982," *Orient*, 24 (1983), 589–609; U. F. Abdallah, *The Islamic Struggle in Syria* (Berkeley: 1983); R. Hinnebusch, "The Islamic Movement in Syria: Sectarian Conflict and Urban Rebellion in an Authoritarian Populist Regime," in A. E. Hillal Dessouki (ed.), *Islamic Resurgence in the Arab World* (New York: 1983), 138–69; A.R. Kelidar, "Religion and State in Syria," *Asian Affairs*, 61, pt. 1 (February 1974), 16–22; also the Muslim Brethren's publication *al-Nadhir*.

7. R. Avi-Ran, *Syrian Involvement in Lebanon (1975-1985)* (Hebrew; Tel Aviv: 1986), 77–125.

8. On Sadr's disappearance, A. R. Norton, "The Origins and Resurgence of Amal," in Kramer, *Shi'ism, Resistance and Revolution*, 211–12. There is no single authoritative explanation for Sadr's disappearance but it is generally believed that Colonel Mu'ammar al-Qadhdhafi was annoyed with Sadr's neutrality during the Lebanese civil war. According to other speculations, it was the shah's secret police, the SAVAK, who were behind Sadr's disappearance. Contrary to these theories, a pro-Iraqi Lebanese weekly charged that Khomeini's own agents were involved in the disappearance. See A. Nurizade, *al-Dustur*, 25 February 1985.

9. On Syria's isolation following Sadat's visit to Israel, *MECS*, 1977–78, 735–39.

10. *MECS*, 1977–78, 221–24.

11. *MECS*, 1978–79, 244.

12. *MECS*, 1979–80, 479.

13. For an analysis of Syria's motivations to support the invasion, see B. Maddy-Weitzman, "The Fragmentation of Arab Politics: Inter-Arab Affairs since the Afghanistan Invasion," *Orbis*, 25 (Summer 1981), 393–99.

14. *Al-Nadhir*, May 1980, cited in Abdallah, 185.

15. I. al-Din al-Faris, *Iranian-Syrian Relations; The Myth and the Reality* (Concerned Muslims of Northern California; Berkeley: n.d.), 9.

16. A statement by Ayatollah Sadeq Khalkhali, April 1980, quoted in Abdallah, 183.

17. Radio Damascus, 1 December 1979—SWB, 3 December 1979; *al-Thawra* (Damascus), 2 December 1979.

18. Y. Hirschfeld, "The Odd Couple: Ba'athist Syria and Khomeyni's Iran," in M. Ma'oz and A. Yaniv (eds.), *Syria under Asad* (London: 1986), 107; Voice of Lebanon, 4 May—DR, 4 May 1982; *MECS 1981-82*, 308-13.

19. *Al-Majalla*, 27 March 1982; Ramazani, 81; *al-Watan al-Arabi*, 13 January 1983.

20. *MECS*, 1979–80, 618–620.

21. *IHT*, 17 December 1981.

22. *MECS*, 1981–82, 706–07.

23. On Islamic Iran's relations with the Kurds, see the chapters on Iran in *MECS*, since 1979; David Menashri, "Khomeini's Policy toward Ethnic and Religious Minorities," in Milton Esman and Itamar Rabinovich (eds.), *Ethnicity, Pluralism and the State in the Middle East* (Ithaca: 1988), 215–29. On Ba'thist Syria and the Kurds, see I. S. Vanly, *Le Problème Kurde en Syrie: Plans pour le Génocide d'une Minorité Nationale*, (n. p.: 1968); C. More, *Les Kurdes Aujourd'hui* (Paris: 1984), 201–09; *Al-Tali'a al-Arabiyya*, 14 April 1986; *al-Ghuraba*, June 1986.

24. Hirschfeld, ibid.

25. *MECS*, 1980–81, 587–89.

26. *MECS*, 1981–82, 596–99.

27. *MECS*, 1983–84, 479–82; the PNDF was formed in 1980, was backed by Syria and included Kurdish elements, Ba'th dissidents and the Iraqi Communist Party (ICP). See *MECS*, 1980–81, 586.

28. On the Iranian offensive in the Sulaymaniyya region, see Radio Tehran, 15, 16 April—DR, 15, 16 April 1987.

29. *MEED*, 13 March 1982.

30. *EIU*, Country Profile, Syria, 1986–1987, (London: 1987), 36. The number of Iranian tourists swelled from only 12,300 in 1982 to 157,200 in 1984. In 1985, it fell back to 132,578, out of a total number of tourists of 486,629.

31. *MECS*, 1981–82, 847–55.

32. Al-Faris, 10–11.

33. Syrian Television, 8 April 1982—SWB, 13 April 1982.

34. Ramazani, *Revolutionary Iran*, 81.

35. On Iranian-Syrian oil negotiations, see chapters on Syria in the various volumes of *MECS*.

36. On Iraq's military potential, see M. Heller, D. Tamari, Z. Eytan (eds.), *The Middle East Military Balance—1983* (Hebrew; Tel Aviv: 1983), 186–98.

37. *MECS*, 1981–82, 861–62.

38. *Al-Thawra* (Damascus), 2 January 1982.

39. Radio Baghdad, 6 January—SWB, 8 January 1982.

40. *MECS*, 1981–82, 247–53.

41. On the Amman resolutions regarding Egypt, see Radio Amman, 12 November—DR, 12 November 1987.

42. *MECS*, 1981–82, 229.

43. Radio Damascus, 3 October—DR, 5 October 1981.

44. SANA, 22, 23 December—DR, 25 December 1981.

45. Radio Tehran, 30 December 1981—SWB, 1 January 1982.

46. *Tishrin*, 15 May 1982.

47. Radio Damascus, 23 May—SWB, 25 May 1984.

48. SANA, 14 July—SWB, 26 July 1984.

49. *MECS*, 1985, 655, and *MECS*, 1986, 616–17.

50. Radio Monte Carlo, 2 August—DR, 3 August 1987.

51. On this and the ensuing Syrian-Jordanian crisis, see Maddy Weitzman, ibid.

52. *MECS*, 1981–82, 861–62.

53. AFP, 10 September 1982; On the Fez anti-Iranian resolution, see Dishon and Maddy Weitzman, ibid., 256.

54. On the omission of the anti-Iranian resolution, see the Syrian communiqué, AFP, 10 September 1982. On Ahmad's statement, see SANA, 14 September—SWB, 16 September 1982.

55. On the Casablanca resolution, see KUNA, 9 August—DR, 9 August 1985.

56. For the Iranian plea, see IRNA, 6 January—DR, 7 January 1987.

57. Radio Amman, 11 November 1987. On the Algiers Summit resolution, see *al-Ra'y*, 9 June 1988.

58. *Al-Thawra*, (Damascus), 14 November 1987.

59. *Akhbar al-Usbu*, 16 June; *al-Usbu al-Arabi*, 4 July 1983; AFP, 16 September 1983 (respectively).

60. *Al-Majalla*, 25 June 1986.

61. *Foreign Report*, 19 June 1986.

62. Voice of Israel, 4 May—SWB, 5 May 1987.

63. *Al-Ra'y*, 10 November 1987.

64. Iraq recaptured Fao in April 1988: see IRNA, 17 April—DR, 17 April 1988 and regained lost ground east of Basra immediately afterwards.

65. *MECS*, 1983–84, 458.

66. Al-Faris, p. 12.

67. IRNA, 2 January–DR, 4 January 1982; Radio Beirut, 10 November 1987 (respectively).

68. See Y. Olmert, "The Shi'is and the Lebanese State," in Kramer, *Shi'ism, Resistance and Revolution*, 196–201.

69. For a good analysis of Syria's policy in Lebanon, see I. Rabinovich, *The War for Lebanon 1970–1985* (New York: 1985); A. I. Dawisha, *Syria and the Lebanese Crisis* (New-York: 1980).

70. *MECS*, 1979–80, 620.

71. *Le Matin*, 28 May 1982; JPRS, 23 June 1982: on Musawi's group, see M. Deeb, "Militant Islamic Movements in Lebanon: origins, Social Basis and Ideology," *Occasional Papers Series*, (Center for Contemporary Arab Studies, Georgetown University: 1986).

72. Ramazani, 156.

73. *NYT*, 18 July 1982.

74. *MECS*, 1981–82, 715–18.

75. *Al-Nahar*, 6 December 1982.

76. Voice of Lebanon, 27 November 1982.

77. Voice of Lebanon, 10 December 1982: AFP, 16 December 1982, *al-Nahar*, 21 December 1982.

78. Voice of Lebanon, 4 March 1983—SWB, 8 March 1983: IRNA, 5 March 1983—SWB, 8 March 1983.

79. A detailed report about Iranian activities in the Biqa appeared in *al-Amal* (Beirut), 19 May 1984.

80. *Ma'ariv*, 27 March 1983.

81. *Al-Dustur*, 25 April 1983.

82. *Ma'ariv*, 28 October 1983.

83. *Foreign Report*, 27 October 1983.

84. Radio Tehran, 13 February 1984—SWB, 15 February 1984.

85. Radio Tehran, 3 February 1984—DR, 7 February 1984: on Fadlallah's see M. Kramer, "Muhammad Husayn Fadlallah," *Orient*, 26 (June 1985); see also a long list of interviews given by Fadallah in 1983 and 1984. Among them: *al-Nashra*, 21 November 1983; *Afkar*, 21 November 1983; *Nouveau Magazine*, 5 May 1984; *al-Safir*, 29 May 1984; *al-Shira*, 16 July 1984; *al-Sharq*, 18 July 1984; *Monday Morning*, 21 October 1984. See also Hizballah's publication, *al-Ahd*.

86. *MECS*, 1983–84, 545–46, 551–54, 559–60, 562–65.

87. *Ettela'at*, 21 December 1983.

88. *The Times*, 23 February 1984.

89. On Amal's change of heart, see C. Bailey, "Lebanon's Shi'is After the 1982 War," in Kramer, *Shi'ism, Resistance and Revolution*, 219–236: A. R. Norton, "Making Enemies in South Lebanon: Harakat Amal, the IDF and South Lebanon," *Middle East Insight*, 3 (1984).

90. *MECS*, 1985, 547–48.

91. Radio Damascus, 29 December 1985—SWB, 1 January 1986.

92. On Hizballah's military build-up, see Ze'ev Schiff, a prominent Israeli military analyst in *Ha'aretz*, 23 September 1986. On Iranian financial investment in Lebanon, see *JP*, 22 July 1987; *al-Musawwar*, 17 September 1987; Voice of Lebanon, 29 October—DR, 30 October 1987; Radio Monte Carlo, 30 October—DR, 3 November 1987.

93. *Al-Nahar*, 17 May 1987; *al-Ahd*, 31 May 1987; *Ma'ariv*, 13 December 1987. For a detailed account of Hizballah's terrorist activities in Lebanon in 1986-1987, see chapters on "Lebanon" and "Armed Operations" in *MECS*, 1986, 470–73 and *MECS*, 1987, 530–31.

94. *MECS*, 1986, 619–21.

95. *Al-Shira*, 3 November 1986.

96. Radio Beirut, Voice of Lebanon, Voice of the Homeland, 10 December 1986.

97. On Hizballah's motivation to wage a *jihad* against Israel see A. Kurani, *Tarikat Hizballah fil-Amal al-Islami* (Beirut: 1986).

98. See Fadallah's interviews in: *Middle East Insight*, 5 March 1986; *MAD*, 10 March 1986; *Jomhuri-ye Islami*, 20 May 1986; *al-Shira*, 26 May 1986.

99. On the ongoing clashes in Tripoli between Syrian-backed militias and Sha'ban's movement, see chapters on Lebanon in previous volumes of *MECS*; on recent contacts between Sha'ban and the Iranians, see *al-Siyasa* (Kuwait), March 1986; Radio Free Lebanon, 24 December 1986.

100. On Waite's kidnapping, see Radio Free Lebanon, 26 January—DR, 26 January 1987.

101. *Al-Anwar*, 24 February 1987.

102. On the February events, see *MECS*, 1987, 418–19, 643–45, 523 respectively.

103. On Glass's kidnapping and subsequent release, see Voice of Lebanon, 18 June—DR, 18 June 1987; R. Free Lebanon, 4 August—DR, 4 August 1987.

10

The Iranian Impact on the Islamic Jihad Movement in the Gaza Strip

Elie Rekhess

One of the most striking characteristics of the Palestinian uprising which began in the West Bank and the Gaza Strip in December 1987 is the saliency of Islamic fundamentalist groups. One such an organization, the Palestinian Islamic Jihad, played a major role in fomenting the riots. Its structure and ideology pose a problem of a special kind: a militant Sunni movement, steeped in Sunni action and traditions, yet inspired and emboldened by the Shi'i revolution in Iran.

It is the object of this chapter to discuss the meeting points as well as the divergencies between the doctrines of the Palestinian Islamic Jihad and the basic tenets of the Iranian revolution. It aims to examine to what extent perceptions characteristic of Khomeini's world view have, in actual fact, been internalized and absorbed by the Islamic Jihad. An epilogue discusses the effects of the Palestinian uprising on these issues.

The Rise of Islam in the Occupied Territories

An Islamic resurgence was evident both in the West Bank and the Gaza Strip since the late 1970s.[1] As in other parts of the Arab Middle East, it was related, to a large degree, to the disappointment with the secularist notion of revolutionary Arab nationalism. For all Arabs, defeat in the 1967 War was a turning point in this respect; but for none so much as for those Palestinians who now came under direct Israeli rule. Loss of faith in secular Arab nationalism now combined with bitter opposition to the Israeli military occupation. Growing despair over the seemingly endless duration and the prolonged Jewish-Muslim disputes over places sacred to both religions (e.g. in Jerusalem and Hebron), were the breeding-grounds for Islamic revivalism. Through the "return to Islam," the local population expressed its rejection of the "corrupt" westernized life-style that was spreading as a result of closer contact with Israeli society. The Iranian revolution then gave the spread of fundamentalist Islam its final impetus.

This was most dramatically so in the Gaza Strip. Muslim activism developed more rapidly there as a result of several distinctive factors: the traditional, conservative nature of local society; the almost exclusively Muslim population (with no Christian-dominated areas as in the West Bank); the pressing socio-economic conditions; the impact of the Gaza branch of al-Azhar University; the influence of Egyptian radical Islam; and the indirect support in the late 1970s of the Israeli military authorities who considered the more moderate Islamic groupings a counter-weight to the (then) more militant, but secular PLO.[2]

The first Muslim activists in the Gaza Strip were the local Muslim Brothers whose movement dates back to the 1950s. Following the Iranian revolution, the Brotherhood stepped up its activity. Its members began to speak of the establishment of a single Islamic state throughout the Middle East. In 1984, a Gaza group led by Shaykh Ahmad Yasin actually tried to translate such theoretical tenets into practice. The group was uncovered and its members were charged with illegal possession of weapons and with intent to destroy the State of Israel and replace it by a religious Islamic state.[3]

Yasin was released in the May 1985 prisoner exchange.[4] He then revised his earlier views and adopted a non-violent approach, trying to deepen the Islamic roots of the local population through religious education and social activities. He soon became the spiritual leader of *al-Mujamma al-Islami* (hereafter Mujamma), the largest legal religious organization in the Gaza Strip, generally identified as a stronghold of the Muslim Brotherhood.[5] Comprising several thousand active members, the Mujamma continued to adhere to the principle of "uprooting the Zionist entity," but claimed that the immediate struggle should be against the nationalists, leftists and communists. Their attack was directed against left-wing PLO activists whose program, the Islamists argued, was narrowly nationalist and thus diverged from the true goal of setting up an Islamic state. In 1986, violent clashes erupted between the rival factions.[6] The dispute reached an unprecedented level when Muslim activists engaged in acid-throwing attacks, knife slashings and fire-bombings against what they termed secular elements.

The Mujamma worked closely with yet another Gaza-based Islamic group, the *Salafiyyun,* who preached Islamic purism and a return to the customs of Prophet Muhammad's time.[7] Under constant pressure from the various Gaza Islamic fundamentalists, a growing number of local inhabitants began wearing conservative dress in accordance with the precepts of Islam. As the movement gained power, the Muslim activists became more aggressive, vandalizing stores that sold alcoholic drinks, attacking women wearing "immodest" dress or bathing in the sea, and breaking up weddings where western music was played.

Al-Jihad al-Islami—The Organizational Setting

The first cells of the Islamic Jihad appear to have become active in the Gaza Strip in 1979 (a date significant in itself). One early group called itself "The Islamic Vanguard" (*al-tali'a al-islamiyya*) or, alternatively, "The Islamic Revolutionary Trend" (*al-tayyar al-islami al-thawri*).[8] It was headed by Fathi Abd al-Aziz Shqaqi, a physician from Rafah who had come close to Sunni fundamentalist ideas during his student days at Zaqaziq University in Egypt, a known center of Islamic radicalism. Khomeini's advent to power greatly impressed him and caused him to search for ways to apply Khomeini's teachings and his example to the Palestinian scene. He viewed the Palestinian problem as basically a Muslim one—to be solved by means of *jihad* in the literal, i.e. military, sense of the word molded after the Iranian revolution.[9]

He soon gathered a group of militants around him, many of them in the liberal professions like himself; some were former secularists who had become "repentant Muslims." Only a minority had previously been active in Islamic movements. Among these were students expelled from Egyptian Universities for being involved in clandestine Islamic activities there. Such was the case of Shaykh Abd al-Aziz Odeh, like Shqaqi a graduate of Zaqaziq University. When Odeh came back to Gaza in 1981, he became a preacher as well as a lecturer at the Gaza branch of al-Azhar and was soon recognized as the spiritual authority of the group.[10]

The group began to gather new recruits at the mosques, at colleges and at social meetings. Among the founding core of activists were: Dr. Ramadan Shalah; Sulayman Odeh; Fa'iz Abu Mu'ammar (of Khan Yunis); Nafiz Azzam (of Rafah); Fa'iz al-Aswad; Ahmad Muhanna (of Khan Yunis); Sa'id Hasan Baraka; Abdallah Abu Samadina; and Jabir Ammar. Four centers of activity came into being: at the Izz al-Din al-Qassam Mosque in Bayt Lahiya (where Abd al-Aziz Odeh was preaching); at the Muti Anan Mosque in the Mashru Amir neighborhood of Gaza; at the al-Katiba Mosque of Gaza; and at the al-Salam Mosque at Rafah. The group also branched out into the West Bank, but their core remained in the Gaza Strip.[11]

Members were grouped in a clandestine network of cells, usually numbering 5 to 6 activists.[12] The cells were called "families" (*usra, usar*), an organizational term commonly used by Muslim Brothers throughout the Arab world.[13] In late 1987, it was estimated that the Islamic Jihad in the territories had a total of 2,000–4,000 members, supporters and sympathizers. In the Islamic University of Gaza, a stronghold of Muslim militancy, some 200 students (nearly 5 per cent of the student body) were identified as Islamic Jihad followers.[14]

Alongside their overt activities, some of the members began in the early 1980s clandestine preparations for violent action, whether on their own or in co-operation with local *al-Fath* (hereafter Fath) activists. One of their first acts of violence was the murder, in 1983, of a Yeshivah scholar, Aharon Gross, at Hebron. Both Islamic Jihad and Fath men from the West Bank and Gaza participated in the team responsible for the killing (carried out under the name "The Palestinian Islamic Jihad").[15] They were inspired and guided by Shaykh As'ad Bayud al-Tamimi a resident of Hebron and a preacher at the Aqsa Mosque in Jerusalem until deported to Jordan in 1970. Tamimi was known for his close ties with the PLO leadership as well as with prominent figures in Khomeini's regime.[16] He became the spiritual mentor of those among the Islamic Jihad movement who advocated violent action.

Some of the new recruits were recently-released security prisoners, members of various PLO groups, who had become converted to the fundamentalist creed while in Israeli prisons.[17]

A series of further acts of terror followed the 1983 Hebron killing, with responsibility being taken by the Islamic Jihad group using different, but closely similar names. They included the killing of two Ashkelon taxi drivers knifed at Gaza in September and October 1986;[18] and a hand-grenade attack at an oath-taking ceremony for new IDF recruits at the Dung Gate in Jerusalem in October 1986.[19] A plan to blow up a truck filled with explosives in a suicide mission in Jerusalem in August 1987 was aborted by the Israeli security services.[20] (For details on operations undertaken just prior to and during the uprising in the territories, see Epilogue.)

Ideologically, the Islamic Jihad movement in the Gaza Strip cannot be described in terms of a unified, homogeneous organization. Rather, it is composed of separate groupings with varying doctrines and principles—although they all present variations on one basic theme. Methodologically, this makes it more complicated for the researcher to describe the nature of the Islamic Jihad activity in Gaza—a difficulty compounded by the mostly clandestine nature of the group. Their specific tenets are rarely committed to writing and they have no newspapers or periodicals of their own. Their occasional leaflets deal with narrow, immediate issues rather than expose the basics of their world view.

The rank and file find ideological sustenance in two foreign publications illegally imported into and distributed in the Gaza Strip: *Al-Tali'a al-Islamiyya*, a monthly appearing in London and later on as the mouthpiece of the international pro-Iran Islamist movement, and an Egyptian monthly, *al-Mukhtar al-Islami*, reflecting the views of radical militant Islam in Egypt.[21] Both are generally assumed to correspond closely with the Islamic Jihad viewpoint. The following analysis makes use of statements by Islamic Jihad members and sympathizers quoted in these two periodicals, as well as of leaflets, handbills etc., distributed by them in Gaza, and of the writings of Shqaqi and Tamimi.

The Concept of Islamic Jihad

Palestinian Islamic Jihad members adopted views on the principles of *jihad*, martyrdom (*shahada*) and self-sacrifice (*istishhad*) in a way which attested to the strong influence of Shi'i symbolism and of the slogans of the Iranian revolution. To illustrate: members of the Islamic Jihad squad who were tried late in 1986 spoke of themselves as sons of "the disinherited (*mustad'afun*) Islamic nation, seeking martyrdom in the name of Allah [and struggling against] arrogance (*istikbar*,) in the world." "We attach much more importance to death than to life. Either we liberate our land or we die," they said.[22] Commenting on an incident in October 1987 in which four Gaza Islamic

Jihad members were killed, Shaykh Odeh said in a similar vein: "They are martyrs. They will go straight to paradise and their sins will be forgiven as a matter of course."[23] The echo here of Twelver-Shi'a concepts of martyrdom is too obvious to need comment.[24]

Central to the concepts of the Gaza group with regard to the notion of *jihad*, was the idea that Arab society cannot be cured by gradual, reformist action. They rejected the notion of a slow evolutionist infusion of traditional Islamic thinking and practice into all aspects of daily life, a policy which the Muslim Brothers supported. The Islamic Jihad was born, in fact, as an antithesis of the latter's reluctance to launch a comprehensive, immediate struggle against Israel. The new brand of Palestinian radical Islam reflected the despair and frustration of younger and more militant believers and their disappointment with the failures and compromises of the PLO as well as with the comparatively moderate policies of the mainstream Islamic trends in Gaza.[25] Islamic Jihad spokesmen described the Muslim Brothers' quietist approach as "unrevolutionary" and "misguided," while the latter labeled the Islamic Jihad's path as "adventurist."[26]

The differences between the "educational" (*tarbiyya*) path of the Brotherhood and the activist strategy of the Islamic Jihad group were articulated in a political platform distributed by Islamic Jihad supporters during the 1987 student body election campaign at the Gaza Islamic University: "[Jihad means] direct confrontation from the first moment in which the heart feels the truth of God's uniqueness through the saying 'there is no God but God'. The form and the means [to accomplish] this confrontation should be defined according to planning and opportunities of action."[27]

What was actually needed, the Islamic Jihad men claimed, was shock-action by a small elite of vanguard forces (*tali'a*) capable of imposing an Islamic regime through the impact of all-out war against Israel.

The echo of Khomeinism is evident in these arguments. It was further brought out by Ahmad Sadiq, a prominent spokesman of the Islamic Jihad trend, in a lengthy essay published in *al-Tali'a al-Islamiyya* in December 1983. The "victory of Allah's faith" in Iran, he wrote, had made the Arab nation realize that Islam was "the true thesis" of the struggle against Israel.[28] Similarly, Tamimi wrote that until the Iranian upheaval Islam "was absent from the battlefield." The very language used to speak of the war against the enemy, he went on to say, was secular. Instead of *jihad*, words like *kifah* or *nidal* (both meaning "struggle") were being used. Instead of calling the enemy "infidels" or "Jews" they were spoken of as "imperialists" or "Zionists." Only when it was clear that the "parties of heresy"—the socialists, the Free Masons and the secular nationalists—had failed to liberate the "blessed land" of Palestine, only then did Muslims sound the old traditional cry of *jihad: Allahu Akbar!* It was the Iranian revolution, Tamimi concluded, which brought home the old truth that "Islam was the solution and *jihad* was the proper means."[29]

In the view of the Islamic Jihad fundamentalists, it was the task of Khomeini's regime to assist Muslims in the occupied territories in forming what they called "the Jerusalem army"—a force capable of waging a "popular Islamic liberation war."[30] They spoke in terms of a bond of ever-growing strength linking Tehran and the Holy City of Jerusalem.[31] In taking such a stand, they ignored the traditional orthodox Shi'i legal position according to which the waging of *jihad* as an offensive war was the prerogative of the twelfth "absent" Imam. Instead, they adopted a central tenet of Khomeini's interpretation of "the new Shi'a": the constant emphasis of *jihad* as a symbol of activism (thereby contrasting it with the traditional concept of *taqiyya* with its connotation of quietism).[32]

But then reference to Iran and Khomeinism was only one dimension of the multi-faceted Palestinian fundamentalist ideology. Alongside the Jerusalem-Tehran axis with its Shi'i *motifs* reference was constantly made to the Jerusalem-Cairo axis (with its overtones of Sunni orthodoxy). In this contest, the Islamic Jihad developed the idea of a line of historical continuity leading from the Palestinian *jihad* organization of Izz al-Din al-Qassam of the late 1920s to the group of Muhammad Islambuli who led the killers of President Sadat. The line also included the *al-Jihad al-Muqaddas* organization established in Palestine in the late 1940s by Abd al-Qadir al-Husayni, the *Jihad* of the Muslim Brotherhood during the 1948 Palestine war and the *Usrat al-Jihad* organization set up by Israeli Islamic radicals in 1979.

Qassam was held in high regard by the Gaza Islamic Jihad men. An *alim* of Syrian origin, Qassam became Imam at the Istiqlal Mosque in Haifa and, in 1928, set up a clandestine group of religious militants who engaged in acts of violence against Jews and British soldiers. He was killed in 1935 in a clash with a British army unit. In time, he became a symbol of Palestinian resistance against foreign rule.[33] An anonymous and illegally distributed booklet entitled "The Palestine Problem from the Islamic Point of View" devoted much space to Qassam and to the devotion of his followers who fought "holding the book of Allah in one hand and the rifle in the other." The author carried his argument to the point of comparing Qassam's death with that of Husayn b. Ali.[34]

Tamimi, too, presented his theme in terms of historical continuity. After 1948, he wrote, the *jihad* trend receded, but "the shameful defeat" of 1967 caused an Islamic revival which again brought *jihad*-oriented thinking to the fore. This was evident, he argued, in Lebanon, Syria, Turkey, Afghanistan and Egypt, as well as in Palestine. In Tamimi's view, Qassam, the 1983 attack on the US Marines HQ in Beirut, the grenade attack on IDF soldiers in Jerusalem and Islambuli's operation were all part and parcel of one broad picture.[35]

The Palestine Problem and Israel

The basic attitudes of the Islamic Jihad on the Palestine problem and its possible solution draw to a considerable extent on some of the principal tenets of the Iranian revolution. It was that revolution, the Islamic Jihad men argued, that ushered in a new era and made it possible to look at the

Palestine problem from the only angle proper to it: that of Islam. According to Shaykh Odeh, the rise of Khomeini was "an important and serious attempt to achieve an Islamic awakening [and] to unify the Islamic nation." Iran, he maintained, was the only country which truly concentrated on the Palestinian cause.[36]

Tamimi in particular did not tire of reminding his readers that, right from the start, the Iranian revolution inscribed the word "Jerusalem" on its flag.[37] It did so, he affirmed, because Jerusalem, and Palestine, are held to be holy by the Qur'an itself. "From the point of view of Islam, Palestine is not [just] a stretch of land, not [just its] trees and springs, but a country blessed because Allah blessed it in the Qur'an."[38] Khomeini was working tirelessly to restore Palestine and Jerusalem to their Islamic character. Palestine's strategic importance derived from its being situated "in the heart of the Islamic body; it is the soul of Islam."[39]

Ahmad Sadiq took a similar line. The Muslim masses of Iran, he wrote, have brought "Islam back to the battlefield" as a counter-force (*naqid*) to resist the Western and Israeli offensive. Shqaqi saw Khomeini's greatness in his capacity to point to the great culture clash in progress between the Islamic nation with its historical tradition, its faith and exemplary civilization, and the West with its crusading spirit and Communist drive. This was a struggle between the divine (*rabbaniyya*) and the satanic (*shaytaniyya*) forces.[40]

The spearhead of the satanic forces was Israel. It threatened all the "disinherited" and "served the interest of world aggression [as practiced by] the Great Satan, the USA."[41] Israel embodied the dream of expansionism—from the Nile to the Euphrates. It was a direct, daily threat to Muslims because it sprang up in the heart of the Muslim homeland, on "the dead bodies of the Muslim Palestinian people."[42] It was therefore doomed to destruction: "Israel was born to die."[43]

Shqaqi quoted a *fatwa* issued by Khomeini which spoke of the religious duty of bringing about the "elimination" (*izala*) of the "Zionist entity" and allocated the income from *zakat* (almsgiving) for this purpose.[44]

Tamimi based the duty to destroy Israel directly on the Qur'an. In a booklet dealing exclusively with this point, he argued that Israel must be brought to ruin because it was destroying places holy to the Muslims in Palestine, first and foremost the Aqsa Mosque. Israel, he went on, was trying to make the mosque collapse because it stood on the spot where the Jews wanted to rebuild their temple. The Jews were a "despicable" people trying to dominate, and eventually replace others by means of usury, deceit, gambling, prostitution and corruption. They succeeded in stealing the "blessed country" but victory could never be theirs because Allah condemned them to "misery and humiliation."[45] These views on Jews and the existence of Israel reflected too, to a large extent, Khomeini's thought.[46]

The Islamic Jihad men defined the Palestinian problem as "an Islamic, not a national (*wataniyya*) problem, concerning the Palestinians, nor an all-Arab (*qawmiyya*) problem, concerning the Arabs."[47] It was the problem of the "Islamic nation" in its entirety, whether considered from the point of view of history or from that of "sound" Qur'anic consciousness. The failure of the national-Palestinian approach lent redoubled strength to the Islamic concept. Again, these arguments clearly reflected Khomeini's disavowal of the nation-state and of nationalism and his denial (at least in theory) of the existence of peoples and states within Islam.[48]

When speaking of the "proper" solution to the Palestine problem, Islamic Jihad writers made do with rather general statements: there must be a "popular Islamic liberation war" leading to the destruction of Israel and the establishment of an "Islamic state" in Palestine.[49] Their attitudes towards other, secular, Palestinian organizations was often ambiguous, reflecting the ambivalence of Khomeini's attitude towards the PLO and possibly their own. Initially, the Iranian revolutionaries stressed their affinity with the PLO, but later, when Khomeini sought to make the PLO conform to Islamic concepts of the "Palestinian revolution," relations grew distant.[50]

The Islamic Jihad spokesmen in Gaza, such as Shqaqi, praised Khomeini's initial encouragement of the PLO and made much play of the fact that some of his revolutionary cadres received their early training at the hands of Palestinian organizations. They recalled that Khomeini cut off oil sales to Israel and expelled the Israeli diplomats from Tehran, handing their premises to the PLO.[51] Most supportive of the PLO among Islamic Jihad leaders was Tamimi who, as we have seen, advocated co-operation with Fath in all matters of violent action (cf. also below).

At the same time, however, other Islamic Jihad men were critical of the PLO, and of Yasir Arafat personally. They accused him of defeatism, charged him with being ready to recognize Israel and with being willing to accept a "mini-state"—"no larger than a tent."[52] They considered his contacts with "left-wing Zionists" as "criminal" and condemned him for taking credit for terrorist acts actually carried out by Islamic Jihad cells.[53] Thus, for example, Shaykh Odeh, interviewed in November 1987, reproached the PLO for "accepting reconciliation" with Arab leaders, instead of aligning itself with "the most important and effective liberation movement in the region"—the Iranian revolution.[54]

At a more ideological level, Islamic Jihad spokesmen deplored the secular attitudes of the various PLO groups, in particular those with Marxist convictions. They came out against the PLO's declared aim to set up a "secular" Palestinian state (in the well-known formula of a "secular, democratic state of Muslims, Christians and Jews")—a program betraying the "total absence of an Islamic view of history."[55] Again, Arafat was held personally responsible for this trend.

The inter-relation between Palestinian Islamic fundamentalism on the one hand, and Palestinian secular nationalism on the other is complex and multi-dimensional. While spokesmen of the Islamic Jihad relentlessly attacked the PLO for its political stands, other members of the organization co-operated with Fath, carrying out joint terrorist attacks against Israeli targets. (For a partial list of such operations, see above). According to the East Jerusalem newspaper *al-Fajr*, the head of the Fath's elite combat unit known as "Force

17" had "expressed interest in recruiting" Islamic fundamendalists. The newspaper further reported "agreements between Fath and the Islamic Jihad for military training."[56] In late 1988, Yigal Carmon, the Israeli Prime Minister's adviser on terrorism, revealed that one of the PLO's military branches, known by the name of "Committee 88" was directly responsible for operations of the Islamic Jihad in the occupied territories.[57]

Those Islamic Jihad groups co-operating with Fath benefited from its personnel, operational experience, arms supplies, communications networks, logistical support and financial resources. Furthermore, they thought of joint operations as a conduit to make their fundamentalist ideology penetrate the nationalist (i.e., in the Islamic Jihad peoples' view: secular) thinking of the PLO.

Fath's willingness, perhaps even eagerness, to engage in joint ventures with Islamic Jihad elements reflects the strengthening Islamic component in Palestinian nationalism. "In recent years Fath had accurately sensed the pulse of many Palestinians and has reached out to the growing Islamic trend. For the terrorist element inside Fath, Islamic Jihad and its sympathizers have provided a ready reservoir of activists."[58] Each side expected to exploit the other for its own aims.

Between Sunna and Shi'a

For all the strong influence of Khomeinist ideas, the Gaza Islamic Jihad has failed to work the notions adopted from Iran into a coherent and explicit ideology. This reflects the fact that the Islamic Jihad groups are not, in actual fact, a single body but rather a coalition of kindred, yet distinct groupings. Their ideological loyalties are divided between:

a) the Iranian revolution;
b) Muslim Brotherhood doctrines (particularly in the form laid down by Sayyid Qutb);
c) Egyptian radical teachings of the type of the Egyptian Islamic Jihad Organization.

At various times, certain groups emphasized one or the other of these above the rest, or else tried to work them into a whole. Their notions of *jihad* and of self-sacrifice derived from Khomeini's teaching; they detached themselves from the Brotherhood's mainstream concept of *jihad* and thought of themselves as following Islambuli's lead.[59] But the *jihad* notion of the Egyptian radicals owed very little to Khomeini. It was a product of their own school, best summed up in Muhammad Abd al-Salam Faraj's book, *al-Farida al-Gha'iba* ("The Neglected Duty").[60] Furthermore, the first priority of the *jihad* preached by them was not to fight against Israel or for the sake of Jerusalem; their targets were the nominally Muslim but, in their view, "unbelieving" leaders of their own Muslim country. These contrasts were not being adequately dealt with by Gaza Islamic Jihad writers.[61]

Unresolved ideological contradictions were even more salient in their attitudes towards the new Iranian state. The central concept of Khomeini's Islamic Republic, that of *wilayat al-faqih* was not genuinely discussed. The Gazans had little to say on the nature of the Islamic state they propagated and on whether it would be headed by a *faqih* or *alim*. Like other Palestinian fundamentalists they preferred to adopt selectively such ideas which fitted into their broad framework of views and to ignore those that did not.

The tendency to bridge, without resolving, ideological contradictions stood out in particular in their attitudes towards the Sunni-Shi'i schism. They took up the ecumenical tendency preached by the Iranian regime and stressed the latter's pan-Islamic orientation.[62] *Al-Tali'a al-Islamiyya* and *al-Mukhtar al-Islami* abounded in articles on the harmony prevailing, in their view, between Sunnis and Shi'is. Over and over again they denied that the Shi'a was heretical, spoke of it as an integral part of the world of Islam and considered existing controversies as "marginal" matters (*far'iyyat*). They cited with approval the endeavors of Hasan al-Banna and of Shaykh Mahmud Shaltut (of al-Azhar) to bring the various Islamic schools together. They reminded their readers of Banna's meeting with Iranian Ayatollahs, such as Abu al-Qasem Kashani, in an attempt to overcome the schism; and they enlarged on Shaltut's famous *fatwa* of 1959 declaring the Twelver Shi'a to be an orthodox school alongside the four other, recognized schools. They pointed to Shi'is joining the Brotherhood in Iraq and Yemen and commended Khomeini for allowing Shi'is to pray in Sunni mosques.[63]

Both Shqaqi and Tamimi elaborated at length on these themes. The former distinguished between the universal concepts in Khomeini's doctrine and the specifically Shi'i ones. What was important, he affirmed, was that the Iranian revolution was "an Islamic revolution in the broad Qur'anic sense," not a matter for one Islamic faction (*ta'ifa*) only. The controversy over the twelfth Imam and the supra-natural qualities of the Imam, he averred, had no relevance to the revolution. Similarly, Tamimi issued a special *fatwa* declaring that it was untrue to say that Shi'is were calling for a split in Islam. They had no Qur'an other than the Qur'an, he wrote, and prayed in the direction of the *ka'ba* as other Muslims do. What matters, he concluded, was to co-operate with the Iranian revolution, not to get caught up in doctrinal discussions on the nature of the Shi'a. What could be wrong with a revolution, he asked, that applied Islamic law, suppressed prostitution and severed relations with "the Jewish state"?[64]

The lack of ideological cohesion, it should be stressed, did not diminish the attraction of the Islamic Jihad groups in the eyes of their Gaza Strip followers. Their internal political and spiritual elite may have been concerned with an analysis of what brings Sunnis and Shi'is together and what keeps them apart. But such arguments did not worry the rank and file, least of all those who joined in for the prospect of taking part in violent action.

Epilogue: The *Intifada*

As noted above, the popular uprising in the occupied territories—the *intifada*—displayed, right from its inception at the end of 1987, a markedly

Islamic component. Islamic Jihad spokesmen claimed from the start that it had been their movement which had swept the broader Palestinian population towards an "Islamic uprising." The road accident of 8 December 1987 near Gaza and the fatalities it caused (widely considered to have triggered off the first wave of the *intifada*) was described by them as a deliberate act meant by the IDF as a continuation of its earlier clashes with Islamic Jihad men.[65]

In the preceding months, the Islamic Jihad movement had stepped up its operations, causing increased tension between the population and the Israeli authorities. The escape from prison of six Islamic Jihad members in May 1987 had given the movement added prestige in the eyes of many Gaza inhabitants. During the summer months, the movement had further accelerated the pace of its activities, culminating in the murder, in August 1987, of the officer in charge of the military police in Gaza city. In October, the IDF uncovered several clandestine Islamic Jihad cells and found a large arms cache. Some 50 members and sympathizers were arrested. Also in October, several Islamic Jihad men were killed in a clash with security forces just outside Gaza; two of the dead men turned out to be from among the six prison escapees of May 1987. The clash triggered serious unrest at the Islamic University during which two Gaza Strip inhabitants were killed. Further unrest there followed when Abd al-Aziz Odeh was arrested in November and a deportation order issued against him.

This series of incidents made some contribution to creating the overall background against which the uprising started in December 1987. It made it possible for the Islamic Jihad men to claim that its outbreak was "their doing."

Once the *intifada* had begun, the movement played a central role in mobilizing large masses. During the first stage (the early months of 1988) the Islamic Jihad and the (PLO-dominated) "Unified Leadership of the *intifada*" arrived at a measure of co-operation. Later, the Islamic Jihad movement seems to have preferred independent action. The Israeli authorities asserted that it was Shqaqi who led the movement from his prison cell.[66]

Co-operation with the "Unified Leadership" notwithstanding, the Islamic Jihad's appeal to the population was in the name of Islam and, unlike the leaflets distributed by the former, its own proclamations called for an "Islamic revolution . . . to liberate Palestine—all of Palestine."[67] Publications reflecting its views, such as *al-Mukhtar al-Islami*, stressed again and again that the uprising must not be thought of as a Palestinian revolt, but as a wholly Islamic revolution led in its entirety by Islamic activists. It had, *al-Mukhtar* asserted, "issued forth from the mosques."[68] And again: "Here he is, Izz al-Din Qassam; rising from the dead and blessing each stone [thrown against the Israelis]. . . . We swear, oh dear Jerusalem, we shall be back, holding high our books of the Qur'an. . . . Long live Islamic Palestine."[69]

Similar slogans were shouted during mass demonstrations following Friday prayers at the mosques of Jerusalem and Gaza. It is safe to assume that cries like the following came from Islamic Jihad members and like-minded people: *Khaybar, khaybar ya yahud, jaysh Muhammad sawfa ya'ud* ([Remember]

Khaybar, oh ye Jews; Muhammad's army shall yet return);[70] or: *Thawra, thawra ala al-muhtall, ghayr al-mushaf ma fi hall* (Revolution, revolution against the occupier, there is no other solution but through the Holy Qur'an).

The active involvement of the Islamic trends in the *intifada* elicited a forceful response on the part of the Israeli authorities: arrests, administrative detention orders and deportations multiplied. Shaykh Odeh who (as mentioned above) had been arrested in November 1987, just before the beginning of the *intifada*, was deported in April 1988; Shqaqi in July; Sa'id Hasan Baraka and Abdallah Abu Samadina early in 1989. These and other measures affected the operational ability of the Islamic Jihad group and reduced its share in the *intifada* activities.

But Israeli counter-measures were only one reason for the comparative decline of the movement. By the beginning of 1988, it had become clear that the group had lost its monopoly on Islamic activism and violent action. These had now become the common ground of all fundamentalist groupings in the territories, first and foremost the Muslim Brotherhood. The previous argument about the way of struggle and the proper interpretation of *jihad* (see above) had been overtaken by events. The uprising had, as it were, found in favor of the militant Islamic Jihad approach. Initially the Muslim Brotherhood found itself militarily inferior, "outflanked and outgunned"[71] by the activist Islamic Jihad. At an early stage of the *intifada* it opted for the militant alternative. The Brotherhood formed its own military arm: the "Islamic Resistance Movement" (known by its Arabic initials as "Hamas").[72] The newly-adopted path found formal expression in the platform of Hamas, the so-called "Islamic Covenant." The document, published in August 1988, stated clearly: "The day the enemies usurp part of the Muslim land, Islamic Jihad becomes the individual duty of every Muslim. . . . There is no solution for the Palestinian question except through *jihad*."[73]

The Brothers, however, continued defining *jihad* in the broadest sense, stressing its non-military or non-violent aspects as well.[74] The emphasis on "fighting the enemy" was a new departure, attesting to the Brotherhood's drawing closer to the ideas of the Islamic Jihad movement. This was also true of other concepts which had previously divided them. A salient innovation in the "Covenant," for example, was the emphasis laid on the distinctively Palestinian character of Hamas. Earlier Brotherhood writings had not highlighted such a *motif,* while the Islamic Jihad group had done so all along. Now the "Covenant" stated: "The Islamic Resistance Movement is a distinctive Palestinian movement whose allegiance is to Allah and whose way of life is Islam. It strives to raise the banner of Allah over every inch of Palestine."[75]

Another instance of convergence can be seen in the attitude towards the PLO. On the one hand, a kind of fellow-feeling was expressed: "The PLO is closest to the heart of the Islamic Resistance Movement. In it are the father and the brother, the next of kin and the friend. The Muslim does not estrange himself from his father, brother. . . . Our homeland is one, our situation is one, our fate is one, and the enemy is an enemy common to all of us."[76]

But then, on the other hand, the very publication of the "Covenant" was a forceful protest against what the Brotherhood considered the PLO's "compromising tendencies." It rejected in no uncertain terms the secular nature of the PLO and the political path it had chosen. As in the past,[77] the Brotherhood came out firmly against the concept of "the secular state" because, in its view, the land of Palestine is a Muslim trust (*waqf*). The ultimate political goal, according to the new formulation by the Brotherhood following the *intifada*, is the establishment of an "Islamic state" on the entire area of Palestine.[78]

This convergence of attitudes (both of doctrine and practice) does not mean that the Brotherhood has now become susceptible to the Shi'i-Iranian influence. The opposite is true. Other than some coincidental use of terms peculiar to the Iranian revolution, the "Covenant" shows no sign of echoing Khomeini-type thinking and makes no mention of Iran. The *intifada* did not prevent Hamas leader Ahmad Yasin from attacking Khomeini's regime. He told an interviewer: "What the Iranians do is not precisely . . . the right model of an Islamic state, and not only because they are Shi'is and we are Sunnis. . . . If you send people to kill or get killed for the only reason of satisfying the wish of the ruler, that is not Muslim action, that is not Islam."[79]

Moreover, the overall relationship between Hamas and the Islamic Jihad movement has remained one of rather hostile competition. The "Covenant" speak of Hamas' "respect and appreciation" for "other Islamic movements,"[80] but the *intifada* has not caused Hamas and Islamic Jihad to co-operate in practical terms. The latter continues to attack Hamas sharply[81]—possibly reflecting Islamic Jihad's frustration over having seen Hamas appropriating the "senior" position among the Islamic trends which it used to hold itself.

Some observers feel that the new-found stature of the Brotherhood attests to the correctness of their earlier choice of making long-term investments in winning over people's minds and hearts. The broad mass affinity they had created gradually, eventually paid off during the uprising.[82] Once the *intifada* has began, the Islamic Jihad people killed far fewer individual Israelis; rather they engaged in mounting mass demonstrations and clashes with the Israeli security forces. Quite possibly, Islamic Jihad may, at some time or other, revert to the methods of spectacular terrorist action in order to regain its leading position in the radical Islamic movement in the West Bank and the Gaza Strip.

The active involvement of the Islamic Jihad in the Palestinian uprising illustrates the growing overall influence of Islamic fundamentalism on Palestinian society and politics. Islam remains the most authentic identification symbol as well as the most powerful historical, cultural and socio-political framework which lends cohesion to Muslim society in the occupied territories. Twenty years of Israeli rule and a lengthy history of Jewish-Arab disputes over places sacred to both Islam and Judaism have given the Palestinian-Sunni version of militant Islam unique characteristics.

Under these circumstances, Khomeinist activism became most attractive to the population of the West Bank and the Gaza Strip. Despite the fact that the ideas of the Iranian revolution have not been sufficiently internalized and absorbed, it offered Palestinians an authentic Islamic explanation and a perceived solution to both the personal stress of the individual[83] and to the collective situation of living under—Jewish—military occupation.

As the *intifada* continues, opposition to the occupation is becoming more and more intensely charged with Islamic sentiment. It may well mark the Islamization of the Palestinian-Israeli conflict.

Notes

1. On the Islamic revival in the territories see: Jean-François Legrain, "Islamistes et Lutte Nationale Palestienne dans les Territoires Occupés par Israël," *Révue Française de Science Politique*, April 1986, 227–47; Alain Navarro, "Palestiniens: l'Expansion Islamiste," *Les Cahiers de l'Orient*, No. 7 (1987), 51–66; Mohammad Shadid and Rick Seltzer, "Political Attitudes of Palestinians in the West Bank and Gaza Strip," *Middle East Journal*, Vol. 42, No. 1 (Winter 1988), 16-32; Mohammed Shadid, "The Muslim Brotherhood Movement in the West Bank and Gaza," *Third World Quarterly*, Vol. X, No. 2 (April 1988), 658–81; Emile Sahliyeh, *In Search of Leadership, West Bank Politics since 1967*, (Washington: 1988), 137–62.

2. Elie Rekhess, "The Rise of Palestinian Islamic Jihad," *JP*, 21 October 1987; Robin Wright, "Three New Dimensions of Palestinian Politics," *Middle East Insight*, Vol. V, No. 6 (1988), 23–27.

3. *MECS*, 1983–84, 257–58.

4. In the exchange, over 1,000 security prisoners named by Ahmad Jibril's Popular Front for the Liberation of Palestine/General Command were released in exchange for six Israeli soldiers held by Jibril.

5. The Mujamma was founded in 1978 and was legally registered. Its base is at the Jawrat al-Shams Mosque in Zaytun, Gaza. The operational head is Ibrahim Yazuri. Other activists are: Dr. Abd al-Aziz Ghantisi, Dr. Mahmud al-Zahar, Dr. Muhammd Sayyam (Rector of al-Azhar University's Gaza branch.) For a recent interview with Yasin see *al-Sirat* (Kufr Qasim, Israel), Vol. II, No. 9 (January 1988), 19–20.

6. On the initial clashes between Gaza Strip Islamic fundamentalists and left-wing circles see, Elie Rekhess, "The West Bank and the Gaza Strip," *MECS*, 1979–80, 287–88.

7. The Salafiyyun's center is at Khan Yunis. Its founder, Salim Shurab, died in March 1986. Among the group's prominent activists are: Muhammad Sulayman Abu Jam'i, Shaykh Hasan Abu Shakra and Shaykh Abd al-Masri. Two other non-military fundamentalist organizations are also active in the Gaza strip: *al-Jam'iyya al-Islamiyya* (headed by Khalil al-Qoka who was deported in Summer 1988); and *Jam'iyyat al-Salah al-Islamiyya* (headed by Tawfiq al-Kurd).

8. Other names the group gave itself were: *al-Shabab al-Ahrar, al-Jihad al-Islami al-Thawri, al-Mustaqillun*.

9. Shqaqi was imprisoned in 1986 for incitement against the Israeli occupation and involvement in arms delivery into the Gaza Strip. He was deported in July 1988. His ideological and political views were summarized in a booklet published in 1979: Fathi Abd al-Aziz [Shqaqi], *al-Khomeini, al-Hall al-Islami wal-Badil*, ([Cairo:] 1979), 123 ff.

10. Odeh was arrested in 1984 for incitement and sentenced to 11 months imprisonment. He was deported in April 1988.

11. Michal Sela, "Islamic Terror," *Koteret Rashit*, 21 October 1987.

12. Robert Satloff, "Islam in the Palestinian Uprising," *Policy Focus*, No. 7 (October 1988), 3.

13. *Usrat al-Jihad* was also the name chosen for itself by a militant Islamic organization formed in Israel in the late 1970s.

14. Satloff, ibid.

15. The organization was also named: *al-Jihad al-Muqaddas, al-Jama'a al-Islamiyya.* On the murder of Gross see *Ma'ariv, JP,* 8 July 1983. For the assassins' trial see, *Ma'ariv,* 25 May 1984.

16. He visited Iran several times. Tamimi's best-known book is: *Zawal Isra'il Hatmiyya Qur'aniyya,* (al-Qahira: n.d.).

17. For example, Muhammad al-Jamal, a former member of the Popular Front for the Liberation of Palestine, was recruited to the Islamic Jihad while serving a sentence in an Israeli jail. *Hadashot,* 9 October 1987.

18. *Ma'ariv, Davar,* 28 September, *Ha'aretz,* 8 October 1986. On the arrest of the squad and its trial: *Ma'ariv,* 26 December 1986; *Yedi'ot Aharonot,* 16 March; *Ma'ariv,* 18 March; *Ha'aretz,* 13 May; *Yedi'ot Aharonot,* 8, 13 July 1987.

19. The operation was also attributed to the Islamic Front for the Liberation of Palestine (*al-Jabha al-Islamiyya li-tahrir Filastin*) and to the Islamic Jihad Legions in Palestine (*Saraya al-Jihad al-Islami fi Filastin*). *Davar,* 16, 17 October, *JP,* 20, 21 October; *al-Ittihad al-Usbu'i,* 30 October 1986.

20. *Yedi'ot Aharonot,* 3, 30 August, 29 September 1987.

21. *Al-Tali'a al-Islamiyya,* edited by the Pakistani militant Islamist Kalim Sadiqi, was first published in London in December 1982. It ceased to appear in 1985 and renewed publication in October 1987. *Al-Mukhtar al-Islami* appears regularly in Egypt since late 1979. The editor is Husayn Ahmad Ashur. It is published by *Maktabat al-mukhtar al-Islami.*

Foreign observers noted that copies of *al-Mukhtar* are clandestinely circulated in the West Bank and Gaza in their thousands; *Los Angeles Times,* 14 September 1987. According to Shaykh Odeh both periodicals reflect "Islamic revolutionary thought." *al-Fajr,* 23 August 1987.

22. *Koteret Rashit,* 21 October 1987; Robin Wright, 24–25.

23. Hugh Schofield, "Militant Islam: Growing Threat to Israel," *Globe and Mail,* 26 October 1987; Compare with the contents of a leaflet distributed by *al-Ittijah al-Islami* in Gaza on 8 October 1987.

24. On the Iranian interpretation of the *Shahada,* see David Menashri, *Iran in Revolution* (in Hebrew; Tel Aviv: 1988), 47–48, 126–28; Marvin Zonis and Daniel Brumberg, "Shi'ism as Interpreted by Khomeini: An Ideology of Revolutionary Violence," in Martin Kramer (ed.), *Shi'ism, Resistance and Revolution* (Boulder: 1987), 55.

25. *Los Angeles Times,* 14 September 1987.

26. Shadid, "The Muslim Brotherhood," 678.

27. *Al-Jama'a al-Islamiyya—Ra'y wa-Mawaqif,* Gaza, November 1987, cited by Reuven Paz, "The Islamic Covenant and Its Significance—First Study and Translation," *Data and Analysis,* The Dayan Center, Tel Aviv University, September 1988 (Hebrew), 3–4.

28. Ahmad Sadiq, "al-Islam wal-qadiyya al-Filastiniyya," *al-Tali'a al-Islamiyya* (henceforward: *TI*), 1 (December 1983). The essay was reprinted and distributed anonymously in Gaza.

29. Interviewed in *al-Mukhtar al-Islami* (henceforward: *MI*), 53 (June 1987); *Zawal Isra'il,* 61.

30. Editorial, *MI,* 42 (May 1986).

31. *TI*, 1 December 1983.

32. Martin Kramer, "The Renewed Shi'a," in his *Protest and Revolution in Shi'i Islam* (in Hebrew; Tel Aviv: 1985), 145; R. K. Ramazani, *Revolutionary Iran; Challenge and Response in the Middle East* (Baltimore: 1986), 25.

33. See Yuval Arnon Ohana, *The Internal Struggle Within the Palestinian Movement, 1929-1939* (in Hebrew; Tel Aviv: 1981), 263–71; Abd al-Sattar Qasim, *al-Shaykh al-Mujahid Izz al-Din al-Qassam* (Beirut: 1984).

34. *Al-Qadiyya al-Islamiyya min Manzur Islami* (n.p.: n.d.). According to Legrain, the booklet was first published by Izz al-Din Faris and Ahmad Sadiq under the title *al-Qadiyya al-Filastiniyya hiya al-Qadiyya al-Markaziyya lil-Haraka al-Islamiyya*, ft. 1, 237.

35. *MI*, May 1986; Ahmad Qasim, 51 (May-April); Tamimi, interview, 53 (June); 56 (September 1987).

36. Cited by Satloff, 4.

37. Tamimi, interview, *MI*, 53 (June 1987).

38. Ibid.

39. Shqaqi, *Khomeini*, 46; Dr. Fahmi al-Shinawi, *MI*, 40 (February 1986); Odeh, interview, *Globe and Mail*, 26 October 1987.

40. Shqaqi, *Khomeini*, 46–47; Ahmad Sadiq, *TI*, 1 December 1983; 31, October 1987; *MI*, 29 October 1984; Dr. Muhammad Moro, *MI*, 46 (October 1986).

41. Ahmad Sadiq, ibid.

42. Ibid.

43. Muhammad Salih al-Husayni, *TI*, 3 March 1983. For a discussion of Khomeini's attitude toward Israel see Michael M. J. Fischer, "Imam Khomeini: Four Levels of Understanding," in John L. Esposito (ed.), *Voices of Resurgent Islam* (New York: 1983), 154–55.

44. Shqaqi, *Khomeini*, 118.

45. Tamimi, *Zawal Isra'il*, 25, 27, 30, 34, 81, 99, 111, 112. Compare: Arafa al-Sayyid, "Readings in Jewish Thought," *MI*, 54 (July 1987). On the "Jewish destruction" of al-Aqsa see Dr. Fahmi al-Shinawi, *MI*, 56 (September 1987) and *TI*, 31 October 1987.

46. See Ramazani, *Revolutionary Iran*, 147, 151, 153–154.

47. *MI*, 43 (June 1986).

48. Ramazani, *Revolutionary Iran*, 20; R. Hrair Dekmejian, *Islam in Revolution* (Syracuse: 1985), 175. (For a discussion of such views of Khomeini, see chapter by David Menashri above).

49. Shaykh Abd al-Aziz Odeh interviewed, *Globe and Mail*, 26 October 1987; *MI*, 42 (May), 53 (June 1986).

50. On the PLO-Iran relationship see, Huwaidi, *Iran min al-dakhil* (Arabic); David Menashri, *Iran: A Decade of War and Revolution* (New York: 1990), 103-104, 153, 210, 253-54.

51. Shqaqi, *Khomeini*, 47; Tamimi, *Zawal Isra'il*; "Readings in the Roots of the Iranian Revolution," *MI*, 10 (April 1980); Dr. Fahmi al-Shinawi, 48 (December 1986).

52. *TI*, 31 October 1987.

53. *MI*, 40 (February 1986); Ahmad al-Qasim, 51 (March-April 1987).

54. *Christian Science Monitor*, 12 November 1987.

55. *MI*, 40 (February 1987), *TI*, 31 October 1987.

56. Satloff, 11.

57. *Yedi'ot Aharonot*, 13 December 1988.

58. Satloff, 12.

59. On the general doctrine of *Jihad*, see Majid Khadduri, *War and Peace in the Law of Islam* (New York: 1979), 51–133; Rudolph Peters, *Islam and Colonialism, the Doctrine of Jihad in Modern Islam* (The Hague: 1979); Wilhelm Dietl, *Holy War* (New York: 1984); on the Brotherhood's view: Olivier Carre, "The Impact of the Egyptian Muslim Brotherhood's Political Islam since the 1950s," in G. Warburg and Uri Kupferschmidt (eds.), *Islam, Nationalism and Radicalism in Egypt and the Sudan* (New York: 1983), 272–73.

60. See Johannes Jansen, *The Neglected Duty, The Creed of Sadat's Assassins and Islamic Resurgence in the Middle East* (New York: 1986).

61. Salah Abu Isma'il, *al-Shahada* (al-Qahira: Dar al-I'tisam, 1984); Dekmejian, *Islam in Revolution*, 99-100, Rudolph Peters, "The Political Relevance of the Doctrine of Jihad in Sadat's Egypt," in E. Ingram (ed.), *National and International Politics in the Middle East* (London: 1986), 252–71.

62. Emmanuel Sivan, *Radical Islam: Medieval Theology and Modern Politics* (in Hebrew; Tel Aviv: 1986), 190–216; Hava Lazarus-Yafe, "The Shi'a in Khomeini's Political Doctrine" (Hebrew), *Hamizrah Hehadash*, 30 (1981), 99–106; Eitan Kohlberg, "The Shi'a: Ali's Faction," in Kramer, *Protest*, 14, 19–21, 30; Kramer, ibid., 152–59; Ali Abd al-Wahid Wafi, *Bayn al-Shi'a wa-Ahl al-Sunna* (al-Qahira: 1984).

63. A pamphlet distributed in Gaza (*Mawqif ulama wa-qadat al-muslimin min al-shi'a, al-thawra al-Iraniyya*, 31), lists nearly 30 sources to prove the harmony between the two schools. See also: Dr. Izz al-Din Ibrahim, cover story, *TI*, December 1982; *MI*, 43 (June 1986); 47 (November 1986); 55 (August 1987).

64. Shaykh As'ad al-Tamimi, a Sunni Imam, proudly tells of prayers which he himself conducted during one of his visits to Tehran. *MI*, 48 (November 1986). Shaykh Abd al-Aziz Odeh, *al-Fajr*, 23 August 1987; Shqaqi, *al-Khomeini*, 35, 38–39, 48, 56–57; Tamimi, *fatwa*, *MI*, 44 (July 1986).

65. *Al-Islam wa-Filastin*, 1, 15 February 1988, 4–5, cited by Paz, 4.

66. *Ha'aretz*, 10 July 1988.

67. Cited by Satloff, 7.

68. "Thawra Filastiniyya am thawra Islamiyya," *MI*, 63 (April 1988), 42.

69. Editorial, *MI*, 64 May 1988, 2.

70. Khaybar was an oasis in the Arabian Peninsula inhabited by Jewish tribes. It was conquered by the Prophet Muhammad in 628.

71. Satloff, 9.

72. For a detailed discussion of the movement, see Satloff, Paz and Jean François Legrain, "Les Islamites Palestiniens à l'Épreuve du Soulèvement," *Maghreb-Machrik*, 121 (July-August-September 1988), 5–41.

73. *Mithaq Harakat al-Muqawama al-Islamiyya—Filastin*, 18 August 1988, 12, 13.

74. "Jihad is not confined to the carrying of arms . . . a telling word, an effective article, a useful book, support and solidarity—all these are elements of the Jihad for Allah's sake." Ibid., 21.

75. Paz, 10; *Mithaq*, 8.

76. *Mithaq*, 19.

77. Shadid, *Muslim Brotherhood*, 679.

78. *Mithaq*, 10, 20.

79. Interviewed by Ron Ben-Yishai, *Yedi'ot Aharonot*, 16 September 1988.

80. *Mithaq*, 18.

81. E.g., *Ha'aretz*, 24 October 1988.

82. A similar line is followed by the Islamic fundamentalist movement in Israel, headed by Shaykh Abdallah Nimr Darwish.

83. On the effect of personal stress, alienation and frustration as a major motivating source for joining radical Islamic organizations, see Saad Eddin Ibrahim, "Anatomy of Egypt's Militant Islamic groups: Methodological Note and Preliminary Findings," *International Journal of Middle East Studies*, 12 (1980), 448; Zonis and Brumberg, 48, 62.

11

Echoes of the Iranian Revolution in the Writings of Egyptian Muslims

Johannes J. G. Jansen

Early in 1979, Egyptian media described the overthrow of the shah as essentially a victory for Islam—a victory which had ended un-Islamic foreign domination on the part of the Americans.

Ayatollah Ruhollah Khomeini, so the readers of the Egyptian press were made to understand, had achieved a victory over Christian western powers. In particular, this was the view of the Muslim Brothers' monthly, *al-Da'wa*. The octogenarian leader of the Egyptian Muslim Brotherhood, Umar al-Tilimsani (d. 22 May 1986) gravely predicted in his columns that the end of non-Muslim rule over Muslims was at hand.[1] He named, by way of warning, Thailand, Malaysia, Eritrea, Burma, the Philippines, and, of course, Israel.

The subject of Muslim victories over non-Muslims is, of course, non-controversial in the Muslim world, and the greatness of such victories can safely be glorified at all times and everywhere. Yet, in the spring of 1979 the Egyptian public (even if interested) might not yet have appreciated a more detailed and specific résumé of Khomeini's ideology.

In the summer of 1979, Khomeini's revolution had to compete for the attention of the Egyptian public with a bold project of legal reform introduced by President Sadat or, according to the rumors current at the time, rather by his wife, Jihan Sadat. This was Law 44/1979 on marriage and divorce. Several of its articles were at variance with the *shari'a*, thereby evoking widespread public discussion. Many thought it particularly offensive that the law designated polygamy as *darar*, "something which harms." Since Qur'an 4.3 ("Marry such of the women as seem good to you, double or treble or fourfold") is widely understood as evidence that God permits polygamy, many pious Muslims were severely shocked that, despite Qur'anic approval, the Egyptian government spoke of it as harmful.

In May 1985, the law was eventually declared invalid by the Egyptian Higher Constitutional Court[2] on formal grounds. Two months later, the government reacted by proclaiming a new law (Law 100/1985) which annulled most of the changes introduced in 1979.

In the elaborate public discussions on the laws of 1985 and 1979, the Iranian revolutionary example played little or no role. It is, however, quite possible that the revision of 1985 was influenced by the government's desire to put an end to a controversy that could only benefit the propaganda of the radical Muslims.[3]

Since the fall of 1979, Egyptian intellectuals who wished to know what exactly Khomeini professed to advocate, could have recourse to an Egyptian edition of Khomeini's book entitled *Al-Hukuma al-Islamiyya*, privately printed and distributed by Dr. Hasan Hanafi, professor of Islamic philosophy in the University of Cairo in Giza.[4] In his introduction to this basic text of Khomeini, Hanafi summarizes Khomeini's views, but adds six provisos.[5]

(1) Although, according to Hanafi, Khomeini relies on reason (*i'timad ala al-ma'qul*) when presenting his political and religious ideology, he too often looks for support for his views in controversial chapters of Islamic history. Hanafi obviously means Khomeini's references to the early wars between the Sunna and Shi'a, on which Sunni Muslims hold views different from those of the Shi'i Khomeini. Hanafi concludes his first proviso with the following words:

> The need for the formation of an Islamic government is an obvious necessity which does not need to be shown to be true with the help of quotations from the Tradition (*hadith*); neither does the doctrine of the supremacy of the *faqih* need such support or proof; both these theories are clearly and solidly found in the Qur'an (*thabit bil-Qur'an*). It would be all too easy to claim that such supporting Traditions are weak, or to cast doubt on their authenticity.

This objection, one cannot fail to see, fully endorses the essence of Khomeini's political ideology. Hanafi appeals to high authority indeed when he teaches that it is the Qur'an itself which prescribes the doctrine of the Supremacy of the *fuqaha*. His objection only concerns the way in which Khomeini argues his point, not the doctrine itself.

(2) The second objection concerns the metaphysical element in Khomeini's theory: not everyone, Hanafi suspects, may share Khomeini's metaphysical belief in the uncreatedness and pre-existence of the Imams. "Here," he complains, "the theory of the supremacy of the *faqih* looks more like a myth than like a positive political order (*nizam siyasi*)."

(3) Khomeini, so Hanafi writes, concentrates too much on the top of the political and social pyramid, neglecting to discuss the base: social change, he explains, cannot be affected before the present political authorities are removed; and this can only be achieved through revolutionary activities, which are doomed to fail if they have no mass support. It would perhaps be better, Hanafi suggests, to concentrate on enlightening the masses (*tanwir al-shu'ub*), since this is a necessary prerequisite for success in the battle for an Islamic state.[6] Many an old Calvinist will be pleased to note his comment

that man needs to be subject to the rule of the *fuqaha* because "human nature is evil, and man is evil by nature."

(4) Hanafi regrets that Khomeini does not give "detailed theories" (*nazariyyat tafsiriyya*) on such essentials of the social order as class structure, the ownership of the means of production, the relationship between farmer and soil, or between worker and factory, the nationalization of banks and insurance companies etc. Such details, he concludes, are needed to transform Khomeini's doctrine from slogan into practice (*min al-shi'ar ila al-tatbiq*).

(5) Hanafi has his doubts about certain measures which the Iranian Revolution took concerning the *chador* and *hijab*, nightclubs, wine, the execution of prostitutes, etc. In these measures, so he thinks, traditional ethics play a large role. Have political Islam and the ethics of Islam kept the same pace, he wonders. Is Khomeini's revolution not essentially a revolution of the oppressed and the hungry, and should it not give priority to the war against poverty and unemployment. Hanafi chooses his words with great care, and every now and then his remarks become rather obscure. He certainly does not want to write anything capable of being construed as an attack on the alleged cruelty of some of Khomeini's measures; nor does he want to be suspected of defending those reprehensible forms of human behavior to which Khomeini's regime put an end. This dilemma dims his clarity of expression.

(6) Hanafi agrees with Khomeini on the necessity of preserving an Islamic identity but feels that to reject all things western goes too far: rationalism, parliamentarism, humanism, progressivism, and a host of other isms may nowadays seem to be western, but according to Hanafi if properly understood and reconstructed in the Islamic way, they are all original Islamic trends (*ittijahat islamiyya*) which the west took from Islam in the Middle Ages.[7] The Great Islamic Revolution is therefore not only a reaction against the west, not exclusively an anti-western movement; to regard it as such would be to belittle it. Rather, it is a movement, so Hanafi concludes, which in principle is capable of fusing (*yumkin al-talahum*) with revolutionary movements all over the world, "the revolution of the priests of Latin America" not excluded.

Hanafi's six remarks are, of course critical, but it is criticism of a kind than can only be called constructive: it implies an endorsement of Khomeini's views. Hanafi, furthermore, teaches that it is the Qur'an which prescribes these views, and that textual support from the different collections of Prophetic Traditions is superfluous and needlessly controversial. By doing so, he lifts Khomeini's doctrine of *wilayat al-faqih* above the Sunni-Shi'i divisions: as far as Traditions are concerned, Sunni and Shi'i Muslims have their differences, but the text of the Qur'an is above any denominational or sectarian difference.

Let us take a short look at the Qur'anic proofs which Hanafi proffers. First, the motto of Khomeini's book,[8] taken from Sura 27.34:

Kings, when they enter a town, corrupt it, and make the noblest of its people the lowest; so they will do.

Here as elsewhere,[9] "town" (*qarya*) is understood as a Qur'anic near-equivalent of the modern word "state"; "kings" (*muluk*) probably has to be understood as "profane rulers." It would not be surprising if many understand "the noblest of its people" (*a'izzat ahliha*) to mean the *ulama* and *fuqaha*.

The other examples[10] all presuppose belief in the truth of the well-known and much quoted Tradition which runs in Arabic "*inna al-ulama warathat al-anbiya*" ("the *ulama* are the heirs of the prophets"). Muhammad, so the Arabic version of Khomeini's book entitled *Al-Hukuma al-Islamiyya* teaches,[11] was a "head of state" (*ra'is dawla*) and so should his heirs be.

In Sura 57.25 we read: "We sent down with [the Prophets] the Book and the Balance, that the people might dispense justice." According to Khomeini, this means that the *ulama*, as true heirs of the prophet, have now inherited the duty to dispense justice, i.e. to rule.

The same is true of Sura 8.42: "And know that if ye take anything as spoil—that to God belongs a fifth of it, and to the Messenger." Like Qur'an 9.104: "Take of their goods a *sadaqa*," this is used to establish beyond doubt that the prophet was not only a preacher telling people about their duties but also had a divine mandate to see that they were carried out (*ma'mur bil-amal bihi wa-tanfidhihi*). As his heirs, the *ulama* should do the same: the executive power is theirs by divine right.

About the relevance in this context of Qur'an 4.62 ("Obey God and obey the Messenger and those of you who have the command")[12] differences of opinion are, of course, possible, since the wording in this verse is (as so often) ambiguous. It should, however, be noted that already the totally uncontroversial Sunni Qur'an commentator al-Baydawi (d. 1260) thinks that it is possible that "those of you who have the command," (*ulu al-amr minkum*) refers to the *ulama*.

A philologist trained in the west may not be impressed by the Qur'anic evidence adduced, and it may well be that Hanafi's main motive is to lift the discussion about *wilayat al-faqih* above the level of the Sunni-Shi'i controversies by boldly reading it into the text of the Qur'an; but we cannot overlook that in the eyes of an Egyptian Sunni Muslim intellectual it appears to be quite possible to make a case for the Qur'anic character of the *wilayat al-faqih* doctrine.

Not much is known with certainty about the views which the Sunni Egyptian Muslim extremists hold, but one of their (rare) uncensored testimonies, *al-Farida al-Gha'iba* ("The Neglected Duty"), the creed of Sadat's assassins, shows no familiarity with this doctrine.

Al-Farida al-Gha'iba was published for the first time in December 1981, and though certainly drafted earlier, it is highly improbable that it was written long before the Iranian revolution. It contains what is probably a reference[13] to events which took place between the summer of 1977 and the spring of 1978. Since it is hard to imagine that Khomeini's revolution would have remained unmentioned if it had already taken place at the time it was written, the most probable date of its composition would appear to be between the spring of 1978 and the end of that year.

Its author, Muhammad Abd al-Salam Faraj, holds views that are remarkably similar to those of Khomeini, but these similarities cannot be explained by assuming the direct influence of Khomeini and Khomeinism. Both the *Farida* and Khomeini's doctrine teach that a good Muslim has the (too often neglected) duty to participate in the struggle (*jihad*) against unbelief (*kufr*), oppression (*zulm*) and imperialism (*isti'mar*) that threaten the world of Islam. But such notions are common to all Muslim revolutionaries, and will crop up in any other religiously formulated Islamic critique of the existing order.[14]

The *Farida* document, however, differs conspicuously from the theory of Khomeinism on one point: the *ulama* are treated with respect, but are certainly not seen as people whom God has chosen to rule the universe in His name. The author tries to present his argument in a way that will look convincing to the *ulama* (see, for instance #63) but nevertheless holds them largely responsible for the state of degeneration into which according to him, Islam has fallen. The *ulama*, so the document tells us, are either vain or do not know the ways of the modern world (#140), and are hence incapable or ill-suited to lead the struggle of Islam against the un-Islamic powers ruling the Islamic world.

The leadership of the Islamic revolutionary movement, so the *Farida* implies in a clear contradiction to Khomeini's world view, can consequently not be in the hands of the *ulama* alone. In #93 we read that "command must go to the best Muslim," irrespective of whether such a potential leader may have received secular or religious training. "The qualities which such a leader may lack can be supplemented" (#94). The earliest generations of Muslims conquered the world by the sword, not the pen (#64). Moreover, the *ulama* either neglect their duties as far as *jihad* is concerned, or feign ignorance of them (#3). Of what use was the learning of the *ulama*, so the author of the *Farida* asks (#64), when Napoleon and his soldiers entered al-Azhar on horseback?

After all this, Khomeini's contention that the ink of the men of religion is more precious (*afdal*) than the blood of the martyrs,[15] pours (one would expect) balm on the wounds of the Sunni *ulama*.[16]

It is well-known by now that the essence of the preaching of modern Muslim radicals lies in their belief that Muslims are under the obligation to set up an Islamic state. In such a state, Islamic law must by necessity be the law of the land, otherwise it would not be truly Islamic. Khomeini took the argument a step further than any other Muslim revolutionaries. According to him, nobody knows the laws of Islam better than the Muslim scholars who study them professionally. Hence, ultimate authority in an Islamic state will have to be in their hands.

Politics is part and parcel of daily life, and so at least to a good Muslim, is religion. Human logic dictates that if this is so, there can be no separation between politics and religion. The basic concepts which Khomeini refers to here are common to both Sunni and Shi'i Muslims. Khomeini himself may be an Iranian Shi'i, and most Muslims in the Middle East may be Arab Sunnis, but it is doubtful whether these two differences make them unwilling to listen to Khomeini's message.

Many informed diplomats assume that linguistic and denominational differences make Arab Sunnis immune against Iranian Shi'i propaganda, but it is doubtful whether this is quite true. To Hanafi, at least, writing in 1979, Khomeini's revolution is a Muslim revolution, not an exclusively Shi'i one: the difference between Sunna and Shi'a, so Hanafi maintains, "has been played with by imperialism and Zionism . . . but Khomeini, like Afghani, leads a truly Islamic revolution that surpasses these sectarian borders. . . . Its *élan* goes back to the first revolutionary achievements of the earliest phases of Islam."[17]

Khomeini's book *Wilayat al-Faqih* originated in a series of lectures which he delivered, early in 1970 at Najaf, to Arabic speaking students. This book is distributed in the Arab world. It is therefore only partly true that differences of language and denomination place Khomeini at a disadvantage when he attempts to be heard in the Arab Middle East. One should be careful not to make too much of the language barrier Khomeini's message has to overcome. Unlike the political language emanating from Moscow or Washington, the political language emanating from Tehran needs little cross-cultural translation before it is understood by Arab Muslims: for obvious reasons, only few of them have, for instance, any difficulty in envisaging what life under the shah must have been.

Moreover, already the very wording of Khomeini's doctrine known as *Wilayat al-Faqih* betrays a certain carefulness on the part of its spiritual father to avoid hurting Sunni-Shi'i sensitivities. Shi'is call their men of religion *mujtahidun* or *ayatollah*, whereas Sunnis prefer the term *ulama*. The word *faqih*, however, is common to both and is readily understood on both sides of the division.

It is psychologically improbable that Khomeini's gospel of the supremacy of the men of religion is not being received with interest by Sunni Muslims. As long as the war between Iraq and Iran continued, any expression of sympathy with Khomeini's ideology from citizens of countries taking Iraq's side came close to treason. Hence, expressions of sympathy with, interest in or agreement with Khomeinism were, admittedly, rare in published writings in the Arab world. Nevertheless, tourists and journalists report that Khomeini's portrait was regularly seen in coffeeshops and teahouses in solidly Sunni regions.

In the wake of the riots preceding the *hajj* pilgrimage in Mecca in 1987, the London Arabic-language weekly *al-Tali'a al-Arabiyya/L'Avant-Garde Arabe* published an article listing official Egyptian condemnations of Iran's role in these disturbances.[18] Short interviews indicated that all Egyptian political and religious dignitaries unanimously blamed Iran. Only the spokesman for a group called "The Islamic Alliance" (*Al-Tahaluf al-Islami*) held different views.

The spokesman for this alliance of the *Hizb al-Amal* and the Muslim Brothers, a certain Shaykh Mustafa Asi,[19] advocated considering the possibility of transforming the *hajj* into a mass conference for discussing the problems of the Islamic world (*tahwil tajammu al-hajj ila mu'tamar sha'bi yabhath qadaya al-alam al-islami*). But he added that he, too, disapproved of violence as a matter of course.

Asi's careful formulas came close to but did not coincide with the Iranian point of view, nonetheless the editor of the weekly simply concluded that the Alliance now sided with Iran in its struggle against Iraq, a country desperately defending its borders. According to the weekly, to show any understanding for the Iranian position went against the consensus of the Egyptian religious and political establishment and Egyptian public opinion. But if the Alliance really reflects the Muslim Brothers' view, it is doubtful whether this is true. It is difficult indeed to imagine the Muslim Brothers and their heirs dissociating themselves from a broad consensus.

However, even Asi was quoted by the weekly as having said: "I believe that the Iranian attempts at exporting the revolution, and with it the special understanding of Islam of the Ayatollahs, will fail (*sawfa tafshal*)."[20] But he went on to caution the Arab states that they would have to do something in order to make it fail and should not wait until failure came about by itself (*dhatiyyan*). It is regrettable that the weekly did not report which measures Asi would have considered appropriate to that end. Could he have meant that the Arab states should step up anti-Iranian propaganda? Or that they change their societies in such a way as to make the Iranian message superfluous?

The Egyptian religious weekly *al-Liwa al-Islami* illustrates another aspect of the possible impact of Khomeinism on Sunni Islam. In an editorial of 18 April 1985, it defiantly demanded from the well-known and much-translated Egyptian writer Tawfiq al-Hakim (or anybody else who would care to answer) to give just one example of an act that is not subject to "the values of religion." Human life in all its aspects, the weekly maintained, is subject to religion, and Islam does not recognize any limitation to the sway of its authority. To a sensitive ear, a vague phrase like "the values of religion" may well be a code for "the specific rules of Islamic law."

The axiom that human life in all its aspects falls under the authority of Islam is not a matter of dispute between Sunnis and Shi'is (or any other Muslim group, a few modernists excluded). It provides the kind of common ground that may well make a fusion of Khomeinism and Sunni Islam thinkable.

The above-mentioned editorial continues with a complicated set of formulas, sometimes hard to interpret, but all open to the understanding that the responsibility for the well-being of the Islamic community lies not with the individual Muslims or the social forces which they collectively generate. Indeed, it lies exclusively with the person or persons who exercise ultimate political authority. Those in authority "should remember God's instructions whenever they sign a law or decree. . . . They should remember the beauty of their religion, and show this beauty to the people. . . . It is, however, only by their example that they can effectively show the beauty of Islam. . . . Those who are in power now should remember that there is Someone who is more powerful than they are . . . who can take away in minutes what they gathered and collected in years."

Who, one can not help wondering, are better equipped to show "the beauty of their religion" to the public than the professional men of religion? Is there really an unbridgeable gulf between the attitude expressed in this and numerous other articles, and Khomeinism? Could Khomeinism not easily become complementary to the insistence, on the part of the Muslim Brothers and their spiritual descendants, on the total application of Islamic law in all its details?

The *Farida* document shows that the extremists who assassinated President Sadat in October 1981 were desperately obsessed by the absolute necessity for a *hakim muslim* (a Muslim ruler), who, like a Messiah, would lead his people to salvation in this world and the world to come. They almost completely disregarded secular influences on human society and human life; they may not even have prepared their attempted *coup d'état* properly since they believed God would take over once they had fired the first shots.

They are actually reported to have attempted to find a "man of religion" to lead their group and to have neglected other aspects of their society. It is difficult not to see the parallel with Khomeinism which at least in theory equally concentrates on the top: if the leadership of the Muslim state is in the right hands, i.e. the hands of the men of religion, God will automatically put things right—so Khomeini wants his disciples to believe.

It is perfectly reasonable to doubt whether the Egyptian public at large is fully aware of the contents of Khomeini's message, and in particular of the *wilayat al-faqih* doctrine. Many a taxi driver will be inclined to put his fare, whether tourist or journalist, at ease by assuring them that according to him Khomeini is not even a Muslim and that Shi'ism is a synonym of terrorism. One may even meet this sentiment in the semi-official religious press: *Al-Liwa al-Islami*, too, assured its readers that Shi'ism is only a kind of extremism.[21]

If, however, the great preacher Shaykh Muhammad Mutawalli al-Sha'rawi supposes the general public to be familiar with the *wilayat al-faqih* doctrine, one may safely assume that this is the case. For over a decade, Sha'rawi[22] has been an extremely popular and effective preacher, who at times appears more often on Egyptian television than the Egyptian head of state. He effortlessly appeals as much to those who like to think of themselves as modern people, as to those who think of themselves as holding on to all that has been good in the past. Few Muslims are capable of so expertly exploiting the possibilities of the television screen to serve the cause of Islam.

A sermon by Sha'rawi, published in *al-Liwa al-Islami* on 6 August 1987, indicates that according to him the Egyptian public can be supposed to have at least an idea about the *wilayat al-faqih* doctrine. The Shaykh does not attack Khomeini's doctrine outright, or mention it by name, but his guarded formulas are clear enough. He reminds his listeners that God ordered the prophet to ask his audience: "Shall I choose as a *wali*[23] any other than God?"[24] It is only natural and human, so he explains, to need the help of a *wali* in times of weakness: when we call our *wali*, he comes to assist us.

It is wicked (*munkar*) to take a *wali* other than God. God's work as man's *wali*, God's *wilaya*, is manifest in the co-operation and mutual assistance of the believers: "The believers, male and female, are each the *wali*[25] of the other."[26]

Consequently, so the Shaykh goes on, God distributed different gifts amongst men, in order to guarantee the continuation of his creation. Examples follow: Medical men need engineers, engineers need doctors, and both need farmers. "No one unites in himself all talents (*mawahib*), every man is master (*sayyid*) in one corner (*zawiya*) of the many corners of life . . . and this is why God said: It is We who have divided out amongst them their livelihood in the present life."[27]

Perhaps such passages do not look very convincing in an English translation. In Arabic, the repeated use of the term *wilaya* makes it difficult not to be reminded of Khomeini's *wilayat al-faqih*, especially in the last lines the Shaykh devotes to this subject:

> Faith in God gives us the insight we need in order to be able to choose our *wali*; a believer must choose the *wali* whom he finds when he is in need of one; hence, believers only choose God's *wilaya*; not the *wilaya* of any one else (*wilayat Allah, la wilayat al-aghyar*). A human *wali* may be absent (*gha'ib*),[28] or ill. . . . The Qur'an does not disapprove if man takes himself a *wali*; But the True God wants us to know that only He is a True *wali*, since this is the real *wilayat Allah*.

The reference to different professions (doctors, lawyers, engineers and farmers) all being each other's *wali* makes it clear that Khomeini's *wilayat al-faqih* cannot be implied since according to this doctrine ultimate authority over all fields of human activity lies with the *faqih adil* (the righteous *faqih*), whereas this sermon makes each man *sayyid* (master) over his own chosen field. Yet, if the believers are *wali* to each other, are not the best believers the best *awliya*? And who, after all, are better believers than the professional men of religion? It would not take much homiletical acrobatics to turn even this sermon into an endorsement of Khomeini's *wilayat al-faqih* doctrine.

Elsewhere in *al-Liwa al-Islami*[29] we find a statement that is a little clearer. It is *iftira* (malicious slander) to teach, "as some do," that real Islamic government can only be established if all power goes to the professional men of religion. Those who teach so deliberately misrepresent Islam. But then the author adds:

> We should, however, draw attention to a very important point: for every position a certain amount of experience and knowledge is required . . . when we have two [candidates] who are equal in experience and knowledge but one of the two holds on more firmly to his religion (*akthar mutamassikan bil-din*), then that one is to be preferred.

Here again, not much is needed to transform a refutation of the *wilayat al-faqih* doctrine into an endorsement of it. A professional editor boldly put above these words the caption "Ultimate social and political authority should not be in the hands of the *ulama* alone." Such clarity is perhaps more in accordance with western secularized taste than with the intentions of the writer.

In 1987, there were at least three attempts to assassinate Egyptian functionaries involved in the struggle against Islamic militancy. All three failed. On 5 May, an attack was made on Hasan Abu Basha, ex-minister of the interior; a week later, the Egyptian government closed the Iranian Interest Section at the Cairo Swiss Embassy. Rumor had it that the police inquiries had uncovered links between the Iranian chargé d'affaires Mahmud Mohtadi and members of Egyptian radical groups investigated following the attack on Abu Basha.

However, in June the editor of *al-Musawwar*, Makram Muhammad Ahmad, was attacked, and on 17 August another ex-minister for the Interior, Nabawi Isma'il, became the victim of an assassination attempt.

As far as it can be established, it is not completely clear whether the Egyptian Prosecutor Muhammad Abd al-Aziz al-Jundi will attempt to prove Iranian involvement in these attacks, since they continued after the expulsion from Egypt of the Iranian diplomat.

At the trial of 33 extremists opened in Cairo in early April the prosecution demanded the death penalty for 15 of the accused. The defendants were accused of membership in an organization which tried to overthrow the Egyptian government, and of membership in the *hijra* movement.

The last part of this indictment implies that the defendants would have used force (or, at least, were ready to use force) in order to implement a set of beliefs including the following: (1) that modern Egypt is as pagan as pre-Islamic Mecca, (2) that true Muslims should leave Egyptian society the way the Apostle of God left Mecca, and (3) that true Muslims should prepare for a triumphant return as conquerors the way Muhammad conquered Mecca in 630.

If the trial confirms that they indeed held such views, it remains to be seen whether they followed the teachings of the extremist leader Shukri Mustafa or whether their ideological inspiration came, mainly or partly, from Khomeinism. (Mustafa was hanged in 1978 for the murder, in 1977, of Shaykh Muhammad Husayn al-Dhahabi.)[30]

Ideological sympathy with Khomeinism is at times abundantly present in the pages of the Egyptian opposition newspapers *al-Sha'b* and *al-Ahrar*. These newspapers (originally of leftist persuasions) have recently identified themselves closely with Islamic aspirations. Their representatives visited Iran in 1986 on the invitation of the above-mentioned Mahmud Mohtadi. Enthusiastic reports about their visit can be found e.g., in *al-Ahrar* of 13 October 1986: "The mosque . . . is the center of the command"; "the Islamic republic does not want war"; "the Muslim armies show the greatest possible determination," etc. *Al-Sha'b* of 24 June 1986 writes: "The [new] rulers of Tehran live as simply as they did before"; "the leaders walk [without bodyguard] amidst the masses"; "[Khomeini] takes no luxurious foods," etc.

The emphasis in this feat of propaganda is, however, on well-known clichés like the simplicity of the new rulers, the enthusiasm of the masses for the New Order, popular hatred for the expelled oppressors, etc., rather than on the *wilayat al-faqih* doctrine.

In retrospect, success in wars and revolutions often looks historically inevitable, and seems to be determined by the social forces affecting the revolutionaries or belligerents. In reality, however, this is not the case. The outcome of a revolution or war is determined by a multitude of factors, many of which are completely accidental. It would be pleasant to believe that things are otherwise, and I envy everyone who does.

The impossibility to predict religious, military and political developments seems to preclude answering the question "Will the Muslim world in the near future be struck by a continuing series of Khomeini-type revolutions?" But it is quite possible to read what our Muslim neighbors preach and write. Their sermons and articles suggest that—no matter how many official condemnations of Khomeinism one may encounter—the distance between Khomeinism and radical and/or activist Islam elsewhere is not formidable. Even the official Islam of the establishment uses, every now and then, phrases that differ only minimally from the slogans of Khomeinism. Moreover, Egyptian opposition newspapers demonstrate a purely political sympathy for Khomeinism, in which religion plays practically no role.

Even if Khomeini and Khomeinism were to lose all credibility within Iran, this does not necessarily mean that the oppressed elsewhere could not continue to hope for global salvation through Khomeinism, and act accordingly. Stalin and Stalinism supply an interesting parallel: long after Stalin had lost his credibility within the Soviet Union, millions of devoted communists in Europe continued to see him as the liberator of the exploited and the hope of the masses.

The activities of Hasan al-Banna's Muslim Brotherhood gave rise to a growing consensus within the Arab Sunni world that Islamic law, the *shari'a*, must be translated from theory into practice. Will this consensus become the hand that fits into the glove of Khomeinism? Only time will tell.

Notes

1. *Al-Da'wa*, 34 (March 1979), 5c.
2. *Al-Jarida al-Rasmiyya*, 16 May 1985.
3. See *Les Modifications du Code Egyptien de la Famille*, (Bulletin CEDEJ; Cairo: 1985); and N. Kruijs Voorberge, "De Nieuwe Egyptische Wet op het Personeel Statuut," in *Recht van de Islam*, 5 (Rimo: 1987), 3–19.
4. Al-Marja al-Dini al-A'la al-Imam al-Mujahid al-Sayyid Ruhollah al-Khomeini, *al-Hukuma al-Islamiyya* (i'dad wa-taqdim Dr. Hasan Hanafi; Cairo: September 1979).
5. Khomeini-Hanafi, 26–29.
6. Dr. Hanafi's suggestion concerning the lack of enlightenment of the masses may imply that, according to him, the general public in Egypt does as yet not support radical Islamic policies.
7. According to Dr. Nikki R. Keddie, this idea was first developed by Jamal al-Din al-Afghani, see her *al-Sayyid Jamal al-Din "al-Afghani": A Political Biography* (Los

Angeles: 1972); and *idem., An Islamic Response to Imperialism: Political and Religious Writings of Sayyid Jamal al-Din "al-Afghani"* (Los Angeles: 1968). The idea has since then become a much repeated cliché.

8. Khomeini-Hanafi, 33.

9. E.g., J. J. G. Jansen, *The Neglected Duty: The Creed of Sadat's Assassins and Islamic Resurgence in the Middle East* (New York: 1986), 111.

10. Khomeini-Hanafi, 68–69.

11. Ibid., 85.

12. Ibid., 69 and 103.

13. My op. cit., 11 and 187.

14. Cf. Bernard Lewis, "Islamic Revolution," in *The New York Review of Books*, 21 January 1988.

15. Khomeini-Hanafi, 149.

16. E.g., *al-Liwa al-Islami*, 16 July 1987, 19b, accuses the extremist Muslims of despising the *ulama*.

17. Khomeini-Hanafi, 25.

18. *Al-Tali'a al-Arabiyya* (London), 17 August 1987, 16–8.

19. *Amin al-lajna al-diniyya fi hizb al-tajammu.*

20. It would be interesting to know why, in this statement about the future, the obligatory *in sha Allah* formula was not used. Does the responsibility for this omission lie with Mustafa Asi or with the editors?

21. Cf. *al-Liwa al-Islami*, 27 August 1987, 1; "Shi'ism is a kind of extremism," *al-shi'a . . . naw min al-tatarruf.*

22. On Shaykh Sha'rawi and some of his critics, see my op. cit., 121–50.

23. Richard Bell here translates *wali* as "patron," see his *The Qur'an Translated* (Edinburg: 1937).

24. Qur'an 6.14.

25. Richard Bell here translates the plural of *wali* as "friends."

26. Qur'an 9.71.

27. Qur'an 43.32.

28. It is tempting to suppose that Sha'rawi here alludes to *al-Imam al-Gha'ib*, the hidden Imam of the Shi'is.

29. Article by the religious writer Ahmad Zayn, *al-Liwa al-Islami*, 24 September 1987, 5.

30. See, e.g., my op. cit., 13 and G. Kepel, *Le Prophète et Pharaon* (Paris: 1984), 70–100.

12

Sunni Polemical Writings on the Shi'a and the Iranian Revolution

Werner Ende

In his famous work *Umm al-Qura*, the fictional proceedings of a secret Pan-Islamic congress alleged to have been held at Mecca in 1898, Abd al-Rahman al-Kawakibi presents the "charter" of a permanent body which the "congress" had decided to establish.[1] Two from among the principles of that body, the *jam'iyyat ta'lim al-muwahhidin*, as laid down in the charter, relate to the existence of "schools" (*madhahib*) in Islam and to the attitude of the *jam'iyya* towards them. Paragraphs 16 and 17 read as follows:[2]

(16) "The Society (*jam'iyya*) is in no way affiliated to any particular *madhhab* or religious party (*shi'a*) of Islam," and (17) "The Society adjusts its religious course of action to the moderate Salafi school of thought (*mashrab*), to the rejection of every addition or innovation in [the realm of] religion, and to [the principle] to argue over (religious matters) only in the best [or: kindest] possible (*illa bi-llati hiya ahsan*)" (see Qur'an 29:46).

There can be no doubt that at the turn of the century, when Kawakibi's book was published, there was a widespread feeling in the Muslim world—at least among the modern-educated urban elite (both Sunni and Shi'i)—that any dispute over religious issues should be avoided. If that proved impossible, it should at least be carried out in a spirit of Muslim solidarity. The main argument was that the enemies of Islam, i.e. western colonialism in all its different forms, would exploit the lack of Muslim unity in order to perpetuate its influence throughout the world of Islam. Even today, this is the standard argument used by all those who would like to see a friendly dialogue between Sunnis and Shi'is—and who would like that dialogue to result in a *rapprochement*.[3]

The argument that communal strife among Muslims is likely to invite outside interference is certainly not altogether unjustified. However, in the minds of some Muslim writers and of many of their readers this argument develops into something like an obsession. Communal strife cannot always be avoided, especially in countries with a confessionally mixed population such as India and Pakistan. When it happens, some spokesmen of both Sunni and Shi'i Islam are eager to prove that imperialism is always plotting behind the scenes in order to split the ranks of the *umma*, using for its own purposes naïve or evil-minded elements from this or that Muslim community. For a number of reasons, conspiracy theories, i.e. speculation about the enemies of Islam hatching plots of all sorts against the *umma*, are very popular in the modern Muslim world. Many of these theories—if "theory" is the right word—are a strange mixture of more or less distorted views on:

1) The history of Islam and other religions;
2) Traditional ethnic and/or religious prejudice (more often than not corroborated by fragments of western ideologies, opinions of orientalists etc.); and
3) An exaggerated belief in the role and capabilities of secret services in international politics, past and present.

In the case of the precarious relationship between Sunnis and Shi'is in the 20th century, presumed foreign conspiracies are often cited to explain, or explain away, the many setbacks the Muslims suffered on the road to unity or, at least, to a mutual *rapprochement*.

Many of the more fanciful explanations may never appear in print, but some find their way into the vast (and in most Muslim countries semi-clandestine) market of booklets and periodicals where traditionalists, militant fundamentalists and secular chauvinists propagate their ideas. Many of these explanations remain unknown to the public at large. But spectacular events such as the bloody incidents of Friday, 31 July 1987 at Mecca, involving Iranian pilgrims (see chapter by Goldberg), do prepare the ground for media "disclosures" which, under other circumstances, would not have been made. This holds true both for the Iranian and the Saudi media.[4] As an example from Iran, we may cite here an article published—a few weeks after the clashes at Mecca—in *Kayhan-e Hava'i*. It described the Wahhabiyya as a doctrine which British imperialism, represented by an agent of the East India Company, had instilled in its founder, Muhammad ibn Abd al-Wahhab, with the aim of deepening the rift between Sunni and Shi'i Islam to the benefit of the British.[5] The article seems to present the gist of a book first published in Persian whose author claimed that his information concerning that agent of the East India Company, one "Mister H-m-f-r," was taken from an Arabic book printed many years earlier in Beirut.

Some Sunni polemicists, on the other hand, do not hesitate to portray Khomeini as a secret ally of the United States and Israel and to describe his revolution as part of an international "scenario." In proof of that, the most far-fetched "clues" are offered not only by politicians and journalists, but also by academics and religious writers. For instance: an assistant professor of Islamic Studies at Yarmuk University tries to prove, in a book published in 1983, that an unnamed orientalist connected with Princeton University and working for the CIA is the real author of Khomeini's famous booklet *Al-Hukuma al-Islamiyya*.[6]

Examples of this kind of wild speculation could easily be multiplied. But I only wanted to give an idea of the atmosphere in which *religious* polemic articles, pamphlets and books, in the present case against the Shi'a, are being written and distributed.

In what follows I would like to address myself to two subjects:

1) The main issue of Sunni-Shi'i controversy in modern times; and
2) the way in which the various topics of dispute are handled by Sunni polemicists, especially in recent years.

If not stated otherwise, references to Shi'is will be to the *Shi'a Imamiyya*, (the Twelver Shi'a or *Ja'fariyya*)—by far the largest contemporary group of Shi'is.[7] With regard to the topics chosen by today's Sunni polemicists, obviously a number of issues treated in great detail in mediaeval Muslim heresiography etc. are no longer discussed by present-day authors or have become marginal. This is true, e.g., of the problem of *mash ala al-khuffayn*, i.e. whether or nor Muslims are allowed under certain circumstances to retain their footwear during the ritual ablution.[8] From a comprehensive survey I made of Sunni polemical writings composed and published in Arabic from the beginning of this century onward, it becomes clear that one or two topics of dispute have become salient (at the expense of others) or rather, have acquired a new dimension as a result of modern developments. As will be shown presently, the question of prophet Muhammad's companions is a case in point. However, *all* these points of dissent have already been basic issues of dispute in the past. In other words: some *motif*s have passed into desuetude, but no new ones have been added.[9]

The live issues can be subsumed under the following general topics:

1) The Qur'an and its interpretation, as well as the integrity or alleged distortion (*tahrif*) of its text.[10]
2) The authenticity of the prophet's traditions (*hadith*s) and what Shi'is consider to be the *hadith*s of their Imams.[11]
3) The image of the Prophet Muhammad's companions, the *sahaba*, including A'isha and the other "mothers of the believers."[12] The Shi'i view that the majority of the *sahaba* committed a grave sin by not supporting Ali's claim to the caliphate is unacceptable to Sunnis.[13] Closely linked to this topic is the question of how to define the concept of the "people of the house" (*ahl al-bayt*).[14]
4) There is, next, the history and concept of the Imamate (*imama*)—in fact the central issue of controversy between Sunnis and Shi'is. All other points of dispute are derived, in one way or another, from it. The Shi'i belief in, and extreme veneration of, the Imams as leaders of the community, appointed by God, the belief in the Imams' infallibility and sinlessness (*isma*), in their potential knowledge of all hidden things past, present and future are all seen by Sunnis as

historically wrong and theologically untenable and dangerous, if not altogether too close to polytheism.[15]

5) The Shi'is' concept of the *imama* has direct repercussions on their view of history,[16] including the question of legitimate power.[17] But in a somewhat intricate way, it is also linked to

6) certain legal details such as the endorsement in Ja'fari law of temporary marriage (*mut'a*), a much-discussed topic in recent years.[18]

7) The example of the Imams is also the basis of the Shi'i theory and practice of *taqiyya*, i.e. the dissimulation of one's real religious belief in circumstances of danger.[19] There is, finally,

8) The wide range of Shi'i lore and practice,[20] such as the processions and self-flagellations of Muharram or the holiday of Ghadir al-Khum etc., which most Sunnis see as unlawful innovations (*bid'a*) and as expressions of hatred against non-Shi'is.

To this list of main topics, I would like to add two observations: 1) The *motifs* mentioned here are all, in one way or another, inter-related. At their root lie different views of early Islamic history. Sunni-Shi'i disagreement on its interpretation appears to be as strong as ever—in spite of (or rather, because of) the fact that there have been certain pro-Shi'i tendencies in modern Sunni thought. By this I mean an inclination among Sunni writers, especially at the time of Jamal Abd al-Nasser, to defend and support contemporary revolutionary socialist policies by partially repainting the picture of early Islam. In this new picture, Ali and his supporters, especially Abu Dharr, became representatives of the "left," and the Umayyids with their allies were cast as the counter-revolutionary "right wing."[21] As this interpretation touches directly on the image of the *sahaba*, it was, and is being, attacked by Sunni enemies, whether traditionalist or fundamentalist, of ideologies such as Nasserism. When these critics came to realize that the view of Islamic history propagated by the Sunni "socialists" was being applauded by Shi'i authors, they began to interpret it as a *de facto* move towards Shi'ism and as a betrayal of Sunni principles and presented it as a lamentable success for modern Shi'i writings. Abu Dharr—a companion of the prophet and a supporter of Imam Ali, a fierce critic of Mu'awiya and Uthman and the supposed founding-father of Shi'is in Syria and Lebanon—figures prominently in the religious propaganda of the Iranian revolution. Thus the old issue of the integrity of *all* the *sahaba* (despite the civil war in which they were involved) viz. the long-established Sunni opposition to passing a negative judgment on one or some of them, has become an issue of current political relevance. In other words: defending the religious and moral integrity of *all* the *sahaba* entails refuting the Shi'i view of history as well as that of the modern Sunni "Islamic-socialists" who, among other things, dare to criticize some of the most famous *sahaba* for the wealth they amassed.[22] By citing from Shi'i works vilifying the first three caliphs and many prominent *sahaba*,[23] the polemicists hope to discredit the whole Shi'i (and, implicitly, the modern Sunni socialist) interpretation of history. (Some of those vilifications, it must be said, are bizarre by any standard).

2) My second observation concerns the function of *taqiyya*. The lawfulness of *taqiyya* for Shi'is serves Sunni polemicists as the ultimate argument against all assertions (whether from Sunni or Shi'i supporters of a *rapprochement*) of there being a new, conciliatory attitude on the part of the modern Shi'a toward controversial issues. All statements made by Shi'i spokesmen to the effect that there is no disagreement on this or that issue (such as the integrity of the Qur'anic text in the redaction supervised by Caliph Uthman), that disagreements are a matter of the past, that they arose only from a misunderstanding or concern only minor points—all this can be discounted by pointing to the principle of *taqiyya*: whatever Shi'is might say, so the polemicists argue, they dissimulate and Sunnis cannot trust them.[24]

Nonetheless, beginning from the start of this century, Islam has witnessed a number of attempts by both Shi'i and Sunni *ulama*, intellectuals and politicians to achieve unity or, at least, a *rapprochement* (*taqrib* or *taqarub*) between the two communities. At the same time, however, some individuals and groups on both sides, but especially among Sunnis, have been campaigning against these efforts. It is interesting to note that Sunni and Shi'i critics and/or enemies of *taqrib* use similar arguments to defend their position. The most important one is that, while unity of the Muslim world must indeed be the aim, it can be arrived at only on the basis of what is religiously correct, not by a false compromise. Since, in the view of such critics, the topics of dissent between Sunnis and Shi'is are fundamental, in fact: irreconcilable, *taqrib* would mean that one of the two *madhhabs* must give up its doctrine more or less completely or, alternatively, that a new sect would arise from this ill-conceived attempt at compromise. The latter would mean a new evil for Islam.[25] Some Sunni polemicists who have been speaking out against the ecumenical movement in recent years tend to point to the experience of certain prominent earlier Sunni writers who worked for *taqrib* but finally became disillusioned. Muhammad Rashid Rida, the editor of *al-Manar*, and Mustafa al-Siba'i, the founder of the Muslim Brotherhood in Syria, are mentioned as typical examples, and their bitter comments on the failure of such ecumenical attempts are quoted with satisfaction by present-day Sunni enemies of *taqrib*.[26]

It remains true, nevertheless, that at certain times in this century the Muslim ecumenical movement made some progress. Broadly speaking, one can say that until the mid-1920s, there was a widespread (but never undisputed!) readiness among Sunni and Shi'i religious leaders to unite under the banner of pan-Islam (until 1918 sponsored by Ottoman Turkey) and avoid controversy whenever possible. The public support shown by a number of Shi'i *ulama* for the Ottoman Sultan before World War I—some of them even addressed him as "caliph"—is a case in point.[27] The leading journal of the Sunni Salafiyya, *al-Manar* of Cairo, again and again expressed itself in favor of a *rapprochement*.

One should not forget, however, that this ecumenical spirit had no deep roots. When, in 1908, *al-Manar* published an article by an anonymous Iraqi who, among other things, warned of the consequences of Shi'i missionary work among the Sunni tribes of his country, a Lebanese scholar, Sayyid Muhsin al-Amin, wrote a sharp reply.[28] In the twenties, we find the same person in the front line of those Shi'i authors who, from 1924/25 onwards, complained bitterly about the Saudi-Wahhabi takeover in the Hijaz and attacked those Sunni scholars and writers who (like Rashid Rida) were now coming forward in defence of the Wahhabis and their newly established rule over Mecca and Medina.[29] Even some friendly words and gestures at the pan-Islamic congress in Jerusalem in 1931 which was attended by a number of Shi'i religious leaders, could not heal the fresh wounds.[30] Not a few of the polemical works published by both Sunni and Shi'i authors in the second half of the 1920s and in the 1930s have been reprinted in recent years and are quoted at length by today's polemicists.

From the late 1940s to the 1960s, however, there was much hope that a *rapprochement* would be possible, and would include an understanding on theological as well as political issues. Some scholars and intellectuals from both sides did in fact enter into a dialogue, e.g. by exchanging letters on problems of dogma. Others composed fictitious protocols of imaginary ecumenical discussions.[31]

In 1948 a society was established in Cairo which for some time became the most important center of ecumenical activities: the *jam'iyyat al-taqrib bayn al-madhahib al-islamiyya*. With an Iranian divine, Muhammad Taqi Qomi, as its founder and secretary-general, it had the support of a number of prominent *ulama* of al-Azhar and also of some Egyptian politicians. Both Sunni and Shi'i authors published articles on religious topics in its journal, *Risalat al-Islam*, but for the most part avoided the most controversial ones.[32] Until his assassination in 1949, Hasan al-Banna, the founder of the Muslim Brotherhood, was in contact with the *taqrib* society and even participated in some of its meetings.[33] Until today, Shi'i writers rarely fail to mention this when writing about the society and its work. Members and sympathizers of the Brotherhood, on the other hand, tend to pass it over in silence or explain it away.

The greatest success of *jam'iyyat al-taqrib* was a *fatwa* issued in the summer of 1959 by the then Shaykh al-Azhar, Mahmud Shaltut. It declared worship according to the doctrine of the Twelve Shi'a to be valid and recognized the Imamiyya as a *madhhab* within Islam.[34]

From the very beginning of its activity, however, the *jam'iyyat al-taqrib* came under fire from several directions, and especially from Wahhabi-Salafi circles. The most radical spokesman of those circles was Muhibb al-Din al-Khatib (d. 1969), a Syrian-born publisher, journalist and editor of classical works living in Cairo (see below). For Khatib as well as his partisans and disciples, the *jam'iyyat al-taqrib* was nothing but a Shi'i missionary institution designed to make converts in Egypt and elsewhere, and its Sunni supporters no more than an unholy alliance of simpletons, opportunists or adventurers.[35]

Among the things which embittered Khatib and like-minded men, was the fact that *Dar al-Taqrib*, an institute established in Cairo by the *jam'iyya*, started distributing Shi'i literature printed in Iran, Lebanon and Iraq. From the late 1950s onward, moreover, Shi'i books printed in Egypt itself appeared on the market there. There is, e.g., *Matba'at al-Najah*, a Shi'i publishing house (probably originating in Iraq) which has re-printed a number of modern Shi'i classics in Cairo. Among them were: Shaykh Muhammad Hasan Muzaffar's *Dala'il al-Sidq*, Sayyid Hasan al-Sadr's *Al-Shi'a wa-Funun al-Islam*, and Sayyid Abd al-Husayn Sharaf al-Din's *Muraja'at*. Also included were Tawfiq al-Fukayki's defence of temporary marriage (*mut'a*), and Shaykh Abdallah al-Subayti's *Tahta Rayat al-Haqq*, a scathing critique of what Ahmad Amin had written on the Shi'a in his *Fajr al-Islam*.[36] All these are apologetic Shi'i writings, and not a few of them are violently polemic.[37]

That these works were reprinted in Cairo before and/or after the Iranian revolution is worth noting. So is the parallel development of the formation of religious circles which, in one way or another, seem to support Shi'i missionary work or at least actively to propagate a Sunni-Shi'i *rapprochement*. While *Dar al-Taqrib* had already lost much of its momentum in the second half of the 1960s and quietly disappeared from the stage after the departure from Egypt of Shaykh Muhammad Taqi Qomi about 1979, some new, though smaller, institutions appear to carry on at least part of its mission. There is, e.g., *jam'iyyat ahl al-bayt*. A Sunni author, As'ad Sayyid Ahmad, expressly mentions its activities in Cairo—where he says it has been registered since 1974—as one reason for his editing a series of pamphlets defending the *sahaba* against what he considers to be slanderous Shi'i attacks. The series is called *Ma ana alayhi wa-Ashabi*. In his foreword to pamphlet No. 3 in the series, a booklet by Muhammad Malallah, Ahmad puts Shi'i religious and cultural activities in Cairo into the wider—and rather fanciful—perspective of an international conspiracy. For this he sees proof in a general Shi'i congress alleged to have convened in Paris in 1973, and, of course, in the victory of the Iranian revolution and in some of the circumstances attending it.[38]

With the outbreak of the Gulf War in 1980 and the political developments resulting from it, some Sunni polemicists found it necessary to point to what they see as bridgeheads of Shi'i influence in the realm of Sunni Islam. In a book published in Cairo in 1983, *Wa-ja'a Dawr al-Majus*, Abdallah Muhammad Gharib presents a detailed account of the number of Shi'i mosques, *husayniyyas* and bookshops in Kuwait, mentioning names, addresses etc.[39] Given the general tendency of the book—the author claims that the Shi'a of modern times is even more dangerous to "true" Islam than the Shi'a of the past—this sub-chapter amounts to an outright denunciation of the Shi'i community in Kuwait as a dangerous "fifth column."[40]

Another aspect of recent Sunni polemical writing is caused by the apparent fascination of not a few—especially younger—members of radical "Islamist" Sunni movements with Khomeini's achievement. Moreover, many members of those movements have become aware that Hasan al-Banna, Sayyid Qutb and other Sunni Muslim radicals of the past are considered there as being among the martyrs who prepared the ground for Iran's "Islamic Revolution."[41]

After some initial hesitation, however, the leadership of most of the Sunni "Islamist" movements turned critical of, and finally attacked Khomeini, his regime and his ideas, thereby, so they claim, "opening the eyes" of their followers to the "reality" of Shi'ism.[42] This decision was of course influenced by developments in Syria, i.e. by what most Sunni "Islamists" view as the suppression of the Sunni majority of that country by a Shi'i regime in alliance with Iran. Not a few of the anti-Shi'i books and pamphlets published in recent years in Jordan, Egypt and elsewhere were obviously written by persons belonging to (or connected with) the Syrian Islamist groups in exile. One feature they have in common is that they equate—and denounce—all Shi'i groups, past and present. In other words, they totally deny any real difference between the Imamiyya on the one hand and "extremist" sects (ghulat) such as the Nusayris or Alawids of Syria on the other.[43] All statements to the contrary by Imami or Sunni authors are dismissed as a result of taqiyya or, on the part of the Sunnis, naïveté.

Another cause of embarrassment for the polemicists lies in the fact that books and articles in favor of taqrib are still being published by Sunni authors not belonging to any of the Islamist movements who are therefore not easily impressed by arguments appealing mainly to a fundamentalist frame of mind. Rather, their authors appear to be "moderates" with both a traditional Muslim and a western education. To illustrate: in 1984, Dr. Abd al-Wahid Wafi, an Egyptian sociologist and educationalist, published a book called Al-Shi'a wa-ahl al-Sunna;[44] also in 1984, Dr. Mustafa al-Rafi'i, a Lebanese judge, diplomat and scholar, published Islamuna fi al-tawfiq bayn al-Sunna wal-Shi'a which calls for a renewed ecumenical effort.[45] Both authors, incidentally, studied in Paris.

Wafi's book was fiercely attacked by a Pakistani author who can be described as the most prolific Sunni polemicist in recent years: Ihsan Illahi Zahir, the editor of a religious journal called Tarjuman al-Hadith (published in Lahore). He was fatally wounded in March 1987 when a bomb exploded in Lahore during a rally of jam'iyyat ahl al-Hadith, a Wahhabi movement of which Zahir was secretary-general. He died a few days later in Riyadh, where he had been flown for treatment, and was buried at Medina.[46]

Zahir seems to have considered himself to be the heir of Muhibb al-Din al-Khatib as a campaigner against the Shi'a and against all Sunni sympathizers of taqrib.[47] He [Zahir] describes Wafi as someone who, at best, is ignorant of real Shi'ism and who has fallen into the trap of modern Shi'i apologetics. Zahir claims that Wafi never read a single line of the mediaeval Shi'i works which he mentions in the bibliography of his book. And it is these works one has to know in order to understand Shi'ism and its danger for true (Sunni) Islam—not only the modern Shi'i apologetical writings which are all designed to lead naïve Sunnis astray.[48]

The accusation of ignorance, as far as mediaeval Shi'i sources are concerned, may not be wrong in the case of Wafi. The same could, however, also be said of quite a few partisans of Khatib and Zahir, i.e. hardline Sunni polemicists of today, since it is obvious that many of them draw most of their information on Shi'i belief and practice from a rather limited selection of Sunni sources. They may possibly include a few classical works such as Ibn Taymiyya's *Minhaj al-Sunna*, alongside a small number of 20th-century polemical writings. Of special importance in this respect are Khatib's commentaries on two mediaeval works he edited, namely: *Al-Awasim min al-Qawasim* by the Andalusian *qadi* Abu Bakr Ibn al-Arabi (d. 1148), and Dhahabi's *Muntaqa min Minhaj al-I'tidal*, a *mukhtasar* of Ibn Taimiyya's *Minhaj al-Sunna*. Together with Khatib's *Khutut Arida*—a pamphlet seething with hatred, in which he describes the Shi'a as another religion (*din*), not just a *madhhab* within Islam[49]—these are the main sources of information for many Sunni polemicists.[50] While Zahir had read widely in both mediaeval and modern Shi'i literature, including some works in Persian, the majority of contemporary Sunni polemicists look somewhat amateurish in their attempts to corroborate their judgments on Shi'ism by quoting Shi'i sources. The same holds true for their writings on the history of Iran, the place of the Shi'a in Iranian history and the roots of Khomeini's revolution. Even their description of what they call the plight of the Sunnis in post-revolutionary Iran is, in general, rather sketchy.[51] An additional reason for that may be the fact that almost all the Sunni polemicists have fundamentalist convictions. They must therefore be critical of all manifestations of secular nationalism within Islam and prefer not to touch on them. They do not, for instance, deal with Kurdish nationalism. Were they to do so, they would have to admit that—much like under the shah—the situation of the Kurds in the Islamic Republic cannot be described solely, or even mainly, in terms of a sectarian clash between Sunni Kurds and Shi'i "Persians." But to support the Kurdish movement for what it is, i.e. a largely secular-nationalist movement, is something they cannot bring themselves to do.

To end this survey, I would like to say a few words about the Iranian Islamic constitution of 1979 as seen by Sunni observers, even though a full discussion of this issue cannot be given here.

Many Sunni polemicists content themselves with showing that the figure of the *rahbar* (leader) and the concept of *velayat-e faqih* are deeply rooted in Shi'i thought and/or Iranian tradition, and are therefore altogether unacceptable to Sunnis.[52] Some of them were delighted to discover that even some Shi'i divines such as Ayatollah Kazem Shari'atmadari and the Lebanese scholar Muhammad Jawad Mughniyya have criticized Khomeini's interpretation of *velayat-e faqih*.[53] One Iraqi polemicist hints at the fact that Khomeini has been accused of plagiarizing (in a distorting way) the main points of his theory from an Iraqi Shi'i scholar, Ali Kashif al-Ghita.[54] (Cf. chapter by Baram).

A rather interesting criticism of the 1979 Iranian constitution was published by the Islamic Liberation Party (*hizb al-tahrir al-Islami*) in August 1979, only a few days after the *Majles-e Khebregan* in Tehran began its discussions of the original draft.[55] In a memorandum, *hizb al-tahrir* (a somewhat old-fashioned, Sunni pan-Islamic movement) objected to a number of basic principles and fundamental statements in the draft, including the fact that the constitution was obviously meant for Iran as a national entity. It assumes a state capable of concluding treaties with other Muslim and non-Muslim states; it declares Persian (rather than Arabic) to be the official language and the Twelver Shi'i *madhhab* to be the official religion of the country; and it stipulates that only an Iranian can be president. (For all these points, see chapter by Menashri). Furthermore, *hizb al-tahrir* criticizes the draft for clearly being inspired by western concepts such as "democracy," "republic," "public opinion" etc. A real Islamic constitution, it argues, would be based on truly Islamic principles, be structured according to classical (Sunni) law and place the caliphate at the center of the state.[56]

The document is not polemic in its tone, but rather written in a mood of disappointment. Earlier in 1979, representatives of the Liberation Party—which is banned in all Muslim countries because of its radical rejection of the national state and its institutions—had made contact with Khomeini and other leaders of the revolution in order to look for common ground in an attempt to re-establish the universal caliphate. Their critical memorandum may be seen as a last attempt to influence developments in Iran.

It is evident that the memorandum of *hizb al-tahrir*, critical though it is, was still written in a spirit of basic solidarity. Since then, it seems that hard-line polemicists have gained the upper hand and may have it for some time to come—even after the cease-fire in the Gulf war. Kawakibi's appeal, based on a verse of the Qur'an, "to argue over religious matters only in the best [or: kindest] way possible," now appears a far cry from reality. Perhaps it will not be forgotten altogether.

Notes

1. Martin Kramer, *Islam Assembled: The Advent of the Muslim Congresses* (New York: 1986), 30–35.

2. Muhammad Imara (ed.), *Al-A'mal al-Kamila li-Abd al-Rahman al-Kawakibi* (Cairo: 1970), 282–83.

3. For a general survey of the attempts to reach a *rapprochement*, see Werner Ende, "Sunniten und Schiiten im 20. Jahrhundert," *Saeculum*, Vol. 36 (1985), 187–200; also Hamid Enayat, *Modern Islamic Political Thought* (Austin: 1982), 18–51.

4. As an example see the many reports in the Saudi daily *al-Jazira* concerning an alleged alliance (not only an arms deal) between revolutionary Iran and Israel (e.g., 26 September 1987 and 4 October 1987), and the summary of a panel discussion organized by that paper on the topic of Khomeini's "extremism" and its roots (*al-Jazira*, 21 September 1987). See also ibid., 17 and 28 February 1988.

5. *Kayhan-e Hava'i*, 9 September 1988: article by M. H. Rajabi, "Wahhabiyyat, Armaghan-e Este'mar."

6. Dr. Mahmud al-Khalidi, *Naqd Kitab al-Hukuma al-Islamiyya lil-Khomeini* (Amman: 1983), 56 ff. This view is also often taken by Iranian opponents of Khomeini.

7. Moojan Momen, *An Introduction to Shi'i Islam: The History and Doctrines of Twelver Shi'ism* (New Haven: 1985).

8. The Sunni *fuqaha* allow this. Zaydi and Imami Shi'is as well as the Kharijis reject it. See Rudolf Strothmann, *Kultus der Zaiditen* (Strassburg: 1912), 21–46. For modern Shi'i statements see Najm al-Din al-Askari et. al (ed. Murtada al-Radawi

al-Kashmiri), *Al-Wudu fi al-Kitab wal-Sunna* (Cairo: 1961), 125–160; Abd al-Husayn Sharaf al-Din, *Al-Mash ala al-arjul* (etc.). The same also in idem, *Masa'il Fiqhiyya* (Sidon: 1951; and other editions).

9. A survey of these issues—as seen by a Sunni polemicist—is to be found in Saeed Ismaeel, *The Difference between the Shi'i and the Majority of Muslim Scholars,* ed. by "A Muslim Group" (Carbondale: 1983?).

10. Etan Kohlberg, "Some Notes on the Imamite Attitude to the Qur'an," in S. M. Stern, A. Hourani and V. Brown (eds.), *Islamic Philosophy and the Classical Tradition. Festschrift for Richard Walzer* (Oxford: 1972), 209–24; see also Momen, op. cit., 172–73. One of the many recent Sunni polemics concerning the alleged Shi'i belief in alteration of the Qur'anic Text is Muhammad Malallah, *Al-Shi'a wa-Tahrif al-Qur'an* (Amman: 1985), preface by Dr. Muhammad Ahmad al-Najafi [sic]). Almost all the Sunni Arab polemical writings mentioned in the following footnotes contain sections on *tahrif.*

11. For the Shi'i definition and point of view see Seyyed Hossein Nasr's introduction (5–11) to William C. Chittick, *A Shi'ite Anthology,* selected by Allamah Tabataba'i (Albany: 1981); see further Momen, op. cit., 173–75. Sunni polemics against the Shi'i *hadith* collections (and also against the way in which Shi'i scholars are using Sunni *hadith* literature in order to corroborate their own interpretation) can be found in many of the books and pamphlets mentioned in the footnotes below, especially Nos. 13–15.

12. Etan Kohlberg, "Some Imami Shi'i Views on the Sahaba," *Jerusalem Studies in Arabic and Islam,* V (1984), 143–75; for Muslim discussions of this issue in the 20th century, see Werner Ende, *Arabische Nation und islamische Geschichte* (Beirut and Wiesbaden: 1977), 53–55, 92–94, 129.

13. For the Sunni point of view see, e.g., Muhammad al-Arabi al-Tabbani, *Ithaf Dhawi al-Najaba bi ma fi al-Qur'an wal-Sunna min Fada'il al-Sahaba* (Cairo: 1949, reprinted Cairo about 1982 by Dar al-Ansar); Muhibb al-Din al-Khatib, *Hamalat Risalat al-Islam al-Awwalun* (Cairo: al-Matba'a al-Salafiyya, numerous editions); Abu Mu'awiyya ibn Muhammad (a pseudonym), *Hukm Sabb al-Sahaba* (based on Ibn Taymiyya and others; Cairo: 1978); Abd al-Muta'al Muhammad al-Jabri, *Hiwar ma'a al-Shi'a hawla al-Khulafa al-Rashidin wa-Bani Umayya* (Cairo: 1985); Ali Umar Furayj, *Al-Shi'a fi al-Tasawwur al-Islami* (Amman: 1985); Abu al-Hasan al-Nad(a)wi, *Suratan Mutadadatan (. . .) inda Ahl al-Sunna wal-Shi'a al-Imamiyya* (Cairo: Dar al-Sahwa, 1985); Muhammad Ibrahim Shaqra, *Shahadat Khomeini fi Ashab Rasul Allah* (Amman: 1987?).

14. Ihsan Illahi Zahir, *Al-Shi'a wa-Ahl al-Bayt* (Lahore: 1982). About the author, see below.

15. This is the central thesis of a number of polemic works such as Ali Ahmad Salus, *Athar al-Imama fi al-Fiqh al-Ja'fari wa-Usulihi* (Cairo: 1982).

16. Ende, *Arabische Nation,* 113–69.

17. Anne K. S. Lambton, *State and Government in Medieval Islam* (London: 1981), 219–41; for modern developments and discussions see Tilman Nagel, *Staat und Glaubensgemeinschaft im Islam* (Zurich and Munich: 1981), Vol. II, 266–329; Enayat, op. cit.; Karl Heinrich Goebel, *Moderne schiitische Politik und Staatsidee* (Opladen and Hamburg: 1984); N. R. Keddie (ed.), *Religion and Politics in Iran: Shi'ism from Quietism to Revolution* (New Haven: 1983). For recent Sunni polemics against Twelver Shi'i legal and political theories in general and Khomeini's views in particular, see note 42 below.

18. Werner Ende, "Ehe auf Zeit (*mut'a*) in der innerislamischen Diskussion der Gegenwart," *Die Welt des Islams,* XX (1980), 1–43 (mentioning, *inter alia,* Sunni

polemics); Shahla Haeri, "Power of Ambiguity: Cultural Improvisations on the Theme of Temporary Marriage," *Iranian Studies,* XIX (1986), 123–54.

19. Etan Kohlberg, "Some Imami Shi'i Views on Taqiya," *Journal of the American Oriental Society,* V (1975), 395– 402; Egbert Meyer, "Anlass und Anwendungsbereich der taqiyya," *Der Islam,* 57 (1980), 246–80; for recent Sunni polemics, see note 24 below.

20. Momen, op. cit., chapter 13 (*The Popular Religion,* 233–45); for Muharram practices and burial regulations see Jean Calmard, "Azadari," in E. Yarshater (ed.), *Encyclopaedia Iranica,* III, fasc. 2 (New York: 1987), 174–77 and the literature mentioned there.

21. Ulrich Haarmann, "Abu Dharr—Muhammad's Revolutionary Companion" in *Muslim World,* 68 (1978), 285–89.

22. Ende, *Arabische Nation,* 210–21.

23. See the publications mentioned in note 13.

24. See, e.g., Khatib, *Al-Khutut* (note 49 below), 9, 14, 31; Zahir (notes 47 and 48), passim; Furayj, op. cit., 150–67.

25. Khatib, *Al-Khutut,* passim; Muhammad Rashad Salim, introduction to his edition of Ibn Taymiyya, *Minhaj al-Sunna* (Beirut: 1962) Vol. 1, 50–59; according to a Lebanese Shi'i scholar, fear of a total disappearance of the Shi'a as a result of *taqrib* does exist among Shi'is; see Muhammad Husayn Fadlallah, "Al-Shi'a wal-Wahda al-Islamiyya," *al-Irfan,* Vol. 71, No. 7 (September 1983), 3–14, esp. 5–6; also in *al-Tawhid* (Tehran), Arabic ed., Vol. 2, No. 7 (1404hq), 120–26. (For Fadlallah's role in Lebanon, see chapter by Kramer).

26. Abdallah Muhammad Gharib (see note 39 below), *Wa-ja'a Dawr al-Majus,* 146 ff., 149–51; also Zahir, *Al-Radd* (note 42 below), 22–24.

27. Abdul-Hadi Hairi, *Shi'ism and Constitutionalism in Iran* (Leiden: 1977), 88–90, 125, 242 f.; Werner Ende, "Iraq in World War I: The Turks, the Germans and the Shi'ite Mujtahids' Call for Jihad," in Rudolph Peters (ed.), *Proceedings of the Ninth Congress of the Union Europénne des Arabisants et Islamisants* (Leiden: 1981), 57–71.

28. Al-Sayyid Muhsin al-Amin (al-Husayni al-Amili), *Al-Husun al-Mani'a* (Damascus: 1910, reprinted in Beirut: 1985).

29. Al-Sayyid Muhsin al-Amin, *Kashf al-Irtiyab fi Atba Muhammad ibn Abd al-Wahhab* (Damascus: 1927/28); a reply to Rashid Rida's *Al-Wahhabiyyun wal-Hijaz* (Cairo: 1926). Sayyid Muhsin's book, in turn, was fiercely attacked by the then Wahhabi writer Abdallah al-Qasimi, *Al-Sira bayn al-Islam wal-Wataniyya,* 2 vols. (Cairo: 1938; reprinted Cairo 1982—probably without the author's consent—with a passage on the title page appealing to Khomeini and his followers to read this book carefully).

30. Kramer, *Islam Assembled,* 132 f.; Ende, *Arabische Nation,* 117.

31. One of the less known examples is Khalil Azmi, *Bayn al-Shi'a wal-Sunna* (Baghdad: 1952).

32. Ende, *Arabische Nation,* 117 f., and idem, *Sunniten und Schiiten,* 196–200 and the literature mentioned there.

33. A photograph showing Banna together with al-Hajj Amin al-Husayni and some other Muslim dignitaries at *Dar al-Taqrib* in Cairo is to be found in a volume edited by Abd al-Karim Bi-azar al-Shirazi, *Al-Wahda al-Islamiyya aw al-Taqrib bayn al-Madhahib al-Islamiyya* (Beirut: 1975), 17.

34. Arabic text in Shirazi, ibid., 22; an English version was published by Dar al-Taqreeb, *Two Historical Documents* (Cairo: 1963/64).

35. See al-Khatib's article "Kalam Sarih wa-Kalam Mubham" in *al-Fath*, Vol. 18, No. 862 (October 1948), 3–6.

36. These books are advertised at the end of Sayyid Murtada al-Radawi, *Ma'a Rijal al-Fikr fi al-Qahira* (fourth edition; Cairo: 1979).

37. For more information about the authors and titles mentioned, see Ende, *Arabische Nation*, index, and (concerning Fukayki) idem, *Ehe auf Zeit* (note 18 above), 18–21.

38. *Matariq al-Nur Tubaddid Awham al-Shi'a* (Cairo: 1979), "Fatihat al-Kitab," 3–13.

39. *Wa-ja'a Dawr al-Majus* (Cairo: 1983), 319–35.

40. This term (in Arabic: *tabur khamis*) is already used by Khatib, *Al-Khutut* (see note 49 below), 28.

41. Concerning Qutb, see, e.g., article "In Memory of Seyyed Qutb," *Echo of Islam*, Vol. 7, No. 1 (June 1987), 12–13 (showing a postal stamp issued in 1984 "on the memory of the Seyyed Ghotb's martyrdom" [sic]).

42. See, e.g., Furayj, op. cit., 11; Dr. Ahmad al-Afghani, *Sarab fi Iran; Kalimat Sari'a hawl al-Khomeini wa-Din al-Shi'a* (N.p.: 1982), 13–16, 54–62. For the term *sarab* in the Arabic title see Qur'an 24:39. See further Dr. Muhammad Ahmad al-Turkumani, *Ta'rif bi-Madhhab al-Shi'a al-Imamiyya* (Amman: 1983), and Gharib, 105–13; Shaykh Muhammad Manzur Nu'mani, *Al-Thawra al-Iraniyya fi Mizan al-Islam* (Amman: 1987), foreword by Muhammad Ibrahim Shaqra, 5–10. (Nu'mani is a Sunni Muslim scholar from India). Also Ihsan Illahi Zahir, *Al-Radd ala al-Duktur Ali Abd al-Wahid Wafi fi Kitabihi "Bayn al-Shi'a wa-Ahl al-Sunna,"* (Lahore: 1985), 14 ff. For general surveys of Arabic literature concerning revolutionary Iran, see Rudolph Matthee, "Arab Commentaries on the Iranian Revolution," *Iranian Studies*, Vol. 17 (1984), 303–12, and idem, "The Egyptian Opposition on the Iranian Revolution," in Juan R. I. Cole and Nikki R. Keddie (eds.), *Shi'ism and Social Protest* (New Haven: 1986), 247–74.

43. Two examples from among many are Yusuf Darwish Ghawanma, *Ghulat al-Shi'a al-Batiniyya fi Bilad al-Sham* (Amman: 1981), and al-Husayni Abdallah, *Al-Judhur al-Tarikhiyya lil-Nusayriyya al-Alawiyya* (Cairo: 1980). For a background analysis see Martin Kramer's "Syria's Alawis and Shi'ism," in Kramer (ed.), *Shi'ism, Resistance, and Revolution* (Boulder: 1987), 237–54.

44. The book was published in Cairo by Dar Nahdat Misr. For some time the author was dean of the Faculty of Education, al-Azhar University.

45. The book was published in Beirut by Mu'assasat al-A'lami; a short biography of the author is to be found in pp. 5–8.

46. *Arab News*, 31 March, p. 2, and 1 April 1987, p. 2.

47. His first book on the issue of Sunni-Shi'i relations, *Al-Shi'a wal-Sunna* (Lahore: 1973), is a response to Lutfallah al-Safi, *Ma'a al-Khatib fi Khututihi al-Arida*. Safi's *radd* was written about 1962/63 and has since been reprinted several times. See also his *Sawt al-Haqq wa-Da'wat al-Sidq* (Beirut: 1977). An English translation of Zahir's book was printed at Lahore in 1984 (Ehsan Elahi Zaheer, *The Shi'ites and the Sunna*).

48. Zahir, *Al-Radd* (note 42 above), 8–9, 211-12.

49. First Arabic edition (there was an earlier one in Urdu), Jeddah 1960/61, several reprints in Cairo, Riyadh and elsewhere.

50. About Khatib and his "school" see Ende, *Arabische Nation*, 91–110.

51. Gharib, 478–81.

52. Dr. Ahmad Matlub, Shaykh Amin al-Naqshbandi *et al.*, *Nahj Khomeini fi Mizan al-Fikr al-Islami* (Amman: 1985); Sa'id Hawwa *et al.*, *Fada'ih al-Khomeiniyya* (Baghdad: 1987; this is a publication of Munazzamat al-Mu'tamar al-Islami al-Sha'bi). Further

Nu'mani, *Al-Thawra al-Iraniyya*. There is also a translation (by one Muhammad al-Bundari) of Khomeini's *Kashf-e Asrar* into Arabic, with polemical commentaries by Salim al-Hilali and an introduction by Dr. Muhammad Ahmad al-Khatib, a member of *Kulliyyat al-Shari'a*, University of Jordan (Amman: 1987).

53. Mughniyya, *Al-Khomeini wal-Dawla al-Islamiyya* (Beirut: 1979); see Goebel, op. cit., 128–37.

54. Abd al-Jabbar al-Umar, *Al-Khomeini bayn al-Din wal-Dawla* (Baghdad: 1984), 5; concerning Mughniyya's and Shari'atmadari's criticism, see ibid., 46 ff. and 144 ff., respectively.

55. Fritz Steppat, "Islamisch-fundamentalistische Kritik an der Staatskonzeption der Islamischen Revolution in Iran," in Hans R. Roemer and Albrecht Noth (eds.), *Studien zur Geschichte und Kultur des Vorderen Orients. Festschrift für Bertold Spuler zum siebzigsten Geburtstag* (Leiden: 1981), 443–52.

56. For a preliminary study of the genesis of the constitution see Silvia Tellenbach, *Untersuchungen zur Verfassung der Islamischen Republik Iran vom 15 November 1979* (Berlin: 1985), with German translation of the first draft (11–46) and of the final text (47–107). See also Hamid Algar (trsl.), *Constitution of the Islamic Republic of Iran* (Berkeley: 1980), preface (7–10).

PART 4

Across the Northern Tier: Containment from Within

13

Iranian Policy Toward Afghanistan Since the Revolution

Zalmay Khalilzad

An account of the interaction between Iranians and Afghans in the aftermath of the Iranian revolution should be approached with caution. We do not know enough of the Iranian policy-making process or of the interaction of Iranian and Afghan *mojahedin*. Some of the following conclusions, therefore, are necessarily speculative. But we are on fairly safe grounds when we say that regarding Afghanistan, as with many other important issues, there are differences of view within the Iranian leadership and that, as a result, Iranian policy has changed over time. We can discern four major considerations that have continually had an impact on Iranian policy. The first derives from strategic reasoning; the second is the internal factional politics within Iran; the third is sectarianism; and the fourth factor could be called ideological considerations on the part of the Iranian leadership.

My view on the first factor is that Iran faces a lasting dilemma in developing a policy on Afghanistan. The dilemma springs from the fact that, on the one hand, Iran has a persistent northern concern grounded in its historical suspicions *vis-à-vis* the Soviet Union. The Soviet invasion of Afghanistan reinforced those suspicions, and there was a widespread belief among the Iranian leadership that the Soviet presence in Afghanistan directly affected Iranian security: that the invasion may, in part, have been motivated by a desire to move further south from Afghanistan—a move affecting Iran even more gravely. On the other hand (and especially during the war with Iraq), there was a southern concern and that southern concern, had been dominant in Iranian policy and in turn affected Iranian policy toward Afghanistan in a significant way. It caused Tehran to follow a cautious policy designed to avoid a direct confrontation with the Soviet Union and the pro-Soviet Afghan forces on the northern or eastern front at a time when Iran was involved in a major war with Iraq. The Iranians did not ignore the Afghan situation entirely during this period, but their policy was low key in terms of material support for the Afghan resistance.

One indication of the importance of the Gulf war was Iran's purchase of military equipment from the Soviet Union even in the immediate wake

235

of the invasion of Afghanistan. Similarly, economic relations with the Soviet Union increased in 1980–81 when US-Iranian relations deteriorated after the hostage crisis and the US economic embargo. During that period, Soviet and Iranian interests coincided to some extent because the Soviets did not want to see Iran defeated by Iraq. This situation led to economic co-operation and to some Iranian military purchases from the Soviet Union. But even then, probably to the surprise of the Soviet Union, strategic and military co-operation was less than the Soviets would have liked. In addition to their historical suspicions, Iranians harbored ideological hostilities that also stood in the way of better co-operation; the Soviet invasion of Afghanistan was clearly another factor.

Toward the end of 1982, when the Iranians began to do better in the war, interests diverged and Soviet-Iranian relations deteriorated again; the Soviets opposed the Iranian continuation of the war after the Iraqis had been thrown out of most of the Iranian territory they had previously held. As relations between the Soviets and Iranians worsened, the Iranian policy toward Afghanistan changed. In the period after 1982 there was, I think, a modification of Iranian tactics regarding the Afghan war, the most important elements of which were greater public and diplomatic Iranian effort against the Soviets in Afghanistan; the development of major radio programs, broadcast from Meshhed, by the *Voice of Iran;* more Iranian attention toward the Afghan war in its own publications as well as in its programs to other Islamic and Middle Eastern countries; and an Iranian increase in material aid to the Afghan resistance (mainly given to Shi'i groups; see below).

This phase in Soviet-Iranian relations probably continued until sometime in early 1987 when US-Iranian relations again began to deteriorate significantly as a result of the "reflagging" of Kuwaiti ships and the increase in the US presence in the Gulf (see chapter by Kazemi and Hart). The US attempt to contain the Iranian revolution dated back to its early years, but until 1987 the efforts were low key. In 1984, the United States tried, in part because of Afghanistan, to develop some contacts with Iran. At this time the United States sold arms to Iran in a move to establish ties with Tehran. But revelations about these contacts caused a political scandal in the United States and resulted in a new low in US-Iran relations.

In 1987, with the initiation of the US reflagging and deployment of substantial naval assets in the Gulf, the containment policy took on a more prominent role. This situation created, to a certain degree, a renewed convergence of Iranian-Soviet interests with respect to the war zone and the Gulf; both wanted the US forces to leave. Moscow protected Iran against immediate sanctions by the UN Security Council when Iran refused to accept Resolution 598. (The resolution, adopted in July 1987, called for immediate cease-fire, withdrawal of both armies within their own borders, and the formation of an impartial body to allocate responsibility for the start of the war.) Consequently, the Iranians tried to adjust their policy on Afghanistan, reflecting, at least in part, their desire to improve relations with the Soviets. Again the Iranians made tactical modifications: The Iranian press played down coverage of the Afghan war; attacks against the Soviet Union decreased (in fact, the Soviet position on the Gulf gained some praise); Iranian efforts at promoting a settlement in Afghanistan developed in a way that would exclude the United States; and, most importantly, the Iranians participated, at the official level, in some ceremonies sponsored by the Kabul regime, which was a major departure from previous policy.

My general assessment, however, is that these changes were purely tactical and perhaps meant to signal to the US and others that if Tehran was pressed too hard, it might have to move closer to the Soviet Union and modify its Afghan policy. In other words, Iran indicated a possible change in its Afghan policy in the hope that this would have an impact on US policy toward the Gulf and Iran. But, overall, the earlier level of material support for the Afghan resistance was maintained. In fact, because of the following factors, there was an effort to expand Iran's ties within the Afghan resistance—including the Sunni parties as well as the Shi'is.

With the Soviet troop withdrawal from Afghanistan and Iran's acceptance of a cease-fire in the Iran-Iraq war, the strategic factors shaping Iran's Afghan policy changed. The Gulf continues to be the dominant security concern. However, unlike in the past, Iran is in a weak position in the region because its armed forces and its economy are devastated. Of course Iran does not like the current situation and wants to reverse the balance in the Gulf, but it needs outside support to do so.

One possible source for outside support is the Soviet Union, as Moscow is willing to be helpful. The overall changes in Moscow and, of course, the Soviet military withdrawal from Afghanistan have decreased Tehran's perception of threat from the Soviet Union. These factors and Iran's continued hostility with the West worked together to give Moscow the opportunity to improve its ties with Tehran. However, the northern concern is still important in Iran. Tehran is likely to try to balance its improved relations with Moscow with similar improvements with the West.

The improvement in relations with the Soviets has negatively affected Iran's willingness to participate with Pakistan and to encourage the Pakistan-based Afghanistan resistance leaders to build a new regime in Afghanistan. Iran appears to favor a regime that lacks strong ties to either Moscow or the United States. It has facilitated a dialogue between Moscow and the Shi'i parties; it also continues to communicate with Pakistan and the Pakistan-based Afghan Sunni parties. It is using its ties with Shi'i parties as a bridge with both Moscow and Pakistan, but its basic concern appears to be to protect Shi'i interests in post-Soviet Afghanistan.

The second factor that affects Iranian policy is the internal conflicts in Iran. These have been very important, in my view, in terms of shaping Iranian policy on Afghanistan. In the early stages of the revolution the more moderate leaders such as Ayatollah Kazem Shari'atmadari, Mehdi Bazargan, and Sadeq Qotbzade were more vocal in their support of the Afghan opposition. After they were eliminated, although the Iranian foreign ministry continued to play a role, control over Afghan policy fell largely into the hands of Ayatollah Husayn Ali Montazeri and the Islamic Liberation Movement headed by Mehdi Hashemi. Initially Montazeri's son, Muhammad, was involved in control over Afghan policy as well. Muhammad took much interest in Afghan affairs and at times seems to have thought of himself as an Afghan *mojahed*. He traveled frequently to Afghanistan and even participated in combat there. He died in 1981 in the bombing of the Islamic Republican Party headquarters, and after that control of Afghan policy remained essentially with Ayatollah Montazeri and Mehdi Hashemi.

This shift of control had a major impact on the way the Afghan policy developed because Montazeri's and Hashemi's approach was to set up groups of "followers of the Imam's line" among the Shi'is rather than work with or support existing Shi'i or Sunni groups. They wished to manipulate the Afghan resistance for the benefit of the Iranian regime rather than support it, as Bazargan and Abu al-Hasan Bani Sadr had done in their time. During the latter period, the Revolutionary Guards also started a program for training and arming Shi'i Afghans.

In the aftermath of the arrest and execution of Hashemi (see chapter by Menashri), Montazeri's grip on Afghan policy slackened as part of the overall weakening of his position and increasing importance of the foreign ministry. The ministry's objectives were to seek improved relations with Pakistan, co-ordinate Afghan policy more closely with the overall regional policy of the ministry, and to diversify Iran's ties with the Afghan resistance organizations, including the Sunni groups. Already at the beginning of 1987, the foreign minister invited one of the principal Sunni resistance leaders, Rabani, to Iran and has since invited a number of other Sunni resistance leaders. However, military assistance to Nasr and Sepah (*Sepah-e Pasdaran*) continued (see below).

This was not, however, the first instance of factional politics within Iran that affected policy toward Afghanistan. In the past the foreign ministry, and possibly Rafsanjani, favored greater control over Afghan refugees in Iran (approximately two million). It must be remembered that the presence of a large refugee population gave rise to much resentment on the part of the Iranian public—no wonder, given the traditional Iranian attitude of mistrust toward Afghans. Although Iranians and Afghans share many cultural traits, the tendency among Iranians is to look down upon Afghans and perceive them as a security problem. As a result, strict rules and regulations were imposed on Afghan refugees during 1983–84 that limited their freedom of movement and established prescribed settlement zones for them; however, once an Afghan accepted the Iranian refugee card, he had a substantial degree of freedom of movement. At the same time, the Iranians permitted some international aid to reach the refugees (for instance, from the UN High Commissioner for Refugees) in a manner not allowed before.

At present two organizations appear to play key roles in executing Iran's policy toward the Afghan resistance. At the military level, it is the Revolutionary Guards that provide military supplies and training. This support continues to be limited largely to Shi'i groups established by Iran. The foreign ministry has been active in arranging meetings between the Shi'i parties and the Soviet Union and between the Pakistan-based Sunni groups and the Shi'i parties. The foreign ministry has also sought to gain international recognition for the eight-party Shi'i alliance by arranging foreign travel for its leaders.

The starting point for a discussion of sectarianism, the third factor in Iranian policy, is that Iran did not initially set out to make a distinction between Shi'is and Sunnis; rather, it expressed solidarity with the Afghans—all Afghans—in their struggle. But in Iran's actual policy, in terms of its support for the Afghan resistance, material aid largely went to Shi'i groups. After the fundamentalists in Iran acquired an exclusive hold on the power, their strategy was to establish in Afghanistan groups that were fundamentalist and that accepted the principles of the Iranian Islamic Repubic. As a result, traditional Shi'i organizations, such as *Shura-ye Ettefaq* headed by Ali Beheshti and the *Harakat-e Islami* of Mohsen Kandari, grew weaker. The Iranian offices of a number of Sunni fundamentalist parties were closed.

From among eight Shi'i parties with ties to Iran, two are the most important. The first organization that Iran established under the above policy, the Nasr party, was founded in 1981, and the second, called Sepah, began in 1983. Nasr is led by Mir Husayn Sadiqi and Sepah by Husayn Sadiqi-Nili and Mohd Akbari. There were several additional smaller groups, but Nasr and Sepah were Iran's principal instruments in terms of material support for Afghan groups. Tehran's strategic concept apparently was that as a first step Iran needed to gain control over the Shi'i areas and particularly over Hazara groups. That was the measure by which Iranian support was allocated to Afghan groups, regardless of their contribution to the overall struggle against the Soviet Union.

The second-most successful case of exporting the revolution—after Lebanon—has been Hazarajat, where the two Iranian-backed groups became dominant at the expense of the older traditionalist Shi'i organizations—especially *Shura-ye Ettefaq*. The Hazarajat region was not directly involved in the military action against the Soviet Union—its role in that struggle has been limited. Instead, much of the fighting there has been between various Shi'i groups and has resulted in the emergence of the Iranian-backed elements as the dominant regional force.

The effort to develop closer ties with Sunni organizations came at a time when Shi'i-Sunni relations generally had become strained as a result of developments in the Gulf and, in particular, because of the incidents during the *hajj* (see chapter by Goldberg). The Saudi-Iranian rivalry that led some Saudi religious leaders to declare Khomeini an apostate in turn affected the attitude of Afghan resistance groups.

The Iranian efforts to gain more influence among the Sunni resistance organizations may also have stemmed from a desire to acquire some US-made equipment from them. The suspicion that Iranians were essentially trying to attain equipment had a negative impact on the relationship between the Afghan resistance and the Iranians. The previously Pakistan-based alliance leader of the Afghan resistance, Yunes Khales, whose organization was accused of having "lost" some of its equipment to the Iranians, has been particularly hostile and turned down several Iranian invitations to visit Tehran. In addition, in late 1987 he refused to admit Shi'i groups to the Afghan resistance alliance. But Iran persisted in efforts to improve relations with the Sunnis.

In the aftermath of the Soviet withdrawal and the cease-fire in the Iran-Iraq War, the relative importance of sectarian issues has increased. Like a number of other states in the region, Iran wants to fill the vacuum in Afghanistan left by the Soviet departure. Iran is using the eight-party Shi'i alliance to achieve this objective. The eight parties have been seeking an aggregate of 30 per cent of the seats in any future Afghan government and councils. There are differences among the Sunni leaders toward Shi'is, some being very hostile, and the leaders have rejected the Shi'i demands. They argue that the Shi'is form only 10 per cent of the Afghan population.

Because of this disagreement, Iran has refused to recognize the interim government formed by the Pakistan-based *mojahedin* government; however, Saudi Arabia has recognized the *mojahedin* government. The Iran-based groups walked out of the consultative council that selected the interim government because of disagreements about the percentage of seats for Shi'is.

Sectarian consciousness has increased in Afghanistan. Without some power-sharing arrangement, the likelihood of conflict between the Iran-based and the Pakistan-based groups will be high in case the Najibullah regime is overthrown. At present Najibullah is seeking to exploit these divisions. He has focused considerable attention on the Shi'is by offering them autonomy in Hazarajat and by appointing Shi'is to some key positions in Kabul.

The last factor in Iranian policy I wish to mention is the ideological one. Verbally, at least, the ideological approach has, on the whole, been consistent: Throughout the period, the struggle in Afghanistan has been depicted as a Muslim war against blasphemy. It has been described as a conflict worthy of support and an Islamic cause, and Iran's response follows from its ideological commitment to the cause of Islam worldwide. There has been a substantial degree of consistency on this topic—although the frequency with which the commitment has been asserted and the publicity given to it has fluctuated.

The ideological factor alone is insufficient as a guide for understanding Iran's Afghan policy over the past ten years. More than Islamic internationalism, it has been Shi'i internationalism that has played an important role. However, even Shi'i internationalism is an insufficient guide. Iran has not offered support to all Shi'i groups. In conflicts among the Shi'is, the Iranians have supported radicals against traditionalists: Nasr or Sepah against *Shura-ye Ettefaq*. It is possible that traditionalists were less willing to conform to Iranian guidance. But it is clear that being Shi'i alone was not sufficient to gain Iranian support.

In conclusion, it should be noted that for Tehran, Gulf affairs—in war, in peace, or during cease-fire—will almost certainly take precedence over

Afghanistan. If there is to be a settlement of the Afghan conflict—an agreement among Afghans on a political formula—the Iranian role will be a marginal one. Iran would be capable of making its mark only in a spoiler role; its positive contribution to a settlement is likely to be very limited.

The new government that takes over in Kabul is likely to have a major Islamic dimension; this will be a very dramatic victory for Islam and is likely to reinforce Islamic movements in the area. This view differs slightly with the view that the Soviets are less concerned about Islam now than they were before. On the contrary, the situation in Afghanistan, and the way it is resolved, is likely to augment the impact of Islamic consciousness on the Islamic populations, whether within the Soviet Union or in the adjacent regions (cf. chapter by Ro'i).

14

Khomeinism—A Danger for Turkey?

Ergun Özbudun

Types of Islamic Fundamentalism

"Islamic fundamentalism" is defined here to include all groups which share the aim of replacing the secular republican Turkish state with one based on Islamic law (the *shari'a*). Beyond this common goal, there are important differences of method and substance among them. More precisely, they differ from each other with regard to the way in which the Islamic state will come into existence and to its nature. Some of these differences will be spelled out below. It should be emphasized here, however, that our definition does not equate fundamentalism with religiosity or religious orthodoxy, but only with deliberate efforts to create an "Islamic state."[1]

Two distinct currents can be identified within the fundamentalist camp in Turkey. One, best called "traditionalist" or "accommodationist," rejects secularism in principle, but accepts the democratic regime as the most appropriate means to gradually establish the Islamic state. Indeed, its adherents see democracy as altogether compatible with Islam, even as an indispensable element of the Islamic state. The most typical proponents of this view are the *Nurcu*s.[2] The Welfare Party (*Refah Partisi*; formerly the National Salvation Party) should also be included in this category.[3] The radical fundamentalists, on the other hand, reject democracy as well as any other kind of man-made political regime. In their view, Turkey today belongs to the *dar al-harb* i.e. the domain of the infidels, and all Muslims living there are slaves. To claim sovereignty (which rightfully belongs only to God) for the nation is apostasy. Therefore, the only way to establish the Islamic state is to destroy the existing secular one through an Islamic revolution. They categorically reject partial "reforms" within the secular political system as well as the idea of working within the system to improve it. The most ardent supporters of this view are the Khomeinists. By contrast, such categorical rejection of democracy is strongly criticized by moderate fundamentalists. Thus, a *Nurcu* pamphlet entitled *Islam and Democracy* notes that "today when radical Muslims reject democracy as a blasphemous regime, they receive their inspiration from Ayatollah Khomeini. . . . Khomeini, in his confused views, calls for an uprising against the democratic regime which he sees as blasphemous. . . . Unfortunately, those who act on their emotions instead of using their minds thus contradict the *sunna* of God, and get involved in destructive action both in Muslim countries and the outside world. They do not hesitate to call [their] cruel acts of terrorism an 'Islamic *jihad'*. They do not mind committing unjust murders against innocent people."[4]

Another important difference between radical and moderate fundamentalists is that while the radicals reject all manifestations of nationalism as inherently un-Islamic, the moderates support national values and argue that Islam and nationalism are compatible. The former do not even use the words "Turk" and "Turkish," and refer to themselves as the "Muslims in Turkey." Finally, the two positions differ with respect to the relationship of Islam and science. The radicals see Western science as "false" and "inhuman," and seek a "true" science completely inspired by revelation. The moderates, on the other hand, do not reject modern science and argue that there is no incompatibility between science and the teachings of Islam.[5]

The Khomeinists

In a book published and distributed by the Turkish Board of Higher Education, entitled "The Cause and the Targets of Anarchy and Terror in Turkey," Islamic fundamentalism in general is classed as one of the main threats to the Turkish Republic. Among the Islamic fundamentalist groups operating in Turkey, the book specifically mentions the *Nurcus, Süleymancis, Nakşibendis, Khomeinists,* the *Hizb al-Tahrir* group, and the Muslim Brothers. It has this to say of the Khomeinists: "The Khomeinist groups have singled out the directorate of religious affairs (*Diyanet İşleri Bakanliği*) as the principal target of their action and propaganda. Their fundamental aim is the establishment of the *shari'a* state in Turkey. . . . All these activities are supported by Iran and its representatives in Turkey. . . . The Iranian Revolution was followed with great interest by the reactionary groups in Turkey. Such interest was enhanced as a result of the Iranian propaganda with the aim of exporting the Islamic Revolution. Some people who believe in the possibility of an Iranian-style revolution in Turkey got involved in such propaganda activities. . . . The leadership cadres of these groups in Turkey have established organic links with the government of Iran." These observations are a good reflection of the views and concerns of the official circles in Turkey, since this report consists of the briefings given by senior security officers at the universities.[6]

The activities of the Turkish pro-Khomeini groups have also been carefully researched and documented by the journalist Uğur Mumcu. Mumcu interviewed a number of pro-Khomeini Turkish leaders resident in Germany and other West European countries. The leader of this group is a certain Cemalettin Kaplan who is a former official of the directorate of religious affairs. He served as the *mufti* of Adana until 1981, and was at one time deputy-director of religious affairs. After his forced retirement from the directorate, he went to Germany and was for a while associated with the Milli Görüş ("National View") group which advocates views parallel to those of the

Welfare Party. But in 1983, he broke away from the group and in 1985 formed the pro-Khomeini *Islami Cemiyet ve Cemaatler Birliği* ("Union of Islamic Associations and Communities"). This group is an ardent supporter of the Iranian Revolution. Its monthly magazine *Islam Çağrisi* ("The Call of Islam") is printed in Tehran in Turkish and, together with the Turkish translation of the Iranian magazine *Kayhan*, is regularly distributed among its members. Video-cassettes of speeches by Kaplan and Turkish translations of speeches by Iranian *mulla*s are also widely distributed in Turkey. Mumcu states that there is ample evidence of collaboration between the Kaplan group and the Iranian embassies in Europe, especially the embassy in Rome. Copies of *Kayhan* and the *Call of Islam* are picked up by revolutionary guards from Iranian embassies and consulates, and distributed in Turkish mosques abroad. Numerous copies of audio and videocassettes are manufactured in Iran and distributed among the Turkish communities in various European cities or smuggled into Turkey. These activities are directly organized and financed by the Islamic Republic of Iran.[7]

In Kaplan's view, any attempt to Islamize the government through the actions of a political party is un-Islamic. The only possible and legitimate way to capture the government is by *jihad* or through an Islamic revolution. This is an important difference between the pro-Khomeini group and the proponents of the "National View" who openly support the Welfare Party. Kaplan prepared a draft constitution for an Islamic state which is almost identical, article by article, with the 1979 Iranian constitution.[8]

Kaplan is also vehemently critical of the official *ulama* (i.e., the functionaries of the directorate of religious affairs) since they support the infidel "Pharaonic" (i.e., secular and despotic) state and advocate obedience to its laws. Islam cannot be separated from politics; thus every religious functionary must be a political figure and every mosque a political arena. The only choice for the religious functionaries in Turkey is between Allah and His laws, or the "idols" of the secular state. Those who accept only some parts of the *shari'a* and refuse to obey others commit apostasy. Allah is the only sovereign lawgiver. Those who obey man-made laws instead of the laws of Allah are polytheists and idolaters. Any Islamic land ruled by such laws is *dar al-harb*; consequently, it has to be reconquered and re-Islamized. Kaplan said openly, and allowed himself to be quoted in the Turkish press, that in case of war between Iran and Turkey, he would fight on the side of Iran. These words were strongly criticized by the spokesmen of the "National View."[9]

Kaplan's views closely echo those of Ayatollah Khomeini. For example, in a speech made on 24 August 1986, Khomeini said: "In the Islamic world, the *ulama* were led to believe that they had to obey the tyrants, oppressors, and the holders of naked power. Certain lackeys preferred to obey Atatürk, who destroyed the rule of Islam, instead of obeying the orders of the Prophet. How can a reasonable mind accept this? Today, the *ulama* who are the puppets of the Pharaonic forces teach the people the orders of God and the Prophet, but at the same time call on them to obey Atatürk. . . . How can one argue that this is consistent with the notion of *ulu al-*

amr whom God ordered us to obey? Obviously, *ulu al-amr* in the real sense can only be those who follow the order of God and His Messenger. . . . You send people a religion and then tell them to obey the infidels and thus to become infidels themselves. Is this not nonsense? . . . These deviations are the work of the enemies of Islam.''[10]

Pro-Khomeini views are represented in Turkey by the daily newspaper *Zaman*, and by such magazines as *Şehadet* ("The Profession of Faith"), *Girişim*, *Iktibas*, *Kitap Dergisi*, and *Mektep*. They interpret national and international events in a distinctly pro-Iranian fashion. One typical example is the support for Iran in connection with the Mecca incident in the summer of 1987, in which some four hundred people, mostly Iranians, lost their lives[11] (see chapter by Goldberg.) *Yeni Forum*, a liberal weekly magazine, observed that "a certain section of the press represents, in full consciousness, the ideological, strategic, and political interests of Iran." Some of these radical Islamic magazines "almost compete with each other in worshiping the Iranian regime. . . . [They] puzzle every patriotic Turk, work like an Iranian fifth column, see all national and international events from an Iranian perspective, and consider all opponents of the Iranian regime—even if they are Muslims— as enemies. One wonders why Iran should need to train and send to Turkey its own agents so long as it has such local supporters.''[12]

Electoral Strength

Two indicators may help in measuring the extent of popular support the various Islamic fundamentalist groups command in Turkey. The first one is public opinion polls. One such poll taken in 1986 found that some 7% of the respondents preferred a government based on the Islamic law (a *shari'a* state). This is significant, given the fact that in the same poll about two-thirds of the respondents spoke of themselves as practising Muslims (at least to some degree). The second criterion is the percentage of votes obtained by religious parties. The first national legislative election contested by such a party was that of 1973, when the National Salvation Party (NSP) gained 11.8% of the total valid votes cast and forty-eight out of 450 seats in the National Assembly. In 1977, it received only 8.6% of the vote and twenty-four seats. In both elections, it emerged as the third largest party, in terms of the size of parliamentary representation, although it was far behind the two major parties, the Justice Party (JP) and the Republican People's Party (RPP).

Election statistics allow us to reach certain tentative conclusions on the social bases of support for the NSP in the 1970s. In 1973, the NSP obtained 10.8% of the urban and 12.4% of the rural vote (urban being defined here as residents of towns of 10,000 or more). The relatively narrow gap between the percentages of rural and urban NSP voters suggests that religious voting in Turkey is not peculiar to rural areas. However, the NSP performed rather poorly, compared to its own national and urban average, in the three largest cities, namely Istanbul, Ankara, and Izmir, where it polled only 8.1 per cent. The NSP's relatively good showing in the medium-sized cities of the less developed (i.e., less industrialized) regions (particularly the eastern and southeastern regions) seems to lend support to the view that the NSP voters in urban areas came predominantly from the more traditional sectors of the urban middle classes, namely small businessmen, merchants and artisans. It stands to reason that these groups, being more traditional in their outlook and feeling insecure and threatened by industrialization, responded in greater numbers to the NSP appeal. On the other hand, the party was not nearly as successful in the cities of the more highly developed regions, which suggests that it was unable to make deep inroads into more modern urban groups (industrial workers, white-collar workers, and urban professionals). As for the relationship between the NSP vote and the indices of provincial socio-economic development, such correlations were negative, but not strongly so. The strongest negative correlation obtained was with the rate of provincial literacy ($-.342$), indicating that the NSP received greater, but not predominant, support from less developed provinces in 1973.[13]

In the 1977 elections, the NSP's voting profile showed significant changes. Not only did the party lose about one quarter of its votes and exactly one half of its Assembly seats, but it also became a more markedly regional party. The NSP's losses were mainly in western and central Turkey and in the Black Sea region. In the eastern and southeastern regions, on the other hand, it generally held its own or even gained. As a result, more than half (13 out of 24) of the NSP deputies elected in 1977 were from the eastern or southeastern provinces.

The results of the 1987 elections confirm these observations. The Welfare Party (WP) which replaced the NSP and is presently led by the former NSP leader Necmeddin Erbakan (Erbakan got elected to the party leadership following the constitutional referendum which lifted the ban on former political leaders) obtained 7.1% of the total national vote cast. Since the electoral law of 1983 introduced a 10% national threshold (that is, 10% of the total national vote cast) for parliamentary representation, the WP failed to get any of its candidates into the Grand National Assembly.

Several conclusions can be drawn from the electoral performance of the WP. First, the percentage of votes obtained by the WP was surprisingly close to that section of the Turkish population favoring an Islamic government, as shown by the public opinion polls mentioned above. The two kinds of findings thus confirm each other, and increase the reliability of the public opinion data, although it is certainly conceivable that not all fundamentalists vote for the WP and not all WP voters are fundamentalists. To be sure, this approximately 7% of the Turkish voters include all shades and varieties of Islamic fundamentalism, including those we called moderate or accommodationist groups. This means that radical Islamic fundamentalists or pro-Khomeini groups represent a very small section of Turkish society.

The second important conclusion is that the Islamic vote in Turkey is not increasing, but decreasing. As we have already observed, the NSP vote decline from 11.8% in 1973 to 8.6% in 1977 and to 7.1% in 1987. This is a rather discouraging result for the WP which, in 1987, waged an energetic,

TABLE 1.   Provinces Where the WP Passed the Electoral Threshold:
           Parliamentary Elections of 29 November 1987

	Percent
Diyarbakir	24.8
Siirt	24.1
Bingöl	22.2
Bitlis	21.5
Van	20.1
Elaziğ	17.8
Mardin	16.9
Konya	15.0
Rize	14.3
K. Maraş	13.3
Ağri	13.2
Gümüshane	13.1
Muş	13.0
Sivas	13.0
Kocaeli	13.0
Urfa	12.0
Adiyaman	11.3
Trabzon	11.0
Nevşehir	10.6
Sakarya	10.5

enthusiastic, and especially well-financed campaign. The 10% threshold is likely to discourage potential WP supporters in the future.

Thirdly, entirely consistent with the 1977 pattern, the WP's pocket of strength seems again to be in the eastern and southeastern regions. Table 1 gives the list of the 20 provinces in which the WP received over 10 per cent of the total valid votes: thirteen (if we include Sivas and Gümüşhane) provinces are in the eastern or southeastern regions. The first five, where the WP got more than 20%, are all southeastern provinces. One wonders whether the greater WP strength in the east and the southeast (i.e., the least developed regions in Turkey) is due to developmental factors or to the greater strength of some Sufi orders (particularly the *Nakşibendis*) in these regions. In the absence of statistical data on Sufi orders, there is no way to answer this question with accuracy.

The fundamentalists' relative weakness in the major cities continued in the 1987 elections. Thus, the WP gained 6.1 per cent of the votes in the province of Istanbul, 4.2% in Ankara, and 2.3% in Izmir—all well below the national average. This voting profile does not make the WP look like the party of the future.

Is Khomeinism a Danger for Turkey?

Both the characteristics of the Turkish political system in general and those of Turkish Islam in particular effectively limit the impact of the Khomeinist movement.[14] As to the first set of factors, it is clear that Turkey differs fundamentally from pre-revolutionary Iran. The secularization process started much earlier and penetrated much deeper in Turkey than in Iran. Turkish society is much more integrated, and Islamic fundamentalists are able to play some role within the political system either through their own political parties or by working inside larger conservative parties. A reasonably open and democratic political system, in contrast to the autocratic and oppressive monarchy in Iran, creates conditions much less favorable to a revolutionary upheaval. Turkish politics in the last forty years of multi-party competition have been dominated by secular and moderate parties. True, these parties were unable to cope with the increasing terrorism and political polarization in the late 1970s, and the resulting authority vacuum was filled by the military intervention of 12 September 1980; but post-military civilian politics are once again dominated by moderate political parties and characterized by a now much less polarized political climate. The two consecutive election victories of Turgut Özal's Motherland Party gave Turkey not only a moderate but also a stable government. Unlike in revolutionary Iran, even a temporary alliance between the extreme left and Islamic fundamentalists is extremely unlikely. The military remains strongly committed to Kemalist secularism; if anything, cadets and officers now undergo a more thorough socialization into Kemalist values than perhaps ever before.[15]

Similarly, the characteristics of Islam in Turkey make it less vulnerable to Iranian efforts at exporting the Islamic Revolution. As in most Sunni countries, and unlike in Iran, religious institutions in Turkey have historically been subordinated to and penetrated by the state.[16] This subordination continued and intensified under the Republic, since religious functions were strictly controlled by the directorate of religious affairs. A second factor is that a large majority of Turkish Muslims are Sunnis and consequently view Shi'i fundamentalism with suspicion, if not hostility. Although the pro-Iranian radical writers attempt to play down the Sunni-Shi'i schism and present the Iranian revolution as the guiding light of an awakening in the entire Islamic world, such age-old divisions no doubt still persist. Former Prime Minister Süleyman Demirel wrote in the *Nurcu* magazine *Köprü*, for example, that Shi'ism was nothing but a corruption (*ifsad*) of Islam and that Sunnis had nothing to learn from Shi'is.[17] Similarly, Taha Akyol, a leading neo-conservative journalist, sees in the traditionalist Sunni groups an effective bulwark against Iranian-style radicalism.[18] Although the Turkish Shi'is (*Alevi*s; *Alawid*s) constitute a significant minority (an estimated 15 to 20%) there are important differences between them and the Iranian (*Ja'fari*) Shi'is. The former are much less orthodox and strict in their religious beliefs and practices which were influenced by their nomadic traditions and pre-Islamic Shamanistic religions. Moreover, the discriminatory treatment they endured under the Ottoman state made them the most ardent supporters of Kemalist secularism.[19] The *Alevi*s have generally displayed a tendency to support secular and leftist political parties. In short, they may be considered one of the groups least vulnerable in Turkish society to the appeals of radical Islamic fundamentalism.

At a more fundamental level, we may argue that the major contribution of Kemalism to the development of secularism in Turkey rested on its continuation and intensification of the already existing trend toward the secularization (or privatization) of Islam. In this sense, high levels of religiosity and religious observance in Turkey are no longer incompatible with the secular state, nor do they threaten it. It appears that a great majority of believing and practising Turkish Muslims today keep the two spheres separate and do not make their political choices on the basis of their religious beliefs and values. If this is so, then the ultimate aim of Kemalism seems to have been accomplished.

Notes

1. On different approaches to Islamic fundamentalism, see Bruce B. Lawrence, "Muslim Fundamentalist Movements: Reflections toward a New Approach," in Barbara Freyer Stowasser (ed.), *The Islamic Impulse* (Washington, D.C.: 1987), 15–36.
2. This is a sect founded by Said-i Nursi (1873–1960). A convenient summary of the *Nurcu* views on democracy can be found in their pamphlet: *Islam ve Demokrasi* (Istanbul: 1987). Interestingly, former Prime Minister Süleyman Demirel frequently contributes to the *Nurcu* magazine *Köprü* arguing emphatically that Islam and democracy are compatible and respectfully quoting Said-i Nursi. Some of these articles have been reprinted in the pamphlet mentioned above.
3. On the National Salvation Party, see Binnaz Toprak, *Islam and Political Development in Turkey* (Leiden: 1981); Jacob M. Landau, "The National Salvation Party in Turkey," *Asian and African Studies*, XI, No. 1 (1976), 1–57; Ergun Özbudun, "Islam and Politics in Modern Turkey: The Case of the National Salvation Party," in Stowasser, 142–56.
4. *Islam ve Demokrasi*, 29.
5. "Türkiye'deki Islamci Dergilere bir Bakiş," *Yeni Forum*, No. 198 (1 December 1987), 12–13.
6. *Türkiye'de Anarşi ve Terörün Sebepleri ve Hedefleri* (Ankara: 1985), 82, 84, 87.
7. Ugur Mumcu, *Rabita* (Istanbul: 1987), 15–16, 27–28, 91–96.
8. Ibid., 16–25, 56–60.
9. Ibid., 18–20, 32–47, 75.
10. *Islam Çağrisi*, Nos. 38–39 (November-December 1986), 45–46.
11. See, for example, *Zaman*, 3, 4 August and 7, 8 September 1987.
12. "Türkiye'deki Islamci Dergilere bir Bakiş," 13–14.
13. Özbudun, op. cit., 151–52.
14. For a good discussion on the subject and the views of a number of experts, journalists, and religious leaders, see *Nokta*, Vol. V, 36 (13 September 1987), 13–21.
15. See, for example, Mehmet Ali Birand, *Emret Komutanim* (Istanbul: 1986), 91–113.
16. For a similar argument on Egypt, see Ali E. Hillal Dessouki, "Official Islam and the Political Legitimation in the Arab Countries," in Stowasser, *The Islamic Impulse*, 135–41.
17. Quoted in *Islam ve Demokrasi*, 91–92.
18. *Nokta,*, Vol. 5 (13 Eylul 1987), 14–15.
19. For the best account on the Turkish *Elavis*, see Altan Gökalp, *Les têtes rouges et les bouches noires* (Paris: 1980).

15

The Reception of the Iranian Revolution by the Muslim Press in Turkey

Binnaz Toprak

This chapter is intended to summarize the response of Islamic groups in Turkey to the Iranian Revolution of 1979 as reflected in various Islamic publications.* The question of whether or not Turkey might follow the Iranian path and opt for a radical change of regime occupies the minds of most Turkish intellectuals as well as many Middle East experts in the West. It is closely linked with that of the apparent visibility and strength of Islamic movements within Turkey in recent years. This is of obvious importance both for Turkish citizens who are committed to the secular state and for Western allies of Turkey, especially at a time when Turkey has applied for membership in the EEC.

The viability of an Islamic revolution in Turkey is besides the concerns of this chapter. However, some background on Turkish secularism and on Islamic movements might be useful in order to place the discussion within its proper context.

The secular movement in Turkey is now over a century old. It started in the second half of the nineteenth century with the initiation of westernizing reforms by Ottoman statesmen and intellectuals.[1] However, the radical break with Islam came only after the establishment of the Turkish republic in 1923. The major goal of the early republican period was to replace Ottoman-Islamic by Western civilization. The policies implemented to accomplish this transformation aimed at disestablishing the organizational and functional strength of both orthodox and Sufi Islam.[2] Whereas the orthodox *ulema* (*ulama*) were tied to the state bureaucracy and became civil servants, the Sufi brotherhoods (*tarikat*) were altogether outlawed. However, they did not

*I would like to express my gratitude to my research assistants, Ms. Nuray Mert and Mr. Atilla Öztürk, for their help in the collection of data.

This chapter is part of a larger research project which is being funded by the Middle East Research Competition of the Ford Foundation.

vanish but went underground. At the same time, a number of legal and constitutional barriers were set up against the use of religion for political purposes. In a reaction against this radical interpretation of secularism and against the concurrent westernizing reforms, various Islamic groups rebelled against the republican regime in the 1920s and 1930s. By the end of the 1930s, however, the Republic had effectively suppressed the Islamic opposition. The end of the one-party era in 1946 led to a relative relaxation of secularist policies, but by then militant Islam had disappeared altogether.[3] Less activist Islamic groups, notably the *tarikat*, were fast to catch up with the logic of democratic politics and chose to operate through political parties.

In general, the unique course of secularization has been quite successful in relegating Islam to the private sphere and in containing demands for a change of regime along Islamic principles. Although Islam has remained a significant force in social and political life, there has been no overt threat to central political authority based on Islamic appeals since the late 1930s.

Since 1980, however, there has been a discernible consolidation of power within the Islamic movement as well as the emergence of a new militant discourse. But militant groups are small in size and mostly confined to young people in large metropolitan centers (but cf. chapter by Özbudun). There can be no doubt that the Iranian revolution had a considerable impact on Muslim militancy in Turkey; this in itself is however, insufficient to explain the greater strength of the Islamic movement since 1980.

The major aim of the generals after the 1980 coup was to depoliticize Turkish society. The military's interpretation of the previous decade rested on the belief that the street violence and political instability of the 1970s resulted from an unnecessarily high level of mass politicization, bred by the liberal 1961 constitution. Hence, a new constitution, a new political parties law and a new law of associations were enacted, designed to restrict freedom of association and political activity. In addition, all political parties, radical labor unions and associations were disbanded in 1980. This was followed by a crack-down on underground organizations of the far Left and Right severe enough to leave them utterly broken. Yet despite this systematic and successful effort, Muslim groups flourished after 1980 as they had never done before under any government in the republican era. This apparent paradox needs explanation.

It seems to me that there has been a change of outlook towards Islam at the level of the political elite, and this has manifested itself, for the first time in republican history, in an overt departure from radical Kemalist secularism. This change in ideological commitment and governmental policies concerning Islam goes back to the oil crisis of 1973. Turkey came to feel the need for closer relations with oil rich countries. Accordingly, there was a shift in Turkey's traditional pro-Israel foreign policy in the Middle East. For example, Turkey established official diplomatic contacts with the PLO, minimized formal cultural and diplomatic contacts with Israel and became an active participant in the Islamic Conferences.

A parallel development in the late 1970s was the increasing importance of Turkey's business connections with Middle Eastern countries. A number of major construction companies undertook large-scale projects in Libya and Saudi Arabia. In addition, Middle Eastern countries became important markets for Turkish industrial and agricultural exports. They were also a major source of credits or funds-in-aid for Turkish economic development. On the other hand, a number of commercial organizations from Islamic countries established branches in Turkey in the early 1980s such as the Faisal Finance group, Al Baraka Corporation and the Islam Development Bank. This was followed by the growing importance of Arab tourism as Istanbul, especially, became a summer resort for oil-rich Arabs.

In short, Turkey's foreign relations in the late 1970s and early 1980s underwent a major change. Closer commercial and cultural ties with other Muslim countries in the region in turn necessitated a parallel change of state policy on secularism. State elites gradually abandoned strict secular norms and came to view Turkey's role as a bridge between the West and the Middle East.

These external developments coincided with a crisis period in Turkey's internal politics culminating in the military coup of 1980. Since the coup, there has been a discernible change of outlook towards Islam at the level of the political elite. This stems from two factors: (1) The strength of religious groups within the ruling Turgut Özal government; and (2) the implicit recognition by state elites, including the military, that the solidarity factor inherent in the concept of a Muslim community might prevent ideological conflicts such as those that led to the anarchy of the street in the 1970s. Hence, we are witnessing the emergence of a new state ideology, an effort to arrive at some sort of syncretism between Kemalism and Islam; a state ideology which is trying to accommodate Islam in order to reconstitute a basis of social integration.

This new outlook has strengthened the political importance of the so-called "Turkish-Muslim synthesis." This is an ideological outlook first formulated by a group of intellectuals on the right in a club which they called "The Intellectuals' Hearth" (*Aydinlar Ocaği*). Although formed back in the early 1960s, the club became important only in the 1970s as its ideas were picked up by the ultra-right National Action Party. After 1980, the "Turkish-Muslim synthesis" was incorporated into the state ideology. For example, it found voice in a document prepared by the State Planning Organization in 1983 entitled "The National Culture."[4] In essence, the "Turkish-Muslim synthesis" rejects the pagan Turkism of Kemalist ideology and attempts to combine nationalism with Islam. The "Intellectuals' Hearth" group supports the Özal government and some of its members now hold important positions in the government and in the government-controlled television network, as well as state-appointed administrative posts at Turkish universities.[5]

These changes in state policy made the ground fertile for Islamic movements. The intellectual void which the 1980 military coup created, plus greater tolerance towards Islamic groups at a time when alternative organizations and movements were disbanded has led to the emergence of militant Islam. Thus, for the first time in the history of the Republic, Islamic discourse has become a powerful alternative to secular thought. There is now a wealth of Islamic publications, some of which lay claim to serious intellectual standing.

The new Islamic groups differ significantly from their predecessors in important respects. In the past, Islamic movements were confined to marginal groups: people who were at the periphery of dominant social, political and economic centers of power. Now it has become largely an elite phenomenon. At the same time, the new Islamic movements have important connections with outside groups. Hence, they are no longer a purely local phenomenon. This new elite includes a number of "Muslim entrepreneurs" who use their connections with the Özal government and their connections with Muslim companies in the Middle East to build financial empires for themselves.[6]

Although Islamic militancy has increased since 1980, the numerical strength of groups with a revolutionary outlook is very limited. As the following discussion will show, it is only a small minority within the Islamic movement that supports the Iranian regime or similar revolutionary action. On the whole, traditional Islamic groups, such as the *tarikat*, prefer co-operating with the state and making their weight felt through their support of center-right parties. The same is true of the new Muslim entrepreneurs who are trying to secure a place for themselves in the integration process of Turkey with the world economy by using connections with international Muslim firms or banks. Like businessmen everywhere, they are bound to know that they will not profit from revolutionary upheavals.

In general, political experience has shown that it is very difficult to mobilize the Turkish population purely on religious grounds. This is the case even in terms of electoral competition: Turkish religious parties do not have much of a following among the electorate. The most recent example is the case of the Welfare Party which was able to muster only 7.1 per cent of the votes in the elections of November 1987, although it had the backing of a number of *tarikat*. Indicative of this general attitude against a change of regime along Islamic lines is a recent public opinion poll which found that those who wanted an Islamic state based on the *şeriat (Shari'a)* were only 7 per cent of the total population.[7]

One of the major points made in Islamic writing in favor of Khomeini's Iran has to do with the nature of the revolution there. It is described as having no precedent in modern history: neither the French nor the Soviet revolutions were of the same magnitude. What distinguishes the Iranian revolution from the others is the fact that it is the first such struggle to draw its ideas from sources other than those prevalent in the west. According to this analysis, Western thought—whether in its capitalist or socialist version—proved insufficient to produce a truly revolutionary ideology with the aim of getting rid of domination. On the contrary, the major revolutions in modern times which started out as the struggle of the oppressed ended with a simple exchange of one form of domination with another. The Iranian revolution, by contrast, shows that the only contemporaneous movement capable of doing away with exploitation is one that draws its strength from Islam. The struggle against imperialism and its local collaborators can only be carried out by means of a radical understanding of Islam, taking the period of the Prophet Muhammad as its model. A revolution based on such a belief will enable Muslims to gain their independence and own their resources and will bring about the rule of divine judgment here on earth.[8]

Hence, it is argued, the Iranian revolution will stand as an example to other Muslim countries under the yoke of imperialism. Iran has proved to the Muslim world as well as to all underdeveloped countries that it is possible to set up an independent state free from superpower influence and relying on its own internal resources. Iran has demonstrated that neither might nor technological superiority can overcome a country united around a common purpose and faith. It has made Muslims see the true meaning of identity precisely when Islamic identity was losing ground in the face of a global process of westernization. It is because of its exemplary nature that Iran has become the enemy of both the US and the Soviet Union as well as their allies. The major reason behind their opposition to Iran is the fear that other Muslim states might follow suit.[9]

The perceived anti-imperialist nature of the Iranian revolution undoubtedly occupies a central place in these analyses. In the same context, attitudes of radical Muslims shade over into another assessment stressing Iran's exemplary role for the oppressed peoples who suffered from imperialist policies.[10] Apparently, Khomeini's defiant politics towards the US has caught the attention of radical groups, whether Islamic or otherwise oriented.

A related theme in this literature centers on the revolutionary character of Islam as demonstrated by Iran. The oppressed peoples of the world who found refuge and hope in Marxist ideology came to see that Marxism had not only been insufficient in the fight against imperialism but actually helped to promote imperialist aims. This recognition led to the acceptance of Islam as the only source of revolutionary action. At the same time, Iran taught Muslims not to support governments whose only virtue was their anti-communist stand. The revolution in Iran came at a time when Muslims all over the world were on the point of losing hope for the establishment of a true Muslim community and the founding of an Islamic state. It put an end to the acquiescent attitude of the Muslim world towards the west—an attitude dominant for two centuries. Moreover, it has silenced the view that religion cannot be an important force in the modern world: it has proved the potential of Islam to mobilize the masses.[11]

A third theme that received emphasis is the importance of establishing an Islamic state. Iran is being held up as the only example of a true Muslim community since the *Asr-i Saadet* (*asr al-sa'ada*), literally: "the era of happiness" connoting the period of early Islam.[12] Although there were other Muslim states and movements in subsequent history, only the Prophet and the first caliphs succeeded in establishing a community governed by the principles of the Qur'an.[13] A movement cannot be considered Islamic simply because it is led by Muslims. Nor should legitimacy be given to movements which use the Islamic potential in order to achieve material, worldly gain. A true Islamic movement, the argument goes on, is one that attempts to earn Allah's blessing by setting up a community which reflects divine design. Hence the Islamic *tebliğ* ("message") should enlighten Muslims what living according to Islam means. It is here that Iran has enriched this message by putting into practice the idea of a Muslim state which follows no other path than to embody Islam's true meaning as the submission to God.[14]

A fourth and perhaps the most important issue stressed by writers favorable towards the Iranian revolution has to do with the differences between Sunni and Shi'i Islam. This is a sensitive issue for supporters of the Iranian regime because of the reserved, if not downright critical, attitude of traditional Islamic groups towards Shi'i Iran. Most pro-Khomeini writers now try to explain at length that the Ja'fari branch of the Shi'a is very close to Sunni concepts and that there are no major differences of principle between the two. Apparent differences of belief and practice are minimized and played down as minor issues which should not stand in the way of Muslim unity. In general, the historical memory of Ottoman-Safavid enmity is blamed for the present-day hostility of Turks towards Iran. In fact, these writers point out, most Sunni Turks have a lopsided view of the basic principles of Shi'ism. Lack of knowledge, coupled with historical prejudice, prevent an understanding between the two sects. Furthermore, it is argued, these prejudices are reinforced by the secularists in Turkey as well as by western countries in the hope of isolating Iran and of preventing the Turkish Muslim population from co-operating with the Islamic state in Iran.[15]

Hence the call is for all true Muslims to ignore such superficial difference and defend the Iranian regime which has openly started a *jihad* against both the infidels and the western-oriented governments in the Muslim world. After all, Sunnis should not forget that there were no sects when Prophet Muhammad was alive and that the emergence of sectarian differences after his death was no more than a historical aberration. The major duty of true Muslims is to make sure that sectarian conflict does not stand in the way of the unity of the Muslim *umma*. Sunnis must guard against such an international conspiracy to divide the Islamic peoples through emphasizing sectarian differences. It was Allah's will that the second Islamic revolution after that of the Prophet should take place in Iran and it is up to all Muslims to obey his will.[16] To back up their contention that sectarian issues are of no importance, Turkish supporters of Khomeini quote statements of his to the effect that the Iranian revolution did not work for the success of Shi'ism alone but for the rise of a unified Islam in the world.[17] They point out that the major difference between the two sects is that historically speaking the Shi'a has carried the seed of revolt and revolution against Muslim, but non-Islamic, governments, while Sunnism has been more conciliatory towards the state. Among the several reasons cited for this difference, emphasis is placed on the institution of *hums* under which the Ja'faris pay a certain percentage of their income to men of religion. The financial autonomy of the *ulema (ulama)* from the state ensured by this practice is considered crucial in the success of the revolution in Iran. Hence it is argued that Turkish Muslims should give up the dream that the Islamic movement can succeed only after the community promotes its material fortunes by enterprises akin to the multi-nationals and follow the Iranian example by donating "clean" money to the cause.[18]

The Islamic press favorable towards Iran also carried news about the Iranian regime's domestic and foreign policies. As might be expected, its interpretations tend to justify the Iranian leadership. For example, Bani Sadr's fall from power in 1981 is considered to have been the result of his betrayal of the Islamic cause which eventually made him a counter-revolutionary.[19] The Iran-Iraq war is viewed as the consequence of a conspiracy against the Iranian regime by the imperialist powers who exploited Iraq as a "front" in their fight with Islam.[20] The same powers are accused of turning world public opinion against Iran by labeling the war a Sunni-Shi'i conflict; but since in actual fact Iraq could not be considered a Muslim state, the war should not possibly be interpreted in terms of Muslims shedding Muslim blood.[21] (The Turkish pro-Khomeini press thus follows the indoctrination line laid down by Tehran.) Similarly, the *Ihvan* (*Ikhwan*, the Muslim Brotherhood) are blamed for opposing Khomeini and are accused of doing so from their desire to co-operate with existing governments in defense of the *status quo*.[22] Iran's purchase of US weapons and the ensuing scandal of 1986 (see chapter by Kazemi and Hart) is also seen as part of the imperialist conspiracy to discredit the Islamic revolution.[23] The same logic is used in explaining the events during the 1987 pilgrimage to Mecca[24] (see chapter by Goldberg).

As I have indicated, the number of Islamic groups supporting the Iranian revolution is rather limited. For reasons that will be discussed presently, Islamic groups which are tradition-oriented rather than militant seem either to have adopted a reserved attitude or to oppose it openly. The major pro-Khomeini groups, each small in size and importance, are centered around the periodicals *Şehadet*, ("The Profession of Faith"), *Girişim*, and *Iktibas*. It is perhaps no coincidence that two of these three, as well as a pre-1980 journal *Şura*, are published in Ankara where the traditional *tarikat* do not have a strong network. In fact, I was informed that no *tarikat* shaykh of importance would live in Ankara because being the seat of the government the city symbolizes the secular state.[25]

The reasons for this non-committal attitude of traditional Islam towards Iran are extensively discussed in pro-Iranian publications. Apparently, the most important reason has to do with the Sunni view of the Shi'i practices as heretical. The claim that the Iranian revolution represents the world Muslim community does not find much sympathy among Sunni groups who consider Shi'i political doctrine, and especially the concept of the infallible Imam, contrary to the teaching of Islam. Sunni traditionalists therefore feel that support for the Iranian regime is the wrong course of action since a clash between the two belief systems is held to be ultimately inevitable. Moreover, given Khomeini's explicit goal of "exporting" the revolution to other Muslim countries, Sunni groups seem to fear an Iran strong enough to dominate the Middle East region.[26]

A related reason why some traditionalist Islamic groups do not support the Iranian revolution apparently has to do with the question of leadership within the Muslim community. According to this view, the caliphate belonged to the Ottoman dynasty and this still places Turkey in a unique position *vis-à-vis* the Muslims of the world. Hence the leadership of the Muslim *umma* cannot legitimately be given to a Shi'i country which has never been the seat of the caliphate.[27]

Finally, some of the traditionalist groups, such as the *Nurcu*, which have consistently supported center-right parties with a pro-American foreign policy think of the Iranian revolution as part of a Soviet conspiracy to discredit American influence in the Middle East with the hope of eventually establishing communist regimes in the region.[28]

Indeed, the *Nurcu* have been against the Iranian revolution from the very beginning. For example, the *Nurcu* daily newspaper *Yeni Asya* argued as early as January 1979 that the Iranian people would eventually pay a heavy price for ignoring a basic lesson of history viz. that disorder and instability breed nothing but despotism.[29] *Yeni Asya* columnists pointed out that what went on in Iran under the banner of Islam was nothing more than an emotional explosion with little to do with the teaching of Islam;[30] that Turkish Muslims had a better awareness of history and would not allow Khomeini-type leaders to propel their country into chaos;[31] and that Iran was rapidly moving towards a still unknown end stage-managed by the KGB.[32]

The *Nurcu* attitude towards Iran is summed up in a book by B. Bozgeyik published in 1981,[33] which is a good example of anti-Shi'i feeling on the part of the Sunnis. The author first points to differences between Sunni and Shi'i Islam and argues that the most important characteristic of Shi'ism is its political nature. He finds it to be conducive to exploitation by power-seekers who make use of religious belief in order to strengthen their own power base. He then goes on to a discussion of Ottoman-Persian relations and points out that the Safavid dynasty followed a constant policy of opposition to Sunni Islam, whether through wars at the frontier or through supporting Shi'i rebellions in Ottoman Anatolia. His conclusion is that opposition to the Ottomans was tantamount to opposition to Islam. Iran, he argues, still follows the same course, as exemplified by Khomeini's policy of not recognizing the rights of Iranian Sunnis. In his view, all the revolution has done is to replace the shah by Khomeini, a change that has nothing to do with the principles of Islam. But Khomeini's advent to power is the more dangerous one in that it undermines American influence and thus removes the only guarantee against a Soviet threat to the region. Hence supporting the Iranian regime is tantamount to betraying one's country, cultural heritage and religious belief.[34] The author states that Islam does not accept the concept of revolution; rather it is a reformist religion opposed to all destructive action. It does not require a revolution to glorify the faith since Islam resides but in the souls of Muslims rather than in the state.[35]

In June 1987, the *Nurcu* periodical *Köprü* published a series of articles on Iran. In general, it emphasized that Khomeini's speeches were full of examples of the typical Shi'i enmity towards Sunni Islam and concluded that Khomeini's despotism was the direct result of Shi'i belief in the infallibility of the *Imam.*[36]

Similar to the *Nurcu,* the *Işikçi* have also opposed the Iranian Revolution from the very beginning. Articles in *Turkiye,* the *Işikçi* newspaper, argue that Khomeini is acting like a modern Shah Isma'il in using Shi'i Islam as a weapon against the Sunnis. The newspaper speaks of his revolution as nothing more than a political movement exploiting religious belief. Its point of view is that a Shi'i country cannot establish a Muslim state and that the Khomeini regime will eventually pave the way for the triumph of communism in Iran.[37]

The attitude of the *Nakşibendi*s towards Iran is more complex. Unlike the *Nurcu* and the *Işikçi* groups which are of comparatively recent origin, the *Nakşibendi* draw on a long tradition and are one of the most powerful Islamic groups in present-day Turkey. Originally, the revolution in Iran found support among the ranks of the now defunct National Salvation Party (NSP; *Milli Selamet Partisi*) which was known for its close ties with the *Nakşibendi tarikat.* Throughout 1979, the party daily, *Milli Gazete,* published both news reports and articles which looked favorably on developments in Iran. In general, *Milli Gazete* was enthusiastic about the revolution and voiced the hope that other Muslim states might follow the Iranian example.[38] A NSP parliamentarian, Sener Battal, even made a speech in the National Assembly in favor of the revolution and asked the Turkish government to recognize the new regime, a speech which met with fierce opposition from the ranks of the center-right Justice Party (*Adalet Partisi*).[39]

Apparently, however, the *Nakşibendi* later withdrew their support, even though their subsequent opposition was not as resolute as that of other groups.[40] For example, the periodical *Sebil* published in the 1970s and known for its support of the NSP, carried an article in late 1979 which argued that the Soviet Union had started a war against the US through Khomeini and that Iran was trying to compensate for its underdevelopment and powerlessness by "blind hatred towards the West."[41] The most popular *Nakşibendi* periodical, *Islam,* published since 1983, has avoided carrying news or comments on Iran although it covers all of the Muslim world in each issue in a separate section.[42]

In a similar vein, the *Kadiri* (another *tarikat* with a long history) has preferred in its journal *Icmal* to be silent on Iran. The same non-committal attitude is also true of orthodox Islam in Turkey. For example, *Diyanet Gazetesi,* published by the Presidency of Religious Affairs, had no news on Iran throughout 1979.[43]

A 1987 issue of *Köprü,* the *Nurcu* periodical, published a picture of Khomeini on its cover page with the caption "Khomeini or Islam?" It can be said to state in a nutshell the attitude of traditionalist Islamic groups towards the revolution in Iran. It tells Muslims that they can either choose

Khomeini whose doctrine is a basically revolutionary philosophy hiding behind Islamic themes, or else opt for the true message of Islam.[44] At present, that seems to be the choice confronting Islamic groups in Turkey and except for a small minority, the call for revolution issuing from Iran has not met with sympathy among them.

Notes

1. For an account of these reforms, see Niyazi Berkes, *The Development of Secularism in Turkey* (Montreal: 1964) and Bernard Lewis, *The Emergence of Modern Turkey* (London: 1965).

2. For the secularization program of the Kemalist regime, see Binnaz Toprak, *Islam and Political Development in Turkey* (Leiden: 1981).

3. Toprak, Chapter IV.

4. For the text of the document, see T.C. Basbakanlik Devlet Planlama Teskilati, *Milli Kültür: Özel Ihtisas Komisyonu Raporu* (Ankara: 1983).

5. For the list of bureaucrats who are members of the Hearth, see *Yeni Gündem*, 22–28 February 1987.

6. A good example of the new Muslim entrepreneurs is Prime Minister Turgut Özal's brother, Korkut Özal. Through his connections with the Muslim Development Bank, the Islamic Conference Organization and the Muslim World League, Korkut Özal came to own ten firms, a partnership with Al Baraka Corp., a business center and three endowments, within a period of five years. See the cover story in *Yeni Gündem*, 15–21 February 1987.

7. *Nokta*, 19 October 1986.

8. Mehmed Kerim, *Iran Islam Devrimi* (Istanbul: 1979), 7–9.

9. Zeytin Refref, *Iran's Nasil Bakmak?* (2nd ed.; Ankara: 1986), 53–59; Atasoy Müftüoğlu, *Firak* (Istanbul: 1987), 100. See also the articles on Iran in *Iktibas*, January 1981, May 1982, April 1984, May 1984, January 1985; *Girişim*, February 1986.

10. See, for example, Cengiz Çandar, *Dünden Yarina Iran* (Istanbul: 1981); Ayşegül Dora Güney, *Iran'da Devrim* (Istanbul: 1979); Introduction to Güney's book by the columnist of the daily *Cumhuriyet*, Ilhan Selçuk; Halûk Gerger, "Ortadoğu'da Devrim ve Karşi Devrim," *Cumhuriyet*, 3 October 1980.

11. *Iktibas*, May 1984.

12. *Iktibas*, January 1984.

13. Ubeyd Küçüker, *Nebevi Tebliğ* (Istanbul: 1987), 55–105 and Refref, 53.

14. Küçüker, 15–16, 121–73 and Kerim, 334.

15. Kerim, 311–16; Refref, 63–86; Küçüker, 122–23.

16. Ibid.

17. *Iktibas*, March 1986, April 1986.

18. Küçüker, 141–44.

19. *Iktibas*, October 1981.

20. *Iktibas*, October 1981, April 1982, May 1984.

21. *Girişim*, October 1985.

22. *Iktibas*, June 1983.

23. *Girişim*, December 1986.

24. *Girişim*, September 1987. Also see Ilhan Kaya, *Iran Tuzaği: Bir Süperin Drami* (Istanbul: 1987), 122–36.

25. For information on Islamic publications, see *Yeni Forum*, 1 December 1987. Also see Gencay Şaylan, *Islamiyet ve Siyaset: Türkiye Örneği* (Ankara: 1987), 96–97.

For the pro-Iran attitude of the *Şura*, see the following issues: 18 May 1978; 5 June 1978; 14 August 1978; 21 August 1978; 24 September 1978; 2 October 1978.

26. Kerim, 311–18; Küçüker, 122–23; Refref, 63–82.

27. Kerim, 317-18.

28. Ibid., 308-11.

29. *Yeni Asya*, 18 January 1979.

30. *Yeni Asya*, 27 January 1979.

31. *Yeni Asya*, 17 March 1979.

32. *Yeni Asya*, 2 February 1979; 4 February 1979.

33. Burhan Bozgeyik, *Bütün Cepheleriyle Iran Meselesi* (Istanbul: 1981).

34. Ibid., 250.

35. Ibid., 240.

36. *Köprü*, June 1987.

37. See *Türkiye*, 9 January 1979; 17 January 1979; 20 January 1979; 12 February 1979.

38. See *Milli Gazete*, 29 January 1979; 22 January 1979; 3 February 1979; 12 February 1979; 15 February 1979; 19 February 1979; 1 March 1979; 1 April 1979; 4 April 1979; 13 April 1979; 17 April 1979; 1 May 1979; 23 May 1979; 3 June 1979; 15 June 1979; and an article on Iran in numerous installments in the issues between 9 July–1 September 1979.

39. *TBMM Tutanak Dergisi*, 13 February 1979, 611-14.

40. See the article on Islamic journals in *Yeni Forum*, 1 December 1987, 16.

41. *Sebil*, 10 December 1979.

42. See the issues of *Islam*, 1983–1987.

43. See *Diyanet Gazetesi*, Nos. 203–227, 1979.

44. *Köprü*, June 1987.

16

Iran's Islamic Revolution and the Soviet Muslims

Yaacov Ro'i

For several years Soviet sources contended that the Iranian revolution had no impact on the USSR's Muslim regions. At the time of writing, a decade after the event, however, this is no longer the case. Both the greater Soviet openness (*glasnost'*) and the considerable national discontent that became manifest, in the latter half of the 1980s, in Transcaucasia and Central Asia, with its undisguised religious *motifs*, made further denials irrelevant and absurd. The purpose of this paper is to look at the forms this influence has taken and the ways it has been expressed.

Indications of Kremlin Concern

Concern at the possibility—or perhaps even actual indications—of "a political Islamic opposition" inside the USSR were hinted at as early as the beginning of 1980 (although not in the central press). One Soviet source said that Western propaganda hoped for such an opposition to emerge, while reactionaries in the Muslim countries spoke of the need for it and for "strong bridges" to link them with Soviet Muslims.[1] Certainly Khomeini (whom the Soviets did not at the time officially classify as a reactionary) and the spokesmen of his regime made it clear that they regarded the USSR's Muslims as natural targets for Iranian propaganda and religious activity.[2]

A decade later, the well-known orientalist and publicist Igor' Beliaev, in an article entitled "Khomeini: A Political Portrait," asserted that the Iranian leader's dream was for the Islamic revolution to be victorious throughout the entire Muslim world from Morocco to Indonesia.[3] Beliaev clearly considered the Soviet Muslim areas as included in this. Indeed, Jalal al-Din Farsi, a candidate (later disqualified) in the 1980 Iranian presidential election, had told Beliaev in 1981 that following the Shi'i revolution in Iran there would be a second, Sunni, one in Afghanistan and a third one in the Soviet Union.[4]

A Western reporter, who, in spring 1979, visited Baku, the capital of the Azerbaidzhan SSR, which borders Iran and is virtually the sole Soviet

Muslim region with a significant Shi'i population, quoted diplomats in Moscow as saying that Baku was more vulnerable to political "contagion" from events in Iran than any other Soviet city. His own impressions seemed to confirm this. Taxi drivers turned on music from Iranian radio stations. The city's Muslims had sent a congratulatory telegram to Khomeini when he took power. (He was presumably referring to the Muslim Spiritual Directorate for Transcaucasia, which is situated in Baku.) On the one hand, the deputy editor of a local newspaper told the reporter when he asked about contagion: "What happened in Iran was a purely internal affair that has no relation to the situation in our country. A social upheaval overthrew the monarchy and put Iran on a more progressive course. In the Soviet Union we solved the same problem sixty years ago." On the other hand, longer private discussions indicated that the local Muslims were largely dissatisfied "on religious and national grounds." They complained of a lack of copies of the Qur'an, mosques and *mulla*s, and of other restrictions on religious life. And they accused the Russian minority of dominating the republic's life. True, an intellectual pointed out that it was hardly credible that the political and religious upheaval of Iran would spread across the border. He noted that Soviet leaders who had used tanks to crush dissent in Hungary and Czechoslovakia would be ready to do the same within their own borders.[5] At the same time, shortly after the Iranian revolution, a rural inhabitant reportedly wrote to the journal *Nauka i religiia*: "We in Azerbaidzhan are all very happy about the Iranian revolution, for it has shown the entire world the greatness of Islam. This religion should be introduced among us, too, as obligatory; then everything will be in accordance with the laws of purity and integrity, whereas now, when Islam is forgotten, there is in our ranks much deceit and filth."[6]

Undeniably, the authorities were concerned. In late 1980, both first secretary of the Azerbaidzhani communist party, Politburo candidate member Geidar Aliev, and the head of the republican KGB, Zia Iusuf-zade, called for effective security measures in view of the Iranian events.[7] The following year, the party newspaper of one of the Central Asian republics conceded that there were endeavors to kindle the "flame of the Islamic rebirth," though it attributed them to Western imperialism and foreign Muslim reaction, acting in order to destabilize Central Asia, Kazakhstan, Azerbaidzhan and the Caucasus.[8] At approximately the same period, First Deputy Chairman of the KGB Semen Tsvigun, listing the various activities of foreign intelligence services and "anti-Soviet centers," noted that "reactionary foreign Islamic organizations and centers of ideological diversion were activating their propaganda speculating on the events in Iran and around Afghanistan."[9]

In Turkmenia, another Soviet republic bordering Iran, the population was reportedly listening regularly to religious broadcasts from Iran in Turkmen, beginning very soon after the revolution. These were said to be recorded on tape and played back by *mulla*s before groups of believers throughout the republic, especially, apparently, in areas more distant from the Iranian frontier, where the broadcasts could not be heard directly.[10] Soviet accusations to the effect that Iran beamed clerical anti-communist broadcasts into Azerbaidzhan and Turkmenia were reiterated several times in the following years.[11] By 1987, Iran was producing several hours of daily broadcasts for the Soviet Union, as well as television programs to disseminate "material of an Islamic nature." Moreover, "many inhabitants" were receiving letters from Iran "supposedly from relatives" consenting to perform the *hajj* in their name, and suggesting that the recipients should also persuade fellow-villagers to make the *hajj* by proxy and organize almsgiving (*sadaqa*), prayer meetings and other actions contrary to Soviet law. This campaign made it necessary for the various Soviet counter-propaganda mechanisms to take large-scale "prophylactic" measures involving both the mass media and party activists.[12]

In November 1981, the Soviet communist party Central Committee plenum urged the party to devote more attention to counter-propaganda—"one of the important spheres of party work." Three major conferences then dealt with its various aspects. Suggestions for improving counter-propaganda included the need to target specific audiences and singled out, among others, Soviet Muslims who had responded to pan-Islamic broadcasts from Iran.[13] Very clearly, despite the greater sophistication that anti-religious propaganda had been seeking to practice in the 1980s, it had not countered Iranian broadcasts and other materials very effectively.[14]

A further indirect indication of the prevalence of Iranian propaganda materials was included in the report of a Uzbek-language newspaper in 1986 to the effect that the Tashkent customs authorities had won second place in an All-Union competition among departments of the Main Administration for State Customs Inspections of the USSR Council of Ministers. They had had to contend with numerous attempts to bring in narcotics, valuables, currency and ideologically harmful materials.[15] There can hardly be any doubt that the allusion is to materials from Iran.

In the spring of 1987, Igor' Beliaev wrote a lengthy article in the influential paper of the Union of Writers, *Literaturnaia gazeta*, entitled "Islam and Politics," which opened with a letter from a student asking whether it was true, "as Western politicians believe," that Soviet Muslims were "subject to the influence of their coreligionists in other countries" who were conducting an unflagging struggle against socialism. Instead of addressing himself directly to the question, Beliaev preferred to discuss the rise of Islamic fundamentalism outside the Soviet Union and then look at the strength of Islam within the country. While not committing himself to the actual existence of an Islamic opposition inside the USSR, Beliaev did concede that "Muslim fanatics—Sufis" had manipulated the youngsters who participated in the Alma-Ata disturbances of December 1986 (following the dismissal of Kazakh SSR Party Secretary Dinamukhamed Kunaev). Beliaev cited the late French expert on the Soviet Muslim community, Alexandre Bennigsen, for the view that Sufi propaganda was constantly increasing among Soviet Muslims, and that an "Islamizdat," i.e. a Muslim *samizdat* (an unofficial, uncensored literature) existed, printing and xeroxing writings on religious themes and disseminating tapes with passages from authoritative and sacred Muslim texts. "I would not be surprised," Beliaev quoted Bennigsen as saying, "were I to hear that some of the tapes reach Uzbekistan and Tadzhikistan from abroad." Again, the allusion is surely to Iran. While insisting that Bennigsen was exaggerating, Beliaev agreed that his assertions warranted attention.[16]

Nor was Bennigsen alone in the field. A scholar at the West German *Bundesinstitut für ostwissenschaftliche und internationale Studien* also believed that Iranian developments influenced the USSR's Muslim population meaningfully in the direction of a more virulent feeling of Muslim belongingness and self-consciousness, as well perhaps as actual religiosity.[17]

An article on Islam that appeared in 1989 in *Komsomol'skaia pravda* drew attention to Muslim extremism and fundamentalism and the political organizations which presented such platforms and positions. These considered, for instance, that "power in the countries of the Muslim world should be given to the most authoritative religious activists [the *mujtahidun*]. . . . In conformity with this religious-political doctrine, the most radical wing of the current Iranian political leadership conducts its policy of 'exporting the revolution'." At the same time, the article pointed out, it would be erroneous to "identify Islamic extremism with all of Islam" or even with Shi'ism. Although most Middle Eastern Shi'is may consider Khomeini their spiritual leader, Khomeinism and Shi'ism were "phenomena of a different order." The former might be a significant and influential component of Shi'ism, yet it was not its quintessence. *Komsomol'skaia pravda* did not speak of a direct connection between Khomeinism and Soviet Central Asia, but saw fit to state that "we" should relate to Islam with respect, for it was "not only the religion but also the way of life," a meaningful part of the culture "of our neighbor, indeed of our near kinsman, . . . [since] a considerable portion of our vast territory" being populated by Muslims.[18]

Assessment of Islamic Impact

There can, then, be no doubt that Khomeini intended bringing his radical Islamic message to his Soviet coreligionists and that materials of various sorts were reaching the Soviet Muslim population from Iran. It is much more difficult to assess the impact of this campaign. The increasing strength of Islam in the USSR had been drawing attention in Moscow as well as in the West some time prior to the Iranian revolution.[19] But perhaps precisely because Islam's hold on the population as a whole and on the youth and intelligentsia in particular was so strong, the ground was especially fertile for Islamic Iranian influence and had rendered certain sectors among Soviet Muslims markedly receptive to ideas propagated by and from Iran. In September 1987, at a seminar held in Makhachkala (in the Dagestan ASSR) on "Islam in contemporary Society: Political, Economic and Moral Aspects," three main factors were cited as promoting the continued prevalence of Islam in the Central Asian republics and various regions of the Russian Soviet Federated Socialist Republic. These were the pervasiveness of religious propaganda, the ineffectiveness of atheistic activity and the influence of foreign radio broadcasts.[20]

The foreign broadcasts were not solely or even primarily those from Iran, since other foreign stations (for instance: The Voice of America, Radio Liberty and the Chinese radio) also broadcast to the Soviet Muslim population in its various native tongues, but it is reasonable to assume that the Iranians enjoyed pride of place.

It seems, moreover, to be generally accepted among Soviet experts and officials that events in Iran have had an impact on the Soviet Muslim population. An All-Union scientific-theoretical conference entitled "Islam and Politics" was held in Dushanbe in May 1988, attended by orientalists, turcologists, philosophers and economists from Moscow, Leningrad, Erevan, the republican capitals of Central Asia and, of course, from the Tadzhik SSR (of which Dushanbe is the capital). These scholars had previously been focusing their attention on current developments in the East "where Islam has for a number of national and historical reasons played a great role." In places where Islam is the "official religion," Radio Dushanbe declared, "its propaganda apparatus has been organized very well and its activities have also influenced neighboring regions in the Soviet Union."[21] Since, from among the USSR's three southern neighbors, Islam is (and was in 1988) the official religion only in Iran, the reference is unmistakable. At another conference which I attended in London in April 1987 (the Second European Seminar on Central Asian Studies, ESCAS II) Soviet scholars admitted in answer to questions that Middle Eastern Islamic movements might have some impact on their own "Islamic regions."[22]

In individual cases, Iranian propaganda seems definitely to have had some direct influence. A pensioner in the Turkmen SSR's Krasnovodsk Oblast admitted before a rural assembly that he had begun vigorous religious activity under the immediate influence of Iranian broadcasts.[23] In Tadzhik-istan, a "wandering *mulla*" was charged with "inciting" people to religion. According to a court document, in 1985 this man had told a gathering of some twenty-five to thirty people that on the previous evening he and "a few devout Muslims" had listened to the Iranian radio and heard a prominent Iranian cleric calling on all Muslims to unite under the banner of Islam. The accused had gone on to say: "We should not stay indifferent to this invitation and we should make efforts for the renewal of Islam."[24]

In the same republic there were said to be several dealers in illegal religious literature. These *samizdat* materials included an illegally published newspaper *Islamskaia pravda*, photocopies of speeches by Khomeini and a Pakistani political leader, books by Jamal al-Din al-Afghani, a major theorist of the Islamic revival, and works by founder of the Muslim Brotherhood Hasan al-Banna and other Muslim Brotherhood theoreticians. One dealer in religious *samizdat* obtained some of his material from Osh Oblast in Kirgiziia. Other literature had been obtained locally; while the police had uncovered the membership in a distribution center connected with Baku of an external student at the Dushanbe Pedagogical Institute, who had used the institute's printing shop to produce 12,000 flyers with religious texts and some religious brochures.[25]

Moreover, as *Turkmenskaia iskra* had pointed out, it was not only individuals who were "deceived." The green banner of Islam and pictures of Khomeini were held high by demonstrators not only in Alma-Ata in December 1986, but also in Baku in November 1988, in connection with the disturbances that shook the Azerbaidzhani SSR over, and in the wake of, the Nagorno-Karabakh dispute with its Armenian neighbor.[26] In Baku, too, demonstrators were wearing the red headband, which in Iran is a symbol of holy martyrdom and was worn by soldiers going off to the war with Iraq.[27] The banners and pictures of Khomeini were also noted at demonstrations in Dushanbe in February and March 1989 and in the eastern part of Uzbekistan in June 1989.[28] *Ogonëk* editor Vladimir Korotich told me that he saw not a few Khomeini badges or buttons being worn in Tashkent when he visited there in the winter of 1988-89.

Admittedly, there has been some dispute among Soviet experts as to the forces motivating the nationalist uprisings in the first half of 1989 in Central Asia and Kazakhstan. While one version or school of thought attribute them solely to socio-economic forces, others have suggested that religious and nationalist factors have played a meaningful role. Certainly, today no one would deny the existence of major social and economic problems in the area: large-scale unemployment, a visibly deteriorating health situation, a dearth of housing, serious ecological problems. Such a situation is undoubtedly conducive to unrest and xenophobia on the part of the indigenous population both *vis-à-vis* the Russians, who are considered responsible for what happens, and other ethnic groupings, who live and work in the area at the expense, as it were, of the local majority.

In this atmosphere, religious fanaticism has also been a factor. Just prior to the disturbances in Fergana Oblast, "hooligans" were reported to be intimidating Uzbek women and forcing them to dress and behave in accordance with Islamic law.[29] In this way, although both the Uzbeks and the Meskhetian Turks are Sunni Muslims, frustration on religious grounds appears to have played no insignificant role in fanning "extremism." (Practically all Soviet reports of disturbances on nationalist grounds talk of the central role of "extremists," but do not usually specify the nature of that extremism.) *Moscow News* listed among the reasons for discontent in Eastern Uzbekistan the fact that in all Fergana there was only one working mosque[30]— and surely similar things were true of many other areas as well. A Western correspondent, reporting from Fergana in June 1989, noted that the role of religion in the disturbances was highly controversial; while many dismissed it as a mere pretext, a Russian official maintained that a campaign to launch a pan-Islamic front had sparked the trouble.[31] Another official, Lt.-Gen. V.K. Pankin, head of the USSR Interior Ministry's Main Administration for Criminal Investigation, told a TASS correspondent that the riots were unquestionably preplanned, that members of the unofficial Uzbek national front *Birlik* were active in them, and that the demonstrators' slogans included:

"Hail to the Islamic banner, the Muslim religion and Ayatollah Khomeini!"[32] A political officer (*politrabotnik*), Lt.-Col. V. Eningin, who sought to placate a mob of 5–6,000 in Kokand, most of them fifteen to twenty years old, who threw stones and Molotov cocktails and even fired some shots, also testified that the crowd waved the green flag of Islam.[33]

The same paper that carried the interview with Pankin said elsewhere that a Muslim underground in Uzbekistan disseminated pamphlets directed against Russians, Armenians, Jews and Tatars, warning these "infidels" to leave the republic. (The reference to Tatars may be to the Volga Tatars, who comprise the largest non-Uzbek ethnic group in Tashkent after the Russians; they are traditionally Muslims, but are generally secular and modernist. Alternatively, the reference might be to the Crimean Tatars, who, like the Meskhetian Turks, were deported to Uzbekistan during World War II and have similarly been refused permission to return to their home region; they, too, are probably much less strong in their Islamic faith than the Uzbeks.)

Conclusions

Let us, in conclusion, try to understand the significance of our data. A *priori*, Islamic fundamentalism appears to hold little attraction for a population which, even though Muslim by practice, does not seem to consider events primarily through an Islamic prism or by Islamic criteria. At the same time, Khomeini and his doctrine have become a meaningful political symbol for many, especially young "extremists," including intellectuals. But for the most part, Soviet Muslims do not seem committed to restoring the primacy of *Shari'a* law, so that this basic tenet of Khomeini's is foreign—if not incomprehensible—to them. Yet, at least certain groups among them use "Khomeinism," by brandishing the green flag of Islam and pictures of the Ayatollah, to bring home to the Soviet authorities that they feel affinity to, or may even identify with, a credo of radically different socio-political orientation. Of late (in 1988 and 1989) these occasions have become increasingly frequent and violent in the general context of *glasnost'*, democratization and the nationalist upheavals the country is undergoing.

We may, I think, accept the reservations of the Kirgiz national literary figure, Chingiz Aitmatov, who doubted the existence of a fifth column in Central Asia awaiting the arrival of Khomeini.[34] But the fact is that considerable sections of the Soviet Muslim population are disgruntled, perhaps first of all because of their difficult material conditions, but also in part due to a feeling of frustration on religious or national-cum-religious grounds. This dissatisfaction, while it often tends to manifest itself in conflicts and disputes between local ethnic groupings (Tadzhiks and Uzbeks, Tadzhiks and Kirgiz), still seems increasingly to be directed at the local Russian settlers and officials and the central authorities in Moscow. Undoubtedly, the disturbances in Uzbekistan in May-June 1989, in which the Meskhetian Turks were the immediate primary butt of popular resentment, and in Kazakhstan, notably in Novyi Uzen', in June 1989, where Caucasian workers were the direct object of mob violence, were addressed ultimately to the powers-that-be in the Kremlin. As Alexandre Bennigsen pointed out in analyzing the prospects of Khomeinist influence among the Soviet Muslims, certain of its aspects were particularly likely to appeal to them. Bennigsen referred specifically to its anti-imperialism: neither Khomeini nor some Soviet Muslims have differentiated between Western imperialism and that of the CPSU, especially since Marxism-Leninism is seen by them, not without reason, as a fundamentally Western ideology. He also pointed to its populist character, with its promise to replace the existing bureaucracy with new, more popular leaders.[35]

In other words, the Iranian revolution, especially perhaps because it was condoned at the time by the Soviet regime as liberating the people from the shah's oppression and the American imperialist yoke,[36] has become a symbol which the population of the Soviet Muslim areas may frequently fall back on in the future as well. It seems far-reaching to think that Soviet Muslims, or at least meaningful number or sectors among them, will seriously contemplate the introduction into the USSR of the characteristic features of Khomeini's doctrine. But it will serve them as a radical, legitimate battle-cry, a convenient tool for rallying the masses against what they often see as foreign oppression.

Notes

1. Hasan Ismailov, "Reply to the Soothsayers," *Nauka i religiia*, No. 1 (1980), 40–43, quoted in my article, "Impact of the Islamic Fundamentalist Revival of the Late 1970s on the Soviet View of Islam," in Yaacov Ro'i (ed.), *The USSR and the Muslim World* (London: 1984), 149–87.

2. Khomeini's colleagues, in particular, enlarged on his intentions to export the revolution to Iran's northern neighbor. They called on Muslims everywhere—including specifically those of the USSR—to follow in Tehran's footsteps and appealed to the Soviet authorities to "show greater respect" for their Muslims and to allow them "greater freedom:" *MECS*, 1978–79, 523 and 534. For further references to anti-Marxist statements on the part of the leadership of revolutionary Iran, on the grounds of the basic antithesis between Marxism and Islam, see Zalmay Khalilzad, "Islamic Iran: Soviet Dilemma," *Problems of Communism*, January-February 1984, 1–20. According to this same source, Iranian publications carried hostile commentaries on the USSR's treatment of its Muslims and wrote about increased anti-Islamic activities in Soviet Central Asia and the Caucasus. They reported, among other things, a considerable demand for copies of the Qur'an among Soviet Muslims.

3. *Literaturnaia gazeta*, 13 January 1988.

4. Ibid., 13 May 1987.

5. "Moscow Looks South," *Newsweek*, 2 April 1979.

6. S. Agaev, "The Iranian Revolution," *Nauka i religiia*, 11 (1988), 26. Interestingly, the contents of the letter were published only in 1988.

7. *Bakinskii rabochii*, 19 and 25 December 1980, quoted in Ro'i, *op. cit.*

8. *Sovetskaia Kirgiziia*, 27 December 1981, quoted *ibid.*

9. "O proiskakh imperialistecheskikh razvedok," *Kommunist*, 14 (September 1981), 98.

10. Bohdan Nahaylo, "The Islamic Time Bomb," *Spectator*, 21 February 1981, quoted Ro'i, op. cit.

11. E.g., *Azerbayjan gänjläri*, 21 September 1987, quoted in Radio Liberty, 87/88, 2 February 1988.

12. *Turkmenskaia iskra*, 5 September 1987.

13. The conferences took place at Riga in June 1982, at Tallinn in October 1982 and at Kishinev in April 1983.

14. See for example the above-mentioned *Turkmenskaia iskra* article.

15. *Soviet Ozbekistoni*, 14 May 1987.

16. *Literaturnaia gazeta*, 13 and 20 May 1987.

17. Hans Braeker, "The Implications of the Islam Question on Soviet Domestic and Foreign Policy," *Berichte des Bundesinstituts für ostwissenschaftliche und internationale Studien*, 12 (1983).

18. *Komsomol'skaia pravda*, 6 May 1989.

19. See, for example, Hélène Carrère d'Encausse, *Decline of an Empire* (New York: 1979).

20. *Azerbayjan gänjläri*, 24 November 1987, quoted by Radio Liberty, 515/87, 11 December 1987.

21. Radio Dushanbe in Tadzhik, 11 May—SWB, 6 June 1988.

22. *Financial Times*, 14 April 1987.

23. *Turkmenskaia iskra*, 5 September 1987.

24. *Tajikistan-i Soveti*, 24 November—SWB, 20 December 1986.

25. *Kommunist Tadzhikistana*, 13 May 1988.

26. See, for example, Patrick Cockburn, "Dateline USSR: Ethnic Tremors," *Foreign Policy*, Spring 1989, 177.

27. *Izvestiia*, 27 November 1988. In Baku the bands bore the legend "Karabakh."

28. *Kommunist Tadzhikistana*, 13 April 1989, and *Trud*, 15 June 1989.

29. Speech of N.N. Ivanushkina at the 13th plenum of the Uzbek party Central Committee, *Pravda vostoka*, 23 May 1989.

30. *Moskovskie novosti*, 25 (1989), 18 June 1989.

31. *Wall Street Journal*, 28 June 1989.

32. *Trud*, 15 June 1989.

33. *Pravda* 12 June 1989.

34. Aitmatov was, it seems, alluding to Beliaev's apprehensions, in a speech published in *Kyrgyzstan mandaniyati*, 17 December 1987—well before Khomeini's death—quoted in Radio Liberty, 87/88, 2 February 1988.

35. Alexandre Bennigsen and Marie Broxup, *The Islamic Threat to the Soviet State* (New York: 1983), 115–17.

36. For an explanation and apologia of that support, see Agaev, op. cit., 26–29.

Contributors

Amazia Baram, Department of Middle Eastern History, Haifa University.

Peter Chelkowski, Department of Near Eastern Languages and Literatures, Hagop Kevorkian Center for Near Eastern Studies, New York University.

Shahram Chubin, Institute Universitaire des Hautes Etudes Internationales, Geneva.

Werner Ende, Albert Ludwigs Universität, Orientalisches Seminar, Freiburg.

Jacob Goldberg, The Moshe Dayan Center for Middle Eastern and African Studies, Tel Aviv University.

Jo-Anne Hart, Department of Political Science, Brown University, Rhode Island.

Johannes J. G. Jansen, Faculteit der Letteran, Rijksuniversiteit, Leiden.

Farhad Kazemi, Department of Politics, New York University.

Zalmay Khalilzad, Rand Corporation, Washington.

Martin Kramer, The Moshe Dayan Center for Middle Eastern and African Studies, Tel Aviv University.

David Menashri, The Moshe Dayan Center for Middle Eastern and African Studies, Tel Aviv University.

Yosef Olmert, The Moshe Dayan Center for Middle Eastern and African Studies, Tel Aviv University.

Ergun Özbudun, Faculty of Law, Ankara University.

Elie Rekhess, The Moshe Dayan Center for Middle Eastern and African Studies, Tel Aviv University.

Yaacov Ro'i, Department of History, Tel Aviv University.

Roger M. Savory, Trinity College, Toronto.

Binnaz Toprak, Department of Public Administration, Bogazici University, Istanbul.

Index